AF544704

RADICAL ART

AND THE FORMATION OF THE

AVANT-GARDE

RADICAL ART

AND THE FORMATION OF THE

AVANT-GARDE

DAVID COTTINGTON

YALE UNIVERSITY PRESS
New Haven and London

First published by Yale University Press 2022
302 Temple Street, P.O. Box 209040, New Haven CT 06520–9040
47 Bedford Square, London WC1B 3DP
yalebooks.com | yalebooks.co.uk

ISBN 978-0-300-16673-6 HB
Library of Congress Control Number: 2021946780

10 9 8 7 6 5 4 3 2 1
2026 2025 2024 2023 2022

Designed by Tetragon, London
Printed in Great Britain by TJ Books, Padstow, Cornwall

Front cover: Paul Sérusier, *Le Talisman (Paysage au Bois d'Amour)* (*The Talisman [Landscape in the Bois d'Amour]*) (detail of pl. 6), 1888. Oil on board, 27 × 22 cm. Musée d'Orsay, Paris

Back cover: Wyndham Lewis, *Kermesse* (study) (detail of pl. 49), 1912. Ink, wash and gouache, 35 × 35.1 cm. Yale Center for British Art, New Haven

For Linsey, for ever

CONTENTS

ACKNOWLEDGEMENTS

Over the nearly 15 years during which I have reflected on and researched this book I have incurred so many intellectual and administrative debts that the complete list of them, were I to present it here, would tire the patience of any reader. I wish especially, however, to thank the following. Per Bäckström, Stefan Nygård, Marja Jalava, Johan Strang, Benedikt Hjartarson, Tania Ørum and other members of the Nordic Network of Avant-Garde Studies gave me my first opportunity to outline the then-emergent project that its theme addressed, via their 2009 conference 'Historicizing the Avant-Garde' at Copenhagen University, and continued over the next near-decade to enable me to broaden and deepen the development of its argument through their further events and publications. These included a paper, 'Mapping the Avant-Garde: Methodologies and Homologies', for their symposium '(Trans)nationality and Cultural Asymmetry in the Humanities, Social Sciences and Politics, Nineteenth and Twentieth Centuries' at the European University Institute, Florence, in 2013, and a chapter on the hierarchies and networks of the artistic avant-garde in M. Jalava, S. Nygård and J. Strang, eds, *Decentering European Intellectual Space*, Leiden and Boston: Brill, 2018. Béatrice Joyeux-Prunel, whose seminal study, *Nul n'est prophète en son pays? L'internationalisation de la peinture des avant-gardes parisiennes 1855–1914*, Paris: Musée d'Orsay, 2009, provided a crucial foundation for this book, and also gave me the invaluable opportunities to develop and test it, via invitations, first, to a Visiting Professorship at the École Normale Supérieure in Paris in 2011, and, second, to give a keynote paper at a conference on 'Global Art History and the Peripheries/L'Histoire mondiale de l'art et les périphéries' at the ENS in June 2013; her intellectual companionship and generosity have been invaluable throughout. In September 2017, an invitation from Hiromi Matsui of Nagoya University,

Japan, to a two-week Visiting Professorship provided a chance to test an argument about classicism and the avant-garde in two seminars there; in July 2018 a paper for Sarah Turner's conference at the Royal Academy, London, 'Frenemies: Friendship, Enmity and Rivalry in British Art, 1769–2018', allowed me to deepen my understanding of the affective current in this country's avant-gardism; this was matched by an opportunity that October to explore the rival current of professionalisation, via an invitation from Pepe Karmel and Ramón Melero to speak at their conference on 'Picasso and History' at the Museo Picasso Málaga. Each of these papers helped to develop my argument, and I am profoundly grateful to all of these scholars, convenors and curators, without which this book would have been a slimmer affair in every way.

It has been equally nourished by other scholarly friendships and occasions for indulgence in shared enthusiasms for avant-garde studies: with Annika Öhrner of Södertörn University, Stockholm, over several years and dinners, as well as via the symposia at Uppsala University and the Moderna Museet in Stockholm that she suggested and co-convened with me, all of which were illuminating as well as enjoyable. A shared interest with Paulina Ambroży, of Adam Mickiewicz University in Poznań, in the relations between different cultural practices within the networks of the avant-garde fed both into reflections on ekphrasis and its pitfalls, as well as a joint paper on the modernisms of Henry James and Édouard Vuillard for a 2012 conference of the European Network for Avant-Garde and Modernist Studies (EAM) – whose biennial gatherings have also been of great benefit in furthering my ideas – and into much subsequent enjoyable correspondence. Exchanges with Sascha Bru of Leuven University, polymathic scholar of comparative literature and EAM's co-founder, have been a constant stimulus; discussions with Peter Brooker about the London bohemia of the early twentieth century and with Lisa Tickner about the city's popular culture in that decade, with Daniel Grojnowski about the 'Incohérents' and *le rire parisien*, and with Fran Berry about the Nabi circle in the Parisian *fin de siècle*, and with Ruth Livesey on sex, socialism and aestheticism in the British equivalent, have been invaluable as well as entertaining. Ben Angwin, whose 2022 PhD for Kingston University on the entrepreneurialism of Roger Fry and his Omega Workshops has been a mine of information generously shared, and others of my former and current PhD students, especially Dr Lina Stergiou, Dr Rosalind McKever and Eva Manticova, have all offered fresh insights as well as new information from their own research. I am greatly obliged to them for these.

At Yale University Press, from its inception Gillian Malpass gave unerring advice which did much to shape the book; she has been ably succeeded by editors Sophie Neve and Julie Hrischeva, whose acumen and professionalism have been much appreciated. The project itself pre-dates by some years its contractual relation with Yale, but its beginnings lay in the latter's publication of my first book over 20 years ago, whose contextualisation of the Cubist movement in the artistic avant-garde of pre-First World War Paris demanded a sequel that in its turn would contextualise that formation itself. That this has eventually emerged is thanks greatly to them all as well as their team, including picture researcher Alice Blows (whose generosity with her time and expertise was much appreciated) and copy-editor Robert Shore. I'm hugely indebted to Brandon Taylor and (in a personal capacity) Gillian Malpass for reading some chapters and offering invaluable advice on these, to Tag Gronberg for enduring repeated updates on my argument and its progress, and to Yale's two anonymous readers for their constructive suggestions, many of which I took up. I'm grateful to Kingston University's School of Art and its Research Fund for its repeated financial generosity over several years.

Throughout these 15 years, but also so many more, my dear late wife, Linsey, so deeply and constantly missed, was not only the best and most insightful critic of all my thinking in the present book, but my close companion in all the effort that went into it. It simply would not have been written without her, and is dedicated to her with all my heart. Since her leaving us, my sons, Andy and Joe, have taken up her mantle of support, for which to them both my profound and loving thanks.

INTRODUCTION

In the autumn of 2012 Tate Britain mounted an exhibition of the work of the Pre-Raphaelite Brotherhood. Its title, *Pre-Raphaelites: Victorian Avant-Garde*, was on one level – that of marketing – a provocative 'sexing-up' of its subject, its discarding of 'Brotherhood' (the term that the group gave itself on its foundation in 1848) in favour of a more up-to-the minute characterisation harnessing the contemporaneity and progressive connotations of 'avant-garde' to give added appeal.[1] But it was also provocative on a deeper level, in that it pointed to a revisionist art-historical interpretation of the modernity of the Pre-Raphaelites: throughout the exhibition catalogue, essay after essay reiterated the assertion that the group was an early instance of that phenomenon of avant-garde groupings that has come to be seen as a marker of modernist art practice.[2]

The proposed revision was challenging in its aim of rescuing these artists and their work from the conventional view of Victorian culture as 'old-fashioned' by stressing their modernity. It was also, however, at once misleading and instructive. Misleading, firstly, in its teleological character: these assertions of avant-garde status shared an unquestioned assumption that the Pre-Raphaelites should be understood solely in terms of the modernist future towards which, from a twenty-first-century perspective, their grouping pointed. Ignoring the fact of the group's self-identification as a brotherhood, a term with intended retrospective connotations, the authors substituted for this concept a *pro*spective, future-facing one that had not yet emerged in English art discourse in 1848, and a term for it, 'avant-garde', that had not yet been coined. And it was misleading, secondly, in the lack of any evidence for the claim, or analysis of the qualities of 'avant-garde-ness', or even definition of the concept itself.

But it was therefore instructive in two ways too, in that this unreflective teleology and lack of historical specificity underlined two requirements for historians if the significance of the Pre-Raphaelite group's own assertion of its identity is to be understood. The first is to acknowledge the distinctions between a brotherhood and an avant-garde, and the quite different historical circumstances in which each had currency. The second is to place both in a much broader and determining social context and dynamic, that of the spirit of collectivism which helped to drive the modernisation of western societies from the mid-nineteenth century, and of the collectivities to which it gave rise. It is this dynamic, with respect to those collectivities in Paris and London that prioritised aesthetic over social aspirations and orientations or shared these with them, that produced the cultural formation of the artistic avant-garde that is the subject of this book.

In the years of my research since the Tate exhibition that writing it has entailed, it has become apparent both that this revisionist interpretation is an ongoing and collective, if uncoordinated, project, to which there have also been other contributors,[3] and that the issues involved in its revisionism extend beyond academic questions of art-historical and theoretical adequacy, into broader fields of the cultural, and indeed political, significance of 'the avant-garde' as a concept and a historical formation. All of which gives the analysis that follows topicality and, dare it be said, urgency. For 'avant-garde' has become one of the two key concepts (together with 'modernism') around which most of the big questions about the character, historical importance and contemporary relevance of the culture of the last two centuries have turned, and which have effectively determined what works and practices in this period have been seen as canonical.

Yet the concept and its deployment in art-historical and critical writing remain deeply problematic, for all its longevity and strategic importance; it is still a slippery notion, ubiquitously taken for granted but rarely defined. The criteria for its application to artists and/or their work have usually remained unspecified, and such questions as those of when, why and how an avant-garde first emerged in Paris, why and how it became both the principal model of artistic collectivity and the primary arbiter of modernist qualities across first Europe and then the western world have been, with very few exceptions, unasked, let alone answered.

It is with these and other related questions that the present history is concerned, and in seeking answers to them it does two things. First, it offers and develops a set of distinctions in the process of suggesting those answers that allows greater precision and clarity of historical, materialist analysis than has hitherto been achieved. Second, as a means of approaching them, it applies the term 'formation', taken from sociology (via the cultural theorising of Raymond Williams), to describe the collectivity of the avant-garde, and also offers a detailed exploration of how this collectivity, *as* a formation, both shaped avant-garde practices and related to the social history of its time and places. Part of the purpose of this study is to thereby offer a methodological model for further application to studies of the avant-garde.[4]

The first distinction is the most elementary, one simply of grammar. For even within the specialist field of art history its usage too often slips from adjective to noun, from ideology to institution, without distinction or acknowledgement of the differences between these. Thus 'the avant-garde' – meaning the cultural formation – is a concrete noun referencing artists; 'avant-garde', without the definite article, is an adjective that refers to particular qualities; 'avant-gardism' – the ideology – is an abstract noun. Each term in this family of terms has a different meaning, reference, significance and even origin, and to understand them the terms need to be disentangled (yet almost never are), and then held in relation, rather than confused.

A further distinction is one of definition: between an understanding of 'avant-garde' as referring to art *per se*, and one designating some artists but not all – those, that is, who belong(ed) to a community of aesthetically radical artists. It was in France in the years after the restoration of the monarchy in 1815 that social theorists across the political spectrum most profoundly questioned the legacy of the revolutionary years and, finding the resulting political and social settlement wanting, sought ways of improving upon it – of replacing the fossilised hierarchy of the monarchical regime with a social order more respectful both of individual rights and collective identities. One of the most influential groups on the left of this political spectrum was gathered around Count Henri de Saint-Simon, who, shortly before his death in 1825, elaborated a model of a state-technocratic socialism in which society would be led by a triumvirate of professions: the artist, the scientist and the industrialist. Of these, the artist would be the 'avant-garde' – and the term was first used in a non-military context, in this way, by Saint-Simon and his group.[5]

It is the second understanding, however, that is the current one. Within 20 years of this Saint-Simonian neologism, the use of the term had proliferated in other directions than that of politics alone. By the 1850s, wider use of 'avant-garde' as designating some artists but not all had spread to the cultural arena, with writers in particular being described with this epithet, although in ways that as yet kept close to the military sense and, in the case of its best-known early literary use, that by the poet Charles Baudelaire, were also clearly negative.[6] It took another 20 years before 'avant-garde' was applied to visual artists, in critic Félix Fénéon's consciously neologistic reference in 1886 to the group of Parisian painters whom he supported, the 'neo-impressionists' (also his coinage), as 'the avant-garde of impressionism'.[7] For reasons that we shall explore, this was also the first artistic group that constituted *an* avant-garde, not only in the current sense of the term but, further, in the stricter sense of meeting criteria that the present analysis, deriving these from the artistic, critical and art-market discourses of *fin-de-siècle* Paris, develops in more detail.

A governing principle of this analysis rests on a third distinction, between this avant-garde as a 'formation' and avant-gardism as an ideology. Central to the ideology as it developed through the 30 years around the turn of the twentieth century was the principle of *rupture*. It was a cardinal commitment to breaking with the cultural (and often, by extension, political) status quo that members of the Parisian literary and fine-art avant-gardes themselves declared, and in consequence it has been taken as a given characteristic of avant-gardes by their historians ever since. But – as I argue – it, too, rests on a confusion. For the avant-gardes were not products of their ideology alone, could not simply will themselves into existence by the force of this in itself; like any other social phenomenon, they were also the result of contingent factors, the historical dynamics of the conjuncture of their emergence and consolidation. A key component of this conjuncture was the process of that professionalisation of middle-class non-entrepreneurial occupations that was a motor force in the development of western societies in the late nineteenth and early twentieth centuries.[8] I argue that the Parisian fine-art avant-garde of the 1880s and onwards should be seen as both a part of this process, *de facto* by virtue of its position in the art market and to a degree unwittingly, and opposed to it by virtue of its ideology; and that the relation between these two positions, initially implicitly contrary, became increasingly contradictory as the formation became consolidated after the turn of the century.

The avant-garde as a formation needs to be distinguished, therefore, from its ideology. The use of the term 'formation' in this book's title plays with its double meaning, both as the process of 'coming into being' and to refer to the collectivity itself. Throughout, I use 'formation' in the second sense, as introduced by Williams to describe a social collectivity somewhere between a group and a movement, sharing with them an identifiable structural coherence and cohesiveness but not necessarily their self-identification as collectives. Williams himself described a cultural formation's particular qualities as 'a remarkably extending and interpenetrating activity of artistic forms and actual or desired social relations'. He elaborated:

> It is never only a specifying artistic analysis, though much of the evidence will be made available through that, nor only a generalising social analysis, though that reference has to be quite empirically made. It is the steady discovery of genuine formations which are simultaneously artistic forms and social locations, with all the properly cultural evidence of identification and presentation, local stance and organisation, intention and interrelation with others, moving as evidently in one direction – the actual works – as in the other: the specific response to the society.[9]

This exposition of his theory of cultural formations was written in 1986, and Williams died, sadly, less than two years later; the essay was published posthumously. He had already written an analysis of a sample formation, that of Bloomsbury, which had shown how valuable a tool of cultural analysis this could be, but this too was only an essay, and Williams had no chance to offer a more extended application of it.[10] The present study is offered as such – strangely, given the insights both cultural and political that the theory enables, it is the first, as far as I am aware, to do so, in particular with reference to the artistic avant-garde.[11]

Part of the tension within the avant-garde formation between belonging to and opposing professionalisation was due to the gradual way in which, as we shall see, its model of cultural collectivity gained ascendancy, first in Paris and then elsewhere including London, over competing models such as brotherhoods, cenacles, circles and societies, that were grounded either in relations of informal sociability including friendship and fellowship, or in those originating in the pursuit of market advantage, or sometimes both. The process of transition from what I call 'affective relations' to the instrumentalised character of art as a profession – even one alternative to that of the mainstream, as the Parisian avant-garde's was – entailed the emergence of some transitional, or hybrid, groupings; I use both terms, since the boundaries between affective and instrumental models were sometimes porous. For the most part, however, these motivations were clearly opposed, separated by a further distinction within cultural discourse at the *fin de siècle*, between the values of professionalism and those of amateurism. In our present usage the latter is more often a pejorative than a complimentary term, but at that turn of the century these were customarily more evenly balanced; if to be amateur was to be incompetent and inefficient, it was also to be motivated more by love than by money, by aristocratic values as often as by hobbyism.

The distinction between the two was also gendered, in fundamental and influential ways. Underpinned by an habitual sexism that was institutionalised by the accepted principle of 'separate spheres', which confined women to the domestic sphere, and defined both the public sphere and professionalism within it as masculine, it was also naturalised by the ideology of avant-gardism, which licensed misogyny as 'bohemian' sexual freedom for male artists, and granted women access to its alternative professionalism only with reluctance. The combination of these factors gives the history traced here a masculinist character that is repeatedly evident, often determining, and addressed as such in this analysis. The issue of gender, however, is not the primary thread drawn through it, for the distinctions between professionalism and amateurism, instrumental and affective motivations, were more broadly based than on that alone, and it was in their interrelationship that they not only played a central role in the history that this book traces, but also assisted in challenging the hegemony of the Parisian model on the eve of the war, at the very moment when it appeared unassailable.

A further distinction follows from this challenge. The position of Paris as the undisputed capital of contemporary western culture from the mid-nineteenth century was one of the factors that led to the emergence of an artistic avant-garde formation earlier in that city than anywhere else, and thence to the spread, in the decade before the First World War, of a pan-European avant-garde network of which it was universally perceived as the centre, to which everywhere else was, to varying degrees, peripheral. Recent scholarship has interrogated this hierarchical assumption, however; as the late Polish art historian Piotr Piotrowski observed in an influential contribution,[12] 'peripheral' sites of cultural practices are often richer in their creativity than the 'centre' to which they genuflect, precisely because of their obligation to negotiate between the initiatives stemming from that centre and their own local agendas. More than this – and beyond Piotrowski's point – they are often well placed to provoke, over time, a shift in these relations. The history of the emergence of London's avant-garde in 1914 is a case in point, as we shall see.

Another, more socially and politically momentous, is that twenty-first-century realisation of their *global* character, and exploration of the ramifications of this in the tensions and confrontations between a newly acknowledged multiplicity of modernisms and the implacable imperatives of contemporary capitalism.[13] Unlike the issue of gender, however, those of race and colonialism do not have explicit salience in the analysis that follows. This is not because of their peripherality to the dominant cultural discourses of turn-of-the-twentieth-century Paris and London – rather the opposite: that is to say, because of the completeness with which the emergent and consolidating formation of the avant-garde shared the racist and colonialist prejudices of the societies to which it belonged. In so far as these were unquestioned – the very fascination with the alterity of non-European cultures that avant-gardist 'primitivism' articulated was, indeed, rooted in them – they did not have the same agency in distinguishing and separating its formation (in both senses of the term) from mainstream culture as did the factors of professionalisation and shifting gender relations that are the specific focus of my analysis. Much valuable work has already been accomplished in the last half-century in exposing these racist and colonialist prejudices, though not from the formational-analysis perspective offered here. To have attempted to offer this in the book that follows, however, would have broadened and blurred its focus unhelpfully. It is my hope that the methodological model it presents will encourage other scholars to take up that work.

A last point of explanation. My choice, for a comparison with Paris, of London – still the 'world metropolis' in that turn-of-the twentieth-century conjuncture, yet perceived (then and now) as one of the more 'peripheral' satellites of Paris in cultural terms[14] – may seem an unreflective and conventional pairing in light of the reconfiguring of the field of European cultural history over the last 30 years of scholarship. It is, however, a considered one, for two reasons. The first is that these decades of reassessment of the relation between the artistic modernisms of Paris and London by historians of the latter, who have challenged prevailing assumptions of Parisian cultural hegemony, have left present understanding of this history incomplete and confused. Scholars of British art have insisted upon the particularity both of London-based artists' experience of modernity and thus, necessarily, of the character of the modernism through which they articulated it, arguing and demonstrating that the time-honoured question 'why was there no artistic modernism in London before 1914?' was the wrong question, based as it was on exaggerated assumptions of the reach and relevance of the Parisian model. Much of this emphasis has been valuable, some of it mould-breaking. Yet its pioneering degree of attention to the specificities of the qualities and context of modernist art in early twentieth-century London has come at the expense of an equivalent consideration, not only of those in Paris, but of the perceptions of the relations between them that were held on each side of the Channel at that time. The baby has been thrown out, it might be suggested, with the bathwater, and deserves to be rescued.

The second reason is that the particularities of the respective positions of Paris and London, as the two hegemonic powers in the pan-European and, beyond this, global arenas, are of singular relevance. How could London, globally hegemonic in politico-economic terms, be at the same time a 'peripheral' city in terms of its modernist culture to the 'centre' that was Paris in the pre-1914 decade? What is at issue here, fundamentally, is at once the concept and the early, constitutive history of the artistic avant-garde, the question of its agency with regard to the development of modernism in those complex, rich and crucial decades of its flourishing in the visual arts before the First World War – and through this, that of the character of early twentieth-century modernity itself. A close comparison and interrelation of the avant-garde's formations in Europe's two leading cities offers a chance to explore this dynamic, or perhaps dialectic, in the most polarised pairing, in this sense, that that conjuncture presented, and thereby to understand better the choice of roads both taken and not taken into the new century, in both capitals.

1
BROTHERHOODS

IDEOLOGICAL BROTHERHOODS

Brotherhoods have a long history. 'From the Middle Ages forward', in the words of one of their historians, 'fraternalism was one of the most widely available and persistently used forms of collective organization in European and American history.'[1] They were part of a broad structure, in which guilds and corporations were the dominant formations, of collective self-interest organised by agents involved in the production and merchandising of goods and services in the emerging medieval market economy. The qualities of masculinist exclusivity, social elitism and sometimes secrecy that often characterised them reflected their members' concern to defend their status and craft knowledge from competition and adulteration. With the development of capitalism, however, this knowledge and its sustaining values came under increasing attack. During the nineteenth century especially, 'craft ideals were increasingly less possible to realize within the workplace. The rise of social fraternalism closely parallels this decline of traditional craft relations in the work world', Mary Anne Clawson observes. 'If these ideals could no longer be realized at work, they could instead be transferred to a purely social setting, the fraternal order.'[2]

The transference was not straightforward, however; the loss of the occupational functionality of fraternal collectivism brought tensions and sometimes contradictions between aspirations and social realities, such as those of class and gender, and between spiritual and economic concerns, which we shall explore. Yet the fraternal model of collectivity was, from the early nineteenth century, especially attractive to fine artists and other cultural producers across Europe, who were faced by the entrenchment across more and more social domains and relations of what Thomas

Carlyle called the 'cash nexus' of capitalism, and within this, on the one hand, by the growing authority and hierarchical, bureaucratic structures of their national academies, and, on the other, by the replacement of the securities of patronage by the uncertainties of a speculative market for their products. Against such constraints, this traditionalist, elitist, often secretive and esoteric, and almost always (as the term suggests) masculinist fraternal collectivism offered, for significant numbers of artists through the nineteenth century and into the twentieth, an emotionally resonant refuge, an idealist, anti-materialist alternative model for how to live and work.

The study of brotherhoods itself also has a considerable historiography, dating, in sociology, from Georg Simmel's writings of the early twentieth century on individuality and social forms,[3] and in recent years including art-historical studies.[4] From these it appears that the earliest example of an artistic brotherhood in a modern context was that of the 'Barbus' or 'Primitifs', established by students of Jacques-Louis David in the late 1790s.[5] A product of the culture of fraternities that flourished in the Jacobin period of the French Revolution and outlasted the demise of Jacobin power as a revolutionary ideal, the group's foundation was prompted, their principal modern historian George Levitine suggests, by two factors. The first, and more specific to their studentship, was a dissatisfaction with the hierarchical order of art practice that David had by then reimposed in his studio. At the height of the Revolution, David, an active supporter of the Jacobins, had responded to their promotion of *fraternité* by introducing procedures of collaboration with his students on what he saw as common projects that built on the personal friendships he cultivated with them. His abandonment of revolutionary politics with the fall of the Jacobins, however, led him to return to the authoritarian studio procedures of the Ancien Régime. Understandably this was resented by some of the students, who expressed their opposition initially in their criticism in 1798, on stylistic grounds, of David's major painting *Les Sabines* (*The Intervention of the Sabine Women*) (pl. 1). This production was his chief artistic activity between 1795 and its completion in 1799, and its conciliatory theme had a contemporary political relevance, in that critical post-Jacobin moment, to which the nascent group also objected. The thrust of their criticism overall was that *Les Sabines* was no more than 'radical chic' in its neo-classicism, a picture adopting the popular taste for the Grecian primitive while presenting a compromise with Ancien Régime values.[6]

These criticisms (led throughout, it would seem, by their self-appointed leader, Maurice Quay, a market gardener's son who entered David's studio in 1796)[7] went beyond the stylistic, however, in the early period of the Barbus' coalescence, in their publicly presenting a reformist social as well as artistic programme.[8] This was in part the product, Levitine argues, of a second, more general factor: the resentment felt by many young artists about the precariousness of their social and professional status, as their aspirations to the betterment of their professional position clashed with the manual, artisanal character of artistic work, and led to public ambivalence towards, and even ridicule of, the former. Their reformist zeal was conveyed most visibly, however, artistically and sartorially: the first by their influential espousal of the style of Greek vase paintings, statues and bas-reliefs from the most archaic, pre-Phidian period, which they lauded as '"simple", "grandiose" and, especially, "primitive"';[9] and the second by their adoption of a mode of dressing that was perceived as that art's sartorial corollary: cloaks and togas, sandals, long hair and beards (hence the sobriquet). While this dress was widely remarked upon, it was also not unique, nor seen as especially eccentric; Levitine notes several contemporary sources in observing that this type of costume, 'despite its extravagance, was not entirely unfamiliar to the Parisian scene at the end of the eighteenth century'[10] – thus its choice by the Barbus was less clearly 'bohemian' than the prevalence of this epithet in the historiography of the group has suggested.[11] When the group's sartorial performativity had little effect, however, either on art and its institutions or on social practices, its members changed tack. They left David's studio to set up a commune in a disused monastery at Chaillot, then still a wild suburb outside Paris, where they stayed from mid-1801 to early 1803. In this 'hauntingly romantic site', their focus of interest shifted from activism to autonomism: Levitine senses 'an increasingly hermetic, illuministic atmosphere in which the utopian idea of a perfect primitive society takes the form of a poetically conceived, paramonastic, esoteric group'.[12] It was probably the arrival of the novelist Charles Nodier on the scene that was the catalyst for this shift, which was to be of consequence as a model of artistic collectivity for at least the next century. Described by Levitine as 'a well-read, highly talented young writer [with] an irrepressible penchant for esoteric pursuits and conspiracy',[13] Nodier had already caught the post-Revolutionary zeitgeist of clandestine fraternity, having founded a secret society, La Philadelphie, in Besançon in 1796, which lasted until his move to Paris in 1800. This was an association, named in honour of the city that was the spiritual heart of the American Revolution, based on male friendship, probity and philanthropy, which combined help to the needy with discussions on literature and morality. Nodier brought some, but not all, of these traits to the Barbus' commune at Chaillot; among those the collective did exhibit were its retrospective emphasis and its masculinism.

The first of these is clear, both in the group's embrace of perceived 'primitive' qualities in early Greek art, and in their acceptance of the name 'Méditateurs de l'Antique'. We should note, however, that this retrospective identification was not simply traditionalist, nor necessarily regressive. Instead, at that time, the available, thinkable framework for the Barbus' retrospectivism was that rich body of Revolutionary symbolism, from the popular Phrygian cap to the ubiquitous figure of Hercules, that the Jacobins especially developed (and upon which David himself had drawn in the many festivals that he organised as pageant-master to the Revolution).[14] By the time of the Empire, such connotations were no longer acceptable, as an influential reflection of 1808 on the Barbus indicates: a *Rapport sur les Beaux-Arts* of that year for the Institut de France noted 'a sort of delirium' that 'had overtaken some young painters who had formed a sect in order… to introduce naiveté in their manner of painting, they were regressing to the infancy of art [and] only succeeded in achieving oddity'.[15] What could be seen as mere oddity in 1808 is interpreted by Levitine with historical hindsight more specifically, in terms of Simmel's characterisation of secret societies as 'aristocratic'.[16] He sees it as 'an aesthetically spiritual, aristocratic and escapist reaction against the contemporary striving for scientifically defined facts and a scientifically produced optical truth', adding that '[t]his last tendency, linked with the beginning of the Industrial Revolution, represented an essentially popular, commonsensical attitude that found its justification in the proliferation of scientific theories and inventions'.[17] We shall see later how this implicitly elitist reaction re-emerged at the end of the century, alongside avant-gardism and in rivalry with it, as part of a broad opposition to bourgeois taste,[18] and contributed to the emergence of an emphasis on the autonomy and purity of art that formed a major strand of modernism; but it is important first to recognise the conjunctural forces that were shaping the Barbus' primitivism. Unlike the young *romantiques* of the Restoration era for whom, as William Vaughan and others have observed, they provided a genealogy, this primitivism was not grounded on a misread and mythified Middle Ages for which perceived qualities of chastity, piety and community were central, but in a striving for other values: those of simplicity, naturalness and unaffectedness that they found both in Homer and in the ideals of the Revolution.

Where there is greater overlap between the Barbus and later brotherhoods is in their masculinism. As Vaughan argues, part of the group's objection to *Les Sabines* stemmed from its depiction of these eponymous figures as not only active, but politically so, in the public domain, which, he observes, 'must have resonated all the more poignantly [with the Barbus] since the Jacobins had gone to such lengths to deny women a place in public life, suppressing the female Jacobin clubs'.[19] The Revolution had been implacably masculinist, and the sect, suggests Vaughan, sought to maintain this principle, or prejudice. The argument is somewhat sapped, however, by the fact that among the leaders of the group, in terms, it would seem, both of artistic ability and personal charisma, was a woman. Lucile Messageot joined initially (at least partly) for romantic reasons – she married one of its founding members, Jean-Pierre Franque, in January 1802 – but became one of its most prominent figures until her untimely death in May 1803.[20] Not only can it be argued that her membership might have moderated such masculinism in the group had she lived longer, it also suggests that the Barbus' masculinism may not have been as implacable as that of the Jacobins. As with their retrospectivism, the Barbus' masculinist predilections were perhaps less clear-cut than posterity would have them.

In both respects, there was a contrast with the grouping that immediately succeeded the Barbus in further developing their model of artistic collectivity. The group of Viennese artists who in 1809 founded the Brotherhood of St Luke – more familiar as the Nazarenes[21] – may just possibly have emerged out of the Barbus' circle. (The painter Gottlieb Schick and the sculptor Ludwig Tieck, peripheral members of this group, both studied under David at the same time as the Barbus.)[22] They certainly followed the Parisians in rejecting the neoclassical teaching they were receiving, in their case, at the Viennese Academy. In 1810 they set up a commune in the monastery of San Isidoro in Rome, where they had moved when the Academy was closed because of Napoleon's invasion of Vienna.[23] Yet in key respects, as Jason Rosenfeld has emphasised, the Nazarenes 'could not be further from' the Barbus. The earlier brotherhood left few works, an informal and incomplete record of its activities, an indeterminacy of membership and little trace of its members' subsequent lives. By contrast, the Nazarenes – although also named after their style of dress (in this case resembling that of Christ's disciples) – 'had articles of incorporation, a code of ethics and an emblem intended for the backs of paintings'.[24] They not only lived in a monastery, but lived monastically, working in solitude during the day and eating together each evening. They were deeply religious, indeed, saw their collective as a quasi-religious order and themselves as artist-monks.[25] By all accounts (though there are not many that are contemporary with them), the Barbus were not the most conscientious of David's students, and seem to have been more committed to the lifestyle than to the art-making that their collective fostered, whereas the Nazarenes were nothing if not dedicated to the project of reconnecting with both the values and the style of early Italian Renaissance art, taking their hero, Fra Angelico, the painter-monk of San Marco, as a model in both respects (pls 2 and 3).[26] Johann Friedrich Overbeck, indeed, went so far in his search for monkish purity as to reject working after cadavers or naked women. 'I prefer to draw less correctly', he declared in a letter of 1808, 'than certainly damage my feelings, which are the artist's greatest treasure.'[27] The search for purity also led the Nazarenes to value friendship, and the shared protection it gave in the commune from worldly corruption, 'as an act of almost religious chastity and dedication', as Mitchell Frank suggests.[28] Friendship, if not always of such a character, was a feature of nineteenth-century brotherhoods that they shared with other forms of sociability,[29] and it is significant for us not only in its invariably masculinist character,[30] but also and more broadly in its exemplification of the importance, for artistic practices, of that current of affective relations that, as I shall argue, underpinned so much of the collectivism of the later nineteenth and early twentieth centuries, and that played a critical role in the emergence of the avant-garde.[31] In the case of the Nazarenes, friendship was of two kinds, which corresponded with, and shaped, the two phases into which the narrative of this group's history is conventionally divided: the first, from 1809 to 1812, ended with the death of Franz Pforr, the second began with Peter Cornelius's replacement of him as co-leader with Overbeck, and lasted until Cornelius returned to Germany in 1819, summoned to Munich by Ludwig of Bavaria to decorate his new sculpture gallery (although the group lasted, in ever looser and more diluted modes, for another decade).

The distinction between the two periods is seen by historians as more than a matter of personnel alone; the change effected a shift from the communal existence and insularity of the earlier phase to the more outward-looking, socially active and professional association of like-minded artists that characterised the later phase. This shift has, in its turn, been analysed in terms of the categories of collectivism first theorised by the sociologist Ferdinand Tönnies in 1887, of *Gemeinschaft* or community, and *Gesellschaft* or society at large.[32] First applied to the Nazarenes by Nikolaus Pevsner in 1931 and developed by Klaus Lankheit in 1952, this characterisation has more recently been substantiated by Mitchell Frank;[33] it has a useful explanatory value for the present analysis, since it captures well both the nature of the Nazarenes and that of the transition, in the history of artistic collectivism, from the hegemony of the brotherhood model to that of the avant-garde.

It was the arrival of Peter Cornelius in Rome in 1811 and his joining the group the following year that was the catalyst for the 'modernisation' of the Nazarenes and their reorientation towards *Gesellschaft*. The death of Pforr not only robbed the introverted, religious-minded Overbeck of an intense friendship but was accompanied by the relinquishing of both the monastery and the self-designation 'Brotherhood', and by 1813, the departure of all its original members but him from Rome. Cornelius brought a reformist, activist disposition and an ardent nationalism to the group's agenda; most notably, they 'went public' both in their behaviour, joining the other artists of the Roman German colony in café life and lively discussions at its HQ, the Café Greco, and in their art, collectively painting a fresco cycle, commissioned in 1816 by the Prussian consul general in Rome, Jakob Salomon Bartholdy, for the sitting room in his residence, on the story of Joseph from the Book of Genesis. It was completed in 1818, in which year a second cycle was commissioned, this time by the Roman aristocratic patron the Marchese Carlo Massimo, of frescoes illustrative of the Renaissance writers Tasso, Dante and Ariosto.[34] But with Cornelius's departure the momentum of this project flagged, relations within the group became less close, and by the time the work was finished in 1829, the Nazarenes had disbanded.

PRAGMATIC BROTHERHOODS

If it was ideology, whether political or religious, that was largely driving the establishment and elaboration of the brotherhood model of artistic collectivity in the cultural capitals of continental Europe in the first third of the nineteenth century, it was a more openly commercial motivation that led comparable groupings in England. The commercial opportunities on both the supply and demand side, and the spaces in between, of the London market at the turn of that century were increased by the political and economic instabilities of the French Revolution and its aftermath; a still incomplete professionalisation of this market offered artists opportunities both for asserting independence from the Royal Academy, and for using this independence as a marketing ploy.[35] As on the Continent, the term 'brotherhood' was reached for, but the entrepreneurial climate gave it other connotations than those across the Channel. An example is that of 'The Brothers', a group founded by the watercolourist Thomas Girtin at the opening of this new market conjuncture at the very time that the Barbus were coalescing around their residual revolutionary ideology. Girtin by contrast had the emergent commercial purpose of raising the profile of his medium, and of that of a few professional and amateur practitioners of it.[36] Forty years later, in 1837, towards its close (by which time the domination of the market by the dealers and the Royal Academy between them had been consolidated), another group chose a similar title, that of 'The Clique', but its ambitions too belied its separatist connotations, for its members sought only to succeed within this market, rather than to challenge or ignore it.[37]

There was, however, one English group that, although not calling itself a brotherhood, more closely echoed – indeed, may have imitated – the Nazarenes. From the mid-1820s until the early 1830s a group of former Royal Academy students, admirers of the work of William Blake, first met frequently at his apartment in London, and then lived part-time at the house of one of their number, Samuel Palmer, in Shoreham, Kent. Styling themselves 'The Ancients', they sought to escape the commercial society of their city and recreate an idealised rural past.[38] In this, they were probably unaware of the example of the Barbus, but it is likely that they knew of the Nazarenes, whose reputation extended across Europe by then, and who had been the subject of several articles in the London press.[39] Following them, the Ancients promoted the wearing of 'revivalist' smocks, together with beards and long hair;[40] their paintings' subject matter was either biblical or intense, abundant, moonlit landscapes (or the former imagined in the latter). Unlike the German group, they found neither patrons for collective work nor critical support, and their exhibits at the Royal Academy found no buyers; unlike Blake, they were politically High Tory, had no programme for social reform and violently opposed the 'Captain Swing' agricultural labourers' uprising of 1830, which occurred nearby, as a disruption of the peace and harmony of rural life. But their initiative registers if nothing else the reach of the Nazarenes' example by the mid-1820s – although, half-hearted and commercially unsuccessful as it seems to have been, it also indicated the lack of penetration of that model of brotherhood in the English art world.

There is evidence, however, that the feature of brotherhood which the Ancients adopted most readily was its masculinism – and, beyond this, its homosociality; in both of these respects it also followed the Nazarenes, including, it seems, in the religious intensity of the friendship between Overbeck and Pforr, noted above.[41] The tacit homoeroticism of the Ancients' relationships was suppressed in memoirs. Noting that '[i]t is one of the features of breakaway artistic communities of the period that they reveal strong same-sex bonding', Vaughan adds: 'Unsurprisingly, such matters are played down in subsequent accounts, yet there are hints of strong emotions in surviving manuscripts.'[42]

The Pre-Raphaelite Brotherhood, founded in 1848 in London by seven young male artists, sat somewhere between the two continental brotherhoods and the English ones discussed above. Initially they borrowed from the Nazarenes their cultish secrecy, adoption of a common symbolic signature ('PRB'), their idealisation of the assumed primitivism of the early Renaissance and the tacit adherence to agreed – if broadly interpreted – pictorial qualities. But there was more that differentiated them from the German group than made them resemble it; the group's foundation in 1848 came fully 40 years after that of the latter, and since the Nazarenes' disbandment in 1830, its reputation, while spreading across Europe, had lost its ideological specificity, spawned no emulative groupings (other than the tentative efforts of the Ancients) and had more influence on questions regarding the morality of art than on its aesthetics.[43]

Perhaps the biggest similarity was in the masculinism of both – but in this, too, the religiosity of the Nazarenes' homosociality bore little relation to the character of the Pre-Raphaelites' exclusion of women. Crucially, the PRB came at a time when English society had undergone industrialisation, the development of bourgeois hegemony, a heightening of class conflict, the regimentation of daily life and the challenge of secularism to the domination of religious world-views, and the artists who formed the new brotherhood faced correspondingly heightened secular, social, economic and psychological pressures. These focused on their masculinity, for as Victorian society became more emphatically patriarchal, and relations between genders both more unequal and more insistently consecrated as such, men were as increasingly, if differently, circumscribed by gender expectations as were women. As recent scholarship has noted, despite the apparent neutrality of masculinity (its status as the normative gender), it was 'a category which preoccupied Victorian critics, [one that] registered consistently in various discourses of the period'.[44] In this context, the choice of 'brotherhood' as a name for the PRB's collectivity was more than a matter of convention, or the lack of a readier alternative, for its members in 1848. Indeed, for all the attention given, both by the artists and in their reception as a group, to the assertion of a 'pre-Raphaelite' aesthetic, the prevalence of themes of male–female relations in their choice of subjects for their paintings indicates that masculinity and masculine sociality were among their primary concerns.

These preoccupations were registered in their earliest pictures as members of the fledgling group, in true brotherhood manner, on two levels. Thus, for example, William Holman Hunt's *Valentine Rescuing Sylvia from Proteus* of 1851 (pl. 4), a subject taken from Shakespeare's *The Two Gentlemen of Verona*, was explicitly concerned with the theme of reconciliation between two best friends, set against each other by tragedy but visibly seeking to restore their bond. On the other hand, John Everett Millais's *Lorenzo and Isabella* of 1848–49, a work whose theme was taken from John Keats's poem *Isabella, or The Pot of Basil*, painted in the first flush of his commitment to the codes of brotherhood, was laced with imagery that, less explicitly but, for those who shared these codes, unmistakably referenced themes of sexual desire, frustration and incontinence (pl. 5).[45] It was, moreover, an engagement with masculinity in which the perceived – and constructed – inequalities of gender were asserted by the members of the brotherhood without exception in terms of their own lives, careers and desires rather than those of the women whom they depicted, despite the presence and the important work of a number of female artists and writers within their circle.[46] As Jan Marsh was the first of many to observe, while women's faces are seen everywhere in Pre-Raphaelite paintings and drawings, 'their voices are never heard. As depicted, they are silent, enigmatic, passive figures, not individuals engaged in activity but objects to be gazed upon by painter and spectator.'[47]

Yet such exploration and assertion of the dimensions of masculinity in the new secular society was not the only major factor distinguishing the Pre-Raphaelites from the Nazarene model; of equal consequence was their *lack* of the latter's monasticism and fraternal, monkish collectivity. As its numbers grew, the group's Nazarenesque features quickly became dissipated: secrecy yielded to the desire for notoriety, the restricted membership of the Brotherhood to a widening and loosening circle of associates, and the commitment to early Renaissance 'primitivism' to a variety of styles that furthered members' individual reputations and their promotion. It was thus the PRB's 'otherhood', to use Jason Rosenfeld's apposite term – its *dis*unity and the individualism of its members, faced especially with the requirements of the art market and the increasingly commercial pressures it imposed on their careers – that was noted by its first historians as the means of its success.[48] Even the insistent masculinism had an instrumental element in this context, in that the eccentric, bohemian and performatively gendered persona that Dante Gabriel Rossetti, especially, cultivated from the early 1860s[49] at Tudor House, his Cheyne Walk residence, was, as Amelia Yeates and Serena Trowbridge note, 'an important part of what his patrons were buying into when they purchased his works'. As they further argue, this alignment with their patrons (who belonged to a significant fraction of the rising industrial and mercantile middle class) also shows that 'it would be wrong to suggest that in its approach to masculinity, Pre-Raphaelite art and literature were always troubling current gender norms; as a group of predominantly male artists and writers, the Pre-Raphaelites knew and benefitted from the value of hegemonic masculinity'.[50] In short, they shared the cultural beliefs of their class and gender rather than opposing them, and in the middle decades of the nineteenth century these included emergent Victorian attitudes towards women. In opposing the dominance of academic 'post-Raphaelitism', they sought and explored the means to articulate the range of positions that such attitudes entailed for a wide spectrum of young professional men such as themselves.

The Pre-Raphaelites were not alone among artists in their shifting economic orientation. As we shall see, it was *within* this market dynamic, and as a deliberate response to its diversification and liberalisation, not only on both sides of the English Channel but across all of Europe from the mid-nineteenth century, that artists of all aesthetic stripes began to organise and exhibit outside of the salons as well as participating in them (or attempting to, subject to their juries).[51] In an influential observation, the cultural historian and theorist Raymond Williams summarised this response as a progressive one: 'We can distinguish three main phases', Williams proposes,

> which had been developing during the late 19th century. Initially, there were innovative groups which sought to protect their practices within the growing dominance of the art market and against the indifference of the formal academies. These developed into alternative, more radically innovative groupings, seeking to provide their own facilities of production, distribution and publicity; and finally into fully oppositional formations, determined not only to promote their own work but to attack its enemies in the cultural establishments and, beyond these, the whole social order in which these enemies had gained and now exercised and reproduced their power.[52]

Williams's proposed dynamic is appealing in its apparent basis in empirical observation, and as such has brought useful and influential explanatory clarity of analysis to a field that previously lacked it. Yet it is misleading, I suggest, in three ways. First, to the degree that, despite such observation, it has a teleological flavour, betrayed by its ending in 'fully': the dynamic has a logic that is revealed in the character of its 'full' development into outright and total opposition to the social (and by implication political) status quo – on the part of that avant-garde that Williams is concerned to account for in the essay from which this is quoted. Second, it is misleading in its elision of the aesthetic and the social in its ordering of degrees of innovation ('initial', 'more radical') – an elision that assumes that these are jointly calibrated – when, in truth, radical aesthetic innovation could go hand in hand with social conservatism, as we shall see. And third, it assumes that these 'phases' of development were (to the extent that they occurred) monolithic – that all its component groupings shared a common direction as well as temporality – when (again, as we shall see) closer observation can discern a more motley collection of them, often developing in different if not opposed directions and with different momenta, towards sometimes rival futures that were as yet only potential.

The Pre-Raphaelite Brotherhood is a case in point, and a crucial one in the context of that current revisionism that, as I noted in the Introduction, proposes this as 'an avant-garde'. For the dynamic I have identified shows the group as at once the agent of an emergent commercialised, individualist professionalism in the art market and as adhering to the (increasingly residual) values of a homosociality that was implicitly opposed to this; thus, not the breakaway 'avant-garde' grouping that this revisionism claims for it, but a *pre*-avant-garde hybrid, an unresolved (and hence unstable) combination of contradictory values. The reasons why, within the range of alternatives that were then on offer to progressive artists (and other cultural producers), including the PRB, the type of cultural formation that came to turn the potential into the actual, and to dominate the field of modernist art by 1914, managed to do so – these are what this book proposes to explore.

Thanks in part to the contradictions encompassed by the PRB, the religious commitment that had driven groups such as the Nazarenes lost favour beyond the group itself in face of the more economically instrumental concern to optimise the market opportunities offered by collective identities. The stimuli towards this ascendancy came largely from within the market, but in different ways. At one extreme in terms of types of collectivity was the phenomenon of rural artists' colonies. These began to form in the 1820s and grew in size and number through the nineteenth century, peaking in its last two decades and the first of the new century; their most recent and comprehensive historian, Nina Lübbren, calculated that across these 90 years over 3,000 artists worked in one or more of over 80 colonies spread across 11 European countries, of which over 30 were formed in the 1880s, and some of which numbered over 200 residents each.[53]

The reasons for their proliferation and success as foci for artistic practice are both multiple and uncertain, but among them was a recognition on the part of the artists who flocked to them that there was significant advantage in market and professional terms in belonging to one (or more): as an addition to a curriculum vitae, as a part of a necessary professional fine-art education (a supplement, or complement to – and eventually, for many, a substitute for – that provided in urban art schools both state and private),[54] a means of learning those skills of painting that were not (yet) taught in the latter. As Lübbren notes, with few exceptions artists who joined them 'trained and exhibited within conventional institutional frameworks', and tended 'to adhere to middle-class values of respectability and professionalism, with only touches of bohemianism to lend them an aura of "artistic" freedom'.[55] As such, these colonies lie largely outside the frame of reference of the present study of the avant-garde. Yet they are relevant to it in one significant respect, in that their adherents' aspirations and allegiances, both professional and market, position them within that pan-European 'Secessionist' network of artists whose emergence and consolidation in the second half of the nineteenth century was, I shall argue, both an immediate precursor of, and a necessary condition for, that of the avant-garde, which followed closely on its heels.[56]

At the other extreme were the small groups of artists that emerged out of school or studio friendships in mid-nineteenth-century Paris as vehicles initially for sharing work and ideas, then for self-promotion in the market and for career advancement, as the process of the privatisation of such promotion gathered pace. Those to which the painter Henri Fantin-Latour belonged are examples of this sequence.[57] The first, an initiative of his own of 1854–56 while he was still a student at the École des Beaux-Arts, gathered a few fellow students to create a shared album of writings and drawings for their private enjoyment. In autumn 1858 Fantin-Latour set up the Société des Vrais Bons, a convivial but primarily market-facing coterie dedicated to 'the painting of the future' and the exclusion of those not deemed 'truly worthy' – as its statutes declared in orthodox cenacle fashion. At the same time he founded the Société des Trois jointly with James Whistler and Alphonse Legros, whose purpose was yet more single-mindedly focused on mutual assistance in promoting their careers (and of which Whistler appears to have been the linchpin, in what was the first of a sequence of professional initiatives, paralleling his painterly activities, by means of which the American managed his own career).[58] Les Trois was not an innovation as such; the mid-1850s in Paris saw the setting-up by many artists frustrated by the constraints and overcrowding of the annual state-run Salon of their own exhibiting societies, some of them (nicknamed *petits Salons*) intended as 'curtain-raisers' to the major event, others as independent of it and registering a loosening of its monopoly. The most famous was the Cercle de l'Union Artistique, founded mid-decade; its rivals included the Cercle St Arnaud and the Cercle Artistique et Littéraire, both active from the 1860s.[59]

Despite this increasing ascendancy of market-facing groupings, the appeal, for artists, of the brotherhood was not yet exhausted; as the default paradigm for a concept of anti-commercial, idealistic artistic collectivity, it continued to have some purchase late in the century, and even into the twentieth, before it was superseded by the professionalism of the avant-garde model. It did so through a compromise that saw explicit religious faith replaced either by a more generalised pursuit of spiritual experience and its expression, and/or a commitment to the values of male friendship. An example of this continuity, in both respects, is the group of Parisian artists who were drawn in the late 1880s to the anti-naturalistic, decorative painting style, known as Synthetism, of Paul Gauguin, and who chose the name Nabis – from the Hebrew for 'prophet' – as their collective designation. The choice, and the ideology that governed it, were those of Paul Sérusier, a charismatic student at the Académie Julian (the oldest and best-known of the *académies libres*, or private fee-paying teaching studios that were then proliferating in Paris).[60]

In 1888 Sérusier sought out Gauguin in the Breton village of Pont-Aven where he was exploring a painterly equivalent for what he saw as the primitive qualities of peasant culture. Under the latter's instruction Sérusier painted a little landscape, first known as *Paysage au Bois d'Amour* (*Landscape in the Bois d'Amour*) (pl. 6), on a cigar-box lid in flat patches of bright, unmodulated colour. Back in Paris at the start of the new term, Sérusier showed this 'talisman', as he somewhat portentously referred to it and as it would come to be formally titled, first to his friends Pierre Bonnard, Paul Ranson, Gabriel Ibels and Maurice Denis, and then to Édouard Vuillard, Ker-Xavier Roussel and René Piot, who were studying at the École des Beaux-Arts. Capitalising on the kudos that it gave him, Sérusier marshalled these fellow students into a group of which he was tacitly accepted as the leader. As Denis later recalled, he gave them 'a name which, with respect to the studios, made us initiates, a sort of secret society with mystical allure, and proclaimed us to be habitually in a state of prophetic fervour'.[61] The emulation of the Nazarenes that this suggests was underlined in a letter to Denis of 1889: 'I dream, for the future', Sérusier wrote, 'of a purified fraternity made up only of convinced artists who are enamoured of goodness and beauty, investing their works and their conduct with that indefinable quality which I call nabi.'[62] A closer model than that of the German brotherhood, however, was by this time available in the French cultural tradition: that of the literary cenacle, which originated in the Parisian world of letters in the early nineteenth century, and possessed very similar collectivist features but without the

Nazarenes' religiosity. As defined by its recent historians, a cenacle was 'composed for the most part of writers and painters [and] tended, out of a concern for homogeneity, to reject all exogenous elements (women, socialites, journalists)'. It was, crucially, private in character and disposed to secrecy in its behaviour, and its cohesiveness was grounded in fraternity: a solidarity which, 'more perhaps even than mere, fragile friendship', was 'a cénacle's corner-stone. For the *cénaclier* worked at once *for* the cénacle and *through* the cénacle'.[63] In this context, Sérusier's *Talisman* initiative and the Nabi brotherhood to which it led can be seen to have drawn also on this model. Indebted to studio friendships, and to the openness to shared innovation that these fostered,[64] with Sérusier's encouragement the group built on these a superstructure of 'all the instruments indispensable to its sustainability: a name (nabi), social habits (a monthly dinner at a particular restaurant, and a weekly gathering at the studio of one of their number, Paul Ranson, which they re-baptised "the Temple"), and a "manifesto" (the painting by Sérusier, re-baptised *The Talisman*)' – in all of these, as well as in their '*prophétisme*, enthusiasm and mysticism', as Anthony Glinoer and Vincent Laisney observe, 'the nabi movement linked itself directly to the grand tradition of the cénacle, which made of the poet an elect, a being apart, touched by grace'.[65]

As between these two models, it was the distinctly religious significance and motivation that the project held for Sérusier and some others in the Nabi group that suggests the Nazarene inheritance as more influential. Maurice Denis made both of these clear, independently and even before its foundation, describing in his journal in 1885 his dream of leading a group of religious artists in communal church decoration.[66] Following the logic of the title that Sérusier gave the group and the character he proposed for it, the Nabi Jan Verkade in 1897 became a noviciate at the Benedictine monastery of Beuron in southwestern Germany, and spent the rest of his life painting church frescoes; Sérusier himself several times considered doing the same, and translated from the German an account of that monastery's decorative work.[67] For others in the Symbolist milieu the model of the painter-monk, as antithesis to the worldly ambition of the mainstream Salon artists, was held in high esteem; Fra Angelico was frequently invoked.[68] Others, however, followed the secular option offered by the literary cenacles – and it is worth noting this distinction, because it goes some way, as we shall see, to explaining the outcome of these potential, alternative avenues of resistance to (and eventual negotiation with) the developing art market.

Among them were two initiatives that, while they remained unrealised, have been recorded for posterity by virtue of the notability of their authors. Laura Morowitz has rescued that of Émile Bernard. Perhaps the leading Synthetist follower of Gauguin (and, in his own view, the unacknowledged pioneer of this painting style), Bernard proposed early in 1891, in a letter to a painter friend, the establishing of a group he would call 'Les Anonymes', whose aim would be 'art for art's sake. Not glory, not commerce, not reputation: the edification of an idea, of a work.' He explained how it should function: 'Each member contributes his effort to the whole project. Each one could no more be taken away from the group than could a stone from a house.... Thus we aim for appreciation of the ensemble, and not the individual parts.'[69] This anonymity was, for Bernard, the key to successful resistance to the siren song of individual renown: with it, there would be 'no jealousies, no dishonest plagiarisms'; members would be sworn to 'incognito absolu' and would 'renounce all personality in order to contribute to the total project, which would be the synthesis of all the combined efforts'.[70] Yet even this was already proving no adequate safeguard, as Morowitz notes, first, since Bernard himself 'attempted everything possible to ensure that history would recognise his primary role in Symbolism'; second, because the market would soon trump the project's strategy, both by promoting the 'painter-monk' as a sellable artistic identity, and by encouraging a consumer taste for 'anonymous' works by 'primitifs'.[71]

The second recorded initiative from that moment of a secular collective grouping of painters on the cenacle model is the project attempted by Vincent van Gogh. This was clearly motivated, as his numerous letters on the subject reveal, both by a yearning for the friendships that a collective venture such as a brotherhood could foster, and by a keen awareness of the marketing opportunities it might also offer. 'I believe', he wrote in 1888,

> an Impressionist association would be an affair of the same kind as the association of the twelve Pre-Raphaelites in England[72] and I believe it really could be brought about. You also know that in my view the artists would then guarantee one another a livelihood, independently of the dealers, by agreeing that each would give a substantial number of paintings to the society and that both gains and losses would be shared by all.[73]

In July of the same year he suggested:

> the material difficulties of the painter's life make it desirable for painters to collaborate and unite (just as desirable as it was in the age of the guild of St Luke). By safeguarding the material side and treating one another as good friends instead of cutting one another's throats, painters would be happier and in any case less ridiculous, foolish and culpable.[74]

The differences between these two projects of Bernard and Van Gogh are themselves considerable: one was motivated, it would seem, by a spiritual conception of art and art practice, the other ostensibly by marketing considerations. Yet they share a homosocial and secular character that further differentiates both from Sérusier's religious predilections. Putting all of these alternative options for fraternal collectivity in a *fin-de-siècle* context, it would seem that the dynamic of the Parisian avant-garde was with the former two and against the latter, with respect both to its internal development and the political conjuncture. As regards the first, the proliferation of the network of *académies libres* in Paris (and their supplanting, for many aspirant avant-gardists, of the École des Beaux-Arts) encouraged the reprise of something of the Barbus' rebelliousness: as we shall see, a studio culture in which the authority of the *Maître* (usually a professor from the École, moonlighting perfunctorily for the money) counted for less than the example of the most charismatic of the students often fostered groupings offering competing technical innovations.[75] As regards the conjuncture, the failure by the turn of the century of the Catholic *Ralliement* with the Third Republic launched by Pope Leo XIII's *Rerum Novarum* encyclical of 1891, and the polarising effect of the Dreyfus Affair from mid-decade (which in the words of Catholic poet and editor Adrien Mithouard split the emergent literary and artistic avant-garde 'like a drop of acid in a retort'), led to a perception of religious commitment as increasingly hand in hand with right-wing, anti-Dreyfusard politics, which gave Sérusier's Nabism a retrospective colouration. The secular combination of market-orientation and friendship, on the other hand, was strengthened both by the economic imperatives of the first and the Dreyfusard allegiances (in the majority within the avant-garde) of the second; its prospective, progressive colouration was intensified, if anything, by the anticlerical activities of the extra-parliamentary cohorts of the Bloc des gauches (Leftists Bloc) after 1900.[76]

These twin motivations of friendship and market advantage were the primary factors in play, therefore, in the establishment of what turned out to be the last significant artistic grouping on the brotherhood/cenacle model to be attempted in France before this model was overtaken by the gathering momentum of that of the avant-garde.[77] The Abbaye de Créteil commune was small and short-lived, yet it is significant because it achieved a renown in the historiography of twentieth-century French literature beyond either the aspirations of its members or its cultural achievements, and because it did so largely, it would seem, as a result of its hybrid character. It was founded in the winter of 1906–7 by five poets, René Arcos, Henri-Martin Barzun, Georges Duhamel, Alexandre Mercereau and Charles Vildrac, and a painter, Albert Gleizes, on the basis both of friendship and of a shared aesthetic that sought to distinguish itself from the introspection of Symbolism through an engagement with everyday life. It lasted for 14 months. Despite its allegiance to the quotidian, the purpose of the collective (as its members explained in an Appeal for support and funds from within their home milieux of post-Symbolist poetry and post-Synthetist painting, published in late 1906) was to secure a means to focus on their arts without the distractions of the need to make a living from commercial activities such as journalistic writing or illustration.[78] To this end, they rented a run-down mansion beside the river Marne on the southeastern outskirts of Paris in which to live communally and work individually, and they invited a printer, Lucien Linard, a former national military service comrade of Gleizes, to join them to run a printing press that would finance the project, and to which they proposed each to contribute a few hours of artisanal labour every day, leaving the rest of their time for poetry and/or painting.

On the evidence of the Appeal and its members' actions, the group's venture was a straightforward effort to marry the pleasures of friendship and communal living (if not collaborative work) with the economic requirements of the literary and artistic markets; as such it was an attempt finally to realise the aspirations of the previous generation, such as the Nabis, Bernard and Van Gogh. In practical terms it was a naïve and improbable project; the Appeal garnered no funding, and if it had not been for the good luck of making the acquaintance of the would-be literary mover-and-shaker Henri-Martin Barzun, a young writer with money, who provided the rent and joined them in the commune, it would have remained, like the above examples, no more than a pipe dream. Yet the terms in which they pitched their Appeal, and the genealogy that they claimed for it, are significant. The extent of their ambition was (perhaps bathetically) vast: not content with naming the project formally, in the Statutes that accompanied the Appeal, 'L'Abbaye, Association fraternelle d'artistes', in a conscious and widely recognised echo of Rabelais's sixteenth-century imaginary 'Abbaye de Thélème',[79] the group also described it as 'a FREE VILLA MÉDICIS, whose guests may work in complete peace, without any constraint and keeping all their individualism, sharing their enthusiasms, uniting their needs, pooling their resources'.[80] Citing Nietzsche, they saw the property as a '*dwelling [that is] too elevated and too vertiginous for all the impure [to reach]*, and by means of which we shall escape the lower depths'.[81] At the same time, and somewhat contradictorily, the group sought to situate their collective in the lineage of anarchists' communes, which had seen a revival since the late 1890s, describing their proposed work with the printing press, in terms that gestured towards anarchist beliefs, as making of them 'its artisans, thereby giving their intellectual labours the necessary complement of manual labour'.[82] This was no more than a spurious gesture, prompted perhaps by the flurry of communes attempted by anarchists across France between 1900 and 1910; however, although the Abbaye members may have been aware of them, it is unlikely, so brief and unsuccessful were they.[83] Indeed, Barzun, whose professional occupation was related to government, later recalled that he was the only member of the group with any awareness of politics at all, let alone an acquaintance with the history of the *milieux libres*.[84] Moreover, the absence of the printer Linard from any Abbaye group photograph, as well as his unannounced departure from the property the moment the venture was abandoned, never to be heard of again, suggests he was treated more as an employee than as a member of the collective. The Abbaye did publish 28 volumes of poetry, according to its most recent chroniclers, but very few of them were printed there; perhaps as few as two.[85]

Why, then, was the Abbaye de Créteil so fêted during and after its 14-month existence? There were, I suggest, two reasons. First, because despite the declared aspiration to communal self-sufficiency and distance from the 'lower depths' of Parisian art journalistic drudgery, the location of the Abbaye just beyond the southeastern periphery of the city ensured that contact with Parisian literary life and its currents was as easy as ever. Moreover, the Abbaye members were assiduous in building a network of supporters (of varying degrees) both in the burgeoning milieux of the *petites revues* that were the vehicles of so much cultural experiment and criticism, and in the broader news press which was happy to print stories of artistic eccentricity such as this. Members welcomed visitors at weekends, organised fêtes, plays and concerts for them,[86] and seem to have tirelessly worked to obtain wide and regular coverage of them. The establishing of the Abbaye Press not only gave their weekday efforts a material outlet – of the poets, all but Barzun had a volume published by the Press, and Gleizes contributed lithographic illustrations to some – but it also published significant new work by sympathetic non-Abbaye authors, which brought both kudos and wider awareness of the venture.[87]

Second, if astute networking and promotion of the Abbaye were what gave the venture such renown, it was also fortunate in capturing the momentum of a contemporary turn to aesthetic autonomism. A year before its foundation, the collapse of the parliamentary Bloc des gauches, the governmental alliance between the Radical-Socialist and Socialist parties, had also ushered to their end the broad and varied extra-parliamentary initiatives that had given social and cultural expression to the spirit of class collaboration that it fostered: the *universités populaires*, the art education groups such as L'Art pour Tous and so on. Among the participants in this populism were future Abbaye members Gleizes and Mercereau. With the organised working class rejecting parliamentary socialism and retreating behind the stockade of an autonomous class politics, grounded in and symbolised by commitment to building for a general strike, its erstwhile partners in the Bloc initiatives, middle-class artists and writers, reciprocated by substituting aesthetic for social commitment.[88] As a part of this shift, the aesthetic of the Abbaye (to the extent that it was adhered to) placed the group's engagement with social life within their poetry and art, rather than alongside it. As a taking of a position within the cultural field, it resonated with key developments within a Parisian literary avant-garde that was undergoing a generational renewal: replacing both the tenets and the institutions of a Symbolism whose major achievements were a decade or more old, and whose leading authors were either already dead or comfortably pensionable, a cohort of young poets was exploring possible directions beyond it.[89] The Abbaye poets were part of this, and as a collective venture, their initiative appeared as more than the sum of its parts.

If these factors gave the project a renown disproportionate to the group's artistic achievements, they also lend it a historical significance not so much in its originality as in its hybrid (and, as it turned out, transitional) character. For the combination, or juxtaposition, of retrospective gestures to collectivities of the past with prospective self-promotional strategies positions the Abbaye *between* the 'residual' brotherhood model of cultural association and the 'emergent' model of the avant-garde. It was, on one hand, the language of brotherhoods on which the 1906 Appeal drew, in its cloaking of the Abbaye in illustrious associations from French cultural history; on the other hand, the very assiduousness and market awareness with which the group promoted its venture were characteristic of the hyperbole of the new techniques of advertising. Self-consciously modern in both form and functionality, these were adopted by the avant-gardes of the new century, and the Abbaye therefore has some claim to belong to their number. This transitional character and position are features to which we shall return.

The Abbaye was not, in fact, strictly the last artistic brotherhood in pre-First World War France. In the decade before August 1914, as the anarchist movement's *fin-de-siècle* imbrication with the Symbolist literary avant-garde largely gave way to mutual disengagement in the face of rising political tensions and the collapse of the Bloc des gauches that I have noted, most of the avant-garde substituted artistic for political radicalism. But a small splinter milieu of individualistic anarchists held to a position that fused avant-gardism, aestheticism and anarchism, promoting a doctrine of 'artistocracy', an amalgam of Nietzschean elitism, Stirnerian egoism and 'anarcho-individualism'. They founded two brotherhoods, in 1911 the Ghilde Les Forgerons (Blacksmiths' Guild) and in 1913 Les Compagnons de l'Action d'Art (Art Action Brotherhood), and a series of *petites revues* in which they condemned the commercialism of the entire art market including its avant-garde sector, espousing instead a mutualist, anti-commercial policy of artistic practice, support and exchange. This was redolent of the cenacle model discussed earlier, except in the somewhat paradoxical insistence on prioritising the individual freedom of members over the requirements of the collective.

This circle was marginal even within the avant-garde, and in the context of that *avant-guerre* conjuncture its hostility to modernist currents was a residual position.[90] Yet its existence is worth noting, not only because it shows this to have been an available position at that time and place, but also because it appears to have been shared by an equally ephemeral grouping across the Channel that was contemporary with it but of considerably greater historical consequence. In London, where the pressures of a professionalising avant-gardism were as yet less insistently felt (though already impinging on its artistic sociality), and where the inheritance of the brotherhood model was correspondingly both more lasting and more heterogeneous, the cultural legacy of the ideas of Friedrich Nietzsche was at that moment central to the cultural discourse of the nascent milieu of the 'little literary magazines'. The philosopher had already had great influence in artistic and intellectual circles across Europe; in London, in the pages, in particular, of *The New Age* under its editor Alfred Orage, the merits and demerits of his concept of the 'Overman' and its application to artists were energetically debated.[91]

A leading and early contributor to the debate was Allen Upward, a polymathic but little-known poet whose radically individualist and elitist ideas have recently been acknowledged as a formative influence on Ezra Pound in particular;[92] art historian Sarah Turner, among others, suggests that he was 'the much overlooked source behind Pound's recasting of the artist not only as a "genius" but also a divine figure—not as a Christian, but a primitive "shaman" or "priest"'.[93] In a series of three articles of early 1910 in *The New Age* Upward offered a challenging critique of Nietzsche on the provocative grounds, not that the promise of the Overman was unpalatably elitist, but paradoxically that it was not exclusive enough, and he substituted for it a collectivity of such divinities, which he termed 'the Order of the Seraphim'.[94] He developed his ideas in books and articles over the next four years, and in the autumn of 1913 felt ready to launch this collectivity as 'The Angel Club', presenting his proposal for it in *The New Freewoman* at the start of that October.[95] It was this proposal that especially caught the eye of Pound, who fleshed out the principles of such an order of his own in a landmark piece of art criticism entitled 'The New Sculpture'.[96] It represents an explicit application of Upward's elitism to the sculptors with whom he was by then associated, Jacob Epstein, Henri Gaudier-Brzeska and Eric Gill, via a characterisation of the contemporary artist that embraced the primitivism of their sculpture:

> He must live by craft and violence. His gods are violent gods. A religion of fashion plates has little to say to him, and that little is nauseous… there is a recognition of this strife in the arts… of the moment…. We turn back, we artists… to the djinns who were our allies aforetime, to the spirits of our ancestors…. The aristocracy of entail and title has decayed, the aristocracy of commerce is decaying, the aristocracy of the arts is ready again for its service… we who are the heirs of the witch-doctor and the voodoo, we artists who have been so long the despised are about to take over control. And the public would do well to resent these 'new' kinds of art.[97]

Published four months before the debut of *Blast*, the incendiary magazine with which, together with Gaudier-Brzeska and Wyndham Lewis, Pound launched London's first avant-garde 'ism', Vorticism, 'The New Sculpture' is a warm-up for the combative and elitist rhetoric of that magazine. How serious either Upward or Pound were in their ideas for a club or brotherhood as a practical venture is uncertain (although the Abbaye de Créteil offered a recent template in several respects for Pound's); given the degree to which the utopian socialism of 1880s and 1890s Britain had fallen from favour in the early years of the new century,[98] Upward's suggestion may have been as ironic as it was impractical, and envisioned only as an ideal. As Suzanne Hobson has shown, angels were quite in vogue in the decades around 1900, as a trope for imagining elites of various kinds, called into service as safeguards against secular materialism. Perhaps this was its only serious function for both of these poets.[99]

2
AFFECTIVE AFFINITIES

With hindsight, both the Abbaye de Créteil's hybrid character and its consequent instability are plainer than they can have been at the time. We shall see in later chapters why and how, as the market for cultural goods expanded and diversified, the avant-garde model of collectivity whose promotional tactics the Abbaye deployed offered, crucially, an appeal of an instrumental and professional kind, and why this was the case first, and particularly, in Paris. Yet the ties of friendship in which it originated were also a powerful incentive, beyond initiatives such as this, towards new collective identities for cultural producers outside the mainstream – indeed, not only for them, but for a wide spectrum of socially, politically or economically motivated groups. As Sarah Cole notes in her study of its role in modernist English writing in this period:

> Perhaps the biggest mistake one can make in conceptualising friendship… is to assume that it is a private, voluntary relation, governed by personal sentiment and easy communion. It is not. Like any complex social relationship, friendship has its own conventions and institutional affinities (schools, universities, social clubs, as well as more rigidly arranged organisations from the Boy Scouts to the military platoon), and it is shot through with social meaning.[1]

If, therefore, we are to understand the character and history of the artistic collectivities of late nineteenth- and early twentieth-century London in particular, and the emergence within these of an avant-garde formation, we must acknowledge the role played by friendship, or, to frame this more broadly, by the growth of an alternative social and cultural disposition of informal sociability – of a culture of fellowship, expressive of what I shall call an ideology of 'affective relations' – in shaping it. The fabric of these relations was woven by the intertwining of several threads of sociocultural dispositions and collectivities, which ranged from informal friendships to fellowships and associations, and from 'New Life' socialism to vegetarianism and spiritualism. As we shall see, the ideology of affective relations had varying forms of expression and degrees of intensity of attachment, whose significance for artists this chapter explores. Together they progressively enriched and articulated, around a shared commitment to 'friendship' in its broadest definition, a current of adversarial bourgeois opposition to the reduction of social relations under capitalism to the instrumental requirements of the cash nexus that ran through later Victorian English society to the First World War.

AFFECTIVE RELATIONS: AN UNDECLARED COUNTERCULTURE

That an ideology of affective relations was of structural significance for modern English society through the late nineteenth and twentieth centuries has increasingly been recognised in modern scholarship. The interdiscursive character of that ideology, its extraordinary bringing together of seemingly disparate, even opposed, cultural and political attachments, has been addressed by contributors to this in different ways, with different emphases that deserve to be noted. In an essay of 1995, Terry Eagleton bemoans a then-present *fin de millennium* shorn of the politics that characterised that of a century earlier.[2] He notes that the late nineteenth century saw 'an astonishing amalgam of spiritual and material ferment', observing that it was 'the period of Aubrey Beardsley *and* the Second International; of aestheticism and anarchism; of decadence and the Dock Strike', 'the decades of Tolstoyan *simplicitas* and the Fellowship of the New Life, of the garden city and rational diet and dress', but also of a consciousness which 'is now itself a form of alienation [from the post-Darwinian understanding of itself as a senseless material mechanism], and an art which posits the overcoming of this, a performative contradiction'. Henry James's late novels, Eagleton suggests, 'spin a style which tries to capture our experience at its very point of emergence, weaving a syntax so supple and devious that not a single discursive nuance or psychological flicker can escape it'. Pulling this set of apparent contradictions together, he concludes that

> the relations between this and Paterian aestheticism are obvious enough: aestheticism is not just some anodyne cult of *l'art pour l'art*, but the considerably more subversive project of living every facet of our experience, including those conventionally thought illicit, with the passionate intensity of our most precious investments.[3]

'It might seem a far cry from all this', he adds,

> to those gay intellectuals like Edward Carpenter,[4] who were especially enamoured of hunky railway workers and athletic East End policemen; but this is just a more literal version of the symbolic embracing of the 'real', the brawny proletarian as material object with which the estranged intellect must libidinally unite.

A metonymic coupling, one might say, for an oxymoronic cultural disposition that Eagleton summarises, with typical brio, as 'mystical positivism'.[5]

One of the most consequential components of the 'astonishing amalgam of spiritual and material ferment' that Eagleton identifies was that of the rise of the 'religion of socialism'. In the 1880s and 1890s a utopian longing for fellowship uncorrupted by the cash nexus of late Victorian capitalism became one of the drivers of the first phase of the British socialist movement. This was a dozen years in which, against a background of economic depression, deepening social inequalities in British society became inescapably plain; when the consequences of the 1867 Reform Act began to show in the rise of working-class political organisation; and when sections of the middle class experienced a moral crisis, in what amounted to a late Victorian revolt against their class by members of it.[6] Among several self-confessed examples, perhaps the most candid were the future campaigning journalist H.W. Nevinson, who joined the Social Democratic Federation in 1889, and the co-founder of the Fabian Society Beatrice Webb. Nevinson later recalled his repugnance for the comfortable class to which he belonged and his shamed sympathy for working people; Webb confessed to 'a growing uneasiness amounting to conviction that the industrial organisation which had yielded rent, interest and profits on a huge scale, had failed to provide a decent livelihood and tolerable conditions for a majority of the inhabitants of Great Britain'.[7]

In the 1880s and 1890s this spiritual unease, this alienation from its own aesthetically cushioned prosperity that Eagleton identified, 'overlapped with socialism and found a material ally'.[8] The intensity of aspiration that was contained in this shared utopian socialism was epitomised by two of its leading participants. Edward Carpenter was a founder member of the Fellowship of the New Life, a small coterie established in London in October 1883 with the explicit aim of transforming society by setting an example of clean, simplified living and elevated thinking for others to follow. It thus brought into focus the tension between the personal and the political at the heart of this early phase of British socialism, a dichotomy that was also between the spiritual and the material, and which has been seen as both its strength and its weakness. Influenced by the utopian and communitarian ideas of Thoreau, Emerson and Tolstoy, the commitment of most of its score or so of members to pacifism, vegetarianism and 'the good and simple life' drew together a motley collection of commitments to 'the cultivation of a perfect character for each and all'.[9] Carpenter, a socialist poet, philosopher, anthropologist and economist, a campaigner for gay rights and animal welfare, a vegetarian, smallholder and sandalmaker, embodied many of these commitments, and seems to have established a network across all their fields of unparalleled breadth and depth.[10] Carpenter's influence on his contemporaries was varied and enormous; summarising this, his biographer Sheila Rowbotham writes that he:

> was such an absorbent thinker and kept a finger in so many ephemeral fractions, groupings, circles and movements, that his political and intellectual trajectory runs like a roller-coaster ride through the highways and byways of late nineteenth-century and early twentieth-century thought and activism, signalling currents of opinion and patterns of assumption which have dissolved from view.[11]

Carpenter thus represents the reach and richness of this adversarial, alternative ideology of affective relations, and of what many of the actors in Stephen Yeo's account of utopian socialism called its 'special times', a conjuncture of a decade or so when it seemed that, for a number of reasons, these were imminent. 'Socialism will come, of that I feel sure', wrote Robert Blatchford, the author of a hugely influential collection of essays on the subject, *Merrie England*, in 1894.[12]

The figure who best represents the depth and strength of aspirations towards first imagining and then making this epochal change, however, is not Carpenter but William Morris. For Morris was perhaps uniquely placed (as well as equipped by his gifts) to do so; he had, more than anyone else either within the Pre-Raphaelite Brotherhood or outside of it, harnessed the retrospective longing for what were then seen as the better past times of a medieval, pre-capitalist sense of community to the present and future everyday practical concerns of 'how we live and how we might live'.[13] He had not only extended the primitivism of his fellow artists, from the early 1860s, into craft practices and products that inscribed the implicitly anti-capitalist values of handiwork, simplicity and probity, but in his writings from the late 1870s and lectures, until his death in 1896, he seized the momentum of the early socialist movement, and the optimism of these 'special times', to reorient the retrospective, nostalgic imaginings of his early career and beliefs as a Pre-Raphaelite into a prospective vision of a utopia whose values were those of that socialism. The culmination of this project, and conceptually its crowning achievement, was his utopian fantasy *News from Nowhere* (1890), the intense and detailed medievalism of whose 'delight in the life of the world; intense and overweening love of the very skin and surface of the earth on which man dwells'[14] has since been assigned, unwarrantedly, to a genre of naïve and sentimental Victorian historical nostalgia now long out of favour. At its centre, however, is a vivid imagining of a process of revolutionary upheaval, unprecedented and unparalleled in its detail of description and nuanced attention to the potential phases, events and violence of this, which thoroughly breaks the retrospective mould of that genre and offers a readable and instructive prospectus of the possibility of convulsive social and political change in late Victorian capitalist society.

For all the optimism within the early socialist movement, such times did not last; as a participant later recollected, they were too exciting to do so.[15] The Fellowship of the New Life's early split and the resulting founding of the Fabian Society foreshadowed the development of the movement in the mid-1890s into a more pragmatic, instrumental organisation aimed at acquiring political power through the ballot box – via, as it turned out, the Labour Party (founded in 1892 as the Independent Labour Party). This closing down, by the turn of the twentieth century, of the utopian dimension of early British socialism has been seen as a marginalisation of the politics of affective relations in a way that invites a parallel understanding of the emergence and character of the London artistic avant-garde in the same period which I will develop.[16] The 'disorderly catalogues and creative mutations', as Leela Gandhi describes them, of that politics were seen as a unique means of showing society, in Carpenter's words, 'the wealth and variety of affectional possibilities which it has within itself'. Yet 'it was precisely this quality of chaotic admixture that came to signal the impoverishment of utopianism as a viable and effective form of socialist politics, disclosing in place of political versatility an impoverished dilettantism'.[17]

The shift in understanding of it, from celebration to condemnation, began within the movement itself, but gained broader momentum over the next third of a century as socialism entered the parliamentary mainstream in Britain and western Europe, while its failure to do so in Russia provoked revolution. Friedrich Engels's *Socialism, Utopian and Scientific* (1892) laid down the terms of utopian socialism's political disqualification, to which Lenin's *'Left-Wing' Communism: An Infantile Disorder* (1920) added the charges of 'immaturity' and 'eclectic mish-mash', as opposed to 'the science of "conscious organisation on a planned basis"' that serious, mature socialism required. The condemnation was completed by George Orwell in *The Road to Wigan Pier* (1937), whose devastating critique mocked utopian socialism as 'an undiscriminating "magnetic field" that drew toward itself "every fruit-juice drinker, nudist, sandal-wearer, sex-maniac, Quaker, 'Nature-cure' quack, pacifist and feminist in England"'.[18]

In the face of this 100-year-old 'disbarment' of utopian socialism and its outriders Leela Gandhi presents the counterclaim that 'it is precisely their ineligibility for the drama of mainstream politics, their lexical inadmissibility within a "developed" or established political vocabulary, that is the[ir] crucial revolutionary ingredient'.[19] In a post-millennial period of disillusionment with that political mainstream which colours contemporary global politics *a fortiori*, this argument offers a recuperation of *fin-de-siècle* radicalism that turns the terms of critique of it into positives. For its qualities of disorganisation, provisionality, coincidence and conjuncture were what made up the fabric of 'a utopian politics of inventiveness'[20] that gave the ideology of affective relations its appeal for assorted adversaries of the dominant cultural (and social) positions in Victorian bourgeois society. The affinities between the components of this interdiscursive cultural current offered not only an alternative to that dominant bourgeois disposition, but also, I shall argue, the means to a critique of, and alternative to, the developed professionalism of fine-art practices in Paris that shaped that city's artistic avant-garde.

MALE HOMOSOCIALITY AND HOMOSEXUALITY

For British artists, the attachment to affective relations as a foundation for creative practice had an early expression in the Pre-Raphaelite Brotherhood, in the progressive discarding, by most of its members, of that religiosity which had been a component of its emergence; in the replacement of this as a bulwark against the commercialisation of art practice by homosociality;

and in that engagement of several of these artists and writers with the complexities of mid-Victorian masculinity that were noted in Chapter 1. In the second phase of the PRB (from the mid-1850s) a significant, if at the time unanticipated, moment in the consolidation of the role of homosociality in art-group formation came with the founding of the Hogarth Club as an independent exhibiting society in April 1858. This was from the start a practical, market manoeuvre, aimed at gaining some independence within it from the Royal Academy; an early move in this self-promotional direction, it had a chequered history, plagued by discord over its exhibition policy, character and aesthetic orientation(s), and it ended three years later.[21] But also from the start its membership was dominated by the Rossetti wing of the PRB: Millais declined to join as he disliked its explicit opposition to the Royal Academy (Frederic Leighton, not a Pre-Raphaelite, also apparently soon withdrew for the same reason),[22] and Holman Hunt castigated the critics who saw Rossetti's 1859 painting *Bocca Baciata* (pl. 7), exhibited there in 1860, as the 'triumph' of the 'school' that the Brotherhood had engendered. In the eyes of the public, as Jason Rosenfeld notes, by that time 'a certain conception of Pre-Raphaelitism had been firmly established in the public's mind, and it had been linked irrevocably to the incipient aestheticism visible at the Hogarth Club'.[23]

Hunt was not wrong in his implicit criticism of the journalistic association of Pre-Raphaelitism with Rossetti (and growing dislike of what he saw as its immorality),[24] for the Hogarth Club provided the foundation for the establishment in 1862 of a social base for the close group of friends on which Rossetti's circle was by then centred, at Rossetti's new home, Tudor House on Cheyne Walk in Chelsea. For this social base developed the concept of brotherhood on which the Pre-Raphaelite group had run up its flag a decade and a half earlier into a collectivity that went beyond aesthetic strategy or even principle, eventually to challenge the morality itself of mainstream Victorian society. Rossetti was joined at Tudor House by his brother, William Michael, then launching a career as one of the first professional art critics in London,[25] and the poets Algernon Charles Swinburne and George Meredith. The ménage was significant not only in bringing together a cultural group with a shared commitment to the exploration of the relation between aesthetic and sexual beauty (a theme of which the keynote was sounded by *Bocca Baciata*), but equally in exemplifying the role that close friendship – Pre-Raphaelite-style brotherhood without the monkish overtones – could play in fostering creativity. As one recent historian of such relations in Victorian England suggests:

> for a time, Rossetti shaped a productive space with these men. Male domesticity, by Rossetti's lights, interwove friendship, love, and creative production… each would become absorbed in his own task, with occasional glances, sharing of ideas, or commentary on the others' projects (painting, poem, essay). Subtle influences passed from work to work. A form of silent support, a willingness to devote oneself to a task as a form of *being with* another, sharing space came as a deep pleasure for him.[26]

Tudor House was more than a fruitful domestic ménage. The community of these four men quickly became, as Deborah Lutz notes, 'a kind of way station or gathering ground for the great artist eccentrics of the day'; more than this, she observes, it became 'the fodder for legend', and adds: 'If a movement can be said to have a location, early Aestheticism emerged from Tudor House.'[27] The legend, such as it was, was not built on art alone; if the assertive sexuality of *Bocca Baciata* shocked some critics when it was shown at the Hogarth Club in 1860, the volumes of poetry that emerged from Tudor House over the next decade – Meredith's *Modern Love* in 1862, Swinburne's *Poems and Ballads* in 1866 and Rossetti's own *Poems* in 1870 – caused scandals that went beyond the literary, and established for the collective, as art historian Liz Prettejohn notes, a '"bohemian" group identity startlingly at odds with the carefully cultivated respectability of other groupings of Victorian artists'.[28]

Much of the reputation of Tudor House centred on Swinburne, then in his twenties, who was rapidly making a name for himself on two cultural fronts. As a critic, he was playing a central role in the elaboration of

Aestheticist poetic doctrine, introducing the term 'art for art's sake' into English critical writing and insisting upon a radical interpretation of art's autonomy.[29] As a poet, and in his private life as documented in diaries and correspondence, he was exploring the shifting sands of sexuality in directions that scandalised Victorian society. With the publication of *Poems and Ballads*, Swinburne gained an instant reputation for sexual rebellion and perversity; one reviewer remarked that 'all literary London is now ringing with the genius, the blasphemies and indecencies' of the volume.[30] This was hardly surprising: a modern literary historian has listed its themes as including 'necrophilia, anthropophagy, lesbianism, vampirism, sadomasochism… cunnilingus, masturbation, fellatio and anal copulation'.[31]

Swinburne was not alone in these obsessions, even if the list of them is unusually long in his case: a significant and growing number of men of all occupations in the mid-Victorian middle class shared them, as the Christian moral certainties of earlier decades were progressively sapped by secularism, Darwinism, the experiences of Empire and a changing balance of forces around gender relations. They indulged them, moreover, increasingly via the membership of private clubs and social networks: thus Swinburne was a member of the Cannibal Club, a private dining club drawn from members of the inner circle of the Anthropological Society. Both of these were founded in 1863 by the charismatic explorer, translator and polymath Richard Burton; the Society held conferences and published formal papers on mainstream aspects of its subject field, whereas the Club was a space for experimentation, bringing together scientists and men of letters to analyse 'deviant' sexual practices and, as Lutz describes it, to 'encourage one another in personal and artistic investigations into the outer reaches of sexual behaviour'.[32] However, literature and art were perhaps the primary publicly accessible cultural arenas for the articulation of these predilections. As Richard Dellamora notes, it is 'a truism of literary discussion' that 'sexual deviance, especially male homosexuality… [is] associated with being an artist in nineteenth-century England'; more specifically, he observes, 'there is a moment, in the 1860s, when writers make the connection explicit in public, vanguard contexts'.[33] Prominent among such writers, besides Swinburne, was his contemporary Walter Pater, who was by 1870 gaining renown for 'fashion[ing] an art historical-critical discourse expressive of male-male desire as a major medium of cultural expression' in writings such as his 1869 essay on Leonardo da Vinci.[34] Together, Dellamora suggests, these two were 'crucial in the struggle over the direction of adversary bourgeois culture'.[35]

Other sites of this homosocial thread of that struggle were two key institutions of Victorian society, the public schools and the universities. The former achieved an extraordinary expansion in mid-century, from a total of nine in 1841 to 71 in 1873,[36] as both the need for middle-class young men to acquire certification of gentlemanly status, and that of the expanding British Empire to recruit bureaucrats, grew exponentially. Through their emphasis on team sports and 'team spirit' within an ethos of manliness and loyalty, the public schools fostered a culture of hierarchised male community, providing core training for the nation's ruling elite that was both harsh and all-encompassing. Its character and significance were pithily summarised by E.M. Forster: 'Just as the heart of England is the middle classes', he wrote in later life, 'so the heart of the middle classes is the public school system.... With its boarding-houses, its compulsory games, its system of prefects and fagging, its insistence on good form and on *esprit de corps*, it produces a type whose weight is out of all proportion to its numbers.'[37] But the ideological effectiveness of public-school education that this indicates was accompanied by the unintentional fostering of a spirit of opposition to its ethos of muscular manliness and hearty, anti-intellectual comradeship. For those boys (the public schools were, of course, exclusively male communities) who had no interest in team sports and philistinism, friendship could flourish within the protocols of fagging and loyalty, replacing rank with intimacy and team spirit with shared intellectual, spiritual and aesthetic values.

This unwitting incubation by a dominant, strenuously heterosexual masculinism of its very nemesis thus led to a contradiction. As Cole notes:

> on one hand, the creation of networks and alliances, life-long old-boy bonds, and the cult of sport-based friendship were central to the schools' self-concept and mission; on the other hand, many former students maintain that their closest friendships with other boys actually collided with the inevitable cult of *esprit de corps*; these became a means of rebuttal of school form.[38]

More than this, indeed: in some respects the oppositional disposition that such students acquired was inseparable from the intimacy and romanticism of their friendships, and fed, as we shall see, into the dynamic of the emergence of the progressive artistic collectivities of Edwardian London. Ironically, the continuing centrality of classical literary studies in the public-school curriculum reinforced this contradiction: in so far as the schools appropriated the ideals of classical culture in their emphasis on athleticism, they glorified the beauty of the male body in terms that were open to homosexual as well as heterosexual appreciation. Moreover, the centrality in classical Greek culture of intimate tutelary relationships between men and boys offered an alternative model of masculine fraternity.

It was a model that remained influential for ex-pupils in their experience of university. The classical Greek privileging of male intimacy was replicated in the tutorial system; thus the brutality of public-school male community was countered by the fostering of close male friendship. It was this that significantly underpinned the late nineteenth-century growth of secret undergraduate societies at Oxbridge,[39] of which the most notorious was Cambridge University's Conversazione Society, better known as The Apostles. Although founded in 1820, this experienced a heyday of influence and renown in the years around 1900 among England's intellectual and professional elites. Originally 12 in number and evangelical in orientation (hence the nickname), the group members' shared views had widened considerably, to be characterised by its most recent historian, W.C. Lubenow, as 'anti-authoritarian and sceptical',[40] and built on friendship rather than religious conviction; for in the late nineteenth century, as Lubenow notes, '[f]riendship provided the code and social insulation necessary for young people as they sought *Bildung* [self-cultivation] and vocation.'[41] The Society remained self-consciously elitist, however, and at least quasi-secret; joining it was by nomination and election among existing members. The Apostles met weekly in each other's Cambridge rooms to give informal papers on any topic they cared to, which the others would then critique; the experience proved a means both of building character and self-confidence and of bonding. Writing to his mother upon his acceptance as a member in February 1902, Lytton Strachey gave a flavour of its prestige and character:

> My dearest Mama: This is to say – before I am committed to *oathes* [*sic*] of secrecy – that I am now a Brother of the Society of the Apostles. How I dare write the words I don't know! – I was apparently elected yesterday.... The members – past-present – are sufficiently distinguished. Tennyson was one of the early ones.... It is a veritable Brotherhood the chief point being personal friendship between the members.... Angels are Apostles who have taken wings – viz. settled down to definite opinions, which they may do whenever they choose. I feel I shall never take wings. This has once occurred with the apparent result that the Ap. was transported for life![42]

Tacitly, that such membership was also a key foundation for a social and professional network of more instrumental value to post-university adult life was understood. As Lubenow acknowledges, friendship such as that of the Apostles 'was also the bridge young people crossed from self-formation to vocation. It assisted them in dealing with the conflicting cross-pressures of duties to self and to professional obligation.'[43] Indeed, for Strachey himself, it proved of paramount importance in the construction of a social and professional network that was perhaps the chief contribution that progressive culture in London made to the formation of the avant-garde — and which is this city's leading example of the hybrid and transitional kind of cultural collectivity we are discussing. This was the network of the Bloomsbury group.

BLOOMSBURY: FRIENDSHIP, ART AND AMATEURISM

As Adam Kuper has demonstrated, Bloomsbury was initially transitional in another sense, as the last of the great bourgeois 'clans' of Victorian England to be produced by big families, first-cousin marriage and family firms, at the moment when these agents of collective bonding gave way to that of friendship.[44] The foundation of the group was gradual over the five or so years around the turn of the twentieth century, but a significant moment came in 1904 when Virginia Woolf and Vanessa Bell, at that time the unmarried Stephen sisters, and their brother Thoby moved from Hyde Park Gate, Kensington, to Gordon Square, Bloomsbury, on the death of their father. The move, from a high-bourgeois district of central London to a then-shabby, down-at-heel one, seems to have liberated them comprehensively from Victorian bourgeois *mores*, and after the death of Thoby in 1906 the sisters became central to a proliferating network built initially upon the former Apostolic status of most of its male members and the friendships that these fostered after university. Leonard Woolf, who married into it via Virginia in 1912, recalled this character explicitly:

> We were and always remained primarily and fundamentally a group of friends.... There have often been groups of people, writers and artists, who were not only friends, but were consciously united by a common doctrine and object, or purpose artistic and social.... Our group was quite different. Its basis was friendship, which in some cases developed into love and marriage... we had no common theory, system or principles which we wanted to convert the world to.[45]

While Woolf's is perhaps the most frequently quoted of such declarations from within the group, it was also the most minimal in its claims. For others – Lytton Strachey especially, who was one of the group's key figures – there was indeed such a set of principles. They had a cardinal point of reference (indeed, of origin, as a self-conscious doctrine) in Cambridge philosopher George Moore's *Principia Ethica* (1903), central to which was an assertion that would become an article of faith for Bloomsbury: 'By far the most valuable things, which we can know or imagine', Moore declared,

> are certain states of consciousness, which may be roughly described as the pleasures of human intercourse and the enjoyment of beautiful objects. No-one, probably, who has asked himself the question, has ever doubted that personal affection and the appreciation of what is beautiful in Art or Nature are good in themselves; nor, if we consider strictly what things are worth having *purely for their own sake*, does it appear probable that anyone will think that anything else has *nearly* so great a value as the things which are included under these two heads... [but] such mere existence of what is beautiful has value so small as to be negligible in comparison with that which attaches to the *consciousness* of beauty. This simple truth... is the ultimate and fundamental truth of Moral Philosophy... it is only for the sake of these things... that any one can be justified in performing any public or private duty;... it is they... that form the rational ultimate end of human action and the sole criterion of social progress.[46]

Moore's peroration deeply impressed Strachey, John Maynard Keynes and other leading members of the group. Strachey wrote to Moore confessing his 'excitement' at a work that 'has... laid the true foundation of Ethics', while Keynes described it as 'stupendous... *the greatest* on the subject... the beginning of a new renaissance'.[47] Drawing on the developing culture of public-school homosexuality, the Apostles' own homosocial sexuality was given licence, in the post-Wilde trial decade, by Moore's emphatic valuation of personal affection. For, as Kuper notes, it was an essential feature of Bloomsbury that it was a network made up of friends and lovers, and, he adds:

> Friends and lovers are not necessarily mutually exclusive categories. In Bloomsbury they were often hard to tell apart; friends and lovers might also be neighbours, lodgers, painters and subjects, patrons and clients. But there was nothing casual about this confusion. Friendship and love

> were idealised. Friends and lovers were sacred figures in a cult of personal relationships.[48]

Moreover, in the wake of Oscar Wilde's prosecution and savage punishment, those bonds, in particular, of male friendship within which the culture of homosexuality flourished took on an embattled character – became necessarily more privately expressed, and also more implicitly adversarial towards bourgeois *mores*, than hitherto. For members of the Bloomsbury circle, its private network provided an environment in which the latent sexualities of the Apostles could be safely – and, as it turned out, adventurously – explored; indeed, not only their sexualities, but friendship in all its aspects, within and between genders.

In this exploration and affirmation, Moore's principles were complemented by a shared attachment, articulated chiefly by Strachey and Clive Bell, to the sociality of certain French aristocratic circles of the mid-eighteenth century. As Ceri Crossley has noted, members of the group 'recognised themselves in the pre-revolutionary society whose memory they cultivated and whose art they admired. Eighteenth-century France came to function almost as a founding myth', he observes, 'legitimating many of the attitudes which members of the Bloomsbury group placed at the centre of their own lives: a devotion to art, a delight in intellectual conversation, a sense of a shared way of living, a mistrust of conventional codes of behaviour.'[49] Once again it was Lytton Strachey who was most assiduous in constructing this myth, writing of the salon of Mme du Deffand in glowing terms: 'Never, certainly, before or since', he wrote in an essay on this circle,

> have [*sic*] any set of persons lived so absolutely and unreservedly with and for their friends as these high ladies and gentlemen of the middle years of the eighteenth century. The circle of one's friends was, in those days, the framework of one's whole being; within which was to be found all that life had to offer, and outside of which no interest, however fruitful, no passion, however profound, no art, however soaring, was of the slightest account.

These exclusions included, Strachey noted significantly, politics: 'Politics were to be tolerated, so long as they remained a game; so soon as they grew serious and envisaged the public good, they became insufferable.'[50]

For all the apparent depth of feeling in Strachey's endorsement of the values of pre-Revolutionary French high society, however, its representation was, as Crossley terms it, mythic. As the chronicler of this infatuation, Christophe Campos showed, nearly 60 years ago, Bloomsbury's acquaintance with the eighteenth-century Parisian salons was patchy, and its assimilation of their qualities confused and historically inaccurate – which together 'points to the fact', Campos concluded, 'that Bloomsbury was transposing into the past ideals of its own.... The salons were a transposed ideal because of a feeling of exclusion from the present. Bloomsbury felt alien to its surroundings.'[51] Indeed, as Raymond Williams argued in a seminal essay, its alienation can be seen in class terms as that of a dominated fraction of the dominant class: an intellectual elite from 'the professional and highly educated sector of the English upper class, itself with wider and sustained connections with this class as a whole',[52] but one whose values were at odds with 'the ideas and institutions of their class'. The 'particular contradiction' of this relation, Williams observed, was 'between the presence of highly intelligent and intellectual women' within the group 'and their relative exclusion from the dominant and formative male institutions'; the general contradiction, which 'must be taken as defining the particular qualities of this fraction', was 'their significant and sustained combination of dissenting influence and influential connection'.[53]

Of perhaps broader cultural significance, however, was the affiliation that *Principia Ethica* sanctioned, for Bloomsbury, to that current of affective relations that I have noted. The outbreak of war in August 1914 brought to a close the first, most carefree decade of the group's existence; the courageous and principled assertion of conscientious objection to participation in the fighting with which it responded is a clear registering of that alienation from the dominant ideology of its class, as well as of what some of its members were prepared to stake on that dissent.[54] But in that initial decade, their behaviour was more often characterised by a deep attachment to their affective community and a sometimes ludic disregard for the 'vast system of cant and hypocrisy'[55] maintained by many of the institutions of their class. That 'politics were a game' for Bloomsbury – at least before 1914 – and that Bloomsbury's class position as a formation gave it an entitlement to mock it is nowhere better demonstrated than by their extraordinary 'Dreadnought Hoax' of 1910. To recap a now-infamous adventure: one day in February of that year, Virginia Woolf, her brother Adrian and the painter Duncan Grant blacked their faces, donned fake beards and Arabian clothing and, together with three other members of the Bloomsbury circle, hoodwinked the Foreign Office and the British Navy by pretending to be the emperor of Abyssinia (a role played by Woolf herself) and his retinue, who had arrived in London on an official state visit. They *blagued* their way into a conducted tour of the flagship of the Home Fleet, HMS *Dreadnought* – the most formidable, most modern and most secret battleship then afloat,[56] which was anchored off Weymouth in Lyme Bay – fooling admirals and civil servants alike (including, among the latter, Virginia's own cousin, with whom she found herself shaking hands) into taking them around the ship, showing them its guns, range finders and wireless room, acting out their roles using a mixture of pidgin Swahili and half-remembered Latin from Virgil. The spoof was a complete success, and it was not until one of the impostors subsequently took it to the newspapers that it was discovered. There were questions in Parliament, and the Navy, to save its honour, demanded punishment; but this was not forthcoming and the row blew over, laughed off by the First Lord of the Admiralty, and the 'prank' quickly took its place in Bloomsbury legend.

In relation to the present assessment of Bloomsbury's cultural positioning, several points can be made about this singular escapade. First, that it shows the sense of entitlement noted above, not only to differ from the dominant consensus on rearmament but also to ridicule it, that came from their class position – a self-confidence and independence that extended to their sexual morality and their aesthetic practices. Second, that this ridicule was conducted in a spirit of 'house-party' frivolity, reducing the high seriousness of military affairs and international diplomacy to the amateurism of a game of charades (albeit – we should note – one whose habituation to 'black-face' dressing-up is a marker of that dominant imperialist racism that this 'prank' in no way questioned, but instead reinforced). Third, that this was, however, in its own terms a principled amateurism, entirely of a piece not only with their prioritising of affective relations above all else but, beyond this, with that adversarial bourgeois ideology that, as I have noted, flourished in resistance to the impersonal forces of professionalisation. In this context, it is worth recalling that Clive Bell hoped in 1914 for a world in which the artist's audience might be able to appreciate artworks free from professional expectations: 'let everyone make himself an amateur', he demanded in his book *Art*, published that year.[57] And fourth, that this embrace of amateurism can be seen as standing in lieu of that alternative professionalism which the critical mass of the Parisian avant-garde enabled that formation to assert and pursue, but which was unavailable to the tiny population of technically radical artists in London.

In so far as it centred both on university friendships and kinship networks, the Bloomsbury circle encompassed a wide range of professional specialisms including economics (John Maynard Keynes), diplomacy (Leonard Woolf), cultural history (Lytton Strachey), literature (Virginia Woolf) and sexology (Goldsworthy Lowes Dickinson). Yet equally central to it was the love of art. Kuper quotes another member of the circle, Frances Partridge, recalling: 'The two things Clive [Bell, who married Vanessa Stephen in 1907] cared about were art and friends', adding: 'these were indeed the two sacred objects of the creed.'[58] This attachment to art is what both positioned it as a transitional cultural formation in the terms we have been discussing, and has secured Bloomsbury's place in the history of English modernist culture. Fundamental to this, of course, were the painting practices of Vanessa Bell and Duncan Grant (the former studied at the Royal Academy Schools, the latter at the Slade and the Académie de La Palette in Paris, albeit in each case for little more than a year), and of the art historian and critic Roger Fry (whose art training was equally brief, and who was largely self-taught). Additionally, it was Fry's activities as a critic (particularly his curation of the two landmark exhibitions of – mostly French – Post-Impressionism at the Grafton Galleries in London in 1910 and 1912) and especially as an art entrepreneur (his founding and management of the Omega Workshops between 1913 and 1919) that underwrote the reputation of Bloomsbury, then and since, as primarily a modernist art and design collective. These activities were also a key means of disseminating its ideas and products.

In addition to this entrepreneurialism, Fry's own art-historical reputation and his critical enthusiasm for Parisian Post-Impressionism and its legacy combined with Bloomsbury's cultural Francophilia to provide the artists within the group with a coherent, if self-consciously imported, aesthetic position and even a shared style of painting. As such, Bloomsbury began to acquire, in the decade before the First World War, features that, as we shall see in the next chapter, had by then in Paris become characteristics of an avant-garde artistic formation: self-conscious distinctiveness that encompassed shared aesthetic principles (its attachment to Post-Impressionism), the employment (and strategic deployment) of correspondingly distinct commercial and/or professional means of self-promotion (the Omega Workshops), and the establishment of a supporting infrastructure (exhibitions curated, and patronage secured, by Fry).[59] Yet it was both less and more than an artistic avant-garde on these terms that Parisian pre-eminence was imposing: less, in that its painterly practices, and these features of them, were neither the origin of its existence as a collectivity, nor its primary interest; more, in that as a network it existed and grew out of personal attachments that (as the quote from Leonard Woolf shows) they valued beyond even art-making. The latter, for Bloomsbury, was a way of working; cultivating human intercourse and the love of beauty was a way of living. In these attachments Bloomsbury was united by an ideology, but paradoxically one which claimed that individuals should resist ideologies; an assessment that is underwritten by a characterisation offered by one of its leading members, Lytton Strachey, who wrote that Bloomsbury was a collection of 'civilised individuals'.[60]

We should note here a feature of Bloomsbury that will be more fully explored in later chapters. A corollary of both its prioritisation of friendship over explicit commitment to specific innovative painterly practices and the incomplete (in Fry's case, minimal) nature of their art-school education was that their engagement with painting had a character of amateurism as much as of professionalism. There were several reasons for this. First, as we shall see in the next chapter, membership of any profession was, in the late nineteenth and early twentieth centuries (as it still is), dependent on possession of certified competence in its field of practice. In that of art, such certification was provided by art-school qualifications (as it still is), as well as by a foothold on the career ladder demonstrated in the mainstream sectors of the art world by critical recognition and medals in the officially sanctioned salons, and in the avant-garde sector by participation in appropriate exhibitions and membership of innovative art groupings. Second, professionalism was then almost exclusively a male preserve; the sphere of women was perceived to be the domestic, and between the two was a gulf that men and their institutions maintained assiduously.[61] The Bloomsbury artists met these criteria only partially; not only because their art schooling was incomplete, but also because at the group's centre and defining its key values were two women. Moreover (indeed, hence, as it almost inescapably followed), their reasons for painting, and the primary subjects for it, were related to the intimate and often domestic attachments within their family-and-friends network.[62]

In addition, amateur painting was in vogue at several levels of Britain's class structure in the late nineteenth century. At the top, the aristocratic Lord and Lady Coutts Lindsay's purpose in founding (in 1877) the Grosvenor Gallery in London was to support amateur artists of their class who wished to exhibit their accomplishment as well as the artists of the Aesthetic Movement whose work they patronised.[63] Lower down the social pyramid, the flourishing of amateur practices in all cultural spheres in the second half of the nineteenth century, as employment legislation on the length of the working day and week brought greater leisure,[64] was underpinned by the proliferating appearance on the market of easy-to-use materials and tools, including those of painting, and men and women at different class levels sought to 'improve' themselves, or to fill this leisure time, by acquiring painterly skills.[65] Lastly, while present-day connotations of 'professional' and 'amateur' largely value the former over the latter, a term primarily used pejoratively, in the heyday of the rise of the professions either side of 1900, the connotations of the respective terms were more evenly balanced between positives and negatives. Especially for those, gentlemen and above,[66] who expressed their social superiority in not needing to work for a living, professional qualities could be seen as narrowly focused on specialist techniques, rule-bound and inflexible towards expressive individuality. While the members of Bloomsbury did pursue a range of professions, as I have noted, their aspiration to that 'civilised individuality' extolled by Strachey was grounded in an open admiration for that which they saw in the aristocratic salons of the French Enlightenment.[67]

ASSOCIATION, POLITICS AND CULTURE IN FRANCE

The character of French sociality and its consequences for artistic groupings were unlike those in England in several respects. While informal friendships shared most of their features (as is to be expected in two old and closely related western European societies), even here there were differences. Homosexuality had been legal on the other side of the Channel since the Revolution (France became in 1791 the first European country to decriminalise sexual relations between people of the same sex), and although there remained, in some quarters, strong prejudice against its open display, especially between men, the law concerned itself only with questions of 'public decency'.[68] Together with the absence of an equivalent of the English public schools and their culture of muscular heterosexuality (as well as its nemesis), this removed two key factors in the flourishing of male homosexuality in France; in consequence, although there was such a subculture, it did not attain the size or cultural significance of its counterpart in England.[69]

It was on the level of institutionalised, formal sociability that the differences between England and France were more significant. Social historian Jose Harris notes that a French study of the 1870s 'calculated that a large majority of the adult population of Britain belonged on average to between five and six voluntary associations: trade unions, friendly societies, literary, scientific and philosophical societies, savings clubs, co-ops, and innumerable other greater or lesser associations set up for a multitude of purposes', and that 'Britain in 1914 remained a society in which private, pluralistic, and self-regulating social relationships... bulked much larger in everyday life and national culture than relationships determined by organs of central government'.[70] In France, by contrast, which had by the *fin de siècle* lived through a century of revolutions and subsequent political authoritarianism, association was far more narrowly constrained politically. As its recent historian Carol Harrison notes, '[s]ystematic regulation and surveillance of associations were the most significant developments in the relationship between the state and private association in the nineteenth century', and French governments 'reserved... an unusual degree of suspicion for voluntary associations'. Bridget Alsdorf concurs: 'Although postrevolutionary France trumpeted democratic principles of liberty, equality and fraternity, association remained an embattled principle in French culture throughout the nineteenth century.'[71] The Napoleonic penal code of 1810, which stated that '[n]o association of over 20 people whose aim is to meet every day or on particular days to concern themselves with religious, literary, political or other aims may be formed without the authorization of the government', remained in force until 1901.[72]

An equally significant difference from the British culture of associations was the way in which those in France reinforced rather than diminished or blurred the hierarchies of class. Harrison stresses this at length, observing that '[i]n the immediate post-Revolutionary decades, the practice of association served as a crucial strategy for reordering society as the atomised individuals defined by revolutionary law reconstituted social groups and hierarchies', and that '[v]oluntary associations marked the perimeters of these groups and mapped out the boundaries of class society'. She adds: 'As one of a company of target-shooters, *savants*, horticulturalists, or charitable donors, a Frenchman knew his place in the bourgeois social order.'[73] By the end of the century this segregation had hardened: 'Frenchmen found it increasingly difficult to imagine class as a component of a unified and harmonious society', Harrison states. 'Under the Third Republic, voluntary associations reflected rather than concealed class conflict and political difference.... The gulf separating both the white-collar gymnast and the *grand-bourgeois* erudite from the working-class *mutualiste* widened.'[74] Moreover, as leisure activities became increasingly commercialised and, in Paris especially, the urban renewal projects of Baron Haussmann fostered the proliferation of cafés, these became 'potentially the slippery slope of bourgeois respectability';[75] for cafés were populated by people of unknown and uncertain morals. Outside Paris, bourgeois men joined *cercles*, membership of which 'proclaimed a man to be leisured, respectable, cultivated and public-spirited', and at mid-century there were around 2,000 of them across France, with about 120,000 members.[76] They met in the upstairs, bookable rooms of cafés, and did not mix with the clientele of the bars downstairs, since '[t]he decorum of a *cercle* was its most important asset.... Statutes elaborated on members' conduct at length: no member was to enter a *cercle* expecting that café standards of behaviour applied.'[77]

Not only class but gender also constrained the sociality of the French bourgeois: in principle, because the institution of association reflected the gendered opposition between citizen and mother. The public sphere was an exclusively male space, to which their voluntary associations helped bourgeois men to stake their claim, and excluded women from its boundaries. In practice, because, as Harrison notes:

> Even when women did establish their own associations, wrote their own statutes, and elected their own officers, their organizations found themselves excluded from recognition in the public sphere. Although French law made no distinction between male and female associations, administrative practice ignored women in groups.... Female sociability was domestic while male association was civic. Women could mimic the

> practices of citizenship, but their performance did not fool those men who were the natural occupants of the public sphere.[78]

If bourgeois sociability in France was segregated from the working class by its concern for respectability and social hierarchy, increasingly the distancing was reciprocal. During the 1848 Revolution and following a proclamation by the government of the brief Second Republic that ensued, as in the first Revolution, working-class radicals flocked to the neighbourhood political clubs: their modern historian Peter Amman estimated that in Paris there were 34 clubs with, at the peak of this movement, a combined membership of no fewer than 50,000 to 70,000 members.[79] But this was France's only experiment with state-sanctioned freedom of association in the entire century, and it was extinguished by the new emperor, Louis Napoleon, in March 1852; a reversal that was continued in its turn by the new Third Republic when it outlawed the clubs of the Paris Commune early in 1871. The experience of the Commune of March to May of that year, and its bloody suppression, polarised classes and class experience in Paris to an unprecedented degree, and the culture of friendship and association among working-class Parisians was, in the late decades of that century, significantly autonomous and equally politicised.

The world of the Parisian working-class café before 1914 has been explored by W. Scott Haine in a searching and meticulous study, and it offers an example of a class-conscious model of collectivity that is relevant to us in several ways. First, as Haine notes:

> As the crossroads of work, neighbourhood, family, and leisure activities, café sociability… often bridged the distinction between conversation and agitation. The café, where workers rested and reflected upon their common sufferings, fears and hopes, was a vital asset to their political capacities and strategies. Families and friends were not the only groups to take advantage of the privacy and intimacy of the working-class café, for now political clubs and labour unions did too. Through their occupation of these sites,

> workers were able to acquire space for self-expression. In times of political freedom, cafés became incubators of new ideas, organizations, and actions; in times of political repression, they served as shelters.[80]

This imbrication of the personal-private and the political-public was, Haine suggests, distinctive: 'Paris workers, much more successfully than their English counterparts in London, were able to maintain connections among work, family and leisure in such a manner that all three spheres remained politicized.'[81] Moreover, such politicisation would, as we shall see, inform the character of the city's emergent avant-garde. Indeed, as Haine implies, it was partly constitutive of it:

> The crushing of the Commune during the 'bloody week' of late May 1871, rather than destroying this café culture of contestation, invigorated it. Unlike during the first eighty years of the 1789–1914 period, however, the café politics of the late nineteenth century did not precipitate a revolution, although it helped to generate a wide range of new radical movements, in politics as in art and literature.[82]

The implication for the avant-garde nucleus that was the Neo-Impressionist circle in mid-1880s Paris is the more specific in that common to most of its members was an allegiance to anarchism and, as Haine notes, '[a]narchists, more than any other group, put the café at the centre of their politics'; indeed, 'the overwhelming majority' of the 100 or more anarchist groups that mushroomed in Paris between 1885 and 1900 used working-class cafés as their base.[83] At the same time, the cafés played a more complex role in a culture of entertainment that, as noted, was changing rapidly in the wake of the Haussmannisation of the city:

> In addition, during these decades, workers also used cafés to continue the tradition of goguettes [amateur singing clubs], which managed to hold their own against the newer and more commercial café-concerts. There were still approximately 300 such singing societies in the peripheral

> districts of Paris in 1900, and although they often sang the new songs of the café-concerts, they remained communal and participatory. Indeed, with Aristide Bruant a prime example, some of the great commercial singers drew inspiration for their cabaret shows from their experiences in proletarian cafés and goguettes.[84]

This appropriation and commercialisation of a Parisian café-concert culture that had begun in working-class sociability and solidarity was part of a broader development that included also the appropriation of bohemianism, and the substitution of the cultural disposition of affective relations on which this last was partly founded by a professionalism that would shape the emergent artistic avant-garde. This dynamic is the subject of the next chapter.

3

BOHEMIANS AND AVANT-GARDES

FROM ART AS A WAY OF LIFE TO ART AS A WAY OF WORKING

If the close-knit, elitist and often secretive groupings of brotherhoods and the affective impulses of friendship furnished models of collectivity for modern art practice that tended towards withdrawal from society at large, another model was provided by what might be seen as their opposite: the amorphous, sprawling, diverse, contradictory and increasingly notorious 'communities' of bohemians, those populations of the socially and culturally marginalised that proliferated in the major cities of western Europe throughout the nineteenth century. As deeply embedded, despite this marginality, in their host societies as brotherhoods were removed from them (at least in aspiration), these bohemias – especially that of Paris, for reasons we shall explore – became increasingly salient in the cultural life of European metropolises, and their character increasingly mythic, as the century wore on.

As Mary Gluck has noted, the bohemian artist 'came to be seen as the first embodiment of the artist of modernity and the privileged interpreter of aesthetic truths in contemporary society'.[1] Indeed, more than this: once the concept of 'the avant-garde' had become established as dominant in the historiography of modern art, the terms became more or less inextricably associated – even, in some contributions, interchangeable. This is a confusion that needs to be addressed; although the life and art of (especially) pre- or un- or anti-academic artists in Paris was suffused with perceived bohemianism, it is nonetheless vital to avoid collapsing either the later formation or its attributes into the earlier. This is not easy, however, for the overlap between the two was close in several respects, and the assumption of their (near-) identity is common enough for the elision between them to be routine. In Paris, moreover, where the largest population of bohemians first found anchorage after its migrations across Europe, and where the concept of bohemia itself was first recognised, there was a close overlap between its spaces and those of the nascent literary and artistic avant-garde formations. Thus, first the Latin Quarter (home turf of the literary avant-garde) in the mid-nineteenth century and, at the century's close, as the commercialisation of entertainment took over Haussmann's new boulevards, Montmartre (one, at least, of the incubators of the artistic) provided a home for both, and the latter's way of life and cultural practices, in particular, presented a contrast, even a provocation, to those of the city centre at its feet.

What, then, was bohemia, and how did it anticipate the avant-garde? Both its history and its historiography are far too rich and extensive to be summarised here,[2] but some relevant facts can be noted at the outset of an answer. As Robert Darnton has been among the most recent succinctly to note, in the eighteenth century 'the term *Bohémiens* generally referred to the inhabitants of bohemia [the western two-thirds of the present Czech Republic] or, by extension, to Gypsies (Romany), but it had begun to acquire a figurative meaning, which denoted drifters who lived by their wits. Many', Darnton adds, 'pretended to be men of letters.'[3] By the 1840s in Paris, the connotations of 'bohemian' had broadened further: Marilyn Brown cites Théophile Gautier's 1843 use of it to refer to three different types: first, what she calls 'the dubious street people' of that city (Gautier himself called them 'cranky ruffians', 'frightful villains', 'hideous toads who hop in the mires of Paris'); second, the wandering mendicant pilgrims of Spain, 'these tall fellows with fine and nervous countenances, tawny as Havana cigars, majestically wearing rags on bronzed shoulders'; finally,

> foolish youth which lives somewhat haphazardly from day to day by its intelligence: painters, musicians, actors, poets, journalists, who love pleasure more than money and who prefer laziness and liberty to everything,

> even glory; an amiable race full of ease and good instincts… which forgets daily bread for evening conversation.[4]

If this already myth-shapen composite overlapped to a degree with Darnton's figure it was enhanced in two further dimensions: by qualities of political radicalism and resistance to an integrated social role, and by those of the superior but crazed outcast artist. Both were, as Brown observes, largely the creation of the Romantic generation of the 1830s (and the latter dimension was popularised from 1835 by Alfred de Vigny's 'suicidal hero-poet-martyr Chatterton').[5] Other modern historians have been more partisan than Brown in defining the phenomenon: for instance, T.J. Clark locates it 'within the complex social structure of Paris… alongside… the *classes dangereuses*… [who were] social outcasts of all kinds: tramps, street-porters, organ-grinders, rag-pickers, knife-grinders, tinkers, errand-boys, and all those who lived by the thousand little occupations of the streets of Paris'; these bohemians fought alongside, too, the revolutionaries of the June Days uprising in 1848.[6] Against this history, Jerrold Seigel locates bohemia at the other end of the above interpretative spectrum, defining it as '[f]rom the start' shaped in relation to its perceived opposite, bourgeois life, and developing – indeed, functioning – in a close dialectic with it. 'Bohemia has always exerted a powerful attraction on many bourgeois, matched by the deeply bourgeois instincts and aspirations of numerous Bohemians', Seigel argues, suggesting in summary: 'Bohemian and bourgeois were – and are – parts of a single field: they imply, require, and attract each other.'[7]

More recently Gluck has distinguished a 'sentimental' from an 'ironic' bohemia. The first comprised those romanticisations of poverty for which Henri Murger's sentimental stories about penniless artists in the Latin Quarter were paradigmatic. First published serially in a popular literary journal between 1845 and 1849, these reached a rapidly widening audience through their reissue as a book and their reworking as a successful popular musical at the Théâtre des Variétés (in 1849), a novel (1851) and were eventually given mythic status, half a century later, by Puccini's acclaimed opera *La Bohème* (premiered 1896). As Gluck observes, 'Murger had clearly succeeded in producing more than a best-selling play; he had given birth to one of the most enduring stereotypes of nineteenth-century culture.'[8] Her second (and more significant) 'ironic' bohemia was characterised by a parodic and dialogic engagement with a popular culture whose irreverence and formulaic commodification it celebrated as counter to bourgeois art.[9] These latter qualities Gluck sees her preferred bohemia as sharing with an avant-garde whose allegiance to, yet distance from, popular/commercial culture are cardinal features of the modernism that is its product. Although Gluck's use of her key terms is often loose and unhistorical ('avant-garde' and 'modernism' are for her interchangeable), these particular distinctions are helpful, as we shall see. Brown further suggests judiciously that '[w]ithin a complex set of meanings the *bohémien* could occupy multiple positions and contain numerous associations'[10]. It was from the 1830s and 1840s that the artistically as opposed to socially alienated aspects gained a connotative ascendancy; this led first to the privileging of bohemia as a cultural rather than a material social space, and bohemianism as a chosen way of life rather than its associated behaviours; and thence to the elision of it with the avant-garde.

But bohemia was not already an avant-garde, for two reasons.[11] First, because it did not amount to a formation: its structures were too provisional, its markers too few and often ephemeral, its way of life too uncertain. (This last was particularly so in the shadow of France's defeat by Prussia, the brutal suppression of the Paris Commune that followed, and the heavy censorship by authoritarian Third Republican governments of any cultural behaviour they saw as a threat to their rule.)[12] Second, in so far as bourgeois bohemians had cultural ambitions, these were, as Seigel persuasively argues, invariably bourgeois. For them, the consolations of bohemia were equally invariably temporary: as transitory members, these (predominantly) young men from the middle class soon exchanged its licence and informality for the rewards of respectability. What bohemia had to offer was grounded in the marginalised locales of cafés in unfashionable and inexpensive, usually working-class *quartiers* and their ways of life; when commercialised entertainment appropriated even many of these spaces, as it did (with the help of Haussmannisation) especially from the 1870s, the alternatives to acquiescence were (as we have seen) a shift into a more explicitly political register of activity,[13] embourgeoisement or destitution. In contrast, the avant-garde, defined, in ways we shall explore, around an opposition not so much to bourgeois life as to its artistic practices and institutions, was able to develop an identity that was constructed through a complex engagement with those commercial forces and encompassed implicit criticism of them.[14]

Yet in terms of their role in the developing cultural field of Paris the relation between the two collectivities was indeed close, and, as with the relation of the emergent avant-garde to brotherhoods, cenacles and friendship groups, should be seen more as a matter of transition than of rupture. This particular transition was both marked and mediated by a cultural grouping that was unique to Paris in the late 1870s and the 1880s, but that has subsequently proved paradigmatic across many cultures, and whose complex history and significance have only emerged from near-obscurity a full century and more later.[15] Those dozen years saw the flourishing of a literary and artistic subculture based on the 'artistic cabaret' and the humouristic practices of *blague* and *fumisme*. Often glossed with amusement and brevity in the historiography of such subcultures as merely a light-hearted expression of their iconoclastic vitality, in fact these two terms were of cardinal importance in the positioning of the groups of which they constituted crucial elements, as recent scholarship has shown. As such they deserve some explanation here.

As Jeffrey Weiss has demonstrated in a comprehensive etymological analysis, *blague*, defined at its simplest, was practical jokery, but of a kind that encompassed both a wide range of applications and an extraordinary connotative reach in Parisian cultural life in the second half of the nineteenth century, and discussion of it spawned a considerable literature of its own in this period. One contribution to this described *blague* as

> a certain taste which is peculiar to Parisians, and still more to Parisians of our generation, to disparage, to mock, to render ludicrous everything

> that *hommes*, and above all *prud'hommes*, are in the habit of respecting and caring for; but this raillery is characterized by the fact that he who takes it up does so more in play, for a love of paradox, than in conviction: he mocks himself with his own banter, *il blague*.[16]

The irony at the centre of this definition is key, for it is this reflexivity, as it were, that makes *blague* such a subtle and complex humoristic tool. Weiss notes that while its 'core meaning... remains fairly stable, the precise implications could be adjusted or reclaimed to suit the philosophical exigencies of each generation. During the Third Republic, *blague* was refashioned as a vehicle of post-Franco-Prussian War spiritual malaise, an irony of disillusion';[17] it is this context in which it drove the activities of the Parisian *humoristes* of the 1880s. Yet the sobriquet that these activities were given was that of *fumistes*, rather than *blagueurs*, for reasons which help further to characterise the kind of humour, and its connotations, that were in play in this burgeoning milieu. For *fumisme* had its origins early in the nineteenth century in the trade of those artisans who installed or repaired the wood- or coal-burning domestic stoves of the Parisian middle class. The encounter between artisan and bourgeois in the home of the latter was a stock source of jokes about the respective manners and snobberies of these two classes (of a kind that still endures) and, taken up by Parisian vaudeville-theatre comedy in mid-century, *fumisme* became a figure of speech expressive of a latent *interclass* hostility that was otherwise inadmissible, its connotations contested between a working class that enjoyed, in the words of two of its recent historians, 'cooking up practical jokes that made fun of its supposed superiors' and a bourgeoisie that sought to make its implications pejorative.[18] By the 1880s it had, as Daniel Grojnowski and Denys Riout note, 'fallen to "youth" to seize the term as its watchword', yet 'they brandished [this] flag without being too sure about what it was rallying them to'.[19]

This apparent uncertainty led the *fumiste* subculture, as we shall see, into a degree of vacillation as to its beliefs and purposes that is also an indication of its hybrid or intermediate character, as a collectivity that stood between bohemianism and avant-gardism. Anticipated by the nihilism of *zutisme*, to which Verlaine and Rimbaud adhered in its brief post-Commune moment of the early 1870s,[20] this subculture first surfaced into visibility with the founding in 1878 of a literary group, Les Hydropathes ('Water-Haters'), by a minor civil servant with writerly ambitions, Émile Goudeau. Meeting twice weekly in a Latin Quarter café, and for nearly 18 months publishing a bimonthly journal of the same name, the Hydropathes were predominantly writers, with some artists and some who were both, who, as Phillip Dennis Cate has suggested, 'formalised and intensified the role of the cafe as the non-institutional showplace for emerging and recognised figures of an increasingly close-knit segment of the Parisian literary and artistic community'.[21] The group brought together two generations of this community, who presented to each other works characterised, for the most part, by the punning, parody, satire and occasional obscenity typical of *fumisme*.

Two developments of the early 1880s opened these activities to a wider milieu: the opening of the Chat Noir cabaret in Montmartre in November 1881 by Rodolphe Salis with the collaboration of Goudeau, to which the Hydropathes took their custom; and the foundation the following year by Jules Lévy, one of their number, of another group, Les Incohérents, which adopted the Hydropathes' agenda (as well as its participants) and developed it in a visual dimension. The Chat Noir replaced the relative introspection of Goudeau's initial grouping with an expansive self-promotional strategy and an explicitly commercial underpinning, drawing increasing numbers of the elite of artistic and literary Paris to performances of poems, songs and monologues. For these, Goudeau and some colleagues would solicit proposed items for performance from the crowd of diners and drinkers at the start of the session, then select and order them, thereby providing new and unknown writers, singers and actors with a readymade venue and audience. The success both of the format and of the performances was such that in 1885 the cabaret moved, with much fanfare including a street procession, to much bigger premises a few blocks away, where it continued to attract full houses of an increasingly fashionable clientele.[22]

The Incohérents' equivalent for this presentational strategy, and this magnetic appeal, was a series of art exhibitions organised by Lévy, the first of which, in October 1882, was followed by a further six in Paris, as well as several in other towns across France, until 1893. Lévy's original idea was 'to hold an exhibition of drawings by people who don't know how to draw',[23] and while this gave way to the inclusion of work by artists as well as non-artists, from the start the exhibitions were unconventional to the point of provocation. The first was held in Lévy's own tiny apartment on the Left Bank, comprised around 200 exhibits and, it is said, attracted 2,000 invited viewers over the course of the single day it was open, including Manet, Renoir, Pissarro, the composer Richard Strauss and the king of Bavaria.[24] The exhibits had in common not the amateurism originally intended, but humour: they included poet Paul Bilhaud's *Combat de nègres dans une cave pendant la nuit* (*Fight between Black Men in a Cave at Night*), an entirely black picture that Cate suggests was 'the first documented monochromatic painting',[25] and others played with equivalent puns, as well as with unconventional painterly materials, in equally nonsensical ways (fig. 1).

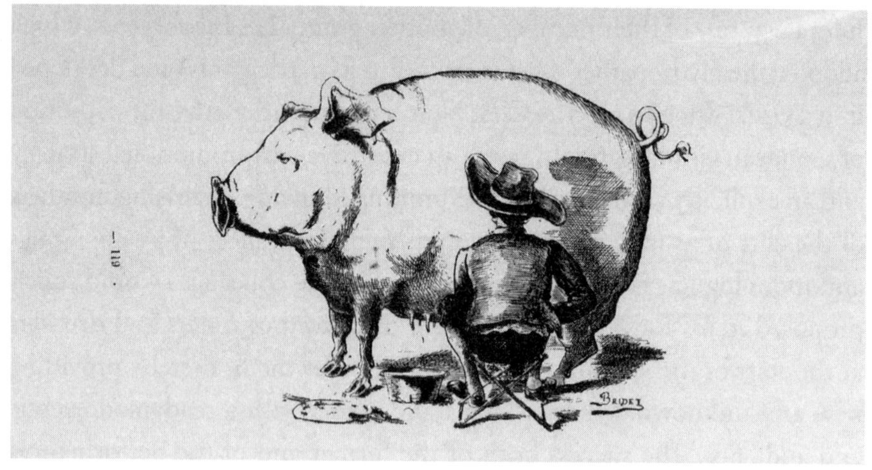

FIG. 1 Boquillon Bridet, *Porc trait par Van Dyck*, 1884. Photo-relief illustration for *Catalogue illustré de l'exposition des arts incohérents*, Paris: E. Bernard et Cie, 1884, 119

If this event sounds like a proto-Dada, avant-garde mockery of 'high art', it was in fact nothing of the sort (although it has been canonised as such by those contributors to the historiography of modernism who have paid it, and the Incohérents in general, any attention). First, because the exhibits (and those in the Incohérents' subsequent exhibitions) took aim not only at Salon art and its conventions (with, for example, a painting of the Mona Lisa smoking a clay pipe that historians have delighted in noting as anticipating Duchamp's *L.H.O.O.Q.* by 35 years, or a drawing entitled *The Husband of the Venus de Milo* that replaced the sculpture's head with that of a bald, bearded man). For at the same time they also mocked the innovations of the 'new art' of the Impressionists and their associates: the amusingly centrifugal composition of Leroy Saint-Aubert's *Rendez-vous au Pont Royal* (1886) is hard not to see as a send-up, specifically, of Gustave Caillebotte's painting *Le Pont de l'Europe* of ten years earlier (pls 8 and 9), while Bilhaud's monochrome *Combat de nègres* mocked not Salon art but the 'all-over' character of some modernist paintings, such as Monet's landscapes and Whistler's *Nocturnes*. Second, this was not proto-avant-garde mockery of high culture, because Lévy went out of his way to deny any artistic intention either on his part or that of his exhibitors: 'We are not making art at all… and have never wished to. We are amusing ourselves, and wish to amuse others', he declared in 1886.[26] This was *humour*, not art; the posters advertising the exhibitions announced as much. Lévy described the humour, moreover, as harmless: 'jokes without malice', 'Parisian entertainment'.[27] Additionally, such humour had, for Lévy, an explicitly nationalistic colouration: 'Gaiety and French *esprit* have been soiled', he asserted. 'It is necessary to rehabilitate this national glory that is known as French wit, and that is why the Incohérents have come.'[28]

It has recently been argued that in such assertions the Incohérents sought to use their 'harmless jokes' to aid in the regeneration of a French society that they saw as corrupted by bourgeois commercialism.[29] Certainly it would seem that their values were often declared in opposition to the latter; Goudeau and some others of the original Hydropathes refused to follow Rodolphe Salis in the Chat Noir cabaret's move to bigger and more commercial premises in 1885, for instance, because they felt that the cabaret was losing its original spirit.[30] As we have seen, moreover, there was at the time a tension between the traditional *goguettes* or singing clubs that met in working-class cafés and the dynamism of the new, commercialised culture of the café-concert. Although the *goguettiers* sang the new songs of the café-concerts, they remained communal and participatory. And it is this characteristic of the Hydropathes' events that their historians have noted as continuing this tradition, thereby juxtaposing values of communal sociability, participation and amateurism against the depersonalised transactions between professional performers and passive audiences in the new commercialised cabarets.[31] Yet the annexation of entertainment by the market was an inexorable development, and to a degree the acquiescence of the *fumistes* in this was inescapable. Indeed, that the cabaret and the Incohérents' art exhibitions had such extraordinary, immediate success in audience terms (the second year's exhibition, held in first-floor rooms in the passage Vivienne, apparently attracted 20,000 visitors over a month's run)[32] is testament not only to the size of their common catchment area (their attendees overlapped closely, by all accounts)[33] – that is, to the existence of a substantial reservoir of cultural consumers responsive to their irreverent and satirical humour. It was testament as well to the acumen of Salis, Goudeau and Lévy in employing so effectively the publicity techniques of eye-catching posters, press notices and social networking whose use was unprecedented in the sphere of art, though entirely up-to-the-minute in that of consumer goods and entertainment.[34]

In both respects, these initiatives mark a development beyond bohemianism: more deliberate and strategic in origin and character, more clearly oriented to a clientele (and in the case of the cabaret, more explicitly commercial in orientation) – yet at the same time retaining the blurred border between these qualities and the participatory, informal cultural modes of bohemian practices in drawing both their performers/exhibitors and core audiences largely from the same community.[35] It was such a development in other respects as well. First, in the substitution of a focused set of aesthetic concerns, both in the art exhibited and the literary works presented in performance, for that elision of life and art, of culture as a whole way of life and as product – life *as* art – that characterised bohemianism: as Grojnowski and Sarrazin note, the culture of *blague* and *fumisme* in which those concerns were grounded was a serious and self-conscious activity, their differences from other kinds of humour, poetry and art theorised by their proponents with exactitude and understood as such by an informed audience.[36] Second, in the self-conscious (at least for some) use of the café, the traditional point of focus for bohemian groups, as a more than convenient and convivial substitute for private premises: while Goudeau's retrospective celebration of cafés embraced them in bohemian spirit as the demotic modern equivalents of the agora and forum of classical antiquity, he saw them also as having 'replaced the Academy, in whose famous garden philosophers walked… declaiming their inductions and deductions'.[37]

In what could thus be summarised as a shift from a way of living to a way of working, the Hydropathes, Incohérents, Hirsutes, Jemenfoutistes and other 'groupuscules' that made up this milieu anticipated the features of the avant-garde formation. But, as Grojnowski observes, they did so 'without having found the recognition that would have consecrated their research'; thus, 'they amounted to an avant-garde without an advance, an artistic provocation without consequence which, in default of making itself felt, remained a simple object of curiosity'. He concludes: 'They demonstrate *a contrario* the determining character of institutions in the transformation of any product into, and recognition of it as, a work of art.'[38] No longer simply bohemians, the Incohérents were not yet (I would argue, *pace* Grojnowski) an avant-garde: for this, they required not only the 'consecration' of recognition but – more crucially, perhaps – a *self*-recognition, an awareness of the import of their 'research', as well as the means to make themselves and their theorised provocations felt. The fact that Lévy insisted upon the non-art character of the Incohérents' exhibitions, and on the harmlessness of the humour, not only annexed these to a recognised national-cultural tradition, but disarmed them as vehicles of a potentially serious critique of the cultural status quo. Grojnowski's point that such a constellation of conditions for avant-gardehood itself required, for its appearance, change at an institutional level is a provocative one, however, for I shall argue that the absence of those conditions, and of that change, positioned the Incohérents as transitional – not only, as I have noted, between friendship groups and the emergent avant-garde formation, but between phases of the development of an institution that would be of cardinal importance both for modern art practice and the avant-garde within it: that of the *profession* of fine art.

PROFESSIONS AND PROFESSIONALISMS

The professionalisation of middle-class non-entrepreneurial occupations was a motor force in the development of western societies in the late nineteenth and early twentieth centuries.[39] It is now clear that whether professions proliferated in this period as the product mostly of market forces, as in the US and Britain, or mostly of central or local state-led bureaucracy, as in much of Europe, the 'liberal professions' (including law, medicine, finance, education and fine art, and their technical equivalents in engineering and the sciences, with architecture straddling both) played a major role in determining both the character and social impact of the occupations that they organised and promoted. Exactly what that role was, however, has been the subject of theoretical dispute among sociologists and historians for decades, but it is now agreed that a distinction needs to be made between the *self*-identity of the professions, and of professionals, as defined by a commitment to the altruistic service of others through the possession of unique skills and competences whose standards it is the obligation of their professions to protect, and a more objective, structural identification of them as defined by their self-interested monopoly control of specialised knowledges, by the training through which these are acquired and by the legal frameworks that underpin both. It is also accepted that professionals occupy a common, prestigious social position, as part of, but distinct within, the dominant class of their host society.[40] In the case of fine artists, the concept has considerable explanatory potential not only in furthering an understanding of the establishment of their practice in late nineteenth-century Europe as a privatised, liberal-bourgeois profession, but also in enabling us to grasp the character of the emergent formation of the avant-garde. The groundwork for this understanding has already been laid. Raymonde Moulin has charted a history of the emergence of the professional artist from that of the artisan, while Robert Jensen has traced the institutional measures by which artists across Europe in the late nineteenth century sought to isolate themselves as providers of special services, and to control a market for their expertise – a collective project, if pursued individually or in small groups with specific promotional aims, that met the criteria for professionalisation almost unintentionally. More recently, and with particular respect to Paris-based artists, Béatrice Joyeux-Prunel has detailed the strategies adopted in thus seizing from their respective state cultural apparatuses the managerial initiative over their own careers. She has shown that from the mid-1850s increasing numbers of artists across the spectrum of positions in the art field recognised the 'leverage' value of establishing a profile outside Paris in default of being able to do so in the highly competitive and overcrowded contemporary market there, and sought opportunities elsewhere to exhibit and otherwise promote their work and ideas, in the process and almost inadvertently creating a pan-European network.[41]

Both Jensen and Joyeux-Prunel offer invaluable analyses of the international dimensions and dynamics of this significant change in the field of contemporary art. They refer to the professional status and character of the art practices it comprehended only in passing, however, and take the concepts of 'professionalisation' and 'professionalism' – as they do that of '[the] avant-garde' – as given, and not in need of analysis, beyond Jensen noting that '[t]he Central European Secessions [those breakaways of artists from their respective academies in 1890s Germany and Austria-Hungary] constituted a unique historical moment when artists attempted to shape themselves as legitimate members of an expanding middle class culture, alongside other residents of professionalism such as doctors, lawyers and university professors'.[42] Jensen's primary concern is to demonstrate the fundamental importance of the market for both mainstream and avant-garde artists and art against the then-conventional art-historical wisdom that set the latter, and its values, in opposition to the commercialism of mainstream art. In doing so, he identifies 'professionalism' as instrumental, in that it 'brought the modernist "left" together with the academic "right"'. 'From widely differing aesthetic positions', Jensen argues, 'the leaders of the official art world and the "avant-gardes" might converge, each as a professional elite, seeking the signs of authenticity through the denial of commercialism.'[43] Between these positions, Jensen identifies an intermediate sector of the field of contemporary art: that of 'juste milieu' or middle-of-the-road art that was made by 'professional insiders rather than radical outsiders', a group that was as such 'a quintessential phenomenon of social and cultural, but not aesthetic, modernism'.[44] These are important insights, and Jensen's introduction of these terms has been valuable for subsequent scholarship; but while 'juste milieu' – a term borrowed from political history[45] – became his principal object of study in a rich and important book, he took no further either his analysis of its professionalism, or that of the European art profession. Joyeux-Prunel has even less interest in the concept, applying it only, and briefly, to the development of a competitive cultural nationalism in art criticism from the 1850s that 'professionalised' an activity until then characterised by dilettantism.[46]

Yet their research enables the occupational and social network that resulted to be seen, not only as a development of the state-governed professionalism of an academic art career, but also as a precondition of the emergence of an avant-garde formation. We should note the significance of the distinction between the two; for if to elide unreflectively these phases of the professionalisation of modern art practice that such work has brought into focus is perhaps slipshod, it is plainly teleological to project the term 'avant-garde' back onto groups active at a time when neither the application of it to artistic practices nor the formation itself yet existed, in that this not only privileges those of its features that appear to have anticipated the key qualities of the clearly consolidated formation, but ignores those that do not, and characterises such groups and practices exclusively in terms of the former. Yet this mistake is routinely made.[47] Is this to say that we must prioritise a period's assessment of itself, and use only the terms of its own discourse? Not necessarily. We should, however, surely pay attention not only to those terms (and, if we supplant them, understand and clarify the reasons for doing so), but also to when 'avant-garde' gained currency, as applied to some artists who were putatively more innovative than others. Isolated uses of the term through the second half of the nineteenth century have been registered, and its employment seems to have become slightly more frequent in art criticism from the 1880s,[48] but, as Riout notes, its appearance throughout that decade was episodic, and its application erratic.[49]

Much more commonly, innovative artists of that time were described as 'novateurs', 'jeunes', 'indépendants', among a host of similar labels.[50] The very plethora of such alternatives pointed insistently to a new type of grouping that was then coming into being but not yet clearly delineated, the competition between them itself indexing an emergence whose specific moment and location have been proposed by Martha Ward as the foundation of Neo-Impressionism in 1886. The adoption by the group of artists around Seurat, Signac and Pissarro of the prefix 'néo-' in that year amounted, Ward suggests, to a 'disruptive strategy of simultaneously historicising, superseding and reviving' Impressionism.[51] In a nuanced analysis of the circumstances of the launch of their initiative that sets this founding moment of the avant-garde formation in the context of Third Republican governments' liberalisation of the press laws, encouragement of artistic independence and emphasis on the public role of art (and design), Ward notes both the spaces already made available by these discourses for such vanguardist gestures, and the clear opposition it signalled, on the part of the Neo-Impressionists, to the developing trend towards the privatisation of the character and consumption of contemporary art.[52] Ward's proposal is underwritten by Joan Halperin's analysis of the role played in Neo-Impressionism's launch by the critic Félix Fénéon, not only in providing the name but also in the manner of his description of the group as 'the avant-garde of impressionism': a self-conscious and tentative coinage whose focus was less on its formational status than on its relation to its then-dominant predecessor.[53] And as Joyeux-Prunel's more recent research has shown, that relation was one of an opposition at once aesthetic and social: aesthetic, in its substitution of a shared and informed engagement with theories of colour science, and the innovations of Pointillist brushwork that this produced, for the empty rhetoric of 'talent' and 'quality' that held together the widening circle of a now middle-of-the-road Impressionism; social, in the Neo-Impressionists' alienation from the networking of an elite for whom social rank and affinities counted for more than canvases.[54]

However, Joyeux-Prunel places that other new grouping of the late 1880s, the Nabis (launched in 1889), alongside the Neo-Impressionists, noting that they were 'more clearly opposed to the impressionist aesthetic'.[55] This implicit positioning of them as avant-garde, while not as developed as Ward's account of the former, affords an insight that can be valuably deepened – namely, into recognition of the *plurality* both of 'spaces available for vanguardist gestures' in *fin-de-siècle* Paris and of what might be called 'trajectories of emergence' of innovative groupings into those spaces.[56] Thus where the Neo-Impressionists favoured a public role for art, the Nabis tended to paint about, and for, domestic environments; where the political associations of the former were clearly anarchist, the latter's politics encompassed the spectrum, from the anarchist sympathies of Pierre Bonnard and Félix Vallotton, through the apparent apoliticism of some including Édouard Vuillard, to (in the case of their spokesperson, Maurice Denis) explicit allegiance to the Catholic and monarchist right;[57] where Neo-Impressionism originated in a shared aesthetic commitment (to colour science and its application to painting), the Nabi group was formed from lycée and art-school friendships. In so far as its members shared an aesthetic commitment (to the expression and exploration of the decorative in art, via the use of simplified shapes and juxtaposed pattern in flattened spaces), their engagement with this also varied greatly in register, from the Gauguinesque rural idylls of Paul Sérusier to the quotidian domestic dramas of Vuillard. Yet the two groups also shared qualities, dispositions and even strategies of 'position-taking' (to use Pierre Bourdieu's term),[58] which we shall explore in a later chapter.

Between Grojnowski's terms of assessment of the Incohérents and this positioning and characterisation of both Neo-Impressionism and the Nabis can be discerned in outline the qualities, and the criteria for the emergence in the mid-1880s, of a Parisian avant-garde formation that, unlike the provocation of *fumisme*, was grounded in self-consciously autonomous art practices. These qualities were those, respectively, of a material and shared social and cultural independence from the dominant formation of the artistic field; commitment to specific aesthetic principles and awareness of their import, as well as to a position outside the mainstream art market; equally independent critical recognition and support; and an institutional framework that facilitated both. We should note, however, that this avant-garde was, as yet, only emergent – one of a number of types of possible formation, and that other, alternative futures for innovative/oppositional groupings hung in the balance in that *fin de siècle*, as un- or anti-academic artists navigated their ways between the shoals of commercialism and expressions of resistance to it (traditionalism, mysticism, elitism, anarchism). We need to make a final distinction, therefore, between the emergence of this avant-garde and its consolidation as a formation, since it was with the latter that both its character and the conditions for its sustainability were established.

As the competition between epithets for them indexed the emergence of the new groups of the 1880s, so the increasingly ubiquitous currency of 'avant-garde' as a collective noun for their multiplying 'isms' indexed that consolidation in the decade before 1914. It was then, and not before, that Parisian critics began to use the term with any frequency, with unmistakeable awareness of it as a neologism and often with evident distaste for the connotations of self-promotional hyperbole that it apparently carried (Louis Vauxcelles writing in 1909 of 'self-styled avant-garde colourists', Roger Allard in 1911 of 'painters who are called "avant-garde", in a childishly bellicose metaphor', and again in 1914 declaring '[a]vant-gardism is not merely ridiculous; it is a plague').[59] The connotations are unsurprising, as this coinage coincided with the flourishing of advertising and merchandising strategies on behalf of a burgeoning, department-store-centred consumerism and the professionalisation of these practices, and the streets and the newspapers were increasingly full of advertising hyperbole.[60] But it also coincided with an extraordinary constellation of interrelated developments within the Parisian contemporary art world. These included the revolution in gallery practices led by the newcomer dealer Daniel-Henry Kahnweiler in his innovations such as exclusive contracts with artists, not holding, or allowing them to participate in, exhibitions of their work in Paris, aggressive networking and promotion of his artists outside France via loans to exhibitions, and the distribution of photographs of their work.[61] More generally, it included a key market development: the consolidation of speculative investment in contemporary art, confirmed by the successful ten-year gamble of the Société de la Peau de l'Ours ('Skin of the Bear Society'), which for a decade from 1904 bought inexpensive work from innovative newcomers, on which it made a 300% profit when it was auctioned in 1914,[62] and the concomitant proliferation of dealers in and collectors of this art across Europe.[63] Institutionally, it encompassed the consolidation also of the Salon d'Automne and the Salon des Indépendants as, together, the accepted 'unofficial' wing of the Parisian Salon provision; the rapid and substantial rise in the number of foreign artists coming to Paris and exhibiting (or, more often, seeking and failing to exhibit) in these two salons;[64] the proliferation, in the five years before the war, of the *petites revues* on art and literature; and the proliferation, also, of those *académies libres* that incubated the new cohorts of the avant-garde and anchored their multiplying networks.[65]

We can, then, summarise and schematise this unprecedented cluster of developments as having provided the two sets of conditions that were necessary for the consolidation, as opposed to the emergence, of that nascent Parisian avant-garde formation. The first was a sense of collective identity, alternative if not always in explicit opposition to the dominant formation of the 'Secessionist' pre-avant-garde, and not necessarily to the dominant social order.[66] This was grounded in a professionalism that was distinct from the bourgeois professionalism of the latter. In the debates over the concepts of 'profession', 'professional' and 'professionalism' referred to earlier, it has been understood that these terms have long had wider connotations than would restrict them to the liberal-bourgeois variant; in recognition of this, sociologist Eliot Freidson suggests that 'profession' should be seen as a 'folk' concept, that is, the product of a changing and broad-based social dynamic in which people 'make… professions by their activities', with 'consequences… for the way in which they see themselves and perform their work', and in which competing 'folk' concepts of professionalism coexist.[67]

It is in light of this broad 'folk' definition that the consolidation of the artistic avant-garde can be seen as a function of, rather than as separate from and opposed to, this late nineteenth-/early twentieth-century dynamic of professionalisation, and an aspiration to professionalism as part of its motivation; only, and crucially, this was an *alternative* to the liberal-bourgeois variant, in both respects – and it was then available as such for the first time. For while the Incohérents and their comrades distanced themselves by their *fumisme* from this bourgeois professionalism in the 1880s, there was as yet, as I have argued, no basis for their collective independent self-recognition *as artists*; hence their retreat to an assertion of an identity as *humoristes*. By 1910, however, the population of artists in Paris who saw or found themselves to be part of a cultural community that operated beyond the pale of the social and occupational network of mainstream art professionals had grown exponentially, thanks to the gravitational pull of Paris as the capital of (western contemporary) art, to number thousands and, crucially, included a substantial minority of foreign artists: if we take participation in the Salon des Indépendants and the Salon d'Automne as a rough guide, as many as 3,000 artists can be included in this formation.[68] These numbers and this international character gave it both a critical mass and a Europe-wide network (large enough to rival that of the Secessionists and by 1914 unprecedented in its density and traffic) of artists for whom the innovations of Parisian painters, particularly those of Fauvism and Cubism, were paradigmatic, and whose own interpretations of which contributed to their significance and polyvalence.

In consequence, avant-gardist artists in Paris could lay claim to what we might term an alternative professionalism, whose status and standards were as carefully guarded as those of the bourgeois professionals, but on radically different terms: a professionalism, that is, parallel to but less institutionally and bureaucratically legitimised than the bourgeois variant. Sociologists have also noted, in addition to the breadth of definition of the term 'professional', that such 'folk' definitions can encompass occupations not generally approved of by their host societies, whose members nevertheless establish behaviour and attitudes indicative of rudimentary professionalisation. One such, for example, is that of thievery, and an analysis of the character of the professionalism of this particular illegitimate occupation is instructive. In a now-classic study of 1937 based on interviews with a successful career thief, American sociologist Edwin Sutherland identified five characteristics of its professionalism.[69] The first, he suggested, is technical skill: like lawyers, bricklayers and physicians, professional thieves possess specific talents; thieves who lack such specific skills 'are regarded as amateurs, even though they may steal habitually';[70] and 'the division between [the two] in regard to this complex of techniques is relatively sharp… because these techniques are developed to a high point only by education, and the education can be secured only in association with professional thieves'.[71] Although he asserted that 'thieves do not have formal educational institutions for the training of recruits', Sutherland noted that '[s]tories circulate… regarding schools for pickpockets, confidence men, and other professional thieves'; if they existed, he thought them 'probably… ephemeral'.[72] The second characteristic, Sutherland suggested, is status. This is based on ability, lifestyle and power: professional thieves are often contemptuous of 'amateur', small-time thieves; indeed, the term 'thief' itself is reserved for professionals, and 'is considered a high compliment'.[73] The third characteristic is consensus: professional thieves 'can work together without serious disagreements because they have…

common and similar attitudes'[74] and develop 'a system of values and 'an *esprit de corps* which support the individual thief in his criminal career'.[75] The fourth is differential association: professional thieves tend to associate chiefly with each other – indeed, mutual recognition as professionals is a necessary and defining characteristic[76] – and to maintain barriers between themselves and the rest of society. The fifth and last is organisation, in that all of the above four entail both a core of knowledge informally shared and a network of co-operation.[77]

I suggest that there are significant parallels here with the consolidated formation of an artistic avant-garde in Paris, and that such a comparison in turn underscores its emergence as a function of professionalisation. This is not, of course, to say that this formation was in any way 'illegitimate', but that its members perceived themselves, *as* members, to be distinct from the mainstream of liberal-bourgeois fine artists in ways that were strikingly homologous with Sutherland's perceived features of professional thievery, and that a comparison with the latter offers a useful heuristic means of exploring the 'alternative' character of the avant-garde's professionalism. Fundamental to this were, I would argue, three features: first, the elaboration of distinctive (energetically promoted and contested) aesthetic principles that were not only different from, but often opposed to, those of the mainstream; second, the emphasis upon, and development of, equally independent technical means and craft inheritances; and third, the mutual recognition of their common and distinctive aspirations – a shared sense of rupture from the mainstream that originated in the mid-nineteenth century with Gustave Courbet, was deepened by the post-Commune subversiveness of *fumiste* culture, and was signalled from around 1910 by the newly available epithet 'avant-garde' itself. In all of these respects – its autonomy, the safeguarding of its skills and knowledge, and its *esprit de corps* – the avant-garde matched the circumstances of an illicit profession such as thievery.

This collective consciousness of an alternative professionalism could not have become consolidated, however, without a second set of conditions, namely those factors that provided independent infrastructural support for its practices and products. The artistic network that developed from the mid-1880s was inseparable from that of the dealers, critics, collectors, exhibiting societies, little magazines, teaching studios and other vehicles of training, promotion and intellectual exchange, which not only underwrote its activities but sustained its alternative and oppositional character, offering the means variously: to combine traditional craft skills with new techniques in experimentation around art's meaning and reach in, and against, modern spectacular society; to explore, share and compare the innovations in studio practices that resulted; and to disseminate and display these for the different audiences, consumers and patrons who helped the members of this formation to make a living. Once again the international dimension of this infrastructure was key, for it provided not only the 'homes from home' in the expatriate and cosmopolitan enclaves of Paris (and later elsewhere) on which the rapidly growing number of foreign artists coming to Paris to study, work and exhibit depended for companionship, solidarity and often credit, but also the web of dealers, collectors and critics whose transcontinental business was beginning to rival that of the Secessionists in energy if not in funds. We shall look at these developments in more detail in the next chapter.

In the context of this chapter, however, there are two points to make about the relation between this alternative professionalism that characterised the Parisian avant-garde, and its relation both to its predecessors and to other forms of collectivist grouping with which it coexisted, at least until its pre-eminence was consolidated. As we have seen, on both sides of the Channel the motivations of a 'brotherhood' model of grouping declared, from the early to the late nineteenth century (from the Nazarenes to the Nabis), through a direct or indirect affiliation to religion, an opposition to the commercial impulse driving mainstream art. This broadened with secularisation into the range of 'affective relations', from friendship to fellowship to efforts at utopian community living, anarchist or otherwise, that was explored in Chapter 2. If the hegemony in artistic practices and production that was won by Paris over other European cities entailed the displacement of such relations by the dynamic of the market, this was at the cost of narrowing the terms of art discourse to questions of rules and techniques: the values of professionalism in art practice were grounded in the competitive advantage that competence in these respects above all gave Parisian artists, whether mainstream or avant-garde. This is not to say that artists in other cities were clearly aware of these costs – their flocking to Parisian art schools in ever-increasing numbers in the late nineteenth century suggests otherwise. However, this cumulative disposition towards genuflection to the terms and values of Parisian avant-gardism would have costs of its own not just for individual artists, but for the scope of art itself in modern societies, as will be discovered.

The second point concerns the relation between bohemia and the avant-garde. For while bohemia had a part in the emergence of the Parisian avant-garde in ways I have traced above, it did not simply 'become' that new formation, nor did it cease to exist after its emergence. From an economic perspective, it could be said that the process of professionalisation of the avant-garde instrumentalised that formation's cultural practices, in so far as the spaces for, and disposition towards, aesthetic innovation that it engendered on the part of the most progressive young artists also diversified the field of cultural production, offering a widening range of products for a flourishing market. But this was only part of a still-broader encroachment of capitalist economic relations into the realm of the aesthetic – and in this process, 'bohemia' as a concept, and bohemianism as a way of life, not only continued to develop, but played a key role. The following section explores the relation of both to consumerism, to questions of the access of women to the avant-garde and the roles they were allocated within it, and to the hierarchies of class in Paris and London in the years around the turn of the twentieth century.

BOHEMIA AFTER THE AVANT-GARDE

Fumisme in 1880s Paris was, as we have seen, a function of several cultural, social and political developments: an extension of bohemian subversiveness into the profitable arena of commercialised entertainment (with the Chat Noir leading the way); a response to the professionalisation of artistic careers – academic, 'liberal-bourgeois' and avant-garde – in ways that 'sent up' all three with ridicule and ribaldry (and, at the same time, a putative avant-garde itself that lacked only the firm ground of an alternative artistic identity); a sublimation of post-Commune opposition to the slowly stabilising Third Republic that, for some of its adherents, drifted into a cultural nationalism centred on perceived French qualities of wit and irreverence.[78] None of these dimensions was superseded by the emergence and consolidation of the avant-garde. Yet in all of them the continued evolution of these broader factors that *fumisme* registered changed its character. Thus the rapid growth of commercialised entertainment, building on Paris's reputation as the capital not only of art but of hedonism and licentiousness too,[79] annexed bohemia and bohemian attitudes to the purposes of making money and attracting tourists, in the process mythifying its subversiveness and otherness into harmless cliché. By 1910 if not before, not only the lower slopes of Montmartre but the village on La Butte itself too were so overrun with tourists flocking to the Lapin Agile bistrot and other overpromoted 'attractions' that many of its artists had already decamped across the city to Montparnasse, there to begin again their role of outriders of the entertainment industries.[80] Those who remained profited from the repetition of *fumisme*'s now-familiar *blaguesque* tropes: for instance, Roland Dorgelès's painting, made (so he claimed) by the tail of the Lapin Agile's pet donkey and exhibited in the 1910 Salon des Indépendants, gained such notoriety that it provided the name ('The Donkey's Tail') for a landmark avant-garde group that was founded in Moscow the following year, as well as the title for the exhibition this group held in 1912.[81] The spoof launched Dorgelès's career (indeed, was perhaps the high point of it); but in a sense this rapid internationalisation of the joke itself marked the commodification of *fumisme*.

This is not to say that the energies or cultural potential either of *fumisme* or of bohemia more generally were exhausted; the examples of Alfred Jarry in the 1890s and Erik Satie through the following decades, both of whom drew on its conventions of humour, absurdity and (in Jarry's case) obscenity to break radically new ground in theatre and music, show that there was much scope in the mingling of the codes of high and low cultural forms. But crucially their reputations, for all their bohemian colour and rich anecdotal quality, were centred on their *work*: without such products as *Ubu Roi* or the *Three Pieces in the Form of a Pear*, their behavioural idiosyncrasies would have been forgotten in weeks. It was no longer enough, when Paris itself had become a signifier (at least for its foreign tourists) for bohemia, for its bohemians merely to live the artistic life.[82] This was all the more the case as the avant-garde formation was consolidated: the imperatives of its, albeit alternative, professionalism, not to speak of the art-market sector that underwrote this, as well as Paris's reputation as the centre of a burgeoning international avant-garde network demanded that its members produce new work, not just new adventures and anecdotes for the mushrooming art press to write about. It might even be said that in the context of this network, there was no longer a space for the bohemia that had been – until, that is, its commodified, 'lifestyle' version was reimported from elsewhere after the First World War, to set up its headquarters in Montparnasse.

It was, indeed, elsewhere that the myth of bohemia both gained much of its traction after the emergence of the avant-garde, and entered into a new social and cultural role. It did so in terms that not only (to use the distinction I suggested earlier) separated bohemia's 'art as a way of life' from the avant-garde's 'art as a way of working', but also, and crucially, shifted the former into a commodified register: from 'way of life' to 'lifestyle'. Of course, bohemia's strategic role in the emerging culture of capitalist modernity would not have been so telling if it were only an agent in this process. As Elizabeth Wilson notes:

> The myth of the bohemian represents an imaginary solution to the *problem* of art in industrial Western societies. It seeks to resolve the role of art as both inside and outside commerce and consumption, and to reconcile the economic uncertainty of the artistic calling with ideas of the artist's genius and superiority.[83]

It was because it also had an inheritance as a potential opposition to capitalist modernisation that the concept, and the way of life to which it referred, had an appeal to those alienated by the commodification of culture. Peter Brooker, writing about the 'social scene' of early modernist literature in London, observes that 'the bohemian inherits much from the figure of the Romantic artist in English and European traditions', taking a lead from Edgar Allan Poe, the French proto-Symbolists Gérard de Nerval, Théophile Gautier and Charles Baudelaire in 'pitting a personal style and aesthetic against the codes and priorities of industrialising societies'.[84]

Such literary Romantic opposition to capitalist social-economic relations also opened, I have argued, into a broader 'adversary bourgeois' ideology. In England, from the Aestheticism of Rossetti's circle on, this adversarial disposition was partly driven and shaped by the increasingly flourishing subculture of male homosexuality, itself an expression of the ideology of affective relations. As such, London bohemianism was less focused on art practices as such than on social and personal values and qualities that stood against the dominant, public school-derived ideology of masculinity. At the same time, as Wilson notes, it 'brought into play all those aspects of daily life that were not central to the production of works of art'.[85] These features came together from the mid-1870s to shift this nascent bohemianism into a register that was increasingly complicit with conventional bourgeois consumerist fashion, yet also characterised by an openness to the exploration and expression of alternative sexualities that challenged bourgeois convention. The Aesthetic Movement was the most notorious cultural instance of this: a merging of art-for-art's-sake attitudes and Arts and Crafts attachment to beautiful hand-crafted objects, for which the vogue around 1880 for collecting blue-and-white Chinese porcelain stood as exemplary, and which became the butt of numerous ribald jokes in *Punch* magazine (fig. 2), its stock cast of dandified men and willowy, androgynous women pilloried mercilessly in the name of bourgeois common sense and conventional heterosexuality.

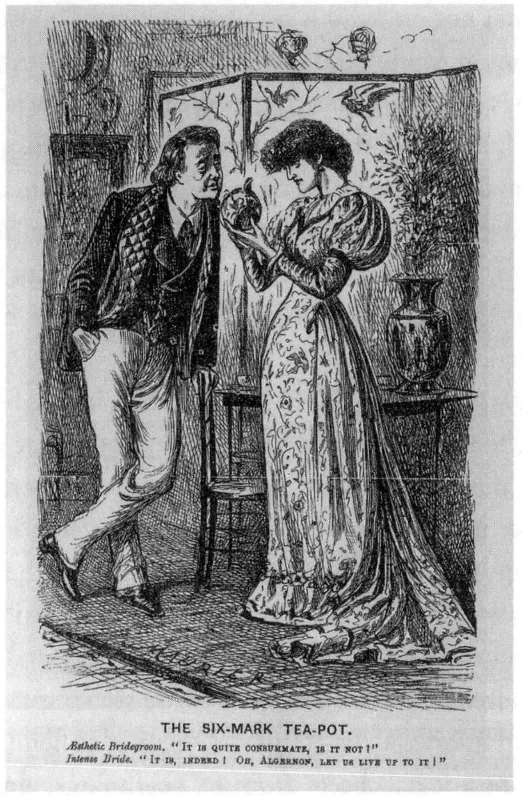

FIG. 2 George du Maurier, 'The Six-Mark Tea-Pot', 1880. Cartoon published in *Punch*, 79, 30 October 1880, 194

As Lisa Tickner and others have noted, such hostility became increasingly acute as the idea and appeal of bohemia spread from Paris to London (and other capitals), and the contradictions noted above by Elizabeth Wilson became sharper.[86] The sanitised and sentimentalised image of Parisian bohemia offered by Murger reached the acme of its renown towards the end of the century, consecrated by the premiere of Puccini's operatic version in 1896. This coincided with the publication of an Anglicised version in George du Maurier's novel *Trilby* (1894), whose story (based loosely on his own experiences 30 years earlier) of three English art students in Paris, the eponymous model and singer with whom they fell in love, and her manipulative 'manager' Svengali, so caught the imagination of the public that not only did it become an instant bestseller but it also spawned a boom in (quite randomly) *Trilby*-themed merchandise, from sweets and songs and saucepans to the soft felt hat that is still a sartorial staple.[87] As Tickner notes, the bourgeois character of his novel's English protagonists stands in sharp contrast to the anti-Semitism of du Maurier's depiction of Svengali as sinister, occult and 'Mephistophelian', and it is this figure, a stand-in, as she suggests, for the perceived 'corrupt and degenerate aestheticism' of Oscar Wilde (whose trial was held the following year), that is the target of the novel.[88]

Yet if *Trilby* was a product of deep-seated and bigoted hostility to the otherness of bohemia, it is also true, as Tickner notes, that Paris's bohemia was changing, not only under the pressures of commercialisation, but also under those imposed by its own reputation, as hundreds of aspirant artists both male and female flocked to the city, where the women found the *académies libres* open to them and even to their studying from the live model (albeit at twice the fees paid by male students). This presence of increasing numbers of middle-class female students contributed to a degree of feminisation and embourgeoisement of bohemia. Through the nineteenth century it had been, from its beginnings, almost invariably not only anti-bourgeois but also male, as a substantial body of modern scholarship has demonstrated. From the *grisettes* of the first half of that century – working-class young women, often seamstresses or milliners, whose attempts at social advancement as mistresses of middle-class male artists were heavily mythicised by Murger – by way of the *femmes de brasserie*, their equivalents of the next generation who supplemented with unlicensed prostitution their inadequate wages from waitressing in the proliferating boulevard cafés and brasseries of Haussmannised Paris, to the models of that new, overwhelmingly male avant-garde of the *fin de siècle* whose aesthetic radicalism was so rarely matched by progressive sexual behaviour, the only roles readily available to women in bohemia were grounded in sexual subservience and exploitation.[89] By the century's end, however, as male supremacy was challenged by 'the new woman' on a number of fronts, women's sense of entitlement to an artistic career was itself a function of their changing social status and an expression of their new freedoms.

While these developments helped women to win for themselves access to a bohemian identity, it nevertheless came at a cost. First, the stakes in choosing bohemia over conventional, usually middle-class, careers or ways of living or social milieux were higher than for men: women risked their respectability, financial solvency and pregnancy, among other social pitfalls. Second, as Brooker observes, if the bohemian life, once embarked upon, meant for some the life of the artist, 'more likely, it meant the role of minor artist or co-worker, editor or sponsor of others' art'.[90] In Paris, where, as I have suggested, the work ethic of the avant-garde placed a premium on gaining a reputation through making and showing art, the latter also entailed a degree of competitive self-promotion that was perceived as unfeminine.[91] In London, where 'lifestyle' signifiers mattered more, it entailed for the more conspicuous female participants 'a life of masquerade in which their leading art exhibit was their own public image'.[92] Some, such as Nina Hamnett and Nancy Cunard, managed to create a myth of themselves as queens of bohemia, but at a time when the perceived determining role of class in Britain was at its height the terms on which these myths were established in each of their cases were significantly different. For Cunard, the heiress to a shipping magnate's fortune, a bohemian 'rebellion' against her privileged, plutocratic background was not far removed from a finishing school: she carried the values of her class to the Café Royal – as Brooker notes, she was a debutante who 'came out' in a different society from one her parents might have had in mind, but one that still deferred to her sophistication and wealth.[93] Hamnett, on the other hand, the daughter of an impecunious army officer, was obliged to work hard both at shedding her provincial middle-class manners and acquiring the reputation for wildness and amorality that she sought; in consequence of which, her considerable artistic talent was, Brooker suggests, neglected, and 'little regarded by herself or others'.[94]

The experiences, and the costs, for young women of seeking attention and reputation in the one-sidedly libertarian world of bohemia, whether in Paris or in London, were thus different not only from those for men – who could enjoy these rewards both for their art and for their behaviour – but also within their gender. In London especially, the decades around the turn of the century that saw the rise of a new business class to social and cultural dominance were those in which the signifiers and determining role of class counted for more than those of an unconventional, artistic 'lifestyle'; the bohemianism of young women was accordingly defined in terms set by those of them born to the new rich.[95] Yet even in plutocratic London there was one respect in which women's bohemianism could be shared across classes. The activism of the suffragist movement – especially that within the Women's Social and Political Union, the suffragettes – both flourished and diversified in the immediate pre-First World War years, and its participants embraced feminism in all the dimensions that it offered to their cause. In so far as the iconoclasms of a bohemian lifestyle helped to loosen the grip of masculinist attitudes to women's public behaviour and roles, they were grist to the activist mill. Thus suffragist magazines such as *The Freewoman* and *The New Freewoman* offered bohemian women a 'women-centred context which gave their art another expression than their performative selves', as Brooker felicitously puts it.[96] Whether such opportunities could gain much purchase on the character of the 'alternative professionalism' of the avant-garde, however, remains to be explored.

4

PARIS: TOWARDS THE AVANT-GARDE

CONTESTING ACADEMIC HEGEMONIES IN EDUCATION AND EXHIBITION

As I noted in the last chapter, a generation of scholarship has traced and assessed the emergence and proliferation, between the mid-nineteenth century and its end, of a Europe-wide liberal-bourgeois professional network of contemporary artists who had broken free of state control of their careers and, like professionals in almost every other sector of the non-entrepreneurial middle class, had taken this over for themselves. Most recently and substantially Béatrice Joyeux-Prunel has shown, with respect to Paris-based artists, how this development began in their struggles in the 1850s to gain a profile in an ever more crowded market, and was driven, over the next several decades, largely by the broadening of their promotional efforts beyond France. While Paris remained the capital of contemporary art, and a Parisian reputation the most sought-after prize in an artistic career, increasingly artists looked for the leverage towards this that successful exposure and critical attention elsewhere in Europe (and later, beyond) could obtain.

As Joyeux-Prunel argues, the network that resulted from these efforts was a social and occupational, rather than an aesthetic, one in which whom one knew and sold to, where one exhibited, and summered and wintered – in short, the society one kept – counted for more than one's ideas about painting.[1] While an engagement with the innovations of Impressionism was common to many of its members, this was a moderated modernism, a 'juste milieu' version (in the phrase adopted by Robert Jensen from French political history and accepted by Joyeux-Prunel),[2] which reconciled

Impressionism's broken brushstrokes and chromatic innovations with more conservative pictorial qualities. What counted, in painterly terms, was practical competence, and the discourse that articulated and shaped its concerns was coloured by a rhetoric of 'quality' and 'talent' – both undefined – whose lack of specificity enabled the encompassing within the network of stylistic options that were in aesthetic terms irreconcilable, in particular those of Impressionism and Symbolism.[3]

This Secessionist network was in place by the mid-1890s. Begun 30 or so years earlier, it obtained its institutional consecration with the foundation in Paris, in 1890, of the Société Nationale des Beaux-Arts, the result of a schism within the Société des Artistes Français, which ran the annual Salon, over the numbers of works by foreign artists admitted for exhibition.[4] Dominated by the leading fashionable artists of the time, the breakaway group and its rival Salon, the 'Nationale' positioned itself in tacit opposition to the conservatism of the Artistes Français, and as such provided a model for a series of similar secessions from their respective academies through the 1890s by comparable artist groups, most notably those in Munich (1892), Vienna (1897) and Berlin (1898). The 'moment' of this consecration was also that of the emergence in Paris of an avant-garde formation, in the milieux that fostered the coming together, in different ways, of the Nabis and the Neo-Impressionists. This was, I shall argue, no coincidence, for the consolidation of the former was in many respects the precondition for the emergence of the latter, and the particular qualities of secessionism and its ideology – the establishment of an international circuit of galleries and artist-organised exhibition societies, the motley of styles, the social networking and status snobbery of the 'liberal-bourgeois' secessionist collectivity – played a key role, as this chapter will show, in producing its opposite and successor in the formation of the Parisian avant-garde. The succession was neither complete nor immediate, however, nor – initially, at least – was the opposition clear and categorical; there was an overlap of more than a decade between the emergence of the nucleus of an avant-garde and the zenith of secessionism. By 1900, indeed, as Joyeux-Prunel argues, the latter's membership of 'socially well-endowed artists' centred on the 'cosmopolitan high society' of Europe dominated the contemporary art world.[5] But by this time, also, it had become increasingly closed to aesthetic innovation, and this left opportunities for a challenge to its hegemony from an avant-garde network of artists that was rapidly consolidating an alternative professional identity and culture.

ACADÉMIES LIBRES: INCUBATING THE AVANT-GARDE

There were several aspects to the causal relation between them. One was the developing structure of the field of contemporary art education in late nineteenth-century Paris. The proliferation of the promotional initiatives of ambitious artists, the growing reputation of the city as the 'capital' of contemporary art, and the loosening of the aesthetic rules and academic codes of practice that was consequent upon the growing challenge to academic hegemony presented by the emergent secessionist network, attracted increasing numbers of would-be artists. Their surfeit led to the proliferation, in turn, of *académies libres*, the private, fee-paying art schools, already referred to in earlier chapters, whose initial purpose was to prepare candidates for the entrance exam of the École des Beaux-Arts (hitherto the institutional gatekeeper to a fine-art career), but which increasingly supplemented that overcrowded establishment. The first of these, the Académie Julian, founded in 1868 by an academic painter, Rodolphe Julian, who had exhibited at the Salon in the 1860s before turning to teaching, was so successful that its initial studio, in the passage des Panoramas in central Paris, was followed over the next 20 years by a dozen or so other branches scattered across the city.

Their success was due initially to two factors. The first was their utility in providing what novice art students needed: a basic introduction to the disciplines of painting and drawing, access to the life model, contact with other artists and informed criticism from a roster of celebrated academic artists, acquaintance with whom might assist an application to the École. The second factor was the willingness of these leading artists and École tutors to act as visiting professors at the *académies libres*, thereby providing their host *académie* with a cachet that would attract students. This was a winning formula, and the Julian was joined by several competitors over the same 20 years: the Colarossi, the Humbert, the Grande Chaumière, the Cormon were the best known of around 20 *académies libres* that made up a flourishing subculture unrivalled anywhere in Europe.[6] Yet the teaching was, to say the least, indifferent – the visits by big-name artists whose 'day job' was at the École were infrequent (if a useful source of additional income to them) – and at worst pernicious, if the recollection of one ex-student, the future novelist and playwright George Moore, is anything to go by: 'That great studio of Julian's is a sphinx', he wrote in 1886, 'and all the poor folk that go there for artistic education are devoured.... After two years they all paint and draw alike, every one has that vile execution – they call it execution – *la pâte, la peinture au premier coup*.'[7] Whether this was true of the rival establishments is not certain – documentation on them is scarcer – but it is likely; it would appear that the Julian's teaching model was ubiquitously adopted.

However, as the population of art students and young artists in Paris mushroomed,[8] and the number of *académies libres* with it, so the character, the significance and the role of the latter changed in important ways. First, as I noted in the previous chapter, their acceptance of women students (decades before the École des Beaux-Arts) increased rapidly, possibly so much that female students outnumbered the men from the 1880s[9]. Second, their evolution from servicing the École's entrance needs to supplementing its teaching – and eventually to supplanting this, breaking its monopoly through sheer force of numbers – changed the character of Parisian art education correspondingly. No longer governed by the formal examination requirements and curricular constraints, the pedagogic discipline and hierarchical culture with which the École safeguarded its status as the premier art school in France (and thus the world), the *académies* were open to a wider range of aesthetic ideas, operated according to looser criteria of quality and produced more artists. Moreover, even though in many cases the same tutors taught at the École as at the *académies*, they often did so, when visiting the latter, with less application and commitment as well as to lesser effect. Émile Bernard, who was a student at Cormon's in the mid-1880s, noted that its teaching 'had nothing academic [about it]: each worked as he wished, staying away on the days of the tutor's corrections',[10] an observation that could probably have been made at other *académies*. Given the indifference of moonlighting professors, it is hardly surprising that the students learnt as much from each other, often from a particular fellow student who was more talented or charismatic than the rest, and could play a more influential role in exploring new directions in painting than did the professors themselves. A case in point is that of Louis Anquetin, a student at Cormon's in the mid-1880s who, as Bernard again noted, 'stood out from all the other students': older than most, at 24 when they met, Anquetin had great ability – Bernard was struck from his first day at the *académie* by a painting of a male torso that showed a grasp of 'great painting' and 'an accomplishment in handling form' – and seemed 'always anxious to become the strongest and the best' artist; Bernard sensed that Anquetin had an ambition 'to be the great painter of modern life, and dreamed of fusing [the qualities of] Manet and Daumier in his own art'.[11]

It is hardly surprising, either, that the friendships made in this environment formed the basis for the emergence of shared attachments to particular innovations, as was the case of Bernard and Anquetin, who were jointly credited with pioneering the 'cloisonné' style of distinguishing the flatly painted forms they favoured by means of black contour lines,[12] and that such studio-hatched techniques were often disseminated across *académies*, developing into often contestatory, and contested, aesthetic position-takings or 'isms' (*cloisonnisme* itself was one such, its relation to Paul Gauguin's invention of 'synthétisme' keenly disputed).[13] Indeed, it was perhaps inevitable that the emergence of such collaborations within an *académie* should lead on to a group gaining a foothold on the teaching roster as a means of promoting its 'ism' – as did the Cubists Metzinger and Le Fauconnier in 1912 when they started teaching at the Académie de La Palette; or even founding its own establishment – as did the Nabis in 1908, when they were sufficiently well known to set up the Académie Ranson, at which several of them taught.[14]

Ultimately, it was in such ways that the *académies libres*, which had begun in the early 1870s as institutions oriented towards the École des Beaux-Arts and its needs, came by the late 1880s to be among the incubators and, as they flourished in the next two decades, among the consolidators of the nascent formation of the avant-garde. Themselves a function of the diversification of the rapidly privatising profession of contemporary fine-art production, they were in turn a necessary condition for the emergence of this formation, helping to create the spaces for its independence from the officially sanctioned fine-art profession in institutional, social and, most crucially, aesthetic terms. They were not the only factor, however: such new initiatives in art education emerged alongside others related to the market that also put in place some of the means towards such independence. Chronologically the first of these was the setting-up by artists frustrated by the constraints and overcrowding of the annual Salon of their own exhibiting societies, some of them (nicknamed 'petits Salons') intended as 'curtain-raisers' to the major event, others as more independent of it and registering a loosening of its monopoly.[15] The most famous was the Cercle de l'Union Artistique, founded in 1860 and known familiarly as the 'Mirlitons';[16] its rivals included the Cercle St. Amand (whose name changed to Le Volney when it moved to the street of that name), the Cercle des Arts in the rue de Choiseul, and the Cercle Artistique et Littéraire in the rue Chaussée d'Antin, all of which mounted collective and solo exhibitions of widely differing current artistic tendencies.[17]

IMPRESSIONISM'S EXHIBITIONS: A HALFWAY HOUSE?

If groups such as the above and the events that they mounted were all oriented, to varying degrees, to the annual Salon and presented themselves as complementary to it, the series of exhibitions organised from the mid-1870s by the group of artists who became known as the Impressionists were different, in asserting an independence that stemmed to a significant extent from dissatisfaction, not only with the increasingly recognised shortcomings of the Salon system (its market inefficiency and chronic overcrowding both of exhibits and of their viewers), but also with the entrenched aesthetic conservatism of its juries. An irregular event held roughly every two years in a diversity of locations, the exhibition series began in 1874 and ended with the eighth in 1886, and although it has become established in the historiography of modernism as the vehicle for consecrating Impressionist painting and the Impressionist group as the first manifestation of an avant-garde, it was, as the initiative of a group of painters facing a complex and changing art market and professional dynamic, neither so clear-cut a departure from then-current custom nor so epochal a phenomenon.[18] Rather, like the proliferation of the above societies, the Impressionists' 12-year project was part of that broad process of the privatisation of the fine-art profession that I have been tracing: in this case, an initiative that from its start sought above all to improve the market prospects for its participants, rather than primarily to declare and cement a specific and new kind of painting.[19]

As Martha Ward notes, 'If the history of [these] Impressionist exhibitions has a beginning, it is not with actual practices but with published complaints', and she cites a letter of 1870 by Edgar Degas printed in the newspaper *Paris-Journal* that 'described what was wrong with the Salon and advised how to fix it'. Instead of 'skying' paintings by hanging them in several rows stretching, frame to frame, high up the walls, Degas suggested, they should be restricted to two rows of works adequately spaced, and artists should be able to specify their placement; in his proposal, 'the primary concept determining installation', Ward observes, was 'the integrity of the individual artist and the individual work.... The Salon should not interfere with the right of each individual to determine his or her own best place on the wall.'[20] Degas's points were taken up in several quarters in the next few years, the critic Paul Alexis recommending in *L'Avenir national* in 1873 the formation of an 'artistic corporation' to counter the Salon system's shortcomings and alluding to plans already under way for such a 'syndicate', an article to which Claude Monet replied in a letter to the same paper, welcoming Alexis's support for ideas that were shared by 'a group of painters assembled in my home' who had together 'read it with pleasure'.[21] Alexis responded in a further published note by stressing the individualism of this informal group and the breadth of its aesthetic approaches: 'these painters, most of whom have previously exhibited, belong to that group of naturalists which has the right ambition of painting nature and life in their large reality', he wrote. 'Their association, however, will not be just a small clique. They intend to represent interests, not tendencies, and hope for the adhesion of all serious artists.'[22]

For all the insistence on individualism in Alexis's note, he also acknowledges that the 'interests' that Monet's group shared had an aesthetic aspect, and this relative coherence around 'naturalism' also underscored the difference between the 'Impressionist' exhibitions and those of the other artists' societies. It has underwritten, too, the still-dominant positioning of this group in histories of modernism as the first avant-garde; for all its longevity, however, this is an assumption that needs to be challenged.[23] The group's shared aesthetic was indeed recognised by contemporary critics, one of whom, Edmond Duranty, responded to the second exhibition in the series, that of 1876, with a lengthy essay that seems to have been the first cogent attempt to address it.[24] Yet, like Alexis, Duranty was at pains to avoid labelling either the aesthetic or the group, identifying only the latter's engagement with innovative stylistic treatments of a wide range of subjects from modern life.

This disinclination to emphasise a more explicit and specific collective position was shared by the group itself in its promotion of the first exhibition in 1874, calling itself in the catalogue simply a 'Société Anonyme des artistes peintres, sculpteurs, graveurs, etc.' In fact, throughout the dozen years that the series spanned, there seems to have been little interest in coining and deploying a specific 'ism' for either the exhibitions or the group itself. While the term 'Impressionism' was in currency by 1876 (and used by Stéphane Mallarmé in his essay on the group in that year),[25] the catalogue for that year's exhibition (the second) avoided using it, as did the third in 1877 (although posters, and the banner over the door of the venue where it was held, promoted it as an 'Exposition des Impressionistes') and the fourth in 1879 (which used only the phrase 'Groupe des Indépendants'). From this persistent eschewal of a collective aesthetic position-taking, art historian Charles Moffett concludes that the group itself 'insisted upon the recognition of Impressionism as only one thread in the increasingly complex fabric of the modern movement', and that '[t]he eight shows were in fact "umbrella" exhibitions for a diverse and complex association' of artists.[26] In the same publication, Stephen F. Eisenman takes this point further, specifying the components of this fabric and thread in political terms. Noting that the initial term given the group by critics was 'Intransigents', and that this label gained in popularity until the third exhibition in 1877, when the group accepted (half-heartedly, it would seem) 'Impressionists', Eisenman explores the etymology and currency in the 1870s of both terms. His analysis reveals that 'Intransigents', deriving from its adoption by Spanish anarchists in the brief civil war in that country of 1873–74, was picked up in France to connote qualities of political radicalism and democracy, while 'Impressionists', deriving from an understanding of impressions as sensual perceptions that was developed by French positivists, in the mid-1870s connoted for the critics 'a vaguely defined technique of painting and an attitude of individualism'. The opposition between these terms and meanings, and the struggles over their usage within the group and among the critics who discussed their work, laid bare deep divisions between their participants, and Eisenman relates these to the political polarisation of republicanism between radicals such as Georges Clemenceau and opportunists such as Léon Gambetta in the still-unstable early years of the Third Republic. His suggestion that this opposition was mirrored within Impressionism by, respectively, Camille Pissarro and Pierre-Auguste Renoir indicates the ideological differences that ran through the group.[27]

This severe précis of Eisenman's argument does no justice to the nuanced visual analysis of Impressionist style that it encompasses, nor to its persuasive situation of this within the political conjuncture of the 1870s; but it does indicate that neither ideological coherence nor avant-gardist aesthetic solidarity were the cement that held the group together for 12 years. In his article of 1986, art historian Jean-Paul Bouillon went further, insisting that the emergence of the Impressionist group 'was less a matter of the maturation of an aesthetic or the logical outcome of the weaving of a network of "friendships"... than the immediate consequence of precise economic givens'.[28] Bouillon argues, first, that the Impressionists remained committed, even as they launched their independent exhibition, to eventual success at the Salon, observing that 'the support of a small number of collectors and of dealers seemed [to them] to offer sufficient grounds in 1874 for an expectation of official recognition through traditional channels', and that the critic Théodore Duret stressed the importance of such channels in a letter of that year to Pissarro in which he advised against the setting-up of a[n exhibiting] society: 'You must take a step further and achieve real notoriety', he insisted. 'You will never get there by means of these private societies' exhibitions. The public never goes to these exhibitions, you will only attract the same small group of artists and *amateurs* who already know you.'[29] Second, Bouillon notes that the plans for this exhibition were made at the time when the French economy was entering what turned out to be years of recession,[30] in which falling prices sapped the finances of this nucleus of support for their work, and particularly those of their principal dealer, Paul Durand-Ruel. 'The "society" approach thus appeared', he suggests, 'as the only recourse for assuring sales via the organising of exhibitions: these were the two chief objectives of the association, as they appear in the founding charter of December 1873.'[31] Bouillon's argument is reductive in its exclusive consideration of economic factors, but the existence of these underlines the common ground between the Impressionists' initiative and those of the other societies.

Indeed, in two respects in particular, some of the group followed closely the same market strategy as the latter in pursuit of recognition (and, in so doing, added an economic dimension to the political divisions within it that Eisenman notes). The first was in continuing to privilege the Salon as the primary status marker in the eyes of the art establishment, until the shortcomings of its exhibitions were exposed by the economic downturn and the decline of sales of contemporary art. This was an orientation confirmed in 1879 when, faced by a new rule introduced by Degas from the Impressionist exhibition of that year that no participant should send anything to the Salon, Renoir, Paul Cézanne and Alfred Sisley opted for the latter over showing at their own exhibition. There was considerable vacillation within the group over this, but Sisley's comment in a letter to Duret that March was succinct: 'We are still far from the moment when we shall be able to do without the prestige attached to official exhibitions. I am therefore determined to submit to the Salon.'[32] The three were joined the following year by Monet, who chose the Salon over the fifth Impressionist exhibition, and in 1881 by Caillebotte. In the same year Renoir justified his choice to Durand-Ruel: 'In Paris there are hardly 15 *amateurs* capable of appreciating a painter without the Salon. There are 80,000 who won't even buy a nose if a painter isn't at the Salon. This is why every year I send two portraits.'[33]

The second respect was in then turning, like the members of the other societies, to the most dynamic galleries as the recession deepened after 1880 and dealers such as Georges Petit responded by targeting the wealthiest stratum of *amateurs* – bucking the recession, as it were, by going 'up market'. The move on the part of the dealers was risky but unavoidable, and one made possible to a great extent by Haussmann's 'refurbishment' of Paris from the early 1850s, which had by the mid-1870s created hundreds of new apartments on his new boulevards;[34] the rising middle class of the young Third Republic (the 'nouvelles couches sociales' announced by Gambetta in 1872)[35] were in the market for them, and were looking also to decorate them.[36] Their aspiration not only encouraged a 'decorative turn' already under way in French art-critical discourse[37] but threw into relief the unsuitability of the Salon environment for meeting the requirements of new *amateurs* such as these. The most common complaint made against the Salon from the 1860s was that it was a marketplace more like those industrial fairs that also occupied the Palais de l'Industrie where it was held after 1855 than an art museum, let alone a private apartment; and, correspondingly, the ambience of the spaces in which the new societies presented their works were coming increasingly to resemble the last of these.[38] Taking their cue partly from across the Channel, where in 1877 the lavish and upmarket Grosvenor Gallery was launched in London to rival the Royal Academy,[39] dealers such as Durand-Ruel and, in particular, Georges Petit from the early 1880s presented their holdings of contemporary art in increasingly plush spaces furnished with comfortable settees and potted plants, all designed to imitate *haut-bourgeois* private interiors.[40] Such 'domestication' of the experience of artworks was accompanied, on Durand-Ruel's part, by an increasingly aggressive marketing policy, including the exportation of Impressionist paintings to exhibitions abroad (in 1883 alone, to London, Boston, Rotterdam and Berlin), as well as the holding of one-artist shows of Monet, Pissarro, Renoir and Sisley in the summer of the same year, in a newly converted, small and comfortably decorated apartment, on the rue Madeleine in the gallery district, that was reserved exclusively for showing Impressionist paintings.[41] These initiatives represented an increase in exposure for Impressionist painting that was designed both to demonstrate his hegemony vis-à-vis his rival dealers in the contemporary art market, and to underscore the entrepreneurial dynamism of the gallery sector relative to the Salon.[42]

Together, these strategies can be seen as driving the process of the 'privatisation' of Impressionism and the absorption of its innovations by the mainstream. Besides such market initiatives, there were two other factors contributing to this absorption, one political and the other visual. With the consolidation of Republican power around 1880, governmental arts policy became more liberal, and measures such as the relinquishing by the state of control over the Salon and reforms to encourage a broader spectrum of art practices opened the way for the official consecration of Impressionism. The price of this artistically was a softening of its style by those more mainstream artists who adopted some of its informalities, and a 'juste milieu' version of Impressionism gradually became fashionable and indeed a common denominator of so much work produced within the Secessionist network that, as I have already noted, by the turn of the century it was its dominant aesthetic.[43] Reciprocally, the Impressionists were gradually persuaded of the benefits of an orientation to a wealthier, wider and more socially prestigious clientele than that of their few dedicated aficionados, and one by one they turned to exhibiting in Petit's gallery. Monet led the way, in 1885 accepting an invitation to show in his annual International Exhibition, alongside artists already identified with the Secessionist network, such as Jean Béraud, Albert Besnard and Henri Gervex, whose company, as Martha Ward notes, 'would have been considered a serious threat to the artistic distinction between the Salon and an Independent show'. Ward adds: 'By 1886, the consequences of the premier Impressionist's participation in this show would begin to unfold. Renoir, Raffaëlli and Monet himself would have to choose between exhibiting with the group or with Petit. All would go after the greater prestige and rewards promised by Durand-Ruel's competitor.'[44] The following year, even the anarchist Pissarro took Petit's franc. As Joyeux-Prunel notes, 'the taking control of several Impressionists' careers by the galerie Petit constituted… a symbolic valorisation without precedent'.[45]

The initiatives of the Impressionists, then, were not the vehicles for a break with the mainstream and the birth of an artistic avant-garde that their historians have assumed, but a register of the gradual disaggregation and liberalisation of the art world that the privatisation of artists' professional status engendered. Yet they did help to bring about some of the conditions that enabled first the emergence, and then the consolidation, of such an avant-garde. To describe the group and its character as a 'half-way house' to the latter would be unduly teleological, however; rather, it offered a way beyond the status quo that had multiple possible futures, of which the emergence of an avant-garde in the groupings of the Neo-Impressionists and Nabis were those realised, in ways and for reasons that we shall shortly explore. The very instigation of a series of exhibitions of an identifiable group, however loosely constituted, independent of the Salon, for all its members' vacillations over the importance of gaining recognition in that forum, established one plank of a platform for more fundamental independence. Their engagement at the same time with the gallery sector, despite the aesthetically compromising association with 'juste milieu' versions of their own innovations that joining Petit's stable entailed, was a step towards the establishment of a viable, more dynamic and effective sector of the market outside the Salon system – one that in less than 20 years would, as we shall see, support speculative investment in the newest art by a new kind of *amateur*.

DEALERS AND *PETITES REVUES*: AN EMERGING INFRASTRUCTURE

It was, paradoxically enough, the deepening of the French recession in 1882, and the need for dealers, if they were to survive, to respond with entrepreneurial initiatives, that precipitated the developments which would provide vital market support for an avant-garde. Petit's lavish new gallery that opened that year and Durand-Ruel's sending of paintings, including Impressionist works, to an exhibition in Boston in the following year introduced their holdings to new collectors and consolidated the shift of gravity within the market towards the dealers as opposed to the Salon.[46] The mushrooming interest from the early 1880s of American collectors in particular, assiduously nurtured by Impressionist-circle painter Mary Cassatt via her social network in the United States,[47] provided a timely boost not only to Durand-Ruel's finances[48] but, more broadly, to the viability of that sector of the contemporary art market that was increasingly oriented to the most innovative work. At both the top and the bottom end of this market, new entrants on the supply and the demand side indicated heightened expectations of profits to be made from speculation in such work. At the top of the supply side, the respected dealer Alexandre Bernheim, since 1863 gallerist and friend of Delacroix, Corot and Courbet, turned his attention to the Impressionists at the instigation of his sons Josse and Gaston. In 1900 they established the Galerie Bernheim-Jeune, where they progressively adopted the mantle of Durand-Ruel in handling and showing – and thereby helping to consolidate the position of – the work of the emergent Parisian avant-garde: among many others, in 1901 van Gogh, in 1906 the Nabis Bonnard and Vuillard, Cézanne in 1907, Seurat and van Dongen in 1908, Matisse in 1910 and the Italian Futurists in 1912. At the bottom end of the supply side, the example of Durand-Ruel's early risk-taking with the Impressionists helped, as it appeared to pay off in the 1890s, to support the emergence of what Robert Jensen has termed the 'ideological' dealer, who combined financial with aesthetic investment in his or her artists, in varying degrees.[49] Such dealers not only steadily expanded the means by which an avant-garde formation could be consolidated as autonomous, opening the contemporary art market to new sales and promotional practices at both ends of it, but also fostered an interest, in both financial and aesthetic senses of the word, in the innovations of modernist art. In truth, Jensen's designation is misleading, for there was a variety of reasons besides ideology for which a small clutch of Parisian dealers pursued these interests in the late nineteenth and early twentieth centuries: for Durand-Ruel, Ambroise Vollard, Louis-Léon Le Barc, Daniel-Henry Kahnweiler and Berthe Weill, to name the most celebrated, dealing was a matter not only of aesthetic discernment but also (even rather) of acute and adventurous entrepreneurship, of the love of a gamble, the enjoyment of patronage, the ties of friendship and – not least – a consequence of the spaces left for each of these in a fairly conservative and hierarchised market.

Perhaps the most notorious of these (partly because of his entertainingly colourful and irreverent account of his activities) was Ambroise Vollard, who in the late 1880s and early 1890s gradually broke out of the chrysalis of clerking for an established dealer, at first getting by hand-to-mouth as an *amateur*-cum-dealer,[50] trading in drawings and prints by lesser contemporary artists, often picked up cheaply from the *bouquinistes* on the quais, before risking all in 1893 by opening his own gallery on the rue Laffitte, then the centre of the trade in contemporary art.[51] Here, in November 1894, he first showed to rave reviews some drawings and unfinished paintings by Édouard Manet that he had shrewdly obtained from the artist's widow.[52] He then raised the stakes further by buying almost the whole output of Cézanne, then the only major member of the Impressionist circle still without a dealer[53] – some 150 paintings – and giving the artist his first show in 1895.[54] Alongside Vollard, the retired shipowner Louis-Léon Le Barc blurred the boundaries between picture dealer and *amateur* in the idiosyncratic manner of his patronage of the Nabis in the 1890s. After establishing a nest egg for his retirement by small-scale dealing in Old Masters, he opened a gallery, Le Barc de Boutteville, combining his own and his wife's names, at the end of 1891. Tiny by all accounts, like Vollard's which it anticipated by two years, it was also, again like Vollard's, in the right place, on the rue Le Peletier, close to that of Durand-Ruel and other dealers in progressive painting. There, over the next six years until his death, he held 15 exhibitions of work by 'Impressionists and Symbolists', in which the Nabis very largely predominated (although there were sometimes Neo-Impressionists too). It would seem that Le Barc was motivated less by financial gain, or even the excitement of speculation in young artists, than by the enjoyment of their company when, as the painter (and future furniture designer) Francis Jourdain later recalled, they happily came to smoke his cigarettes and warm their feet by his stove.[55] Jourdain summarised Le Barc's attachment to the Nabis, writing that he 'found out about this peculiar band, not always understanding its behaviour, and eventually became happily convinced that there was, not a [financially] fruitful project to realise, but a useful role to play in helping the early careers of these young people'.[56]

The risk-taking of these new dealers was underwritten by two factors that were then particular to Paris. First was the existence of a district of the city, the hill-top *quartier* of La Butte Montmartre, which had for generations offered cheap rents and entertainment venues to a socially and culturally marginalised population, and whose steep slopes and *rus in urbe* communality increasingly sheltered young and adventurous artists alongside villains, revolutionaries and the indigenous poor.[57] It now housed an informal ghetto of low-rent studios and art-materials suppliers who took their new paintings, in lieu of payment, which they displayed on their shop walls. Second, the first clear demonstration of interest in the potential profitability of speculation in this art at the bottom end of the demand side came with the founding in 1904 of a collectors' society by 14 *amateurs*, with the express purpose of amassing over ten years, at the cost of 250 francs each per year, a collection of 'important works by young painters or those just establishing some notoriety', and selling it at a profit at the end of this period.[58] Their choosing to name their venture the 'Société de la Peau de l'Ours', after the fable by La Fontaine in which two hunters sell the skin of a bear before hunting – and failing to kill – the animal indicates its dozen members' enjoyment of the gamble this entailed. It paid off: the collection made a profit of over 300 per cent at its sale at Drouot's auction house in 1914. It also underscored the arrival in the market of a new kind of *amateur*, the *dénicheur* or winkler-out of bargains: young professional (usually) men, for whom the financial rewards for their discernment and independence of judgment in discovering for themselves such 'important works by young painters' were equal to those of aesthetic contemplation of the works themselves.[59] Drawn in their search for such art towards the mythical bohemia that Montmartre already stood for, the *dénicheurs* showed little interest in the young unknowns of Montparnasse, those scores of hopefuls from across the world who gravitated, upon arrival in Paris, to the many enclaves of their countrymen and women centred on its boulevard cafés, its *cités d'artistes* and its *académies libres.*[60] Instead, their patronage gave valuable support to La Butte's network of penniless small galleries and bric-à-brac shops, which constituted both the very bottom of the contemporary art market and, as such, the front line of infrastructural support for its avant-garde community. They also served to reinforce gender imbalances, for few of these *dénicheurs* were interested in purchasing the work of women artists, not least because their purchases from the avant-garde enabled them to share vicariously in the heroic identity of the latter. Thus, of the 54 artists represented in the Peau de l'Ours collection at its auction in 1914, only one was female.[61]

Ironically given this last fact, one of the key gallerists on this front line of support for the avant-garde was a woman. Berthe Weill opened a gallery in December 1901. Since she had few assets to help launch her art-dealing career other than an enthusiasm for contemporary art, and was thus obliged to harness this to a search for new talent,[62] it was ideally situated for the bottom rung of the art-market ladder that she perforce occupied, on the rue Victor Massé, halfway between Montmartre and the rue Laffitte. There 'la petite Mère Weill' (which translates as 'little mother' or 'little marvel'[*merveille*]), as 'her' artists fondly called her, held 60 exhibitions of work by unknown young artists in the decade and a half before the First World War, selling not a lot of pictures for about 25 francs each, developing from eclectic beginnings towards the modernists, bringing together the *dénicheurs* and some of their leading representatives.[63]

Between Berthe Weill and Bernheim-Jeune, then, by the beginning of the decade before the First World War a sector of the contemporary market had become established in Paris that provided the infrastructure upon which an artistic avant-garde was able both to build a collective identity as professionals distinct from the mainstream and to make a living. It was a stable hierarchy, itself built on a tacit principle of live and let live, in which a cartel of dealers at the top end, chief among whom was Bernheim-Jeune, supported the activities and products of those below them. Those with least capital such as Weill had too little of it to amass a stock of work, and so could only attempt to sell new work as soon as possible. They might, if lucky, pass their artists up to the tier above them, who might in turn hold onto them for longer, burnishing the reputation of a newcomer by including him (or, more rarely, her) in mixed exhibitions alongside established names – often including a work or two loaned from a top-end gallery in a transaction that both brought added allure to the borrower's exhibition and, for the lender, 'farmed' new work in which it was potentially interested. Eventually a newer name might have won sufficient recognition on this journey up the hierarchy to be a safe bet for Bernheim-Jeune, say, to offer a contract (which gave them first refusal on that artist's new work).[64] As such, it was a benign system, which left market opportunities open to dealers with the ambition to seize them. The first of those to do so was Kahnweiler – with consequences for the consolidation, and the shaping, of an artistic avant-garde that we shall explore in a later chapter.

Even more than the *académies libres* or the market for new art, the history of the flourishing of *petites revues*, or little magazines, in *fin-de-siècle* and Belle Époque Paris has become a substantial research field in itself in recent years. In French literary studies it has beaten its Anglophone equivalent, if not by very many years, to the establishment of a corpus of major publications that have between them surveyed this phenomenon in detail, and have greatly enriched our understanding of the institutional and discursive determinants of Parisian literary modernism.[65] While it is beyond the scope of the present book to summarise the findings of this corpus, its almost exclusive focus on the roles and positions of these *petites revues* within the then-emergent and consolidating literary avant-garde of Paris, as opposed to the broader field of French cultural practices, means that their consequences for its equivalent and contemporary artistic formation are, very largely, yet to be explored.[66] This will be the focus of the following paragraphs.

The number of *petites revues* that were published in the 40 years before the First World War was at first considerable, and then became extraordinary. Between 1872 and 1894, in France as a whole 529 periodicals with *revue* in their titles appeared; of these 325 were published in Paris.[67] More than 250 literary revues alone were listed by Maurice Caillard and Charles Forot in 1924 as appearing in Paris between 1870 and 1914. Rémy de Gourmont's 1900 estimate for literary reviews was at least 100 between 1890 and 1898. Roméo Arbour found over 185 circulating in the capital between 1900 and 1914, over 50 of which were founded after 1910. What were the reasons for this unprecedented (and surely unrivalled, whichever of these counts is preferred) flourishing of a whole little-magazine subculture? Several have been offered, including 'profound social and cultural changes occurring' such as the greater legal freedoms for publishers introduced around 1880, and the democratisation of reading.[68] Among them are four that merit particular mention. The most general, perhaps, is the fact that in the 50 years from the mid-1830s, writing became industrialised in France:

the total number of novels, volumes of poetry and plays published had increased by 50 per cent by the mid-1880s. Of these, novels grew most in that period, by nearly 400 per cent, while the number of plays did not change and poetry volumes declined by 25 per cent.[69]

As the cultural historian Christophe Charle suggests, these differentials register an increasingly clear divorce, over those decades, between the financial success achieved by novelists and the literary consecration achieved by poets and playwrights.[70] Yet as Charle also notes, despite the relative privation of the literary life for most, between 1860 and 1890 the number of writers in France doubled, as – like aspirant painters and sculptors – would-be *littérateurs* flocked to Paris, drawn by its reputation as the cosmopolitan literary capital of the world.[71] Such a population of writers needed the resources to support itself materially; the novelist Gustave Flaubert may well have aspired, as he put it, 'to live as a bourgeois and think as a demi-god',[72] but this still required the means of a bourgeois. Crucially, two material developments of around 1880 helped to furnish these resources, at least for young and impecunious poets. The first was that relaxation in 1881 of the laws governing the French press that I noted above, as the Third Republic, founded only a decade earlier, began to feel less threatened by the monarchist right. This removed the dissuasively large financial deposit required of anyone who wished to publish a magazine, as well as the censorship that had severely constrained press freedom. It was therefore less expensive, and less risky, to publish a wide range of opinions, whether political, literary or both. The second development was a technological revolution in newspaper publishing, which saw rotary web offset printing introduced (invented in 1865, this allowed rotary-fed printing on both sides at once, of paper that from the mid-1870s could be made from wood pulp more cheaply than from the rags that until then had provided its raw material) and the resulting relinquishing of now-obsolete letterpresses; these could be bought by those wishing to print the magazines that they could now afford to set up.[73]

The *petites revues* that resulted were overwhelmingly literary or political, and often both; it was not until the end of the century and after that *revues d'art* appeared in any numbers.[74] They occupied a space in the field of published writing that was distinct from books, from daily papers or weekly periodicals, and from militant pamphlets – and their editors and contributors were endlessly concerned to assert and maintain such distinctions.[75] The philosopher and political theorist Georges Sorel declared that 'the newspapers make journalism; the *revues* make culture; the two should not be confused', while the Goncourt brothers asserted, with even greater provocation, 'a book is a gentleman, a journal is a girl', and Léon Blum, with perhaps more decorum as well as less *hauteur*, suggested that 'the *revues* are not books. It would not be fair to reproach the style of a *revue* article for its hastiness or its superficiality. It does not have the character of eternity. It is not thought in its definitive form. But nor is it a newspaper story that one reads while drinking one's chocolate.'[76] Within the spaces that these and other such distinctions delineated, *petites revues* were founded for any of several reasons, and adopted dispositions that corresponded to them. As Michel Leymarie observes, 'the forms that they took were indeed multiple, the subjects discussed very different, the actors more or less numerous, the readership confidential or broad, the financing hazardous or assured, the relation with publishers variable, the longevity very diverse.'[77] What they had in common, however, was their expression of a sociality that, responding to the steady decline of publishing venues for new writers in the wake of the economic recession of the 1880s, combined occupational and social motives – professional aspirations and ties of friendship – in the nurturing of often fertile collaborations. In her study of the disposition of *La Revue blanche* (1889–1903), which was perhaps the most openly, actively and consistently supportive of new art (that of the Nabis in particular, through the 1890s) of all of the *petites revues*, Janis Bergman-Carton argues that, like its rivals and comrades-in-arms the *Mercure de France* (founded 1890) and *La Plume* (1889), the *Revue* was conceived 'less to exercise an editorial imperative than to extend and professionalize the intellectual and personal communities its publishers, contributors and affiliates had formed as *lycée* students'.[78] Indeed, across this burgeoning sector of writing and publishing, groups of writers, artists, musicians and dramatists gathered around such magazines for conversation, recreation and collaborative cultural production, generating a wealth of projects that brought their respective specialisms not only together but also into contact with anarchists on the one hand and the growing network of art dealers on the other.

Art criticism in particular grew in the *petites revues*, both in status and in volume, as the 'dealer-critic' network expanded, and both the criticism and the artists it addressed benefited correspondingly. Writing for a *revue* was after all an equivalent, for impecunious young would-be *littérateurs* seeking a reputation, of the participation in an exhibition that was essential for aspirant artists. Moreover, writing criticism about new art gave such writers a means to present an aesthetic position alongside their literary works, and to make a name for themselves that sometimes eclipsed what they achieved with the latter. As a result, the *petites revues* quickly came to be, in two ways, a significant means both of support for, and influence upon, the emergent population of innovative artists making paintings and sculptures increasingly independently of the mainstream: first, in simply promoting them, giving their work critical space in their pages; second, in presuming to speak for, as well as to, their artist friends in their critical interpretations of their aesthetic innovations. If the promotion and the exposure were welcome, the interpretations were sometimes more of a mixed blessing; as we shall see in later chapters, the terms in which writers presumed an understanding of visual art were often not those of the artists themselves, and gave rise to rivalries and some hostility. The opportunities for reciprocal presumption on the part of artists were few – to put it perhaps glibly, it was easier to write about painting than to paint about writing – and yet the professional articulacy of writers was also of benefit to artists' efforts to conceptualise their experimental practices (in so far as such concepts could or should be disengaged from studio practice) and to find words for these.

Alongside this contestation of the terms in which the new art would signify, however, the material benefits of such engagement were considerable, and indeed crucial for the emergence of the artistic avant-garde.

For although the conventional wisdom on this development has long set the idealism of avant-garde artists against the commercialism of the mainstream, it has become clear from the more recent scholarship that such an opposition is a myth and that, on the contrary, the integration and even interdependence of experimental art and a fast-developing dealer-based art market was a condition of the avant-garde's emergence.[79] The proliferation of new technologies of visual reproduction such as chromolithography and photogravure, their exploitation both by magazine publishers and by adventurous artists, together with the overlaps between gallerists' promotion of pictures and their publishing of books illustrated by 'their' artists, and with the blurring of the boundaries between advertising imagery and media and those of fine art, all combined to create both a field of new, hybrid art practices and new locations for the exposure of artworks. Bergman-Carton notes that the *Revue blanche* was among several *petites revues* that gave their office walls over to the display of new work by their artist associates, and that in so doing it joined 'an expanding arena of alternative exhibition sites that included small shows in bookstores, art studios, theatre lobbies and artistic cabarets'.[80]

The *Revue blanche* was, as Bergman-Carton's account of it indicates,[81] among the most active of the *petites revues* in its engagement with the work of the emergent avant-garde, and thus its underwriting of that emergence itself. It was, moreover, open in its disavowal of the myth of anti-commerce among the artists it supported, and closely implicated in that support with the dealers who promoted and sold the new art. The move of its offices to the rue Laffitte in 1894, making the magazine a neighbour of the 20 art dealers in this 'street of pictures', as Vollard called it, rather than of other *petites revues*, most of which were based on the Left Bank, must have benefited the dealers, as the rapid appearance, following this move, of reciprocal gestures of 'courtesy' promotion between them testifies.[82] But the relocation itself was perhaps a function of a pre-existing, and deepening, friendship between Thadée Natanson and his then-wife, Misia, and the Nabis, Vuillard and Bonnard in particular. The Natansons' apartment in the rue Saint-Florentin, just off the Place de la Concorde, was both a key centre for gatherings of the *Revue blanche* social circle (and nicknamed by its members 'the Annexe' – that is, to the *Revue*'s offices) and a showcase for new decorative work. The couple were enthusiastic patrons of Vuillard's work above all, buying easel paintings and commissioning decorative panels from him – and introducing him to other leading patrons of new art.[83] As this friendship deepened, its role in shaping the reception of Vuillard's work thus grew; Thadée Natanson's addition of art criticism to the strings on his bow, in the form of several articles on Vuillard's painting and his creativity in general, further raised the latter's profile.[84]

Such multifarious support of new art and artists from within a flourishing subculture whose motivations and aspirations, and sense of distinctiveness from the mainstream in its field (here, the existing, large-circulation periodical press), were common to both parties to this relation, placed the *petites revues* alongside the *académies libres* and the dealer-centred art market as helping to enable the sustainability of an artistic avant-garde in Paris – but with one key difference. The educational and market factors, I have argued, *both* developed the privatised, 'liberal-bourgeois' art professionalism that characterised the Secessionist breakaway from state control of the Parisian art world *and* put in place the conditions for the further breakaway, in turn, of an avant-garde formation from this 'juste milieu' sector. But the *petites revues* were themselves the locus and the expression of such an avant-garde, in this case literary. This is not to claim, however, that the literary formation preceded the artistic – that these little magazines and their *modi vivendi* were already in place and helped, as such, to create the spaces and support for the latter. They were, instead, developments contemporary with each other – closely so, as we shall see: emergent in the 1880s and 1890s, alongside the artistic formation that is the subject of the next chapter.

5

PARIS: THE AVANT-GARDE'S ALTERNATIVE PROFESSIONALISM

As I argued in the last chapter, the development of the 'Secessionist' network of liberal-bourgeois artists across Europe was the precondition for the emergence of an avant-garde. For while the ideology of avant-gardism originated in its modern form in the first third of the nineteenth century in the Romantic movement across Europe and, in France, in the Saint-Simonian opposition to the Bourbon monarchy, it had little purchase on cultural collectivities in the field of the contemporary arts until the institutional and discursive supports for a break with the dominant professions in these arts were in place. The flourishing of the *académies libres* and the *petites revues*, and the establishment of a dealer-centred and speculatively profitable market for innovative art styles, provided, as we have seen, that necessary infrastructure *in potentia* for artistic independence from the mainstream. But it was the cultural politics of the 1880s and 1890s – chiefly, Republican government policies to foster the growth of the creative industries (especially those of design and the decorative arts), the privatisation of art consumption and the polarisation of political discourse towards right-wing nationalism and left-wing anarchism – that provided the spaces and the incentives to actualise them. Actuality came in the form of a crisis in the status of fine art in Paris whose product – or resolution, of sorts – was, as Martha Ward has observed, the emergence of an avant-garde formation.[1] Given the circumstances of its birth, it is not surprising that in the eyes of its adherents, the founding gesture, and the core of its ideology, was one of rupture with the dominant forces of French culture and their management.[2] Yet for all the authority that, as we shall see, this commitment both immediately acquired and has subsequently retained through the long historiography of the avant-garde, the position and character of this formation were both more equivocal: at once a part of the process of professionalisation that not only also produced the 'Secessionist' formation but encompassed many of the occupations of the non-entrepreneurial middle class across Europe, and a break away from it. In earlier chapters I have suggested that this equivocal position and character be seen as those of an 'alternative professionalism'; in this chapter we shall explore the meaning and ramifications of this characterisation in more detail.

AESTHETIC AGONISTICS

Ward's invaluable analysis of the spaces of the avant-garde confines these, and the formation that emerged to occupy them, specifically and solely, in its initial phase, to the Neo-Impressionist group, grounding its mould-breaking separation from the Impressionists in the very name that the group adopted.[3] The emerging avant-garde was, however, I have suggested, part of a more broad-based structure and development than this allows for, one that encompassed a plurality of aspirations to cultural and functional independence, as different groupings across the arts negotiated the options of acquiescence in or resistance to commercialism.[4] Alongside (and rivalling) Neo-Impressionism it was the Nabi group that, in fine art – as well as in other associated visual practices – made of this navigation a trajectory of emergence into the avant-garde formation, and survived to have a progeny. The differences between them, as I have noted, are clear. Thus where the Neo-Impressionists favoured a public role for art, the Nabis tended to paint about, and for, domestic environments; where the political associations of the former were clearly anarchist, the latter's politics encompassed the spectrum from the anarchist sympathies of Bonnard and Vallotton to Denis' explicit allegiance to the Catholic and monarchist right;[5] where Neo-Impressionism originated in a shared aesthetic commitment, to colour science and its application to painting – thus, for example, Pissarro was drawn to Seurat by his interest in the latter's innovative Pointillist style of brushwork (pl. 10) – the Nabi group was formed from friendships. In so far as its members shared an aesthetic commitment (to the expression and exploration of the decorative in art, via the use of simplified shapes and juxtaposed pattern in flattened spaces), their engagement with this also varied greatly in register. Yet the two groups also shared a commitment to aesthetic innovations, and to the rupture with dominant 'juste milieu' Impressionism; both were closely related to the literary avant-garde that was then also emergent, and made use of this relation for promotional purposes (just as, reciprocally, the writers championed their work for position-takings of their own in the literary arena);[6] both largely avoided exhibition in the mainstream salons (the Neo-Impressionists preferring the jury-free Salon des Indépendants, the Nabis exhibiting almost exclusively at the quasi-amateur gallery of Le Barc de Boutteville through the 1890s, and undertaking decorative commissions for friends).[7]

In consequence, the character of the avant-garde has to be seen to be rather more complicated and internally differentiated than a shared attachment to an ideology of 'rupture' would itself suggest. Indeed, it encompassed not only that commitment to 'advance' that the adoption of the military term implies,[8] but also a position that has been taken to be its opposite, that of 'arrière-garde', entailing a residual allegiance to putatively outmoded values. Within the Nabi group, a notionally 'arrière-garde' position – that of Maurice Denis in his 1890 essay 'Définition du néo-traditionnisme'[9] – was able to coexist with a commitment to 'rupture' from the dominant mainstream aesthetic that was deepened by the dynamic of art-market forces. Moreover, while the complexity of the character of the avant-garde formation as it emerged – and began to distinguish itself – from the framework of liberal-bourgeois professionalism is evident from the coexistence of these rival trajectories of the Neo-Impressionists and the Nabis, it was made yet more complex as the formation became consolidated (through the agencies that I have noted, of the developing *académies libres*, dealer-centred art market and *petites revues*). The consolidation did not happen overnight, but gradually as the impact of each of these agencies was worked through. By the end of the first decade of the new century, however, the qualities of a perceived independence, the prioritising of commitment to aesthetic innovation, and attachment to a distinct (and alternative) artistic lineage had come both to be articulated in a collective identity, and underpinned by the critical and market support and investment that I discussed in Chapters 3 and 4. As I noted, this identity found expression in the use, as meaningful linguistic currency and no longer a neologism, of 'avant-garde' as a term to which artists could lay claim, and with which critics could (and did) either belabour or underwrite their efforts, as they chose.

If we are to grasp this dynamic complexity it is important to underline that the avant-garde was not simply what its ideology of rupture led it to think itself to be, nor did it will itself into existence through the force of that ideology alone; rather, it was a product of *contingent* – accidental and/or external – factors *as well as* the originary, motivating one of ideology. Thus, the distinguishing commitment to specific and innovatory aesthetic principles that I have noted was also to a self-conscious, implicitly (and often explicitly) contestatory espousal of these. Although such commitment has been unanimously taken by historians as amounting to a principle of rupture with a presumed aesthetic status quo, the contestatory expression of it was manifested as much *within* the nascent avant-garde formation, between declared innovations, as between this and the Secessionist formation: that is to say, the 'rupture' was not so much a matter of principle (or of ideology) as a rhetorical trope used as a way to enhance position-taking around a specific, purportedly new 'ism'. The Secessionist network – which was already dominant, as Joyeux-Prunel argues convincingly, by the late 1880s, and still broadening its reach – was uninterested in such a commitment; what mattered to it was technical and social 'competence' of a generic and conventional kind.[10] While these qualities were broad, their limits were policed assiduously by means of exclusions of any works of art that transgressed them from those exhibition societies – such as the Cercle de l'Union Artistique – that were the new vehicles for shaping the legacy of Impressionism, and that were discussed in Chapter 4. It was in part the very refusal of interest within the Secessionist formation in specific and shared aesthetic principles that engendered a reciprocal insistence on them by ambitious young artists as a rallying point for their developing sense of a collective 'avant-garde' identity.

The consolidation of this identity was crucial for the future of the formation, as the next chapter will show. The qualities it cemented, however, were emergent from the 1880s, as I have noted. The coalescing of a grouping around shared aesthetic principles – the prioritising of these over friendship as its *raison d'être* – was registered, first in the literary avant-garde and then in the artistic, in the extraordinary flourishing of position-takings, or 'isms', from that decade: in 1912 the literary critic Ernest Florian-Parmentier noted at least 35 literary 'isms' that had been declared since 1885. A year later, Serge Diaghilev, writing in the newspaper *Comoedia*, launched a tirade against an even greater number of artistic 'isms', bewailing that '20 *Écoles* [the term 'ism' had not then caught on] are born every month'.[11] Although the assertion was clearly a rhetorical exaggeration, this itself underlines the perception of excessive auto-promotion by artists that motivated his article. If the concurrent flourishing of the French advertising industry and of its promotional techniques were furnishing a model for such widespread auto-promotion,[12] the advantages for an artist of sharing the declaration of an innovation with like-minded colleagues were voiced 20 years earlier on behalf of the Post-Impressionist generation by the critic Gabriel-Albert Aurier, who coined the term 'synthetism' and supported the group of artists led by Gauguin whom he identified by it.[13]

Such advantages were inseparable from the rapid rise in the valuation of aesthetic innovation *per se* that occurred from the 1880s.[14] As Clément Dessy observes, the rise in critical support from those who wrote about 'les novateurs' among new painters in the *petites revues* was noteworthy and widespread. Among the most outspoken of these was Lucien Mühlfeld, who wrote on art for *La Revue blanche*. 'I have explained elsewhere *à propos* writers', he reminded his readers in 1893,

> the value of an innovative artist, and that one is an artist to the extent that one is a *novateur*. As regards the newcomers among painters, only one question needs asking: 'Are they truly *novateurs*?' (Useless to add this problem: 'And are their novelties preferable?', for all the worst have been made, and the new will inevitably be better.)[15]

To Mühlfeld's vague and somewhat tautological approval of innovation, the critic Maurice Cremnitz added some specificity a few months later, in a review of the Nabis' exhibition in December 1893 at Le Barc de Boutteville:

> They are being called *novateurs*, and they seem, in effect, to merit this term by their praiseworthy care to free themselves from tyrannical conventions, to escape the jail of frightful current formulae in order to work, in the full integrity of an artist, according to their instinct alone, and with no other rules than this integrity and the concern to make a work of art.[16]

The qualification in Cremnitz's final phrase implies an appeal to an (albeit undefined) professionalism, thus allowing the critic to embrace both the individualism of the artists concerned and avant-gardist collectivism at the same time. It was for the lack of a professionalism defined in more conventional terms that the Nabis' most serious detractor, Alphonse Germain, criticised their work, writing that they 'reject perspective and modelling with a serene lack of awareness, and seem to take pride in deforming to the point of ugliness'. 'Let them therefore first learn the mysteries of their art', he added, 'these 20-year-old *novateurs*, these young people who don't know how to construct a head.'[17] Reciprocally, it was perhaps in implicit criticism of such aesthetic conservatism that Thadée Natanson wrote an article for *La Revue blanche* embracing precisely the opposite qualities: dedicated to the Nabi painter Édouard Vuillard, his essay on 'Le Don de contredire' took aim at the 'tyranny' of an art education whose 'frightful apparatus' led the 'maîtres' – of the École des Beaux-Arts, presumably – to 'submit [the] poor, tender, defenceless brains' of their students to the uniformity of their time-honoured methods; against this Natanson exalted 'the precious, dangerous, glorious gift of contradiction' that characterised real artistic creativity.[18]

That the enthusiasm for technical innovation was a *distinguishing* feature of emergent avant-garde discourse is evident both from the insistence with which the Neo-Impressionist group pursued and presented new ideas and techniques, and from the way their critic-supporters promoted them in reviewing their exhibitions, each year and each new exhibition bringing new 'firsts' in the putatively science-led refinement of colour combinations for enhanced luminosity.[19] It was registered explicitly in the coining of a new term for such technical innovation – *technie* – by the young critic Félix Fénéon in writing, in September 1888, about the polychromy of the Neo-Impressionist Paul Signac's poster promoting psychophysicist Charles Henry's new book *Cercle chromatique* (pl. 11). 'This poster is the first application of rational polychromy established on rigorously mathematical principles by the author of the *Cercle*', Fénéon declared, adding: 'this production by the young polychromist allows one to anticipate what new and complex impressions can be expected from a *technie* served by skilful lithographers and competent chemists'.[20] Borrowing the term from the early nineteenth-century Polish mystical scientist Józef Maria Hoene-Wroński, Fénéon clearly saw it as a key concept, for he explained:

> I say *technie* and not *technique*, after a neologism of Wronski's meaning an absolutely new and unknown idea. Polychromy is as old as humanity; and polychromatic *techniques* began with the first civilisations.... But *polychromatic technie* was born with the theory of colour sensations and could not have been born before.[21]

It was a coinage whose criticality for avant-garde discourse will become apparent in later chapters (and Fénéon's own crucial role in fostering Neo-Impressionism's investment in it was registered implicitly in Signac's extraordinary portrait of him two years later) (pl. 12)[22]. Its relevance at the time is evident also in a negative fashion, from the indifference with which this enthusiasm for aesthetic innovation was greeted by the critics of the newspaper press. These were interested enough to give the Neo-Impressionists wide exposure, but did so more for the purpose of outdoing each other in the invention of outlandish names for the Pointillist technique with which to amuse their readers, than from an interest in its scientific basis.[23] The technical particularities of the style and obsessions of the group were either ignored or disdained by them – an example of the latter being Gustave Geffroy's observation in 1888 that '[t]he religion of an immutable process is not a sign of progress and artistic revolution. It is truly of no consequence whether the mixture of colours occurs in our eye or exists already on the observed canvas.'[24] It would seem, moreover, that such innovation was a quality prized and promoted as much by the new critics of the *petites revues* as by the artists themselves. For as I noted in the previous chapter, it played into their competition for position and status in their own avant-garde literary field: thus Aurier made his reputation for his support of Gauguin and his theorising of 'synthétisme' around the latter's paintings;[25] thus too Germain offered Maurice Denis his services in the formulation and expression of his theories as soon as he had read Denis's debut essay, 'Définition du néo-traditionnisme', in 1890, while in the same year Maurice Beaubourg courted Seurat for similar purposes.[26] If a consequence of such jockeying in the literary avant-garde was thus a factor in the emergence of key groupings committed to aesthetic innovation within the artistic formation, this relationship was nonetheless a complex and fluid one, and the hegemony (if it was that) of the literary field was not permanent. The consolidation of the artistic avant-garde shifted the balance of forces between these two formations in fundamental ways; we shall return to it in the next chapter.

AN INDEPENDENT HERITAGE

Regardless of the interests, both vested and otherwise, of Parisian literary avant-gardists in supporting and interpreting the innovations of their artistic comrades, the independence of their formation from the liberal-bourgeois professionalism of the Secessionist network – its commitment to an alternative professionalism – was secured also by adherence to and declaration and elaboration of a separate and distinctive set of technical means and craft- or *métier*-based inheritances. Indeed, the iteration and establishment of these was equally critical for the artistic avant-garde's resistance to the compromising embrace of *littérateurs*. There were two principal inheritances, one of which was that of classicism. As Richard Shiff and Edward Fry argued in different ways over 30 years ago, the common inheritance of classicism that was the backbone of French high culture from the seventeenth century through to the twentieth was at one and the same time a means of ordering the visual representation of the world according to a rational, clear and perceptible system, and of anchoring contemporary painting in a time-honoured tradition.[27] Which of these alternatives artists inclined to, and what they made of each, were at once indicators and determinants of their position within the fine-art profession, between mainstream (whether academic or Secessionist) and avant-garde sectors. They were not mutually exclusive interpretations, but the commitment to technical innovation and experiment that distinctively characterised the avant-garde disposed its adherents more readily to a classicism whose ordering of perception was increasingly open to display, and even interrogation, than to one that provided, above all, ostensible anchorage for the consecrated conventions of academic art.

The key figure in the establishment of this distinction, whose initiatives enabled the artists who followed Impressionism both to build on its perceptual insights and to claim classicism as their own independent legacy, was Cézanne, whose aspiration, as he expressed it, to 'make of Impressionism something solid and durable, like the art of the museums', is familiar to any art-history undergraduate.[28] As Shiff summarises Cézanne's precepts, the painter 'warned [Émile] Bernard and others to follow the venerated masters of classical style only as guides to solving technical problems. The modern artist's classicism should not be *made* in imitation of the masters, but must be *found* in his own sensation, in his direct experience of nature.'[29] Shiff's close reading of Cézanne's landscapes reveals how the painter's concern for detailed observation and the faithful transcription of aspects of the natural scene before his eyes and easel was articulated through the development of a unifying system of repeated brushwork patterns and compositional geometries. This leads him to argue that Cézanne established a 'technique of originality' that married his attachment to Impressionism with techniques that drew inspiration from the mid-seventeenth-century landscapes of Claude Lorrain (pls 13 and 14).[30] The interpretations of this achievement offered by two leading theorist-painters of the next (and the first avant-garde) generation, Émile Bernard and Maurice Denis, in writings over two decades from 1890 based (if sometimes loosely) on interviews with Cézanne, did much to consolidate his systematisation of individual perceptions into a classicist technique that had wide and flexible appeal across the avant-garde and, thus, to position Cézanne, even before his death, as the anchor of one strand of the specific inheritance of the formation.[31]

If Cézanne's example, as Shiff explains, offered the emergent avant-garde the means to fashion a distinctive and innovatory classicism, it was the Cubist movement, whose developed technical aspirations were, as we shall see, characteristic of the formation's consolidating phase in the decade before 1914, that instigated its interrogation and completed its modernist renewal. As Edward Fry argues, 'the special achievement' of Cubism, 'and above all of Picasso, was to reinvent classical, mediated representation, and in that reinvention also to transform it so as to reveal its central conventions and mental processes'.[32] Picasso's achievement, and to a lesser extent that of the other Cubists, Fry suggests, 'was that of the classical mind's becoming aware of its means for thinking and representing the world even as it carries out that representation'.[33] More recent research has added valuable detail to the ways in which Picasso in particular repeatedly and probingly interrogated the rules of classical order embodied in proportional systems of anatomical drawing, in his art before and through the Cubist years.[34] But what also needs to be recognised is that as the avant-garde's engagement with classicism developed, so the interpretation of it became more flexible: thus Picasso's invention of a reflexive classicism was complemented by members and supporters of the 'salon Cubist' wing of the Cubist movement, as is shown by the poet-critic supporter of this group, Roger Allard, whose ingenious and persuasive attempt in an article of 1911 to fuse classical qualities with the Bergsonian flux that would appear to be its opposite we shall explore in the next chapter.[35]

Classicism was not the only inheritance, of course, and it was the one most clearly shared, if differently, by artists of all stripes; but it is these differences in their engagements that help to distinguish the professionalism of the avant-garde. Another inheritance, of equal significance, was provided within the Parisian avant-garde itself, in the very theorising and sustained experimentation of the Neo-Impressionist group. Its members' rivalries in researching the science of colour, and in offering as the result of such research ever more punctilious painterly applications of recent theories of optical sensations,[36] helped to underpin their collective identity and separateness from both Impressionism itself and its 'Secessionist' moderators in the mainstream. More than this, they offered the next generation a distinct, innovative and steadily diversifying arsenal of painterly techniques and theoretical rationales for these that served, along with other factors, to consolidate the emergent formation and underpin its collective identity – as Guillaume Apollinaire noted, observing in 1913 that 'Pointillism [one of the several terms for the Neo-Impressionist brushwork technique] was responsible for liberating the artistic consciousness of the younger generation'.[37]

Central to this strand of its inheritance was Paul Signac's monograph, *D'Eugène Delacroix au néo-impressionnisme*, which appeared in serialised form in *La Revue blanche* in 1898 and as a book in 1899.[38] This presentation by the *de facto* joint leader, with Seurat, of the Neo-Impressionist group (and sole leader after the latter's death in 1891) of a history of nineteenth-century art alternative to the dominant academic narrative, which ran from Delacroix's colourism via Impressionism to the 'advances' of Neo-Impressionism, was, as Catherine Bock observes in her 1981 study of the influence of that movement on Matisse, 'written for just the painters in Matisse's situation, who had no perspective on the confused *mélange* of movements in the late nineteenth century.... In some ways', she writes, 'Matisse [in the late 1890s] was a beginner in need of basic instruction; Signac's treatise could provide just that.' Signac himself felt the need, Bock suggests, 'to provide a history of modernism whose keystone was impressionism', adding: 'He also sensed the need for such an account to be written by a painter, in painter's terms, with the emphasis on pictorial method, especially after a decade or more of general theorising on art by poets, critics and *littérateurs*.'[39] As Bock notes, Signac's history is a selective one, French nineteenth-century art seen through Neo-Impressionist lenses, but, she observes,

> it helps him to shape a closed, self-contained account of the development of modern painting. It enables him, moreover, to isolate that history to a reductionist emphasis on the elements of painting alone, the tools of its distinct language. Since symbolist painting was without a proper style and distinguished itself by themes and subjects, it was left to divisionism to champion a style that arose from concentration on the essential elements of the art.[40]

Signac's treatise was thus a key instrument in securing the independence of the nascent formation of the Parisian avant-garde. Like Picasso's engagement with classicism, Matisse's *rodage* with Neo-Impressionism was characteristic – indeed, a function – of the consolidation of the Parisian avant-garde's alternative professionalism. Like Picasso's Cubism, his approach to painting was driven by a focus on innovations (in his case with regard to colour relations and Divisionist theory) that were increasingly developed, specialist and technically informed.[41] We shall explore these qualities in the next chapter.

Signac's treatise was important in this respect not only in itself, but also in lending its authority to the dissemination across Europe, within two or three years, of a technique of painting that gave licence, for many of the new adherents to the avant-garde formation before 1914, to the replacement of manual dexterity by theoretical sophistication and/or decorative effect as the principal criteria of the 'advanced' status of a painting. In the context of that project of 'de-skilling' that was a component of avant-gardist discourse in the decade after 1900, the application of mosaic-like dabs of pigment had for many novice painters the twin advantages of facility and fashionability.[42] The spread of Neo-Impressionism across the burgeoning network of the avant-garde in the first decade of the new century was thus both a register of its consolidation and a factor in this. For such painters as – aside from, as we have seen, Matisse – Robert Delaunay, Wassily Kandinsky, Frank Kupka, Jean Metzinger, Piet Mondrian and Gino Severini, to name but a few, Signac's treatise provided a history of modern painting, and the Divisionist technique a schooling in the use of colour.

If these twin legacies were the most important, they were not the only ones that were available to and distinctive of the avant-garde. The environments of the *académies libres* and the *petites revues*, noted earlier, fostered others that produced their own *technies*, such as the *cloisonné* outlining of flat forms that Louis Anquetin, then still the charismatic student at the Cormon *académie* whom we have already encountered,[43] drew in the late 1880s from an exploration of medieval stained-glass methods and promoted (in competition with Émile Bernard) as the next big thing. Or the expressionistic style adopted by Anquetin's classmate and friend Henri de Toulouse-Lautrec, whose caricatural simplifications of form – quickly observed, cutting in tone and attuned to social decadence – in paintings and posters of cabaret dancers were foundational for the artistic articulation of modernity in Montmartrois culture (pls 15 and 16).[44] This style was indebted to the engagement with popular and commercial culture, as well as with the oppositional culture of anarchism – both shared also by Nabi artists such as Bonnard (who, like Lautrec, designed posters)[45] – and probably a product also of the need of the *humoriste* magazines that flourished in the Belle Époque, such as *L'Assiette au beurre* (founded 1901), for illustrations with just such qualities, in the interests of their topicality and sharp political and social critique. Increasing numbers of avant-garde artists turned to such work as a means of financial support.

A COLLECTIVE IDENTITY

The above two factors of aesthetic innovation and independent lineage could be described as necessary but not sufficient for the consolidation of the Parisian avant-garde. What was crucial in securing that consolidation, and enabling their dissemination across the formation, was a third, namely the collective identity – the mutual recognition among members of this community of their common and distinctive artistic aspirations – that they helped to establish in the two decades around 1900, and that was registered both within and beyond the formation by the use of the term 'avant-garde' itself.[46] This identity had two foundations. One was the sheer critical mass that the Parisian population of aspirant aesthetic innovators – incubated by the *académies libres*, supported by the *petites revues* and occasionally sustained by risk-taking dealers – had achieved by the *avant-guerre*, and which allowed it not only to distance itself from but for the first time to rival the mainstream professional formation.[47] As I noted earlier, whereas the iconoclasm of the Incohérents of the 1880s fell back upon their *humoriste* collective identity in default of any available alternative ground from which to challenge the terms of that professionalism, the generation that followed thus had the means – the numbers – to mount such a challenge.

Yet this identity had a second aspect. Such self-conscious rivalry with mainstream professionalism had its risks, as well as the benefit of heightening the sense of autonomy from it. For in offering an alternative to the mainstream, it tacitly acknowledged the values of professionalism itself and thus, by extension, its own absorption of them. For *soi-disant* avant-garde artists, to lay claim to the validity of their experimentation with the technicalities of aesthetic representation was to assert their specialist entitlement *as* professionals to do so – and thus to acquiesce, ultimately, in the assimilation of its expertise to the evolving capitalist social order that the process of professionalisation both epitomised and was driving. In other words, the embrace of such an identity was a first step along the road to the institutionalisation of the avant-garde formation within that social order, and co-option by its hegemony. This assertion of professionalism, however, was in potential conflict with the ideology of avant-gardism which, as noted earlier, was the other fundamental determinant of the formation: the commitment to the prioritisation of imagination and 'thinking otherwise' in aesthetic terms not as 'legitimate' specialist expertise but as an expression of opposition to the 'cash nexus' values of capitalism itself, and a vehicle for the articulation of these. On one level 'rupture' was a trope that figured the contestatory disposition that was shaping the marketplace in aesthetic ideas *both* within the burgeoning formation of the avant-garde (the competition between 'isms', for each of which its rivals were outmoded) *and* between it and the status-driven social network of Secessionist professionalism. At the same time, on a deeper level it was – in the eyes of many of its proponents – a tacit embrace of political alternatives to the bourgeois Third Republic itself. We therefore need to be clear about the character, implications and outcome of this as yet (in the *fin de siècle*) still only potential contradiction between the formation's alternative professionalism and its motivating ideology.

The study of the close relationship between technically radical artists in all media and extra-parliamentary politics in late nineteenth-century Paris was a staple of its cultural criticism from the 1890s, and has been acknowledged throughout a subsequent rich historiography; within this, the reiterations of the anarchist sympathies of avant-garde writers and fine artists, in particular, in that *fin de siècle* have left us in no doubt of either their extent or their sincerity.[48] What remains less certain, and is at issue in this book, are three questions: what was the character and motivation of those sympathies, what was their relation to an artistic avant-garde formation then emerging, and what was the outcome of this dynamic for the consolidation of that formation in the decade before 1914? We shall explore each of these in turn.

On the face of it, and despite the historiography, there was no intrinsic relationship between Symbolist literary practices and anarchism; although both had emerged in Paris before 1880, French anarchism's leading historian, Jean Maitron, argues that this 'did not become a political current that was distinct and independent from other socialisms' until early in the decade that followed[49] – a detail that, as Richard Shryock observes, undermines any supposition that Symbolism was fundamentally anarchist. Indeed, Shryock suggests that any link with leftist politics in that decade is problematic, noting that 'an important group of Symbolists supported General Boulanger's attempts to come to power in the late 1880s'.[50] As he argues, grasping the character of the relationship depends upon how 'politics' are (and were then) understood. In the *petites revues* that addressed political as well as literary issues and themes, and to which the Symbolist writers gravitated, the term referred primarily to parliamentary politics, which most of them rejected in favour of a more revolutionary affiliation – for the problem with the former was not only that it was perceived as irredeemably corrupt, but also that 'it did not bring about *enough* change'.[51]

It was, Shryock argues, at least partly in response to the rightward turn of Third Republic governments that the politics of Symbolist literature evolved.[52] Having seen off the threats posed by the monarchist right, by the early 1880s the politics of the Republic were increasingly controlled both by and for the bourgeoisie, and the imperative to impose its values extended to the putting in place of new cultural policies. As Miriam Levin notes, the Republicans' art theory 'was an integral part of an ideology which made art a major force influencing public values and economic behaviour'.[53] The criteria of good citizenship, social solidarity, 'family values' and patriotism were applied alike to programmes for decorative murals in public buildings and the books chosen for public libraries, constructing cultural norms for a political agenda that sought to meet the challenge of socialism and anarchism not by confronting the inequality and poverty endemic to capitalism but, as a 'true social tranquilliser' in the words of one modern historian, to 'unite the poor with the rich, the illiterate with the scholar'[54] in an awareness of the duties, as well as the rights, of Republican citizenship.[55] Such an instrumental view of art was anathema to Symbolist writers, whose cultivation of a hermetic language, valuation of aesthetic ambiguity over clarity and attachment to idealist philosophy were fundamentally at odds with Republican materialist norms. As Shryock argues, Symbolism thus *became* political as the Third Republic's politics hardened and this ideological opposition became more evident.[56] 'By 1889, the centennial of the Revolution', he suggests, 'the Third Republic was overdue for a major change. For many – both Symbolists and those reading Symbolist literature – Symbolist writing was thought to have [the] same corrosive effect on Republican ideals as the countless small actions undertaken by anarchists and [to] contribute to bringing down the regime.' Shryock cites Symbolist poet Pierre Quillard's 1892 article 'L'Anarchie par la littérature' as a key contemporary expression of such an idea.[57]

It is an argument that has been taken further more recently by Patrick McGuinness, who observes that 'the Symbolists... appear to have become more politically radical as they became more marginal', adding that this is 'a model entirely consonant with the aesthetic realm, too, where the modern avant-garde becomes more experimental as it becomes less popular and its readership more specialised. In politics as in poetry', McGuinness proposes, 'irrelevance is a licence to experiment... one might even suggest', he concludes, 'there exists a symbiotic relationship between radicalism and depoliticisation.'[58] Despite this somewhat withering assessment of Symbolist politics, McGuinness also offers a nuanced analysis of the Quillard essay cited by Shryock, suggesting: 'Of all the Symbolists, perhaps Quillard most acutely felt the separation between art and politics, in part because of his own poetry's high Parnassian-Symbolism: ceremonial in its formalism, recondite in its diction, and usually set in an indeterminate classical age.'[59] Quillard did not try to bridge this separation, he argues, but to celebrate Symbolist poetry for qualities that were the opposite of those of most political activism: its understanding of 'actions, gestures, words or events [as] all about opening up meanings, making things multiple in their possible interpretations, ambiguous and richly unclear';[60] likening poetry to the Nihilist bomb-throwing that haunted the bourgeois imaginary of the 1890s,[61] Quillard argued (as McGuinness notes) that poetry was 'the ultimate form of anarchist dissemination because it is the least bounded and the most context-transcending'.[62] Ultimately, writing Symbolist poetry was the most far-reaching literary act in its potential effects and, at the same time, the most autonomous literary practice; as Quillard wrote in a review of another poet's work in the same month in 1892, 'any literary work that is free and without bias, which asks for no approval from the bourgeoisie's usual "common sense", implies an act of contempt and revolt towards today's Society'.[63]

The argument about Symbolist poetry and its politics, as presented by Shryock and McGuinness and summarised here, raises some key issues for an understanding of the nascent artistic avant-garde, its character and its collective self-identity. As art historians have registered in a body of work elaborated over the past 60 years, painters in late nineteenth-century Paris were as deeply implicated with anarchist politics as were their poet associates. Indeed, they were perhaps more directly so, in the case of such artists as Camille Pissarro, Paul Signac, Maximilien Luce, Théophile Steinlen and several others, who made illustrations rather than (with some exceptions) writing essays for political *petites revues*.[64] This was at least partly a function of the specificities of their respective cultural practices: if their literary comrades were able to turn their writerly skills to the penning of essays for anarchist *revues*, they did so as intellectuals – as McGuinness notes in passing, the 'birth' of the latter formation was related to this involvement of Symbolist writers in radical politics[65] – whereas the more artisanal image-making skills of the painters put them alongside other manual workers who embraced the values of anarchism. Yet there are clear parallels between the argument made by Quillard for the revolutionary autonomism of Symbolist poetry and that offered by Signac for the Neo-Impressionist painting of which he was the leading exponent. In one of those exceptions just noted, an essay published a few months before 'L'Anarchie par la littérature', Signac argued in *La Révolte*, one of the most widely read of the anarchist *revues*, for 'the revolutionary tendency of the Impressionist painters':[66]

> Technically, they are innovators; they replace the outmoded methods with a logical and scientific arrangement of tones and colours... their works, resulting from a purely aesthetic emotion produced by the picturesque quality of things and beings, have the same social, unconscious dimension that has already marked contemporary literature... only artists gripped by pure art, and in particular the Impressionist painters, whose technique is the negation of old artistic routines, deserve the entire accord of those who applaud the collapse of outmoded prejudices.[67]

While these phrases are a selection from a text in which they are interwoven with emphasis on the working-class and popular character of the subjects of (Neo-)Impressionist paintings, the prioritisation of technical innovation as the basis of the revolutionary character of this art is clear. Signac's repeated emphasis on it suggests that McGuinness's assessment of the 'irrelevance' of Symbolism's technical experimentation (its lack of 'popularity') follows too complacently Pierre Bourdieu's reductivist model of a field of cultural production polarised between 'heteronomous' (renown-seeking) and 'autonomous' (renown-rejecting) aspirations,[68] and that there is more to Signac's motives for it than mere cultural elitism. Given the pressures and necessary distinctions within the dynamic of professionalisation that I have traced, we should instead recognise in such technical preoccupations the aspiration towards that alternative professionalism I have discussed above. As such, the very attempt to reconcile the aesthetic technicism of this with the allegiance to radical politics that both Quillard's and Signac's essays inscribe exemplifies precisely that tension I have noted between the external factors shaping the avant-garde formation's emergence and the ideology of avant-gardism driving its direction.[69]

As yet, however, both the political conjuncture of the 1890s and (as we can see with hindsight) the then-incomplete character of the formation's consolidation prevented this tension from becoming that contradiction that we shall trace in the next chapter. The conjuncture was in turn increasingly dominated, for artists in all media and their comrades on the left, by two developments: the Dreyfus Affair and the growth of an 'Art Social' movement. The former rapidly polarised the politics of the avant-garde in ways that historians of the 'Affaire' have documented,[70] and in doing so heightened its sense of (and commitment to) 'rupture' as it underwrote the aesthetically contestatory disposition of its affiliates with an increasingly confrontational left-political discourse. The Art Social initiative, on the other hand, had a more equivocal – or perhaps, one should say, mutable – character, as well as a chequered history.[71] An idea originating in the post-Revolutionary decade and developed in the Romantic period, it was resurrected in the *fin de siècle* via the Club de l'Art Social founded by a socialist literary critic, Adolphe Tabarant, in 1889 and nourished via a *petite revue* of the same name established in 1891 by an anarchist poet, Gabriel de La Salle. Both had foundered by the mid-1890s without expanding their readership, or their concerns, beyond that of a few leftist writers and artists worrying the bone of how to take art to the people. The initiative and the *revue* were resurrected, however, in the context of the rapidly growing syndicalist movement of the second half of the decade, which mushroomed not so much in numbers (in the late 1890s there were around half a million syndicalists in France)[72] as in the growth and diversification of the network of *bourses du travail* (labour exchanges) that became the focus in each locality for an impressive range of collectivities – sports clubs, book clubs, theatres, choral groups, hiking clubs and social centres. In this context, the possibilities seemed real of progressive artists and writers making common cause with workers, and political activists turned to art as a weapon in the sharpening class struggle. Thus journalist and activist Fernand Pelloutier, founder member in 1892 of the anarchist-oriented Fédération des Bourses du Travail, spelled out in an 1897 lecture sponsored by the Groupe de l'Art Social how art could 'unmask all the social lies, show how and why religions were created, the cult of patriotism conceived, the family constructed on the model of government'.[73]

But with the election of Pierre Waldeck-Rousseau's centre-left government in 1899, dominated by radicals but harnessing the acquiescence of the parliamentary socialists (and the participation of one of them, Alexandre Millerand, as a minister), the parliamentary Bloc des gauches (Leftists Bloc) that this created extended the spirit of class collaboration beyond the Assemblée. Fuelled by its ideology of 'solidarisme', acting via mutualist and other associations, co-opting the above cultural groupings, as well as founding 'universités populaires' in working-class districts, the Bloc stood not for anarchism, syndicalism or socialism but for a centrist politics for which these movements were a threat to social order.[74] The emphasis of the Art Social movement shifted correspondingly: the new cultural groups – L'Art à l'École, L'Art et la Vie, Art et Travail, Art et Science, perhaps above all the Société de l'Art pour Tous – became in the first five years of the new century, in the words of a modern commentator, an 'arsenal built up to challenge socialism for the monopoly of the working class' by bringing workers to an appreciation of the joys of art and the cultural heritage of France.[75] As the understanding of this reorientation became clearer among its adherents in the artistic avant-garde, the tensions between its alternative professionalism and its oppositional ideology became less sustainable, with consequences that we shall explore.

6

PARIS: CONSOLIDATING THE AVANT-GARDE, 1905–14

PAINTING AS *TECHNIE*

In one of his forensic technical analyses of Matisse's painting in the first half of his career, 'On Matisse: The Blinding' of 1994, Yve-Alain Bois tells the following anecdote:

> Shortly after his arrival in Nice [in 1918], Matisse went to visit Renoir, whom he had never met and who hardly knew his painting. The old master invited Matisse to show him something of his work on his next visit. When Matisse brought him some recent canvases, among them certain small landscapes in the vein of those he had done a few months earlier at Clamart, Chenonceaux, or Villacoublay – closer to Impressionism than anything of Matisse's for more than twenty years – Renoir wasn't overly enthusiastic. Yet he couldn't help admiring the way in which, in a view from his room at the Hôtel Beau Rivage in the Promenade des Anglais in Nice [pl. 17], 'the strongest feature' of the painting was 'the darkest tone in the ensemble,' namely the almost black, mahogany curtain rod above the window opening onto 'the rolling, silver-grey sea'.

Bois then quotes Matisse's own recollection of their conversation:

> 'He was surprised to see that the dark tone didn't leap out, but stayed at the distance indicated by its position in the room. He had me move the canvas further away from him, and said, "How do you do that? If I used a black like that in a painting, it would jump out at you." I couldn't come up with an explanation straight away, and yet the explanation is

> very simple: it comes from a combination of forces in the canvas, which is what my generation has contributed. I think it also comes from the feeling of space that I always get when standing before my models, and which even brings me to put myself in this space. It is constructed with an ensemble of forces that has nothing to do with a direct copy of nature.'

'The essential point here, of course', continues Bois, 'is the one concerning "what my generation has contributed": the combination of forces that sutures the surface of the canvas into an inviolable totality.'[1]

The anecdote is both illuminating and intriguing, for it at once indicates the chief concerns of the painter in making this work, and invites further questions: namely, as to what that 'combination of forces' was; why this was the principal contribution (to, presumably, the avant-gardist project of the advancement of painting) of his generation; and what this prioritisation of 'the surface as an inviolable totality' tells us about the character of the Parisian avant-garde formation (or at least that part of it to which Matisse was affiliated) in the first decades of the twentieth century. These questions are the starting points for the present chapter's exploration of the process of consolidation of that formation in the *avant-guerre* decade.

Matisse's generation was, in a sense, a double one. In biographical terms, it was that of the Nabis: he was born in 1869, a year before Denis (1870), and soon after Bonnard and Vuillard (1867 and 1868). Indeed, it was Denis who summarised this generation's 'contribution' (somewhat precociously) in his 1890 essay 'Définition du néo-traditionnisme'. 'We should remember', Denis declared, 'that a picture – before being a war horse, a nude woman, or telling some story – is essentially a flat surface covered with colours arranged in a particular order.'[2] But in career or occupational terms, as a painter, Matisse also belonged to the following generation, that of Picasso and Braque (born 1881 and 1882); Matisse came to painting late, and to fame (as pre-eminent in the Fauve group of painters who took the limelight at the 1905 Salon d'Automne) over 15 years after the Nabis' debut; as a result his career has conventionally been discussed in close comparison with that of the Spanish painter.

The second affiliation is the more appropriate in art-historical terms. For Matisse's affiliation to the 1890s generation was as an informal apprentice – more specifically to Neo-Impressionism and the tutelage of Signac – and it was from that group's attachment to aesthetic technicism, particularly, that Matisse drew his own. I discussed in the last chapter the significance of Neo-Impressionist attachment to technical innovations, and the way Signac's *D'Eugène Delacroix au néo-impressionnisme* codified these and gave them a historical pedigree. In light of these initiatives that, as I argued, marked the emergence of key features of the 'alternative professionalism' that characterised the nascent avant-garde, Matisse's development from apprenticeship to the construction of an innovative technical aesthetics of his own is a marker of one feature of its consolidation. The distance he had already travelled from Nabi approaches to painting by 1905 was registered in Denis's sharp criticism, in his review of that year's 'Fauvist' Salon, of what he saw as Matisse's 'excess of theory'. Earlier in the year, when Matisse had shown his recently completed *Luxe, calme et volupté* (*Luxury, Calm and Delight*) (pl. 18) at the Salon des Indépendants – a work that self-consciously built on, but also departed from, the premises of Neo-Impressionism, and which was criticised but also purchased by Signac – Denis's response had been a combination of encouragement and advice as well as criticism. 'He [Matisse] will not be discouraged by this first experiment [with Neo-Impressionist technique]', Denis acknowledged,

> but it will warn him against the dangers of abstraction. *Luxe, calme et volupté* is the schema of a theory. It is in reality that he will best develop his gifts, which are rare indeed, of a painter. It is in French tradition that he will rediscover a sense of what is possible.[3]

By the autumn, however, Denis's position had hardened, and in ways that are significant in relation to the process of consolidation of the avant-garde. I shall come to them shortly, but first we need to understand this phase of Matisse's journey as a painter in more detail. It is one whose narrative was most recently elaborated in the two decades around the millennium by a succession of American art historians,[4] in a manner that can be summarised as follows.

Catherine Bock's 1981 account of a crisis to which Matisse came, in the mid-1890s, as a young aspirant avant-gardist with as yet more promise than sense of direction, opens this narrative. She argues that Matisse felt his move towards modern painting, resulting both from his seeing the Caillebotte bequest that was finally hung in the Musée du Luxembourg in spring 1897, and from his work of the winter of 1896–97 when he changed 'from an academic to a modernist style', was a daring and uncharacteristic adjustment of direction. 'For him', Bock writes, 'it entailed new goals, new subjects, new techniques, new patronage, and a new self-image'.[5] Matisse himself recalled:

> It was with the constant sentiment of the importance of my decision… that I took fright, realizing that there was no turning back. I therefore charged, with head lowered, into my work, impelled by an unknown force which today I perceive to be foreign to my normal life as a man.[6]

As Yve-Alain Bois then recounts, in two essays of the 1990s (drawing on the evidence of Matisse's own recollections, collaged from numerous interviews over his career),[7] a holiday in Corsica in 1898 opened the next stage: Matisse found himself 'traumatised', Bois suggests, 'frightened' by the 'intolerable brilliance of the Midi'; on his return to Paris he obtained the latest copies of the *Revue blanche* in which Signac's treatise was being serialised, and threw himself into an apprenticeship to its precepts.[8] 'The new technique made a great impression on me', he later acknowledged; 'painting had at last been reduced to a scientific formula'.[9] The luminosity and confident *facture* of the picture *Nature morte: buffet et table* (*Still Life: Buffet and Table*) of early 1899 (pl. 19) was one of the results. The technique allowed him to 'put some order into his sensations'; but, as he later said, he 'knew very well that achievement by these means was limited by too great an adherence to strictly logical rules'.[10] Bois elaborates: 'In following the prescribed rules to the letter, Matisse soon found himself faced with a conflict in his painting between the representation of depth and chromatic order.... He quickly abandoned Divisionism and for several years set about studying volume, modelling and values.'[11] For this study he turned to Cézanne and Vuillard, learning from the former how to unite tonal values and colour hues, from the latter how to combine closely related hues to slow down the viewer's apprehension of a scene and disperse its foci of attention.

In 1904 Matisse was invited by Signac to join him at his home in Saint-Tropez and paint beside him. The second *rodage* with Neo-Impressionism which this experience precipitated found him better prepared both to profit from it and to find his own way beyond it.[12] He discovered the constraints that were unavoidable in its Divisionist system of transcribing traditional modelling and its subtle gradation of colours into a code governed by colour theory. Chafing against these constraints, he made what Bois observes was 'his major discovery in the area of colour, namely that "a square centimetre of blue is not as blue as a square metre of the same blue"'. This 'quantity/quality equation', suggests Bois, 'is what led Matisse to conceive his painting as a given, whole surface', and to recognise that 'each point in [a] picture became as important as any other'. This recognition, the result of his difficulties with 'the Signac system', became the foundation for 'his own colour system'.[13] It was a system that Matisse himself summarised in his keynote 'manifesto' of 1908, the *Notes of a Painter*:

> For me, expression does not reside in passions glowing in a human face.... The entire arrangement of my picture is expressive: the place occupied by the figures, the empty spaces around them, the proportions, everything has its share. Composition is the art of arranging in a decorative manner the diverse elements at the painter's command to express his feelings. In a picture every part will be visible and will play its appointed role, whether principal or secondary.[14]

The key terms used by Matisse in this text – 'expression' and 'decorative' – are notoriously slippery in interpretative possibility, but there are two points that can be made, in the context of the present study, about his use of them. The first is that he touches on – but does not develop – the issue of decoration, whose meanings and significance were a central concern for artists in many media, and in London as well as Paris, in the *avant-guerre* decade. We shall explore in later chapters the differentials between the discourse of 'the decorative' in each capital, and their complex relations with those of 'representation' and 'abstraction'; suffice it for now to note that, while Denis in 1890 had felt it enough merely to insist that a picture was 'a flat surface covered with colours' *before* it represented anything, by 1905, in his criticism of Matisse's latest paintings, he felt obliged to charge these with abstraction *tout court*:

> [what] we find above all [in the room given over to the 'school of Matisse'], in particular *chez* Matisse, is artificiality; not the artificiality of literature, as would be a search for the expression of an idea; nor a decorative artificiality, such as the Turkish or Persian carpet-makers imagined; no, this is something more abstract still; it is painting beyond all contingency, painting in itself, the pure act of painting. All the qualities of a picture other than those of the contrast of tone and line, all that the painter's reason has not determined, all that comes from our instinct and from nature, in sum all the qualities of representation and feeling are excluded from the work of art.[15]

The criticism was sharp, but telling: there is a close relation between Denis's words and those of Matisse three years later. Moreover (and this is my second point), what they both *also* register is the narrowing of the terms of the innovation that characterised the Parisian avant-garde's alternative professionalism, beyond that of Denis himself and his fellow Nabis in the 1890s, to a technicism that threatens representation itself. Here Denis appears to gesture towards the understanding of the *character* of Matisse's technicism that underlies the recent current of analysis that

I have adumbrated above: namely, that its consequence for the viewer of his paintings goes beyond interpretation, and is rather an experience on the level of *affect* – that is, it is a direct physiological response to the work's arrangement of lines, forms and colours, an experience of a kind that is ineluctable and universal, and moreover consciously created by the painter. This is a startling claim to make, and one that reveals the sophistication and complexity of Matisse's technicism in that period.

If Matisse's ever-closer focus on such technical qualities and commitment to aesthetic innovation is, thanks to his many recorded accounts of it, perhaps the most traceable and demonstrable of the leading painters of his (occupational) generation of the avant-garde, he was not alone. His technicism was shared, if rarely matched in its sophistication, by that of others, both individuals and groups, as the Parisian formation grew in the new century's first decade to a size sufficient not only to allow its subdivision into many contesting aesthetic positions,[16] but to foster a widespread preoccupation with the technical advances and conceits that these brandished. This was registered in the ferment of experimentation that was evident as the decade progressed, encompassing *inter alia* a return to classicism, an infatuation with archaic and pre-Renaissance art, an enjoyment of popular-commercial entertainments and the visual clichés of their advertisements, and an engagement with non-European (predominantly African) cultural artifacts and their anti-mimetic provocations. Within this preoccupation the growth of the formation also fostered rivalries not only between 'isms' but between individuals, the most notorious of which was perhaps (and has certainly become) that between Matisse and Picasso.[17] The first major product of the latter's formal experimentalism in the decade before 1914, the *Demoiselles d'Avignon* of 1907, was motivated indeed at least partly by this, conceived as a riposte to the former's *Nu bleu* of earlier that year. Yet Picasso's commitment to these qualities was of a different order from that of his rival: where Matisse was single-minded, even methodical, in putting himself through an apprenticeship to Post- (and particularly Neo-) Impressionism in pursuit of a painterly system of his own, Picasso's precocious graphic talent, early notoriety and bohemianism fed an experimentalism that was open, not only to this inheritance, but also to what could be learned from (among other popular-cultural stimuli) comics and cinema as well as African masks. Thus as the technical introspectiveness of his hermetic Cubist style became ever more pronounced, it was also increasingly matched by a play of wit and irony that acknowledged its seemingly wilful obscurantism, as in *Ma Jolie* (*My Pretty [Woman]*) of the winter of 1911–12 (pl. 20), whose deeply unflattering 'portrait' of the artist's new love, Eva Gouel, carries, written on its surface, a title taken from the favourite popular song of that season.

As I noted earlier, the American art historian Edward Fry's 1988 essay on Cubism and reflexivity demonstrated that this hermetic pictorial vocabulary amounted to a thoroughgoing 'reflexive' transformation by Picasso of classical representation, a revealing of 'the classical mind's becoming aware of its means for thinking and representing the world even as it carries out that representation'.[18] Fry shows Picasso's (and occasionally Braque's) Cubism of *c.* 1910–12 to be a technical *tour de force*, the progressive articulation of a painterly system whose formal sophistication we can see to have been the equivalent of Matisse's. That these two achievements were a product of the same cultural formation and moment is an indication of not only the primacy of *technie* for that avant-garde, but also the degree of formalist radicalism which the consolidation of its professionalism enabled. It was, moreover, the combination of these qualities that afforded Cubism, as a movement and as a style, the hegemonic status across western modernist culture that it attained by 1914. In Paris, the artists who came together in the 'salon' Cubist group in 1911 were drawn by a common investment in the technical devices pioneered by Picasso and Braque as much as by the 'simultaneity' of modern life, whose qualities these innovations could be deployed to suggest. Through their efforts, which complemented those of 'gallery' Cubism, the formal conceits that became the hallmark of Cubism (multiple perspective, the elision of figures and ground, geometric armatures *et cetera*) proliferated, and made it the technicist style *par excellence* of the pre-war moment (pl. 21).

PROFESSIONALISM, COMPETITION, DIVERSIFICATION

The technicism whose growing salience I have traced was at once a product and a determinant of broader dynamics within the Parisian avant-garde. These dynamics together achieved the formation's consolidation and also effected, in the decade before the First World War, a prioritisation of its alternative professionalism over its ideology of political radicalism and rupture, in the conflict between them that lay at its centre. The dynamics had several elements. One was that shift in the character of cultural collectivities that I traced broadly in Chapter 1: a shift from a model grounded in affective relations (of varying degrees of intensity, from brotherhoods to fellowships to informal friendships) towards one built on the more instrumental commonalities of shared aesthetic principle and ambition. This was a cross-media phenomenon: Anthony Glinoer and Vincent Laisney trace the shift in respect of the Parisian literary avant-garde formation after 1900, from 'natural' groupings (a term coined by the critic Charles Augustin Sainte-Beuve in the 1860s) of which the cenacle was the culminating form, based on *fraternité*,[19] to '*artificial* groupings, put together in haste, to assure themselves a place in the sun', whose strategies included declared aesthetic positions, manifestos in the press and soirées.[20] Fine artists employed equivalent, and sometimes identical, strategies: thus the group of painters who joined Matisse in 1905 in adopting a pictorial style of loosely brushed combinations of non-mimetic colour launched themselves as a group at the Salon d'Automne of that year by securing, by dint of lobbying the chair of the Commission de Placement, a shared room for their exclusive use – a tactic that yielded a satisfyingly hyperbolic critical response as well as a group name, 'Les Fauves', courtesy of a critic. The initiative was followed and developed by another emergent group of like-minded painters at the Salon des Indépendants of 1911, when they succeeded in securing the position of Commission chair itself for one of their number, Henri Le Fauconnier, who was able to hang their works together in room 41; once again the result was, as group member

Albert Gleizes later recalled, a gratifying *succès de scandale* that successfully launched Cubism as a public movement.[21] The difference in notoriety that this tactic accorded them vis-à-vis that of the Fauves was a measure of the progress made by the Parisian avant-garde in this aspect of their professionalism. Another such measure was the adoption of explicit obligations on membership, in place of the previous informal and fraternal mutual support of cenacles. Thus when Marcel Duchamp entered his picture *Nu descendant un escalier nº 2* (*Nude Descending a Staircase No. 2*) (1911–12) (pl. 22) for exhibition in the Cubists' rooms (of which there were now two) at the Indépendants of 1912, fellow Cubists Gleizes and Jean Metzinger sought, in the words of another member of the circle, Georges Ribemont-Dessaignes, 'to establish a kind of legislation of the Cubist movement', going so far as to insist on its removal, lest its cinematographic depiction of that nude's descent seem too obvious and too public an acknowledgment of the ideas of the group's upstart rivals, the Italian Futurists, whose debut exhibition in Paris at the Galerie Bernheim-Jeune had only just closed. To Ribemont-Dessaignes this 'appeared a betrayal'[22] – as it must have done for Duchamp himself, for it prompted his leaving the group, his departure for several months' stay in Munich, and a turning point in his artistic career.[23]

Another element in the dynamic was the development of the disposition to principled aesthetic contestation into a more market-aware competitiveness, as the numbers of *soi-disant* avant-gardists mushroomed and rival 'isms' proliferated. To an extent this was also market-led, especially after two key developments of 1906–7. The first was the appointment, noted above, of Félix Fénéon to the Galerie Bernheim-Jeune in November 1906 to lead its engagements with contemporary art. Fénéon brought a network of contacts on both the supply and the demand side of avant-garde painting that few others could rival, and a partisanship towards not only Neo-Impressionist painters but also the Nabis and Fauves that seemed rooted both in aesthetic principles and commercial 'nous'. The second was Daniel-Henry Kahnweiler's entry into the field the following summer, which brought not only the innovations in dealership practices noted in earlier chapters but also a more aggressive entrepreneurial disposition. Together they added rivalry between galleries to that between aesthetic principles, within a mushrooming and increasingly multifarious avant-garde.[24] The competitiveness was prompted also by the models of avant-gardist strategy presented by other groupings within the expanding formation. Surprisingly perhaps, given the Parisian history I have traced so far, the most significant of these came from outside France, when in February 1909 the publication, on the front page of the leading Parisian newspaper *Le Figaro*, of the founding manifesto of Futurism announced the launch upon the city's (indeed, the continent's)[25] unsuspecting artists and public alike of an Italian avant-gardist collective with an apparently cross-media agenda of cultural revolution that threw down the gauntlet to the modernist aspirations of the Parisian avant-garde. Ironically, the manifesto can be seen to be in part a product of this formation itself, and in part a measure of the impact its consolidation was having elsewhere. For its author, Filippo Marinetti, a gifted, ambitious and independent-minded Italian poet and playwright, had learned his literary skills and political ideology in the *anarchisant* milieux of mid-1890s Parisian Symbolist writers, and had joined to these a dissatisfaction with the provincialism and conservatism of contemporary Italian literary culture; it was the differential between the energy and radicalism of an emergent Parisian literary avant-garde and Marinetti's perception of the lack of either in Milan or Rome or Turin that gave this mix a combustible quality.[26] Marinetti was, therefore, at once well positioned between the centre and the periphery, with a foot in each, and well resourced by the technical and political radicalism of the Symbolists to make full use of his own considerable, and uncommon, personal charisma. Not only, moreover, for literary purposes: the manifesto of Futurism may have had an ostensibly literary focus, but it is rarely explicit in this, and it gestures repeatedly to other art forms; as a call to arms it is an appeal to artists in all media. It was, moreover, followed in 1914 by a further 11 manifestos: two on painting, one on sculpture, others on music, cinema, architecture, noise art, words-in-freedom and lust, most of them written by Marinetti himself or assisted by him.[27]

The manifesto's rhetorical force and poetry were not matched by technical specificity, however; where the balance of forces at the centre of the Parisian avant-garde was leaning towards a professionalism whose compass was, as I have argued, itself narrowing to a preoccupation with aesthetic technicism, Marinetti asserted in 1909 above all a broader cultural commitment, alongside those to the dynamism of a violent, masculinised modernity, to a rupture with a past of sorts (albeit one selectively emblematised by museums, libraries, femininity and somnolence) – hence a version of avant-gardist ideology. He would learn from Parisian alternative professionalism over the next five years, however, as his progressive itemisation of a Futurist cultural agenda in his series of medium-specific supplementary manifestos demonstrates. He was quick to grasp that a Futurist programme for visual art, in particular, required some specificity, given the technical advances then under way such as those noted above. Thanks to the domiciled presence in Paris of Italian painter Gino Severini, and his membership of its avant-garde (with the useful credentials of marriage to the daughter of poet Paul Fort, one of the key players in its literary formation),[28] Marinetti was able to marshal a group of visual artists into a Futurist cohort, and with his support they produced two manifestos on art in quick succession in February and October 1910, which together laid out a technical agenda for painting, and a third on the occasion of their debut exhibitions tour of European capitals in spring 1912, which reprised and developed the second. These were followed in April 1912 by one on sculpture, by Umberto Boccioni alone.[29]

The response from within the Parisian avant-gardes, both literary and artistic, was mixed but substantial. On the one hand, the Futurist engagement with everyday modern urban life and its distinctive collective experiential features was cognate with an already emergent current in contemporary French poetry, including Jules Romains's theory of unanimism, the concept of a collective consciousness in which the emotions and impressions of the group as a whole take precedence over the psychology of the individual, launched with the publication in 1908 of his collection of poems *La Vie unanime*. It was cognate too with Robert Delaunay's exploration and celebration of the spatial experience of the modern city, in his series of paintings of the Eiffel Tower, begun in 1909, which owed much to the example of his friend, the self-taught painter Henri Rousseau. In both respects the 'modernolatry' of Futurism encouraged the engagement of the salon Cubists with similar themes and subjects: collective urban events, team sports, fashion, aviation, bright city lights. The two movements shared, lastly, an enthusiasm for the philosophy of Henri Bergson, for which Le Fauconnier's picture *L'Abondance* (*Abundance*) (pl. 23), first shown at the 1911 Paris Indépendants and subsequently much exhibited across Europe before the First World War, became a visual manifesto. On the other hand, the rural setting and classical nude subject of this work stood for much against which the 1909 manifesto had so colourfully declared itself, and which the two subsequent painting manifestos condemned, and as the affair of Duchamp's *Nu descendant* showed, the emphasis on differences between Cubist and Futurist aesthetics was mutual. Moreover, if the salon Cubists in particular found in Futurist painting before 1912 some points of overlap with their own pictorial devices (as in the adaptation of that of multiple perspectives to offer a montaged juxtaposition of spatially unrelated vignettes, rather than merely different diagrammatic views of an object or figure) (pl. 24), they also found much to deride in the technical shortcomings of the Italians. In terms of 'alternative professionalism', too, the response of Parisian avant-garde artists was substantial yet mixed. The Futurists' innovation of Europe-wide manifesto launches reinforced an existing trend towards the use by artists of this literary genre; while manifestos as such were not new, the hyperbolic character of Marinetti's (and those that followed from the Futurists) was so, and while his particular flair and bombast were not easily assimilable, his own borrowings from the fledgling advertising industry fed into a growing recognition in the Parisian formation of their promotional utility. Critics such as Camille Mauclair, Roger Allard and Louis Vauxcelles were not slow to remark (mostly with hostility) on the *surenchérisme* (hype) with which the exhibition of new art in Paris was increasingly accompanied.[30]

Another stimulus to the artistic avant-garde's competitiveness, alongside the quasi-external challenge of Marinetti's strategic assault on its citadel, came in the form of a change in the balance of forces vis-à-vis its literary equivalent. This was registered both by the increase in the critical attention given to Cubism in particular, in comparison with that afforded to previous artistic 'isms' since Impressionism, after the public launch of the salon Cubist group in 1911, and by the character of one component of it. While the newspaper critics continued largely to mock Cubism's technical conceits with the ribaldry that they reserved for avant-garde innovations, and to feature reviews of its exhibitions only to amuse their readers,[31] the poets, essayists and novelists who wrote art criticism for the *petites revues* leaped in unprecedented numbers to offer explanations of Cubism's aesthetic principles.[32] Indeed, so many were the contributions that it would appear to have been a matter of self-esteem for writers to have a published position on the meaning and significance of Cubism. Their enthusiasm for explaining what the painters were doing led some of the latter, mostly from the salon Cubist circle, to offer their own view of this, with articles in the press. This was undertaken most readily by Metzinger and Gleizes, who sought to legitimise Cubism's technical innovations either by insisting on its 'respectable' character (Gleizes) or by stressing its continuation of French tradition, identified either with classicism (Metzinger) or with a perceived vernacular opposition to this (Gleizes).[33]

Increasingly, as the critics' interpretations multiplied, the relationship between the composite and ekphratic 'critical Cubism' that they collectively (and competitively) produced and the paintings, whether Salon or gallery Cubist, itself became ever more tenuous – a fact that underlines the strategic character of the writers' contributions, as being aimed at a literary rather than a painterly readership, each contribution a taking of a position in the literary as opposed to the artistic field. At the same time the emphases of Gleizes and Metzinger on respectability and continuity were aimed, as were those of some of the writers, at assimilating their paintings to traditionalist and classicist discourses already consecrated both in contemporary cultural fields at large and in the narrower fields of the avant-garde. Thus Roger Allard sought, first, to update classicism with a Bergsonian interpretation in his 1911 commentary on the Louvre's recent acquisition of Nicolas Poussin's *Et in Arcadia Ego* (1637–38): it was the balance that Poussin achieved in such paintings between the dynamism implied by the frozen gestures of their figures and the stasis of their compositions, Allard argued, that gave them a living beauty: 'Thus to love the living work for the vital forces that are in it, is to understand and possess nature, since by an act of genius a human thought has known how to contain it whole.'[34] Second, he applied this fusion of the then-fashionable philosopher's key concepts of *l'élan vital* and *la durée* with classical temporality to his analysis of Cubism: an example is his characterisation of Metzinger's *Nu* of 1910, in which 'an art diametrically opposed to Impressionism is born, with little interest in copying a chance cosmic episode, and which, in its pictorial plenitude, offers the beholder's intelligence the essential elements of a synthesis situated in time'.[35]

It was not only the literary supporters of Cubism, however, who presented it as exemplifying, in ways that writers could only learn from, the most significant cultural trends; the 1912 critique of it by Jacques Rivière, editorial secretary of the leading literary periodical *La Nouvelle Revue française*, who was then elaborating a conservative, traditionalist model of literary classicism that was part and parcel of his right-wing nationalist ideology, gave an account of Cubism that, while it was as mocking as it was intrigued, yet in its very negativity acknowledged Cubist painting as a force to be reckoned with beyond the studios of the avant-garde. 'It is my intention to give the cubists a little more freedom and self-assurance by providing them with the profound reasons for what they are doing', he declared, adding: 'True, I will not be able to do so without showing them how badly they have done it until now' – a remark that drips with the then-conventional condescension of the writer for the painter.[36] Beyond this, Rivière showed no understanding either of painting as a material practice or of the reflexive qualities that made Cubism so ground-breaking a contribution to modernism.

Rivière's hostility betrayed, as I have said, an awareness that Cubism marked a turning of the tide in the balance of forces between visual art and writing, and their respective avant-gardes: after decades in which literary Symbolism had set the terms in which painters were obliged to articulate their ideas verbally and writers had policed them (witness the ridicule to which Gauguin was subjected when he attempted to take the contest to the *littérateurs*),[37] his condescension itself registered an anxiety that hegemony was slipping from the writers in Paris; and this in turn reflected the dynamic of an artistic avant-garde coming into its own and setting its own terms for contemporary cultural expression. Rivière's effort was soon followed (and his rearguard effort abandoned) by a cohort of writers, among them Apollinaire, Max Jacob, Pierre Reverdy and Gertrude Stein, who explored the ramifications of Cubist poetry and prose, further securing painting's hegemony in Paris (at least for a while).[38]

A third element in the dynamic that reinforced the artistic avant-garde's alternative professionalism was the increasing diversification of visual practices and projects within its groupings, and the heteronomous character of some of these. Gauguin had pioneered an extension of his studio activities into the field of decorative arts, making ceramic vessels and the occasional piece of furniture;[39] following him, the Nabis had from the start of their careers understood their art practice to include graphic and theatre design. These were largely self-initiated responses to the growth and strengthening of a discourse of decoration that by the turn of the century had brought together the Parisian avant-garde's concerns with painting techniques, the policies of successive French Republican governments of support for applied arts, and the Europe-wide flourishing of Art Nouveau.[40] This discourse underwrote in three respects that consolidation of the professionalising emphases within the new formation that I have been tracing: the first was in its harnessing of some avant-garde artists' concerns to an agenda of national economic competitiveness; the second in turning others towards the tastes and milieux of the Parisian social elite; and the third in assimilating those of yet others into the wave of nationalism that swept France in the decade before the First World War.[41]

PROFESSIONALISM AND POLITICS

The exacerbation to the point of contradiction of the tensions I have been tracing was not, however, a product of the dynamic of professionalism alone; it was, perhaps even more fundamentally, a consequence of the broader political conjuncture of the *avant-guerre* Third Republic. The political dynamic of the decade before 1914 was one driven by both internal and external pressures: those of a sharpening class struggle, as the social and economic inequalities of a supposed 'Belle Époque' turned former allies into potential antagonists, and of the rising tide of nationalism I have noted, whose currents were strengthened by the two stand-offs with Germany over Morocco, in 1905 and 1911. It was the manner in which it was caught in these currents, carried by some and resistant to others, that precipitated the contradiction on which the Parisian artistic avant-garde was consolidated, and that is the subject of the following paragraphs.[42]

As I noted in the previous chapter, the Bloc des gauches that shaped republican politics in the first years of the new century had its most concrete existence and symbolic importance on a parliamentary level, as the basis of support for the Radical administrations of Pierre Waldeck-Rousseau (1899–1902) and Émile Combes (1902–05). The 'government of republican defence' of the former had two overriding policies: anticlericalism, or a commitment to the separation of church and state, which tacitly meant a weakening of the political power and social authority of the church and the dissolution of those religious orders that had been most openly anti-Dreyfusard; and republicanism, which entailed the removal from positions of influence of those supporters of the political right who had sought to undermine the republic by means of the Affair. For Combes, anticlericalism was almost the sole motivation. When this policy achieved its consummation in the Act of Separation of late 1905, the Bloc lost its momentum: it fell apart in the 18 months that followed, and was dead before the end of 1907.

This disintegration was not a product solely of the act, however. The Bloc is incomprehensible without an awareness of both its existence outside parliament and, more generally, the growth of extra-parliamentary forces in this period. For the Affair precipitated the entry into public life of new social strata and groupings, expressing themselves by new means. As Madeleine Rebérioux notes, on the Dreyfusard side, 'the Affair, which had united workers and intellectuals in their aims and even in action, convinced the latter that the consolidation of democracy required their active participation in social life'.[43] For business managers and politicians alike, on the other hand, the tensions accompanying a period, since the mid-1890s, of rapid growth in an inegalitarian society threw the relations between capital and labour into as sharp a relief as those between republicans and monarchists. In the assessment of one modern historian, Sanford Elwitt, 'battalions of businessmen, reformers and politicians mobilised throughout the 1890s to forestall the irruption of working-class unrest' that anarchist and syndicalist activities appeared to threaten.[44] Thus, while on the surface of political life the oppositions generated by the Affair gave the Bloc des gauches a progressive colouration, on a more fundamental level it was less so. Ultimately, it was the conflicts provoked by this ambivalence from 1904 to 1907, rather than the passing of the Act of Separation itself, that brought the coalition to its end. In its heyday, the extra-parliamentary groups and societies attached to it, through which intellectuals effected their participation in social life, reflected this ambivalence: they were both an extension of Dreyfusard comradeship into other arenas and, at the same time, instruments of corporate paternalism, a 'generalised political strategy aimed at fixing the pattern of labour-capital relations'.[45] Its instruments were various: profit-sharing and worker-shareholding schemes, company unions, workers' housing co-operatives, the garden city movement, adult education projects. In the late 1890s, as I have noted, parapolitical organisations for their promotion mushroomed: the Société Française des Habitations à Bon Marché, the Musée Social, the Société d'Éducation Sociale, the Universités Populaires – the gamut of the Art Social initiatives noted in the last chapter. They were recognisably part of the anti-socialist consensus – indeed, central to the programme of solidarism that, with the collapse of the Bloc, became the leading doctrine of republicanism, an attempt to steer a middle road between capital and labour, to moderate the former's social effects in recognition of the fact that these, if unchecked, might produce social strife and eventually socialism.

Allegiances and initiatives such as these, varied as they clearly were, together demonstrate the ways in which, as the antagonisms between classes intensified in France and the currents of nationalism grew stronger, increasing numbers of young French artists and writers in the avant-garde formation found the affiliation to anarchism less integral to their sense of identity and their ambitions than had the preceding generation. As the organised working class withdrew progressively from cross-class collaboration behind the stockade of political and strategic autonomy, many of these artists and writers responded with reciprocal withdrawals. For some, such as those who had embraced Art Social, the subtle shift from comradeship to paternalism – from art as a means of furthering class struggle to one of countering it – was a recognition of their steady distancing from the working class that differences in their respective responses to nationalism were underwriting. The second Moroccan crisis of late 1911, which brought France and Germany to the brink of war, turned this nationalism to a patriotism that was openly shared by most of the nation, and whose relative absence among the working class further widened the distance and provoked, within the avant-garde as without it, a rallying to the *tricolore*. For others in the avant-garde – who by 1912 included a significant and rapidly growing minority of foreign artists for whom the appeal of either nationalism or patriotism was, to say the least, somewhat less telling[46] – the reciprocal response to syndicalist autonomism was an espousal not of nationalism but of a correspondingly autonomous artistic identity, centred on that alternative professionalism whose consolidating practices I have been tracing.

An illustration of this shift is offered by the case of Henri-Martin Barzun. At the time of the collapse of the parliamentary Bloc he was secretary to a rising star in the Radical Party and a founding member of its Comité de la Démocratie Sociale, Joseph Paul-Boncour, from which strategic position he planned to launch a literary magazine, the *Revue rouge*, to promote 'the literature of the young generation' and to 'support a [solidarist] politics of reform'.[47] By the end of 1906, however, he had abandoned both his post and his proposed publication and joined Gleizes and his friends in the communal venture of the Abbaye de Créteil, whose brief and ostensibly utopian existence he underwrote financially, despite his disparagement by other members as 'un jeune politicien'.[48] By the time of the high tide of pre-war patriotism, Barzun's commitment had changed again: in the first issue of his new publishing venture, a *petite revue* launched in late 1912 entitled *Poème et drame*, he declared his aim to be to 'federate intellectually the young creative elites of the whole world'.[49] This was an internationalism explicitly at odds not only with the national mood, but with political engagement itself; his editorials condemned '"revolutionary" [poets who had] become unfortunately misled into making social statements [and] who confuse aesthetic research with class struggle', and proposed instead an autonomous artistic avant-gardism – 'the creative drive *forward* can only come from the poetic instinct', he asserted. This he presented as the high and heroic calling of a putative elite whose members had become brothers 'through the anguish, the privations, the dangers of their adventure, through the hostilities of the fat cities that exile them, through the hard-won victories that will one day be the inheritance of everyone'.[50] It is interesting that this elevated tone, and the associated idealisation of the avant-garde artist, is close to that offered at the same moment in London.[51] But the rhetoric was perhaps deceptive, for the *revue* was part of a strategy of self-promotion whose instrumental professionalism is clear: the 'programme and goal' of *Poème et drame* were to provide a forum for Barzun's 'creative elite', an anthology of its works, and opportunities for networking via bi-monthly banquets.

A final register of the increasing dislocation between the narrowing, technicist professionalism of the artistic avant-garde and the oppositional politics to which the Neo-Impressionist painters and Symbolist writers had been affiliated lies in the efforts of those few among the new literary avant-garde who declared and elaborated an explicit allegiance to the revolutionary syndicalism to which the anarchism of the *fin de siècle* had given way. The autonomism of the syndicalists was hard to bear for those writers whose loyalties remained with a working class that seemed not to want them, and in a few *petites revues* of the last three years before the war, primary among them Jean-Richard Bloch's *L'Effort*,[52] some of them sought to delineate the features of an autonomous proletarian art, while others, such as Léon Rosenthal (in the parliamentary Socialists' paper, *L'Humanité*) and Henri Guilbeaux (in the radical socialist *Hommes du jour* and the satirical *L'Assiette au beurre*) carried their socialist sympathies into their salon reviews. But their allegiances among fine artists remained with the Neo-Impressionists and their immediate heirs, bastions of the Salon des Indépendants. From this left-wing perspective the technical innovations of aesthetically radical avant-garde groups such as the Cubists were trebly suspect: first, because, accompanied as they increasingly were by the apparatus of publicity, they smacked of commercialism and hype; second, because, as Madeleine Rebérioux has suggested, for a generation of young bourgeois who had the same cult of the humanities and the same rhetorical training, such formal obscurities nourished obscurantism of thought and opened the door to irrationalism, mysticism, thus even to nationalism itself;[53] last but not least, because the autonomism of painterly *technie* was precisely intended to exclude writers like them.

7

LONDON BEFORE 1912: A PRE-AVANT-GARDE CONJUNCTURE

LONDON ART AND THE LURE OF PARIS

The field of contemporary art production in late nineteenth-century London was a part of that broad process of the professionalisation of non-entrepreneurial middle-class occupations that characterised the modernising economies of the western world at the time. It was so, both in the generic sense of the manner in which, as we shall see in this chapter, the members of this field broke away, in ways that paralleled other occupations, from the structures that had previously governed it and took control of its procedures, and in the specific sense of its participation in that growth and diversification across the major cities of Europe of a privatised, loose but self-consciously professional formation of 'Secessionist' artists that I discussed in earlier chapters.

As Béatrice Joyeux-Prunel has detailed, this growth was centred on Paris, which was seen to have replaced Rome early in the nineteenth century as the 'cultural capital' of Europe.[1] It began in the mid-century struggles of Paris-based artists to gain a profile in an ever more crowded market (as well as, for those who had dealers, in the efforts of the latter to find new markets), and was driven, over the next several decades, largely by the broadening of their combined promotional efforts beyond France. This was not the only source of the professionalising dynamic, of course; in each city with a significant field of contemporary art production, artists were professionalising in ways that were shaped also by its particular dynamics. Yet a Parisian reputation remained the most sought-after prize in an international artistic career, and increasingly artists looked for the leverage towards this that successful exposure and critical attention elsewhere in

Europe (and later, beyond) could provide. One of the consequences of this dynamic was to weave a loosely connected population of artists into a pan-European formation, in which the relations between its artists, dealers and collectors in its major cities were in themselves as significant for the setting of the terms on which contemporary art was practised, and directions in which it developed, as were those practices themselves. A second consequence was to cement Paris's pre-eminence as the centre of this formation: well before the century's end, it had become the global centre for the making, exhibiting, selling, collecting and critical appraisal of contemporary art.

As such it was also the city above all others in which to study art – a fact that aspirant artists in London were as quick as those elsewhere in Europe and beyond to recognise and act upon, although perhaps the first significant Anglophone artist to do so was an American. James McNeill Whistler, the son of a globe-trotting railroad engineer, born in Massachusetts, educated in Russia and at West Point, arrived in Paris from Baltimore in 1855, the year of the city's first Exposition Universelle. He enrolled both in its then-leading private teaching *atelier*, that of academic painter Charles Gleyre, and in the ranks of its bohemia. He stayed until 1859 when he moved to London, where he lived for the rest of his life, although he returned frequently to Paris. Whistler's importance for artistic links between these two cities was as dependent on the friendships he made in bohemian milieux as on those made *chez* Gleyre. From soon after his arrival he established himself at the centre of an Anglo-French network of artists and collectors which, though it broke up in the mid-1860s, created new cross-Channel contacts: first as the leader of a 'Paris Gang' of young British artists, then as the founder of a 'Group of Three' with French painters Alphonse Legros and Henri Fantin-Latour.[2] It was Whistler who introduced Fantin-Latour to a London clientele comprising a number of plutocratic Europeans, among them the Ionides family (patrons of the Aesthetic Movement, and Whistler's own clients; Luke Ionides had been a member of the Paris Gang) and Stavros Dilberoglu, for whom, from the mid-1860s, Fantin-Latour painted copies of Old Master pictures before establishing a substantial reputation for floral still lifes.[3] It was Whistler, too, who recognised, reciprocally, the value to London artists of nurturing institutional links with the Paris art market. Aware of the rapid growth there from the 1860s of the number of self-managed artists' exhibition societies, as well as of the growing importance for London of the increasingly pan-European Secessionist network, he worked hard to develop such links, and to bring Parisian installation innovations across the Channel.

His influence was felt in both of these directions. From the 1860s through to the First World War, scores of aspirant British art students followed the trail Whistler had blazed, flocking to Paris for an art education and enrolling, as we saw in earlier chapters, in the proliferating number of *académies libres* that supplemented, and eventually supplanted, the École des Beaux-Arts in furnishing the skills and credentials necessary for a successful artistic career. By the mid-1890s this path had become so well trodden as to represent not only a familiar route but also, as the huge success of George du Maurier's *Trilby* (1894) showed, a mythical journey, and had spawned a literary sub-genre of 'the Parisian student/bohemian memoir' which had consequences of its own for the emergence of an avant-garde in London in further entrenching the perception of the latter's subalternality.[4]

But this city's membership of the burgeoning Secessionist network centred on Paris had already been signalled, and indeed secured a decade earlier. Among the members of the Paris Gang (and Whistler's fellow student at Gleyre's *atelier*) had been Edward Poynter, who in 1871 became the first professor of fine art at the newly established Slade School of Art (whence he moved in 1875 to become principal of the National Art Training School in South Kensington).[5] As Edward Morris notes, the chief lesson that Poynter took from his art education in Paris was its superiority to that available in London; he found the drawing skills of most of his compatriots there to be poorer than those of their French fellow students, and at the Slade he introduced a new régime of art teaching that drew tacitly – and, with his replacement four years later by Legros, explicitly – on an experience of the Parisian model. (Poynter's single-minded study of life drawing and the Old Masters in the Louvre would become fictionalised in *Trilby* in the character of Lorrimer.)[6] By the mid-1880s this régime had produced a cohort of artists whose own attachment to putatively Parisian aesthetic and technical values was declared in the establishment, in 1886, of the New English Art Club by 15 young painters, most of them graduates of both the Slade and the Parisian *académies*. The NEAC was founded in express opposition to the perceived conservatism and insularity of the Royal Academy, an opposition that was reflected in its modelling of its constitution on that of the Paris Salon, and on the assumption that, as young artists recently returned from study in Paris, they had a manner of painting[7] sufficiently common to all of them to justify an initial proposal to name themselves 'The Society of Anglo-French Painters'. Yet the group was divided from the outset into at least three factions, each indebted to one of the several coexisting currents within Secessionist circles in Paris. It thus shared the character of other groupings of the members of that pan-European network, of being more significant as a promotional and positional vehicle within the rapidly growing and diversifying contemporary art market, than as a declaration of a shared aesthetic principle.

London's dealers in contemporary art were also increasingly oriented towards Paris.[8] Edward Morris notes that since the 'Paris Salons provided both a more effective market and a larger and more inclusive display space for contemporary art than did the Royal Academy in London', independent galleries in London 'faced less official competition than in Paris', and 'dealers' exhibitions led in the promotion of French art in England'.[9] From the 1880s, Kenneth McConkey notes, London dealers benefited from 'the ripple effect' from Paris, where, they recognised, 'groups of artists directly staging their own exhibitions stimulated a lively trade in contemporary art'. In response, Bond Street galleries such as Agnew, Colnaghi, Deschamps and Tooth imported Salon paintings, and even went so far as to band paintings together for exhibition as produced by notional groups even though they were simply items of current stock.[10] As Morris observes, there was little reciprocation of this attention: in late 1870s and 1880s Paris there were almost no galleries where the work of even established

British artists could be seen outside official sites such as the Expositions Universelles of 1878 and 1889.[11] The novelist and sometime critic Henry James compared new British painting unfavourably with French; reviewing the inaugural exhibition of the Grosvenor Gallery in London in 1877, he observed that '[t]he pictures, with very few exceptions, are "subjects"; they belong to what the French call the anecdotical class', and in his review of the Royal Academy's Summer Exhibition the following year he noted that 'you immediately see that the exhibition is only in a secondary sense *plastic*; that the plastic is not what English spectators look for in a picture, or what the artist has taken the precaution of putting into it'.[12] Richard Thomson concludes from such observations:

> British painters… shied, it might be argued, from gearing advanced pictorial devices and concepts to the complexities of the modern metropolis…. Whistler, like James an expatriate American, was arguably the only artist to have consistently attempted this in London during the 1870s…. French artists, however, did have the [technical] representational means and the aesthetic notions that could engage with the contemporary city in ways which their British colleagues, as yet, could not.[13]

Given the commercial and critical openness of the London market to the qualities and renown of Parisian painting, it is not surprising that Parisian artists and dealers alike took advantage of it. Paul Durand-Ruel was the first of the dealers in contemporary art to attempt this: when the Franco-Prussian War and the siege of Paris brought that city's art market to a halt in 1870,[14] that December he opened a gallery on New Bond Street, founding the Society of French Artists[15] and holding an exhibition of paintings from his stock, including works by Monet and Pissarro whom he had only recently met. This was followed over the next five years by further such exhibitions. The British art public showed little interest, however,[16] and Durand-Ruel closed the venture in 1875. Meanwhile Degas was making overtures on his own initiative, and with more success, exhibiting a substantial number of paintings in England from 1871, and making important sales, including to the wealthy merchant Constantin Ionides and, perhaps surprisingly, to a former volunteer soldier, Captain Henry Hill, who had made his fortune supplying the army with bedding. Retiring to Brighton, Hill began an eclectic art collection (mostly of contemporary work), and in 1876 bought seven of Degas's paintings.[17]

In 1882 Durand-Ruel was back, and by the middle of the decade had secured a foothold; he was accompanied in showing French paintings in London by another Parisian gallery, that of Goupil, which was then expanding across Europe and into the USA, opening branches in Berlin, The Hague and New York as well as London. From this point Parisian engagement with the London market gained ground steadily. This was not surprising, since this market was itself burgeoning, and also diversifying, offering artists a widening range of exhibiting opportunities and their audiences the means to view their work, from the formal structures of juried exhibitions organised by artists' societies to commercial art dealers and *ad hoc*, newly emergent formations. By the end of the first decade of the twentieth century, indeed, London's was the biggest art market in Europe, with over 300 commercial art galleries – an index of the city's concentration of art capital that closely correlated to its position as the leading international financial centre – compared to about 130 in Paris at that time.[18] This number encompassed a wide variety of firms, however, from picture restorers, paint and frame suppliers who dabbled in selling pictures on the side, by way of well-established commercial dealers whose stock-in-trade was Old Master art, to those who were beginning to invest in contemporary work.[19]

THE GROSVENOR GALLERY: ARISTOCRATS, AMATEURS AND AESTHETES

Despite the more scattered, less focused character and structure of the London market vis-à-vis that of Paris, it was a London initiative that opened perhaps the most significant avenue of development for the immediate future of both, indeed for the European Secessionist network as a whole. In 1877 the Grosvenor Gallery was launched in London by Sir Coutts and Lady Blanche Lindsay, an aristocratic couple with a deep interest in art and its patronage who were also amateur artists of some skill in their own right, and possessed of a network of family and friends that was intertwined with those of the later Pre-Raphaelite circles.[20] One of the first institutional registers in London of the growing dissatisfaction in these aristocratic and aesthetic milieux with the conservatism of the Royal Academy, the perceived debasement of its aesthetic standards and the commercialism of the current art market, the Grosvenor also positioned itself apart from the mainstream exhibiting societies and dealer-led galleries, as a private venture that was more discerning and distinctive both socially and aesthetically. In doing so, it at once replicated the recent increase in the importance of aristocratic and *haut-bourgeois* 'cercles' in the Parisian art market that I noted in Chapter 4, and yet also refracted, in the cultural sphere, a specifically British social dynamic: that of the efforts of its embattled and declining aristocracy to resist the social ascent and challenge to its pre-eminence of the industrial and mercantile middle classes, and of their cultural values.[21] As such, the initiative of its creation deserves exploration in some detail. As we shall see, the gallery was at the centre of a discursive matrix that drew together some of the threads that this book is tracing.

The ostensible reason for the Grosvenor's establishment, as declared by its proponents both at the time and in recollection, was to supplement the Royal Academy by offering a venue for artists who had until then been unable to gain space for their pictures at its annual exhibitions. Sir Coutts Lindsay took to the art press and the papers with explanations of this to coincide with the launch, declaring his support for those who were 'either unable or unwilling to exhibit elsewhere',[22] and (as *The Times* reported) in his toast at the inaugural banquet voiced his gratitude for the RA's co-operation in the venture;[23] his assistant Charles Hallé later insisted in his memoirs that the gallery had not been founded in opposition to the RA.[24] Yet Lindsay also signalled, if diplomatically, an orientation to a different artistic community, tacitly criticising the RA's perceived vulgarising policies: 'There are several thoughtful men in London', he wrote in the *Art Journal*, 'whose ideas and methods of embodying them are strange to us: but I do not think strangeness, or even eccentricity of method, a sufficient excuse for ignoring the work of men otherwise notable';[25] and in the *Times* piece he was quoted as distinguishing these as too 'ascetic' and of a too 'sensitive fibre' for the RA's exhibition walls.[26] The clearest expression of the Lindsays' antipathy to the Royal Academy and its perceived populism, however, was voiced by Joseph Comyns Carr, co-assistant with Hallé, a year before it opened. Writing to Dante Gabriel Rossetti in April 1876, Carr solicited the latter's participation in what he described as a proposed 'exhibition for the higher kind of painting which the Academy has either failed to represent or has represented unfavourably and imperfectly', a failing, he explained, that the establishment of the Grosvenor Gallery itself was intended by Sir Coutts to redress. 'There is to be no attempt to serve a popular taste', Carr continued, 'but rather to protest against the concessions which have been made to popularity at the expense of poetical art.'[27] As this suggests, the project was both more ambitious, and a more deep-seated challenge to everything that the Royal Academy's exhibitions represented and furthered, than its proponents publicly acknowledged.

This is indicated in a number of ways. First, the financial outlay made by the Lindsays in setting up their gallery was very substantial: approximately £6.5 to £10 million in today's figures,[28] a huge amount to come entirely from their personal funds, and a sum that suggests motives greater than altruism alone and points towards more strategic objectives (although profit was apparently not a motive; the sole income from the venture seems to have come from admission ticket and exhibition catalogue sales)[29]. Not that the Lindsays were short of inherited wealth – Sir Coutts acquired his name, his title and his fortune from his grandfather Sir Coutts Trotter, a partner in the bank Coutts & Co., while his wife, Blanche, was a scion of the Rothschild banking family. Significantly, however, the size of their investment was matched by the lavishness of its deployment in the decoration of the Grosvenor's premises both externally and internally.

On one level this opulence signalled in the most visible and material of ways[30] an alliance between high finance and the aristocracy that was a key part of the strategy of the resistance of the latter to the social ascent of the industrial and mercantile bourgeoisie. For as Youssef Cassis and others have detailed, in the upper levels of the interclass *rapprochements* that were a central driver of Victorian social developments, it was important to distinguish not only the aristocracy but also those members of the upper middle class whose wealth came from finance (and sometimes a profession) from those for whom it came from factories and trade. In contrast to the entrepreneurial values of hard work and sweated brow, the combination of wealth and leisure that intermarriage between baronial and banking families achieved gave access to purportedly higher values beyond the cash nexus. Between the mid-nineteenth century and its end, high financiers were progressively assimilated into the aristocracy;[31] in this process, both partners to this relation gained access to the cultural capital of occupations and dispositions that signified those higher values, including amateurism and the pursuit of beauty. Thus, the Lindsays' aim in so lavishly fitting out their new gallery with an elite address on Bond Street, impressive premises (immediately dubbed a 'picture palace' in the London press)[32] and an opulent suite of exhibition rooms (whose spaciousness and luxury were intended to emulate those of the Italian Renaissance patrons to whom Sir Coutts Lindsay himself was compared)[33] was, in part, to underline the project's elite status, its distinctiveness from the perceived increasing vulgarity of the Royal Academy.

On another level the Grosvenor project represented a clearer commitment than the Royal Academy was showing to artistic values and artists' interests.[34] Here too its aristocratic connotations were clear and significant. From its outset the gallery provided a means of exposure and encouragement to aristocratic amateurs such as the Lindsays themselves, especially those – many of them women – who excelled in the medium of watercolour, deemed more suitable for them than 'messy and undignified' oil painting, with its inappropriate professional connotations.[35] This aim was successful, for a substantial number of works at the gallery's annual exhibitions were by titled amateurs, as reviewers noted. As Paula Gillett observes, 'The presence of these aristocratic amateurs and of others who exhibited later, as well as the numerous portraits of titled sitters featured in the annual shows, strengthened the powerful aristocratic ethos conveyed by [its] palatial architecture and opulent décor.'[36] The amateurism and feminism were not only as significant as the aristocratic identity, but for the Lindsays inseparable from it; thus, also from the start, the Grosvenor was characterised by an orientation to not only the artistic, but also the social and political roles of women. Not only did its exhibitions include twice as many female artists as did those of the RA,[37] but also – founded in a decade in which women's opportunities and rights were matters of increasingly urgent debate – it attracted the support, and often participation, of leading hostesses in London 'Society' as well as leading campaigners for women's suffrage.[38] At the same time, this was also a period when the struggle for social status, as between the aristocracy and upper middle class, was conducted across the boundaries of 'Society', entrance to which was governed by access to its key social circles and their events, and these were controlled by its socially most senior – necessarily aristocratic – women.[39] In this context, the role of Blanche Lindsay in the promotion of the gallery during its first six years before the couple's separation was crucial: her success in attracting a stellar set of Society celebrities (including the Prince of Wales, 'professional beauties' such as Lillie Langtry and actresses such as Ellen Terry) to the private events that the Grosvenor sponsored both burnished her own status at the top of its aristocratic hierarchy and underwrote the gallery's elite character.[40]

It did more than this, however; for the role of Society hostess was a key element not only of the high-end social *rapprochements*, but also in the bringing together of aristocratic circles and their values with those of the cultural bohemia whose steady growth through the nineteenth century was another expression of hostility to the bourgeoisie. The Lindsays recognised in bohemia a disposition that they could harness for its own purposes. As Elizabeth Wilson has noted, artists in mid-nineteenth-century England were less defiantly hostile to the social order than French bohemians, partly because the artist was a more marginal figure and thus less liable to upset that order *tout court* – indeed, as she also notes, English bohemianism was closer to upper-class raffishness and eccentricity than examples elsewhere[41] – and the social elite that the Grosvenor Gallery's activities attracted could safely enjoy what one of the gallery's historians has called the 'intriguingly suspect aura' of bohemia. Blanche Lindsay was not alone in 'raiding bohemia to add zest to a luncheon', Gillett observes, '[b]ut the Lindsays' mingling of the aristocracies of birth and artistic talent was not occasional but programmatic', and reached as far as the royal family itself.[42]

The 'raiding' of bohemia was, it should be noted, part of a more general raiding of art *per se* for its cultural capital – one that sought not only to harness but also redefine art to its own advantage via an alignment with the Aesthetic Movement. This redefinition encompassed three aspects, closely interrelated and together underwriting the social pre-eminence of the aristocracy they sought to safeguard. One was an explicit pursuit of aesthetic beauty as a spiritual quality, which raised art above the prosaic and material qualities of everyday social life, as an autonomous realm of culture by implication accessible only to an elite of *cognoscenti* (Comyns Carr's 'higher kind of painting... a poetical art', noted above). A second was the consequent revaluation of artists – and especially those such as Rossetti, Whistler and Burne-Jones, whose work explicitly celebrated this autonomy – and of their gifts as creative individuals. This commitment was demonstrated in the Grosvenor project not only in Sir Coutts's consideration for 'eccentricity', quoted above, but in a display policy that, in sharp distinction to the overcrowded jumble of the Royal Academy's exhibitions, grouped the entries of each artist together in a sympathetic, uncluttered space – a shift in favour of their interests that paralleled those reforms to the Paris Salon's display policy proposed a few years earlier by Degas, noted in Chapter 4.[43] A third was an espousal of decoration, and of the decorative role of art, as the expression of its spirituality. This too privileged the artists of the Aesthetic Movement, but it also expressed the Lindsays' own aesthetic predilections: in the early 1880s Sir Coutts himself undertook a decorative scheme for Dorchester House, the Park Lane home of his brother-in-law Robert Holford, a commission that made his name as an amateur artist of great talent,[44] and he took this interest into the Grosvenor initiative, which consequently became a key point of institutional reference for decorative art practice in the late Victorian period. As Charles Hallé later recalled:

> it was to maintain this decorative value of pictures that Sir Coutts built and furnished his Gallery in a sumptuous manner, and had the pictures arranged for public exhibition as nearly as possible as though they formed the decoration of the walls of the house he lived in, and could live in with pleasure.[45]

Once again, the aristocratic values that the espousal of the decorative purpose of art above all others indicated were clearly read by the gallery's public and critics, as Gillett notes: 'Reviews of the Grosvenor's opening implicitly recognised this meaning by ascribing Sir Coutts' funding of the Gallery to his spirit of noble generosity – the aristocrat sharing his cultivated taste and inviting his countrymen to delight in art works in a setting of palatial opulence.'[46]

Yet it was the connotations of bohemia and bohemianism that were especially worth seizing by the Grosvenor, in so far as the alliance this cemented had been itself developing for a generation or so, as an expression, in part, of that ideology of affective relations that was growing in opposition to those fostered by the cash nexus. From the early 1860s there had begun to flourish elite groups of aristocrats with the money to indulge in art patronage and the leisure for an interest in intellectual pursuits associated with artists. One such circle was that of Little Holland House in Kensington, where the 'Holland Park set', centred on the aristocratic Holland family who owned much of the borough, included the painters G.F. Watts and Frederic Leighton, and the photographer Julia Margaret Cameron, and where Sir Coutts Lindsay met Blanche as well as some of the Pre-Raphaelite painters.[47] This 'set' had a distinctive social tone, succinctly described by Liz Prettejohn as 'aspiring to the aristocratic, venerating the arts, cosmopolitan and with a hint of Patrician moral laxness'. Comparing it with the more outrageous bohemianism of Rossetti's circle at Tudor House, Chelsea, she notes that 'the two groupings were alike in their repudiation of bourgeois respectability', and that contacts between them were 'frequent and friendly'.[48] If such groupings were in the van of the aristocracy's assimilation of at least the upper reaches of London's bohemia in the 1860s, by the 1880s this co-option of them by the Grosvenor on behalf of its aristocratic network was well under way: in her later *Reminiscences*, Comyns Carr's wife, Alice, who saw herself as a bohemian by way of her marriage, could relish how '[i]n these fine rooms, hung with crimson damask, [the Lindsays] certainly gathered together the *élite* of the great world as well as all the brilliance of a select bohemia', and noted that 'a regular attendant' at these Grosvenor parties 'was James McNeill Whistler'; 'more than once', she noted, 'his audacious remarks did much to jeopardise the *rapprochement* between the social and Bohemian worlds'. She recalled that Blanche Lindsay 'always liked knowing artists and musicians, and herself dabbled in both these arts, though later the pen of an easy writer claimed her affections and she published much Society verse. But', she added, 'we of the Bohemian world were never deceived into thinking that she *really* included us in the "inner circle" of her own friends, and Jimmy Whistler, in particular, loved to make social *faux pas* at her parties.'[49] Thus the Grosvenor was instrumental in the consolidation of that category of 'high Bohemia' that was unique to London in its annexation of its social alterities to the requirements of 'Society', and which, as we shall see in Chapter 9, helped a quarter of a century later to shape the character of the city's avant-garde.

Thanks in part to the Lindsays' long-standing acquaintance with the Pre-Raphaelites of the Holland Park circle, it was the painters of the Aesthetic Movement who benefited most, among the artists who exhibited there, from the Grosvenor Gallery's establishment; reciprocally, it was through exhibitions of the second-generation PRB (although Rossetti declined to participate) that it gained its heady early success and its reputation as 'the residence of Aestheticism' and 'the private Palace' of the movement.[50] The international reputation of Edward Burne-Jones in particular was achieved very largely through its exhibitions and support,[51] a Europe-wide fame that was unique for an English painter in the period, and one that in turn reflected back on the Grosvenor itself. Burne-Jones's continental reputation was secured by the showing of two of his paintings at the 1878 Paris Exposition Universelle, a year after he had returned to the public arena at the inaugural Grosvenor exhibition with a display of eight pictures.[52] This first continental exposure was the start of a 'stellar' rise to fame[53] through successive Grosvenor exhibitions, culminating in the presentation of his *King Cophetua and the Beggar Maid* of 1884 at the 1889 Exposition Universelle in Paris.

It is, then, ironic that the pan-European profile of Pre-Raphaelitism itself was, arguably, achieved largely through the mediation of Paris. As Andrzej Szczerski observes, it was from that city, as the recognised centre of the continent's contemporary cultural arena, that most of the information about the movement was obtained by its followers across central and eastern Europe.[54] French criticism positioned Pre-Raphaelite painting as a branch of the Europe-wide Symbolist movement, while the leading Parisian writer on contemporary English art, Robert de La Sizeranne, whose approbation of Burne-Jones's work did much to seal both *King Cophetua*'s reputation and that of the artist in 1889, made much of the perceived common identity, within Pre-Raphaelite circles, of fine and decorative art.[55] Both of these emphases had wide appeal across Europe.

In the context of the present chapter, we may add the Grosvenor Gallery initiative itself to the PRB in support of Szczerski's argument for British art as an influence on the contemporary European art field. For although its early success with exhibitions of second-generation Pre-Raphaelites and other Aesthetic Movement artists did not last beyond the 1880s, the gallery had by then demonstrated the benefits, beyond those specific to its contribution to the British aristocracy's rearguard strategy, of associating contemporary art with the tastes and environment of the social elite, and it was in consequence a business strategy that was quickly adopted by galleries elsewhere. After the Lindsays separated in 1882, Blanche taking her fortune with her, the gallery struggled until its close in 1890, but its mantle was taken up from 1888 by the New Gallery, which opened in nearby Regent Street, under the management of Sir Coutts's assistants, Hallé and Comyns Carr, who took Burne-Jones and other Pre-Raphaelites with them, and gave the former his first-ever retrospective in 1893.[56] The strategy had by then already long reached Paris: when Georges Petit opened his gallery on the rue de Sèze in its fashionable Madeleine district in 1882, the opulence of its premises, its high-ceilinged, top-lit, chandelier-hung, plushly furnished exhibition rooms emulated the Grosvenor and captured the attention not only of Parisian high society, who flocked to its 'International Expositions' mentioned earlier. These judiciously drew on the new European network of fashionable artists, but also of some of the Impressionist circle, such as Monet and Renoir, who were eager to join and abandoned their own group exhibitions, soon after Petit's premises opened, to do so.[57] It had also reached Brussels: two years after Petit's initiative, the exhibiting society Le Cercle des XX was founded in that city with the aim of offering an elite environment, in conscious imitation of the clubs of London, for the viewing of works by a core of Belgian artists, accompanied by a selection from the modern artists whose names were recognised across the capitals of Europe, above all in Paris.[58] Thus was the Grosvenor Gallery initiative, itself partly based on Parisian *cercles*, assimilated to the professionalism of the increasingly gallery- and Secessionist-driven European market – and London's contemporary art field to the Secessionist, liberal-bourgeois network.

Yet the distinctiveness of the Grosvenor initiative in British terms remained, and should be noted. For its social and cultural affiliations were multiple; indeed, beyond those already traced within the aristocracy as well as bohemianism and high finance, the Lindsays' project both registered and furthered that ideology of 'affective relations' that was gaining ground in the cultural field of late Victorian England, in close relation with the adversarial spirit of those motley movements opposed to the dominant *mores* of the middle classes. The aristocracy and its clans were defined by their genealogies and their familial, kinship networks, and fostered values (as well as protocols and snobberies) for which those affective relations counted more than – and were implicitly opposed to – those entrepreneurial conventions and priorities imposed by capitalist economic relations; and the Grosvenor's combination of social status and 'bohemian aura' underwrote them.[59]

BOHEMIAN SOCIALITIES AND THEIR DIFFERENTIALS

Despite the innovations and cachet of the Grosvenor Gallery, the difference between the scattered, multifarious London contemporary art market and the narrow focus and hierarchy of that of Paris was crucial; even the members of a new cohort of London galleries dealing in contemporary art that opened around the turn of the twentieth century, including the Carfax Gallery (1899) and the Leicester Galleries (1903), blended their displays of modern art, British or French, with those of works by earlier generations such as the Barbizon group, as well as Old Masters and even antiquities.[60] Perhaps the key difference between these markets, though, was the almost complete absence in London, before the First World War, of that category of art dealer who was committed primarily, even exclusively, to buying, promoting and selling the work of particular new and unknown artists in whose work they believed – a category that, by contrast, has attained something of a mythic status in the history of the Paris art market. As I noted earlier, there was a variety of reasons for which a small clutch of Parisian dealers pursued this strategy in the late nineteenth and early twentieth centuries: for Durand-Ruel, Vollard, Le Barc, Kahnweiler and Weill, to name the most celebrated of these, dealing was a matter not only of aesthetic discernment but also (even rather) of acute and adventurous entrepreneurship, of the love of a gamble, the enjoyment of patronage, the ties of friendship and – not least – a consequence of the spaces left for each of these in a fairly conservative and hierarchised market. Their risk-taking was underwritten, moreover, by two factors particular to Paris: first, the existence of a district of the city, Montmartre, with its low-rent studios and art-materials suppliers who doubled as sales outlets for new paintings in lieu of payment by their artists. Second, that small but growing number of *dénicheurs* in the Paris market – those collectors of contemporary art with a social investment in artistic bargain-hunting and an enjoyment at once of the risks this entailed, the identification with artistic creativity and proximity to bohemian culture it offered, and the opportunities it provided for financial investment in it for winkling out or 'déniching' a bargain.[61]

In the more fluid, less specialised conditions of the London contemporary art market, where artists were obliged to negotiate a plurality of exhibiting opportunities, and dealers (both those already established and the increasing number of newcomers) to seize every opportunity to show and sell in whatever venue they could, there was neither much incentive for nor reward from such promotional exclusivity or speculative risk-taking.[62] Before 1914 only the Chenil Gallery pursued such a policy – and it did so on terms that, while comparable with these Parisian innovators, were indicative of the cultural differences between the contemporary art fields of the two cities. Established in 1905 on the King's Road in Chelsea, the Chenil had a studio with an etching press that was used by its artists, and its founder, Jack Knewstub, 'carried on the combined businesses of art dealer, artist's colour-man and picture-frame maker'.[63] Both in this hybrid character and in Knewstub's background – his father had been an assistant to Rossetti and his two sisters were married to established artists[64] – the Chenil was closer to the artists' side of the artist–dealer relationship than to that of the Bond Street galleries (following in this the Grosvenor Gallery vis-à-vis the Royal Academy in the previous generation), being involved in the making of art as well as in the selling of it. The Chenil, moreover, supported artists who 'called on the paradigm of bohemia', in the apt phrase of Anne Helmreich and Ysanne Holt[65] – again like the Grosvenor, only now more radically – setting itself in tacit distinction from (if not opposition to) Bond Street galleries in material and ideological, as well as entrepreneurial, terms. As regards the first of these, its premises were unostentatious in décor, cramped in size and thus differed sharply from the 'pompous' ambience of establishments such as Goupil's, with its 'polished wood and walls lined with crimson damask', as William Roberts described it (in an echo of the response to the Grosvenor a generation earlier).[66] In this respect, it was also both like and unlike the above Parisian *dénicheur* dealers. For while Chelsea's informality and bohemianism suggest (and suggested to contemporaries) an equivalence to Montmartre,[67] the character of this district and the connotations of its name were entirely different: not those of pleasure and crime, villainy and social or aesthetic illegitimacy, but of an anti-bourgeois enclave, home as much to the aristocracy as to aesthetes. Once described as a 'village of palaces', by the late nineteenth century it had become 'a neighbourhood associated with small traders and as yet untouched by... new commercial and residential developments'.[68] Chelsea was always a popular location for the wealthy, artists as much as others, and its particular mix of class and culture gave its bohemianism that genteel English accent that, as we have seen, was a world away from that of La Butte.[69]

As regards the Chenil's ideology, Helmreich and Holt note that the gallery 'signified an identity specific to the Chelsea locality, an alternative social and cultural disposition of informal sociability'.[70] Like the Grosvenor a generation earlier, but without any of its aristocratic affiliations, and more explicitly bohemian in character, it was grounded not so much in professionalism (either that of social status or technical experimentalism) as in affective relations. Partly contributory to this was Knewstub's selecting, for his stable of artists, from the district's local population, which situated the gallery as much in that affective community as in the entrepreneurialism of the art market; but more constitutive of it was the star billing he gave to Augustus John, whose works were permanently on display – William Roberts observed that so dominant was John's presence at the Chenil that it appeared to be run chiefly for his benefit.[71] For as we shall see in the next chapter, John was not only the rising star of English painting at the turn of the new century, but a key figure in the determination of the character of the London formation of progressive artists in its first decade, for reasons that should be explored.

Before exploring them, however, we should note that in this formation there were social as well as financial and art-educational factors that at once drew London's anti-academic artists into the Secessionist network and yet distinguished their sociality from that of Paris. The café culture of the latter city was already notorious long before the end of the nineteenth century, not only for its commercial entertainment attractions but also for its supportive closeness to the milieux of the literary and artistic cenacles of the nascent avant-gardes, with many of the individual cafés' names associated with a specific 'ism', and the whole a network-within-a-network providing succour of an intellectual as well as material kind. It was almost as integral to the nourishment and character of these avant-gardes as were the *petites revues* and the *académies libres*.[72] London had no equivalent: as Cecily Mackworth notes, when Mallarmé came to meet Swinburne and other London literati in 1875, he was frustrated that he was unable to locate them. Mackworth speculates that the Parisian poet 'never quite understood that… one could not simply drop into a certain café or restaurant and be sure of finding a few poets who would tell one where the others were to be found… in London, there were few places of this sort'. The Café Royal was not yet, in 1875, a fashionable gathering place; the Cheshire Cheese had a long past but little vitality even among the small group of poets whose Rhymers' Club met there in the 1890s; pubs were still primarily working-class establishments. 'One needed introductions to the private houses where men of letters gathered', Mackworth observes, 'and even there, things were changing, the old circles breaking up.'[73] Little changed before the turn of the century, however; the poet Arthur Symons, who was the leading spokesperson for French poetry in London, observed in 1899 that when his French friends asked him, on their arrival in London, 'Where is your Montmartre, where is your Quartier Latin?', he would have to reply

> 'We have none'… because there is no instinct in the Englishman to be companionable in public. Occasions are lacking… for the café is responsible for a good part of the Bohemianism of Paris, and we have no cafés…

> nothing in Cafés Royaux and Monicos and the like can have the sort of meaning for young men in London that the cafés have long had, and still have, in Paris.[74]

The Café Royal is, indeed, a case in point, for its steady ascent to a *fin-de-siècle* notoriety unparalleled among the city's fashionable cafés – one that attracted tourists and hangers-on in numbers and of a kind that any true bohemian would seek to avoid – underlines not only the lack of a Parisian type of bohemian sociality in London, but also the specific character of that of London.[75] Its foundation (in 1865, by a Frenchman) in emulation of Parisian cafés condemned it, ironically, to such a subaltern status. Initially patronised by, among writers and artists, only homesick Parisians such as, in the early 1870s, Paul Verlaine and Arthur Rimbaud, and later Gustave Doré, Théophile Steinlen and Jean-Louis Forain, the bohemian reputation of that city on whose gilded reflection it traded[76] eventually brought to the Café Royal not only the showiest artistic performers and their entourages – Whistler was the first, and was soon followed by Oscar Wilde – but, beyond these cliques, a 'multitude of philistines and would-be artists who came… only to sit and stare'[77] at such celebrities. In addition, beyond these in their turn, the Café attracted a variety of non-artistic coteries, including both those for whom admission to the flourishing roster of 'gentlemen's clubs' was not an option because of their lack of that status, and those for whom it was but one of several options allowed by it. Examples of the first were 'bookies, boxers, con-tricksters, moneylenders, tipsters, dashing young subalterns [and] burlesque showgirls', who 'wrote off Whistler, Wilde and company as "the art crowd"', as well as 'a spirited crowd of journalists from papers [that were] sometimes ephemeral, often scandalous, but always colourful'. An example of the second was, as Guy Deghy and Keith Waterhouse themselves colourfully describe them, 'the biggest flock of black sheep ever assembled from the proud folds of Eton, Harrow, Sandhurst and Osborne – the "Boy-Ohs"… described in the newspapers as "sturdy, strapping, ruddy-faced young men, exceedingly well-fed to look at, exceedingly well-groomed and faultless in point of varnished boots and well-fitting coats"'. Within this coterie was another, in that most of its members also belonged to the Pelican Club, which 'embodied the essence of that drinkin', fightin' and bettin' fraternity'.[78] They were the kind of 'young men about town [who] would decide on the spin of a coin whether to go to a music hall or to spend the evening in the Café Royal',[79] each being as entertaining as the other.

The variety and number of its habitués, the reputed glamour of the Café Royal's ambience and its celebrity status indicate that bohemian sociality in London was in part shaped by the flourishing, in the late Victorian and Edwardian periods, of a consumerism that assimilated and commodified its qualities and signifiers, turning bohemia into spectacle and bohemianism into lifestyle. But that sociality was also a register of two other factors, which should be noted here alongside this dynamic. The first was the already existing model of a sociality shaped crucially by the shifting class relations and tensions between and within the upper middle class and the aristocracy, and exemplified by the proliferation and flourishing of broad and formally constituted collectivities, such as those of the 'gentlemen's clubs' just mentioned, the salons of 'Society' discussed earlier and semi-secret societies such as the Apostles, made up of self-selected elites.[80] Following this model, London's bohemian cultural circles were likewise broad, inclusive and often overlapping, collectivities based not on a shared aesthetic doctrine but on commonalities of class, friendship, cultural preferences and political allegiance. Examples from after the turn of the century included the South Lodge, the Kensington circle of Ford Madox Ford, editor of *The English Review,* and his companion, the feminist novelist Violet Hunt; the 'Tuesdays' of critic and poet T.E. Hulme; and the 'Saturdays' of the Fitzroy Street Group of painters led unofficially by Walter Sickert. In each case, the participants were markedly motley, as their chroniclers have recorded. 'At Violet Hunt's parties you met… every intelligent person in Edwardian London worth meeting', recalled Edgar Jepson, one of the regulars of the South Lodge gatherings.[81] 'Everyone at one time or another attended Hulme's Tuesday evenings', observed literary historian Peter Brooker, noting poets Rupert Brooke, Ezra Pound and F.S. Flint, artists Sickert, Wyndham Lewis and C.R.W. Nevinson, among philosophers, literary agents and a diplomat – a roster of which Brooker remarks: 'We're put in mind of Nick Carraway's list of guests at the magnificent parties held by F. Scott Fitzgerald's Jay Gatsby.'[82] Of the Fitzroy Street Group, immediate precursor of the now better-known Camden Town Group, its historian Wendy Baron notes that by the end of 1910 '[e]very progressive artist in London came, at least sometimes, to its Saturday Afternoons. The gatherings were composed of a cat's cradle of strands based on friendship and professional relations.'[83]

The other factor shaping bohemian sociality in London was that of the absence until shortly before the First World War of the form of sociality that, as noted in the last chapter, was exemplified by the avant-garde formation in Paris, whose alternative professionalism replaced the criteria of affective relations – variously defined – with those more instrumental to advancement in the techniques of their respective cultural practices, and thus to renown within the fields of these. Cultural historians Anthony Glinoer and Vincent Laisney have summarised this shift within the Parisian literary field as one from 'natural' groupings to 'artificial' ones.[84] Once London's progressive artists began to feel, for reasons to be explored, the gravitational pull after around 1910 of the new 'sun' of the Parisian avant-garde and its alternative mode of *technie*-driven artistic professionalism, they too underwent a similar shift; but until then, awareness of new art in Paris was assimilated to the protocols of a sociality that was grounded as much in the values of affective community as in those of aesthetic innovation. The epitome of this ambivalence was the Bloomsbury group; in a phrase that I have used before, this was both more than an avant-garde, and less than one. We have explored in an earlier chapter the character of Bloomsbury's attachment to sociability and of its friendship network, which enabled the first; we shall assess the manner, the degree and the artistic consequences of the second – its engagement with Parisian alternative professionalism – in the next.

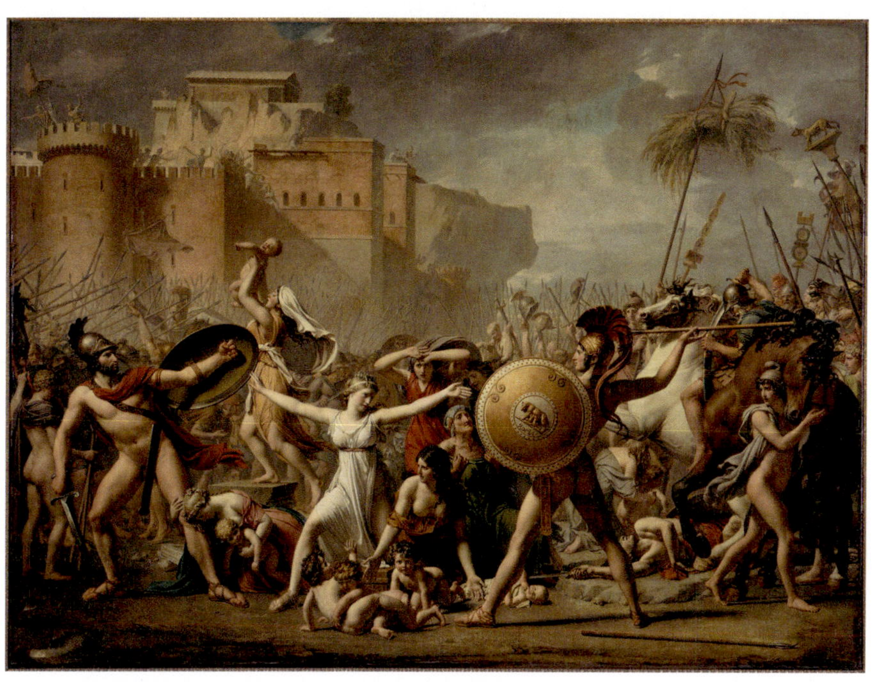

PL. 1 Jacques-Louis David, *Les Sabines* (*The Intervention of the Sabine Women*), 1799. Oil on canvas, 385 × 522 cm. Musée du Louvre, Paris

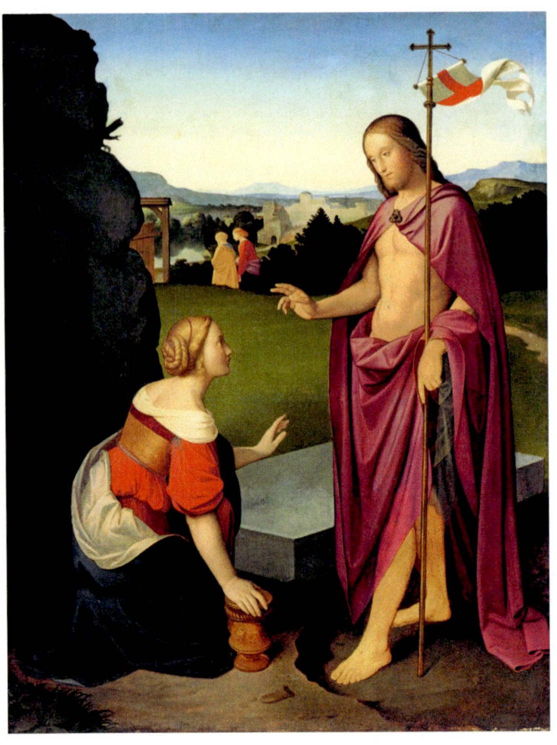

PL. 2 Johann Friedrich Overbeck, *Ostermorgen* (*Easter Morning*), 1818. Oil on canvas, 131 × 102 cm. Kunstpalast, Düsseldorf

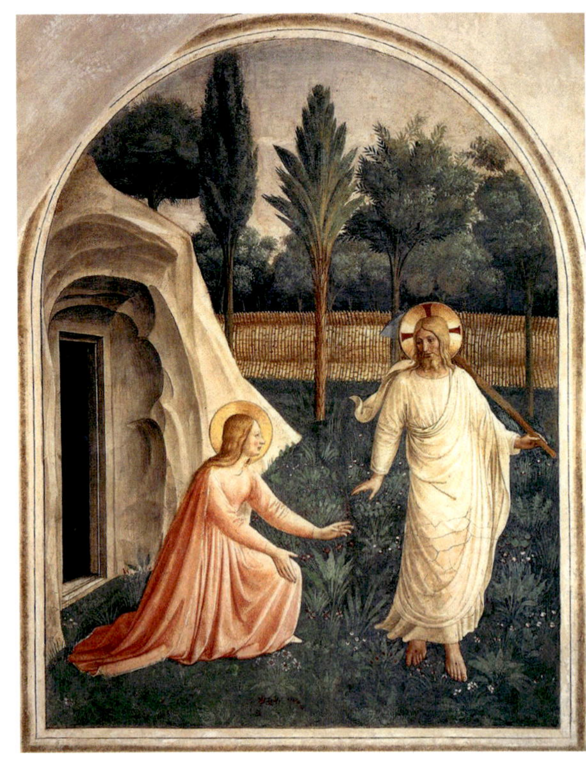

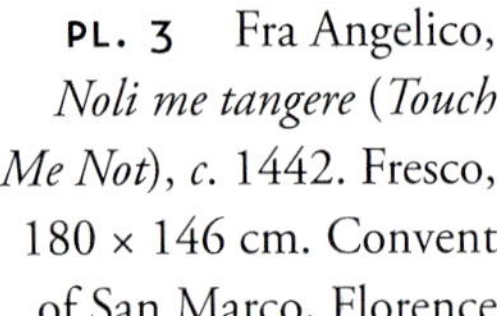

PL. 3 Fra Angelico, *Noli me tangere* (*Touch Me Not*), *c.* 1442. Fresco, 180 × 146 cm. Convent of San Marco, Florence

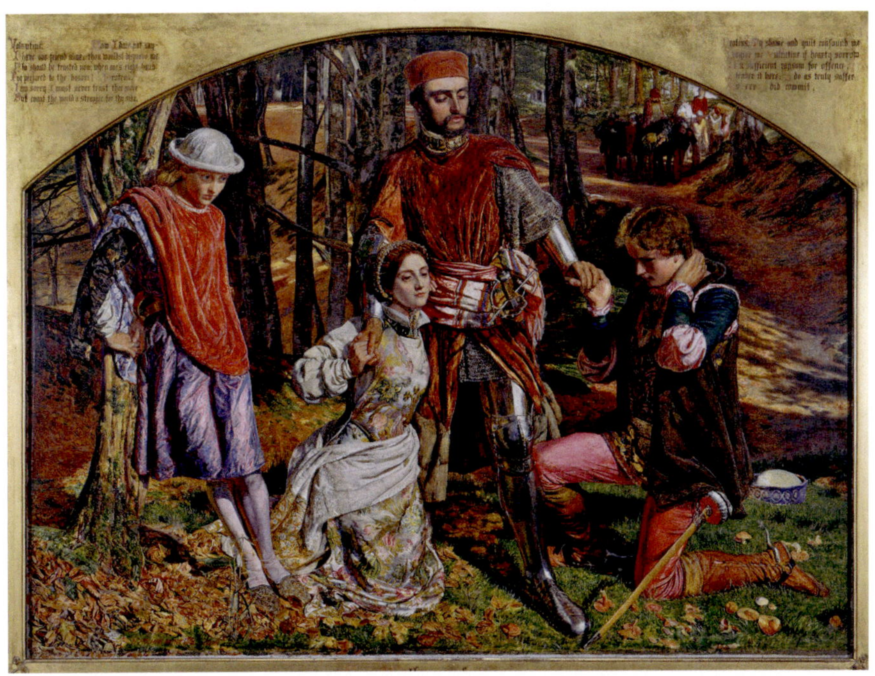

PL. 4 William Holman Hunt, *Valentine Rescuing Sylvia from Proteus*, 1851. Oil on canvas, 100.2 × 133.4 cm. Birmingham Museum and Art Gallery

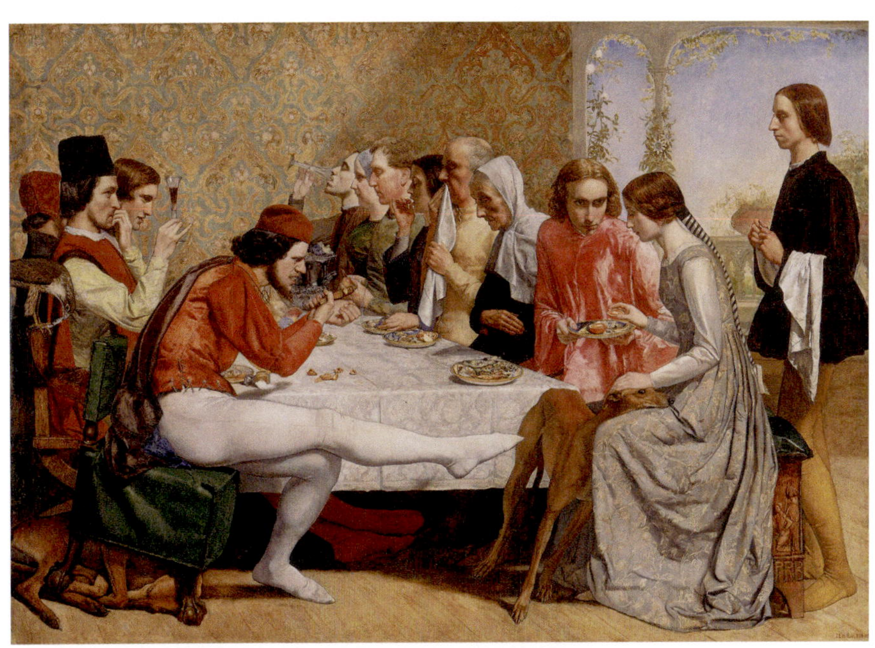

PL. 5 John Everett Millais, *Lorenzo and Isabella*, 1848–49. Oil on canvas, 103 × 142.8 cm. Walker Art Gallery, Liverpool

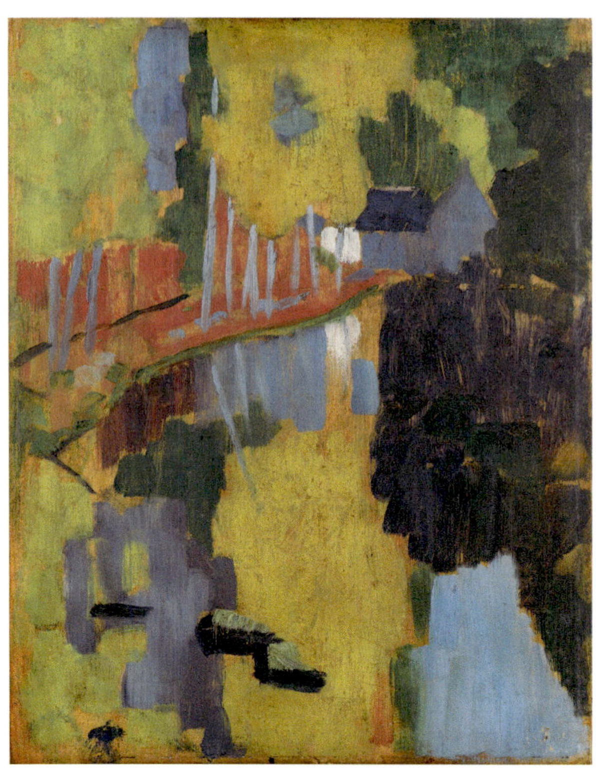

PL. 6 Paul Sérusier, *Le Talisman (Paysage au Bois d'Amour)* (*The Talisman [Landscape in the Bois d'Amour]*), 1888. Oil on board, 27 × 22 cm. Musée d'Orsay, Paris

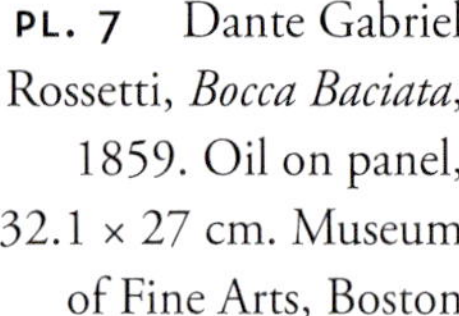

PL. 7 Dante Gabriel Rossetti, *Bocca Baciata*, 1859. Oil on panel, 32.1 × 27 cm. Museum of Fine Arts, Boston

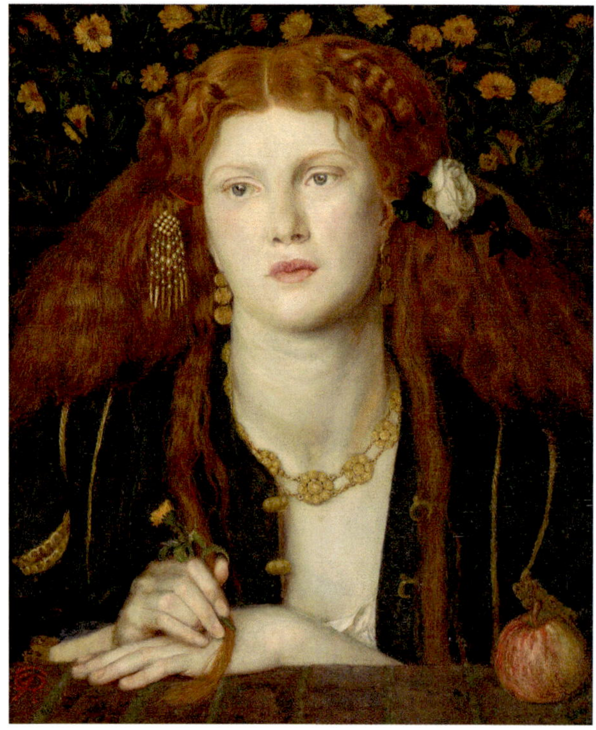

LE ROY SAINT-AUBERT

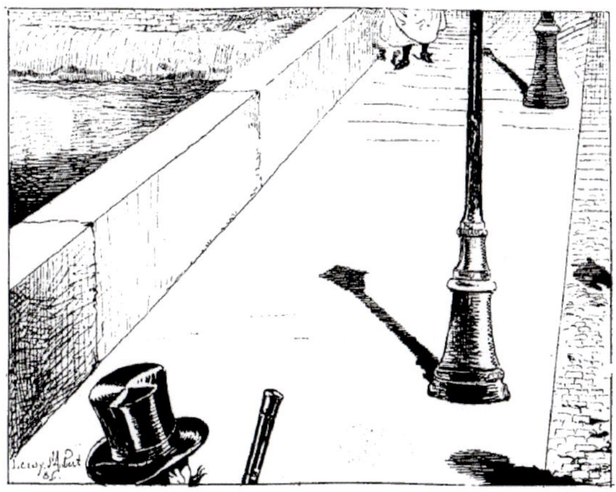

Un rendez-vous au pont Royal.

PL. 8 Leroy Saint-Aubert, *Rendez-vous au Pont Royal*, 1886. Photo-relief illustration for *Catalogue illustré de l'exposition des arts incohérents*, Paris: E. Bernard et Cie, 1886

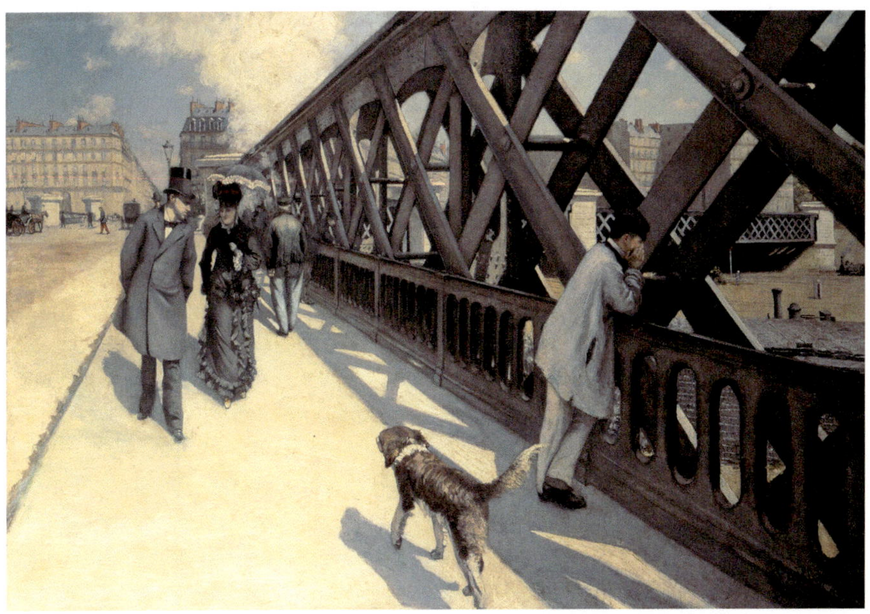

PL. 9 Gustave Caillebotte, *Le Pont de L'Europe*, 1876. Oil on canvas, 125 × 181 cm. Musée du Petit Palais, Geneva

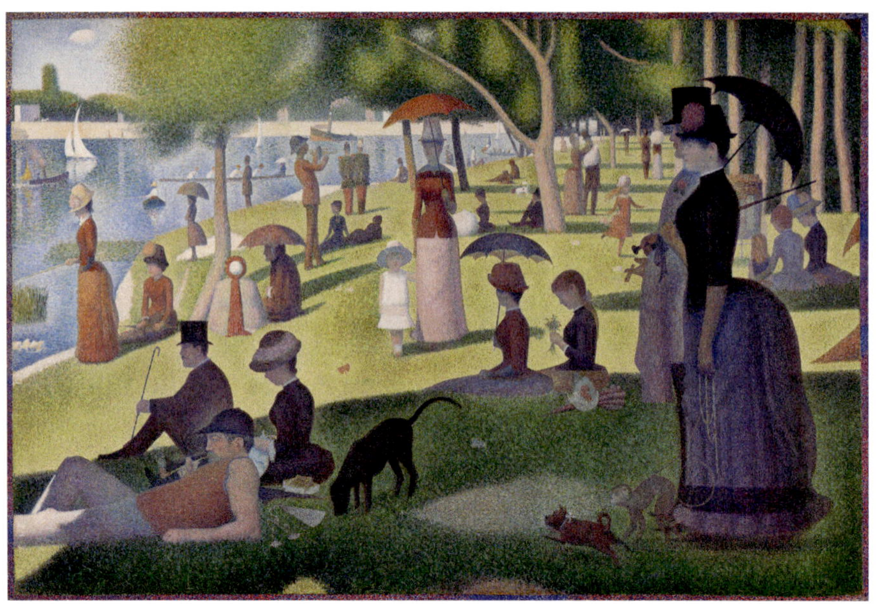

PL. 10 Georges Seurat, *Un Dimanche après-midi à l'île de la Grande Jatte* (*A Sunday Afternoon on the Island of La Grande Jatte*), 1884–86. Oil on canvas, 207.6 × 308 cm. Art Institute of Chicago

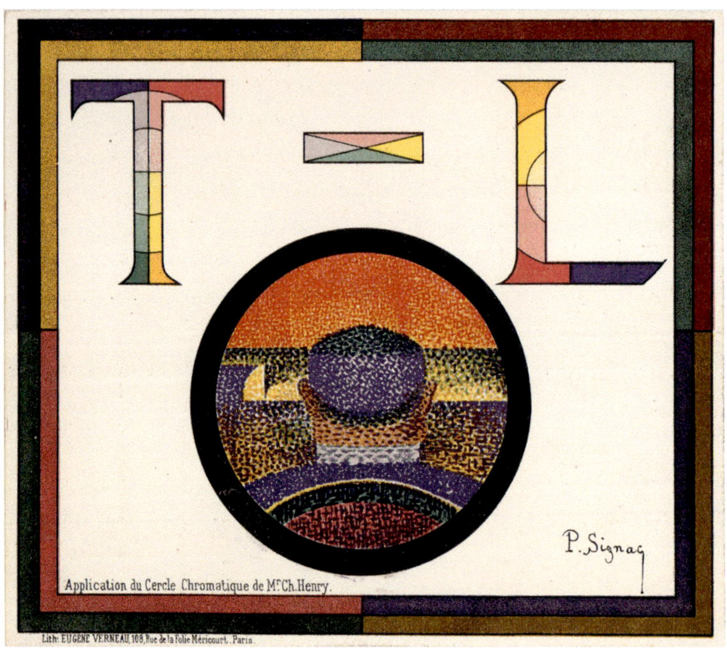

PL. 11 Paul Signac, *Application du cercle chromatique de M. Ch. Henry* (*Application of Charles Henry's Chromatic Circle*), 1888. Colour lithograph on card, 16 × 18.5 cm. Zimmerli Art Museum, Rutgers University, New Brunswick

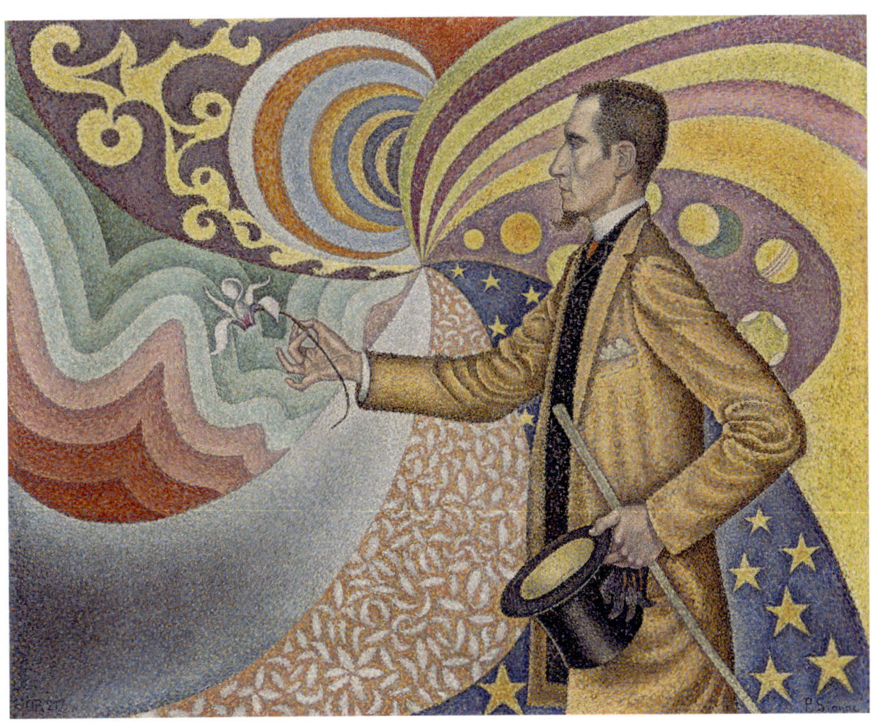

PL. 12 Paul Signac, *Opus 217. Sur l'Émail d'un fond rythmique de mesures et d'angles, de tons et de teintes, portrait de M. Félix Fénéon en 1890* (*Opus 217. Against the Enamel of a Rhythmic Background of Beats and Angles, Tones and Tints, Portrait of M. Félix Fénéon in 1890*), 1890. Oil on canvas, 74 × 92 cm. Museum of Modern Art, New York

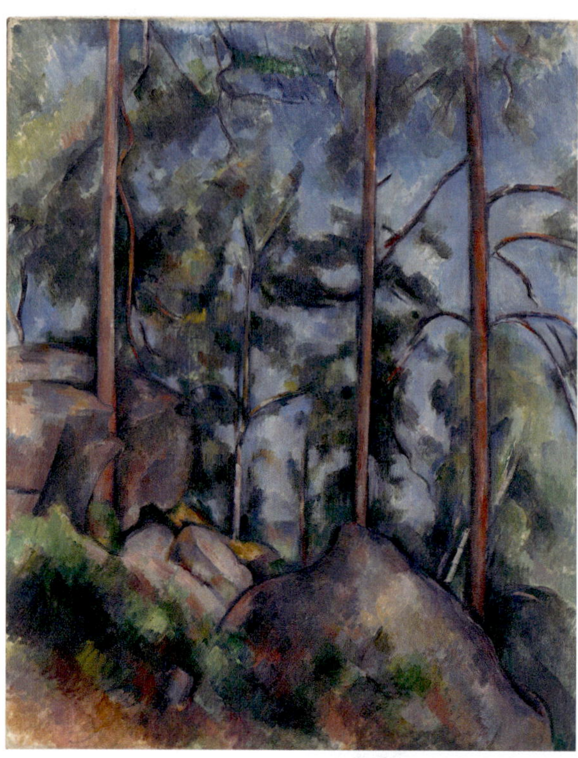

PL. 13 Paul Cézanne, *Pins et rochers (Fontainebleau?)* (*Pines and Rocks [Fontainebleau?]*), *c.* 1897. Oil on canvas, 81.3 × 65.4 cm. Museum of Modern Art, New York

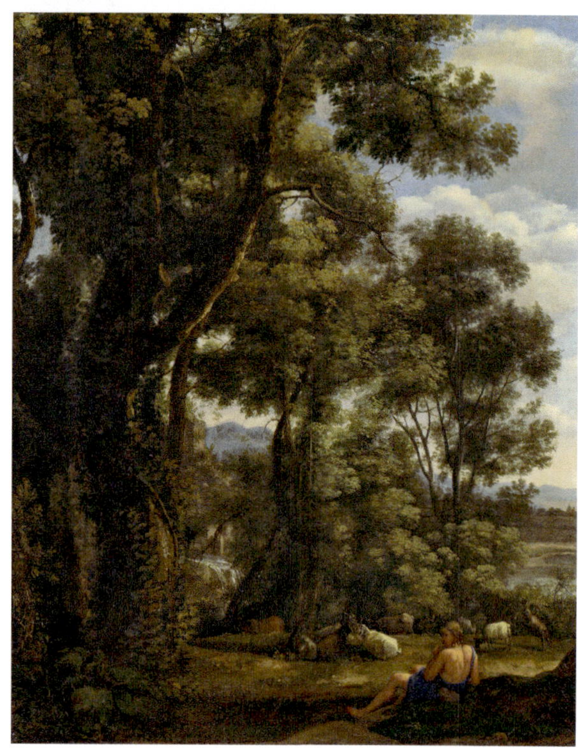

PL. 14 Claude Lorrain, *Paysage avec chevrier et chèvres* (*Landscape with Goatherd and Goats*), 1636–37. Oil on canvas, 52 × 42 cm. National Gallery, London

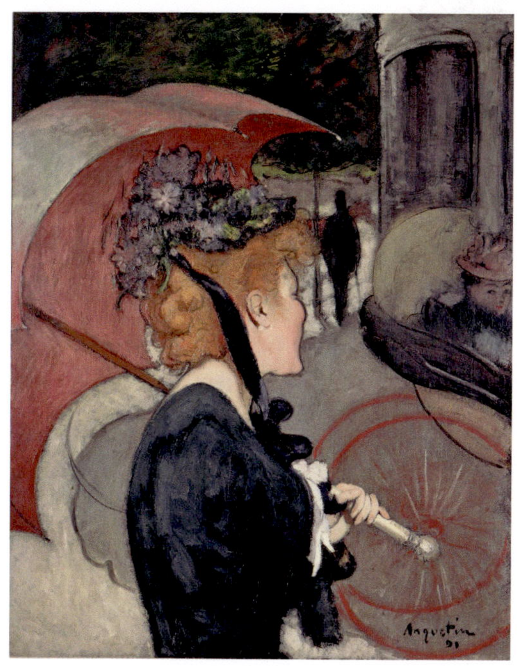

PL. 15 Louis Anquetin, *Femme avec parapluie* (*Woman with Umbrella*), 1891. Oil on canvas, 90.8 × 73.7 cm. Private collection

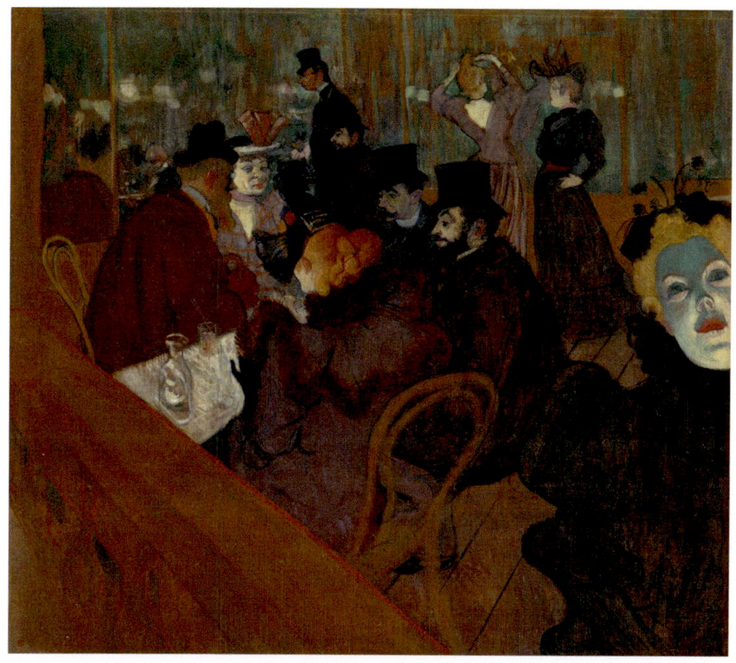

PL. 16 Henri de Toulouse-Lautrec, *Au Moulin Rouge* (*At the Moulin Rouge*), 1892–95. Oil on canvas, 123 × 142 cm. Art Institute of Chicago

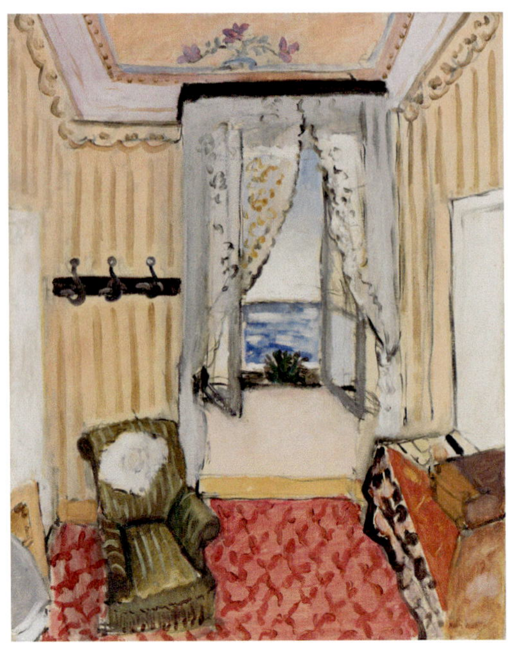

PL. 17 Henri Matisse, *La Fenêtre ouverte (Ma Chambre à l'Hôtel Beau-Rivage)* (*The Open Window [My Room at the Hotel Beau-Rivage]*), 1917–18. Oil on canvas, 73 × 61 cm. Philadelphia Museum of Art

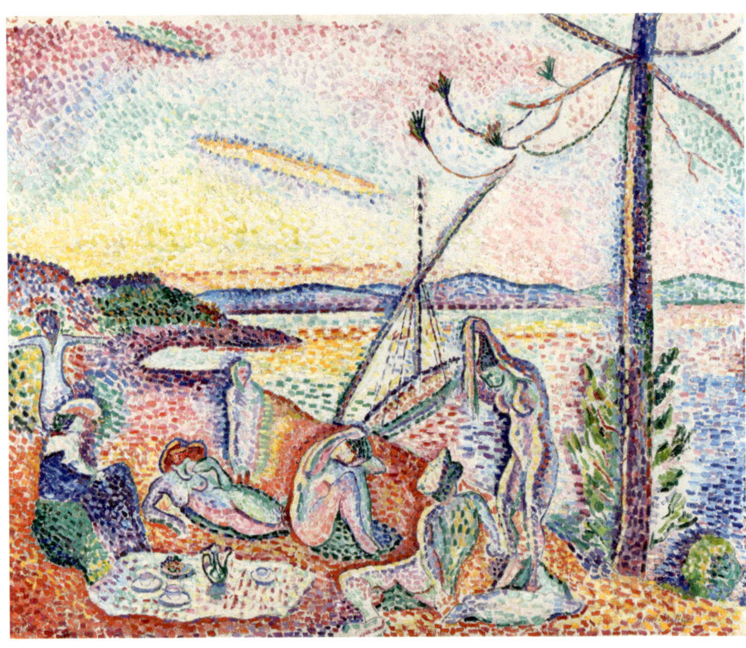

PL. 18 Henri Matisse, *Luxe, calme et volupté* (*Luxury, Calm and Delight*), 1904. Oil on canvas, 98.5 × 118.5 cm. Musée d'Orsay, Paris

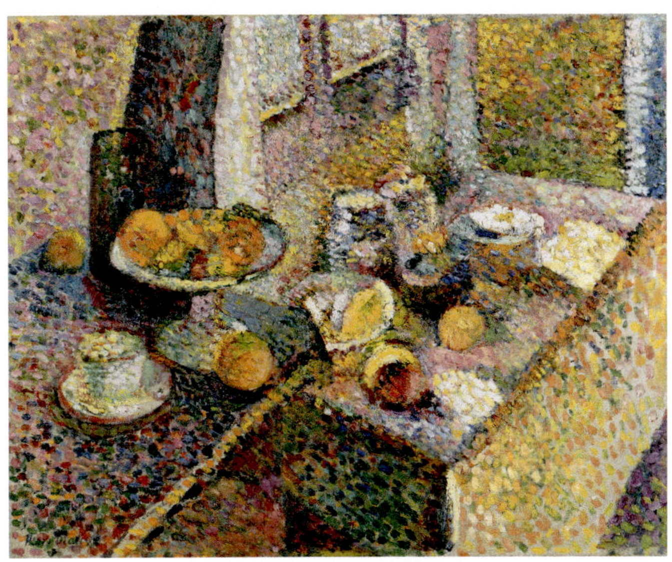

PL. 19 Henri Matisse, *Nature morte: buffet et table* (*Still Life: Buffet and Table*), 1899. Oil on canvas, 67.5 × 82.5 cm. Kunsthaus Zürich

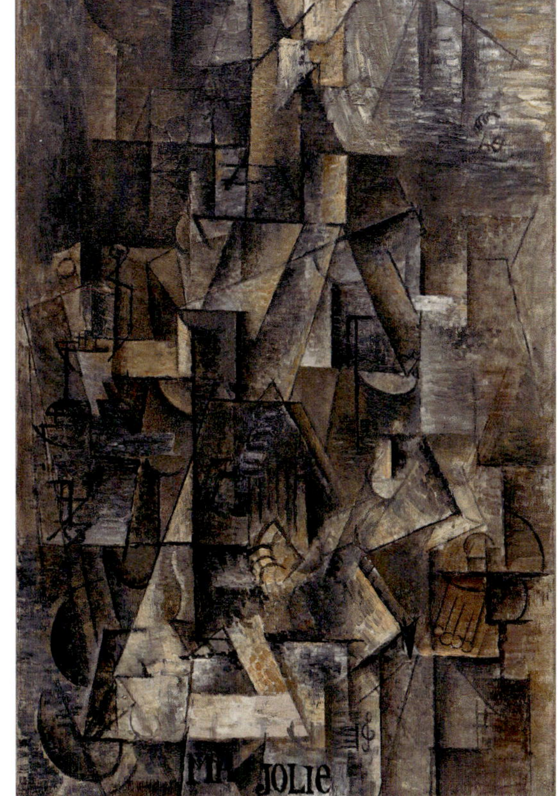

PL. 20 Pablo Picasso, *Ma Jolie* (*My Pretty [Woman]*), 1911–12. Oil on canvas, 100 × 64 cm. Museum of Modern Art, New York

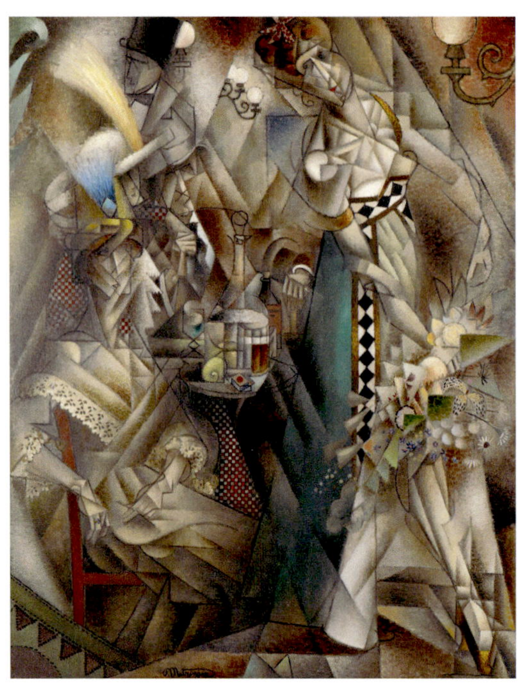

PL. 21 Jean Metzinger, *Danseuse au café* (*Dancer in a Café*), 1912. Oil on canvas, 146.1 × 114.3 cm. Albright-Knox Art Gallery, Buffalo

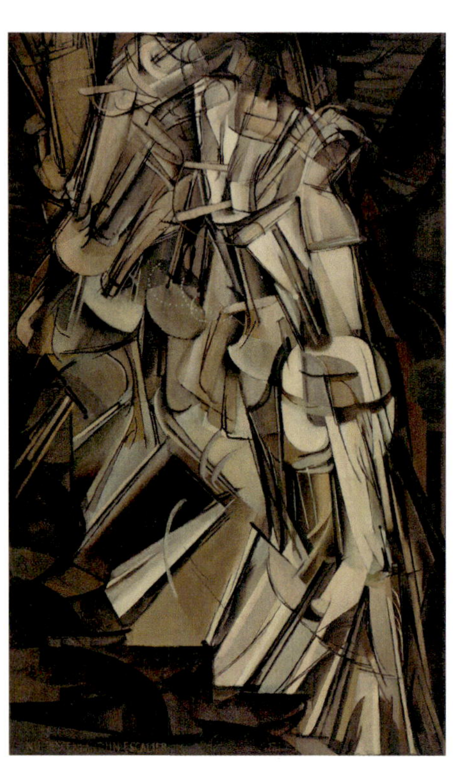

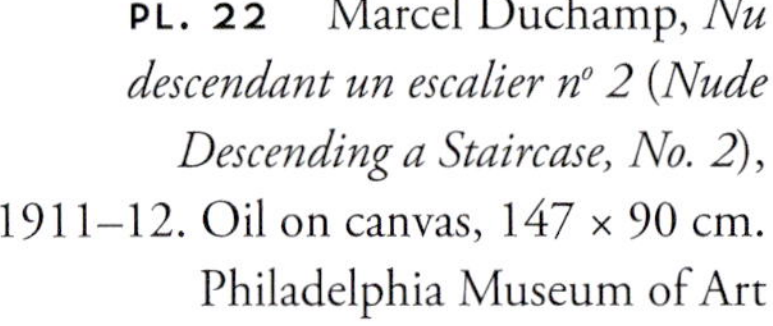

PL. 22 Marcel Duchamp, *Nu descendant un escalier nº 2* (*Nude Descending a Staircase, No. 2*), 1911–12. Oil on canvas, 147 × 90 cm. Philadelphia Museum of Art

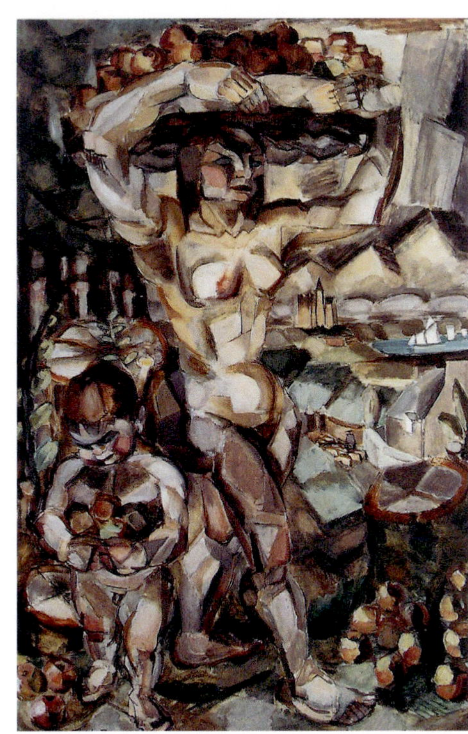

PL. 23 Henri Le Fauconnier, *L'Abondance* (*Abundance*), 1910–11. Oil on canvas, 191 × 123 cm. Kunstmuseum, The Hague

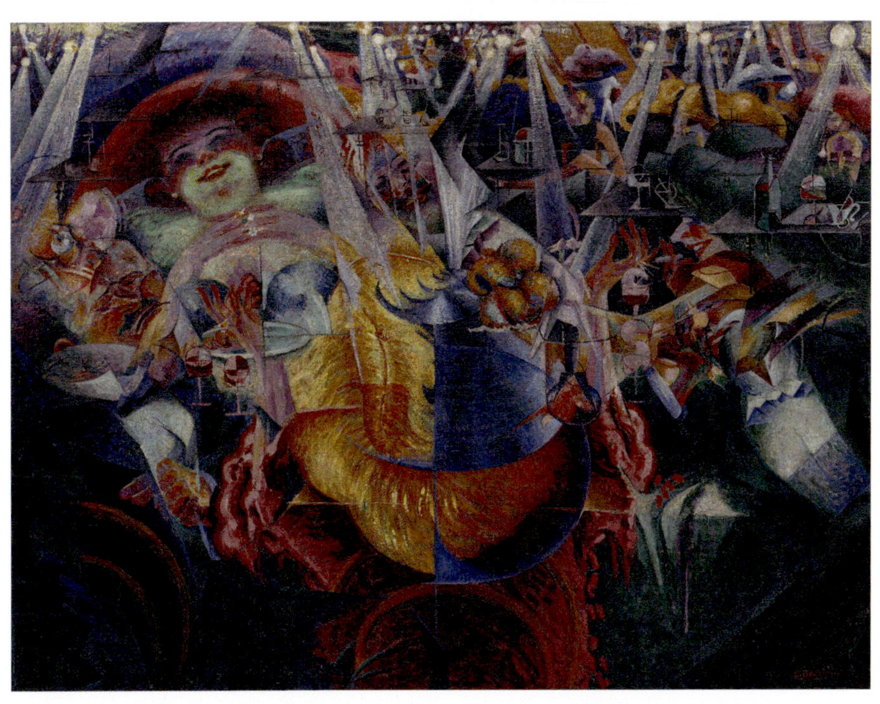

PL. 24 Umberto Boccioni, *La Risata* (*The Laugh*), 1911. Oil on canvas, 110.2 × 145.4 cm. Museum of Modern Art, New York

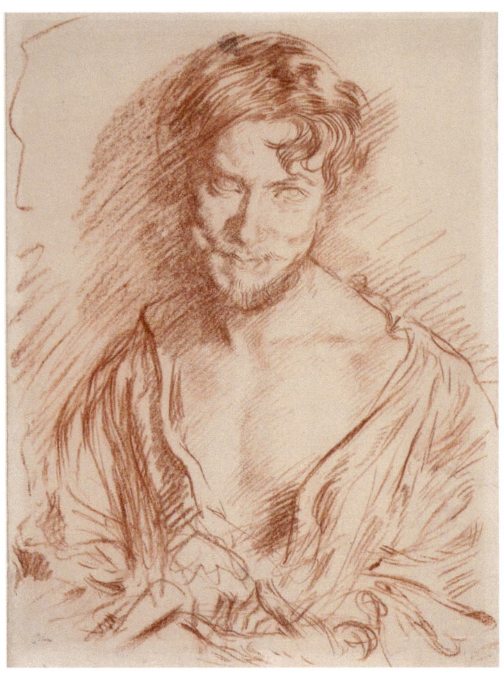

PL. 25 Augustus John, *Self-Portrait, c.* 1898–1900. Red chalk on paper, 37.2 × 24.8 cm. Yale Center for British Art, New Haven

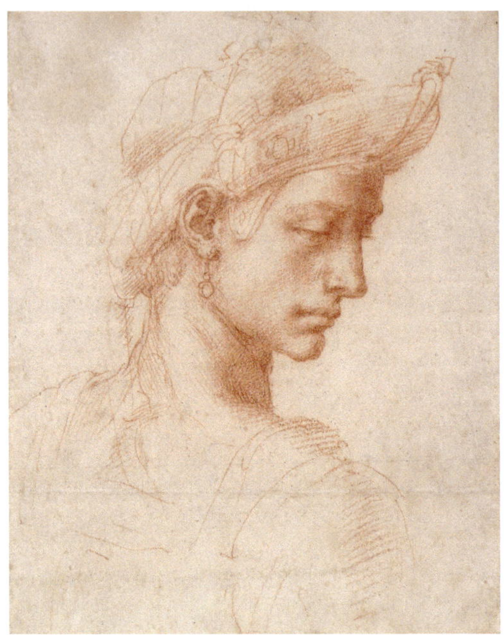

PL. 26 Michelangelo Buonarroti, *Profile with Oriental Headdress*, 1520–25. Red chalk on paper, 20.5 × 16.5 cm. Ashmolean Museum, Oxford

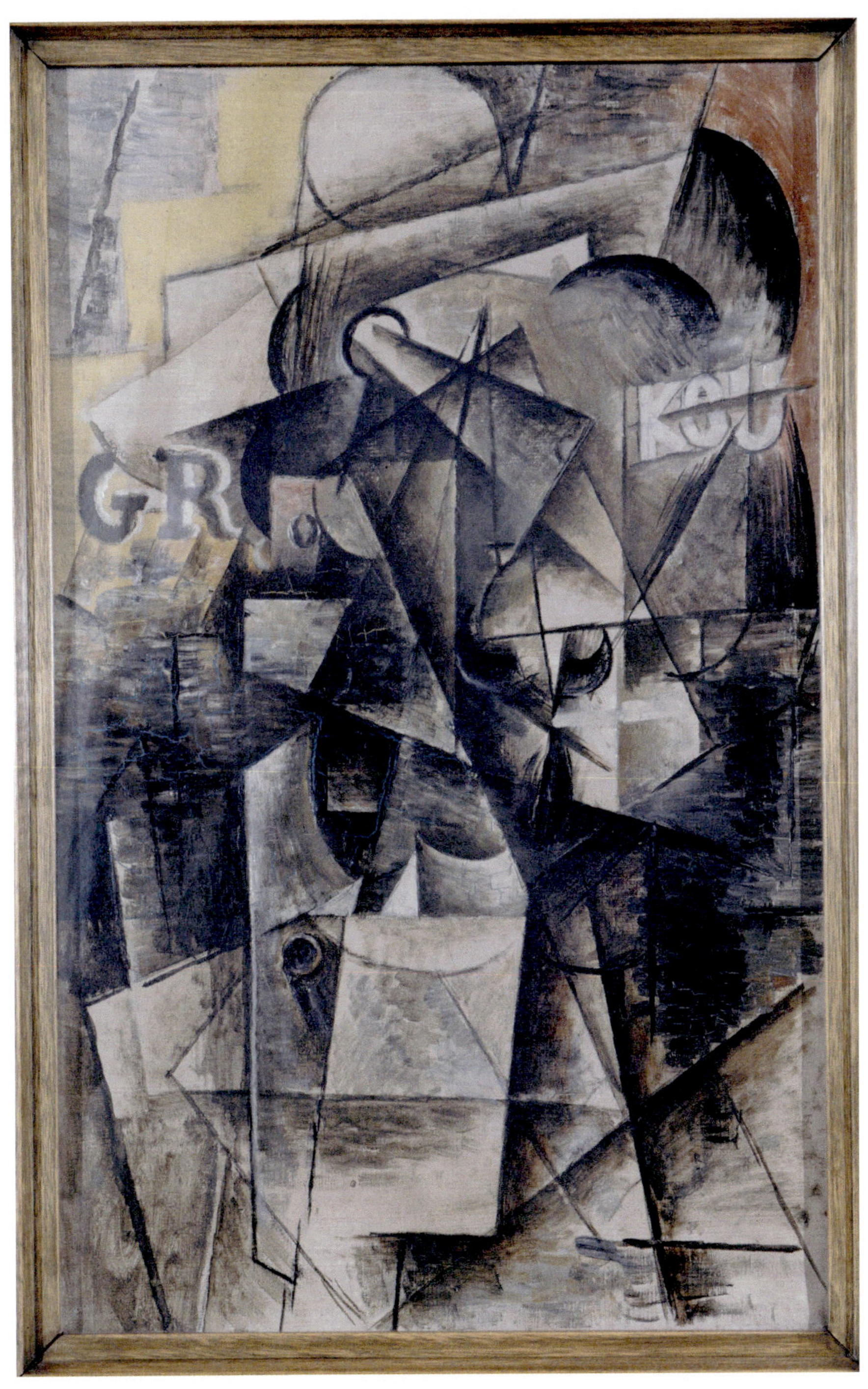

PL. 27 Pablo Picasso, *Tête d'homme* (*Head of a Man*), 1912. Oil on canvas, 61 × 38 cm. Musée d'Art Moderne de la Ville de Paris

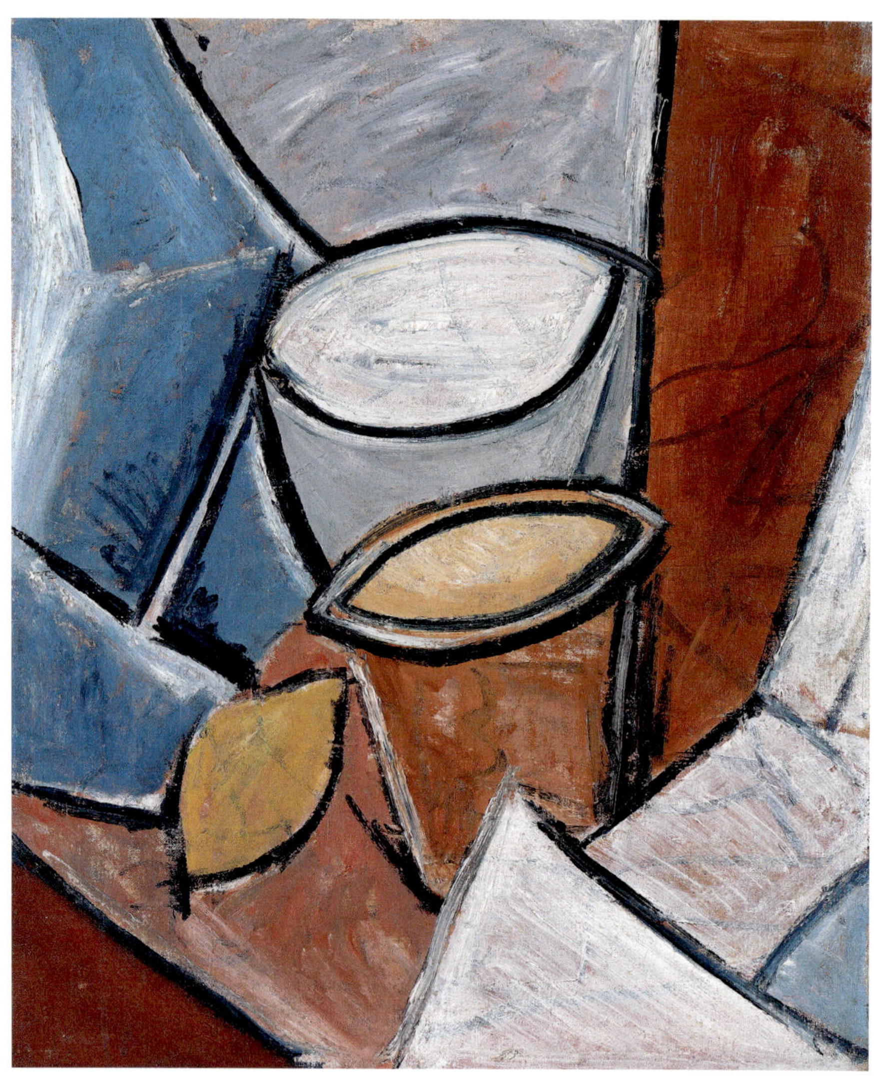

PL. 28 Pablo Picasso, *Pots et citron* (*Jars and Lemon*), 1907. Oil on canvas, 55 × 46 cm. Albertina Museum, Vienna. Rita and Herbert Batliner Collection

8

LONDON: AMATEURISM, PROFESSIONALISM AND FRIENDSHIP

AUGUSTUS JOHN: BOHEMIANISM, THE SLADE AND ANTI-PROFESSIONALISM

Augustus John was not only the rising star of British painting at the turn of the new century, but a key figure in the determination of the character of the London formation of progressive artists before the First World War. The first reason for this was that his reputation, then as now, was grounded more in bohemianism than in artistic originality.[1] The precocity and accomplishment of his skill as a draughtsman were striking and quickly notorious, but rather than serving as the foundation for a personally expressive, let alone innovative, graphic and painterly style, they led instead to the reinforcement of traditional qualities, and to a measuring of his 'genius', both by himself and by contemporary critics, against the standard of the Old Masters (pls 25 and 26). Underwritten and nurtured, as we shall see, by the character of the teaching of the Slade, where John was seen as the outstanding student of his generation, this in turn underwrote a *fin-de-siècle* bohemianism for which his own physical attributes suited him. Charismatically handsome, sartorially louche, sexually voracious, swaggering yet shy in demeanour, John performed the social identity of a modern bohemian artistic prodigy with a conviction that was not only infectious but, further, set the terms in which such a figure signified in popular London culture of the time – as is evident from another item in a 1917 revue to which I have already referred. The *Chelsea Matinée* was brought to a close with 'the John Beauty Chorus' singing in praise of the artist, in terms that had little to do with his graphic precocity itself, and everything to do with his bohemian renown:

> John! John!
> How he's got on!
> He owes it, he knows it, to me!
> Brass earrings I wear,
> And I don't do my hair,
> And my feet are as bare as can be;
> When I walk down the street,
> All the people I meet
> They stare at the things I have on!
> When Battersea-Parking
> You'll hear folks remarking
> 'There goes an Augustus John!'[2]

The second reason was that, in the absence of that infrastructure for a collective artistic pursuit of innovation that I have traced in Paris – the material and discursive supports for an alternative professionalism, in short – John appears to have had little sense of *how*, in technical terms, his unrivalled artistic gifts might be put to use, and given purpose and (modernist) direction. That engagement with *technie* that, as I have argued, characterised the Parisian avant-garde was so completely missing from his awareness of the contemporary cultural environment that he appears to have been bewildered as to what, or how, to paint.[3] Indeed, the very idea of 'professionalism' was anathema to him: writing in 1903 about an exhibition he shared with his sister Gwen, he declared to William Rothenstein: 'Gwen so rarely brings herself to paint! We others are always in danger of becoming professional and to detect myself red-handed in the very act of professional industry is a humiliating experience!'[4] Far more appealing than such application was the alternative of relying on 'genius' alone: 'I've been damnably lazy this summer, but am happily unrepentant', he wrote again to Rothenstein, three years later:

> I fancy idleness ends by bearing [more] rare fruit than industry. I started by being industrious and lost all self-respect – but by now have recovered

> some dignity and comfort by dint of listening to the most private intimations of the Soul and contemning all busy-body thoughts that come buzzing and fussing and messing in one's brain.[5]

This last remark is telling beyond its immediate context as regards John's behaviour both as an artist and as a man, indeed, because it implicitly references the direction he took in his particular resistance to all that 'professional industry' connoted: what might be called John's anti-bourgeois disposition found its profoundest expression not so much in radical art practice as in the radical social practice of 'tramping', which he took up with enthusiasm in his early twenties, and which led him to a lifelong affection for the gypsy culture and way of life that lay at the heart of that practice in the Edwardian period.[6] The gypsies were 'the living antithesis of a society patterned on settled housing, waged labour, landed property and bourgeois proprieties',[7] 'the last romance left in the world… the only free race', in the words of the poet Arthur Symons,[8] and recourse to the adoption of their way of life was attractive for those late Victorians and Edwardians whose responses to the urban and economic modernities of the new century were ambivalent and more. John's commitment was serious: he learned Romany, bought and lived in a caravan with his young family, escaping to it whenever he could in the first decade of the century, and sought out the company of gypsies, with whose nomadic life, kinship communities and apparent existential freedoms he identified strongly. His embrace of it was, one might say, overdetermined: 'bohemian' was a term originally associated with gypsies, after all. But he was not alone: from the 1870s 'tramping' grew into a cult professed by thousands of all classes, if with varying degrees of commitment that ranged from weekend camping to living on the open road, and from George Borrow's *Lavengro* (1851), a semi-autobiographical novel that hymned the gypsy life, to Douglas Goldring's *The Tramp: An Open Air Magazine* (1910–11), which sought to combine 'the literary distinction of *The English Review*… with the commercial success of *Country Life*',[9] writers explored and celebrated its pleasures.

John thus joined, in his embrace of the fellowship of the open road, a loose but broad-based movement that can be seen to have shared key characteristics with that even broader culture of fellowship – of attachment to affective relations and communities of all kinds, from 'New Life' socialism to vegetarianism, spiritualism and beyond – that, as I have noted in earlier chapters, shaped an 'adversarial bourgeois' disposition running through later Victorian English society to the First World War. What makes his affiliation to this especially significant for the present analysis is, first, that given his position as both the leading young London artist of his generation and perhaps the most notorious of its bohemian contingent before the war,[10] John can be seen to represent the bringing together of the discourses of affective relations and anti-professionalism. And, second, that part of his uncertainty as to what and how to paint, in the face of the challenges posed both by modernity and Parisian modernism, was that he was as committed to the pursuit of affective relations as to originality or technical experimentalism as a painter. For John, for all that he was prodigiously gifted as an artist, life meant more than art – in so far as art practice entailed hard work, and experimentation, with its 'busy-body thoughts that come buzzing and fussing and messing in one's brain', especially so. In this dual allegiance – or ambivalence – he was close to that disposition of the Bloomsbury group that we have encountered in an earlier chapter. We shall return to its cultural context later in this.

If such uncertainty was part of John's make-up, it was reinforced by the teaching he received from the Slade. By the time of his arrival there in 1894, this had evolved, from Poynter's assimilation of Parisian academic studio methods that had emphasised study from the life model and the espousal of the formal principles of a classical style, into an obsession, under the leadership of Frederick Brown and his assistant, Henry Tonks, with drawing from the Old Masters combined with the privileging of personal expression.[11] Tonks came to the Slade soon after Brown's appointment as professor in 1892 on the latter's invitation, leaving an initial career in medicine, which had included working as a demonstrator in anatomy at a London hospital, to start a second career as teacher of drawing, in which role he quickly became the dominant influence. As Simon Watney observes, such was the Slade's prestige by this time it could be a largely self-referential institution, and thanks to Tonks, whose antipathy to the fashions of contemporary art across the Channel was notoriously severe, its pedagogical references were to the major figures of European art history. 'Unless a man believe in art he cannot be saved, and everyone must as they did when Donatello lived', Tonks wrote to a friend.[12] As Watney concludes, 'thus it was that young artists emerged into Gower Street [where the Slade was located] able to draw like angels, committed to an idea of Art which by definition bore no relation whatsoever to the society in which they lived'.[13] Tonks's role in this was key, and his authority unchallengeable: 'he came to be remembered as the Slade's super-ego', Andrew Forge notes. '"Even if you passed him on the other side of the Tottenham Court Road", one of his students said not so long ago, "you took your hands out of your pockets".'[14]

The Slade ethos under Tonks was consequential for new British art on more structural levels than those of deferential pupillage and individual expressiveness alone, however. It was at that time the only art school in London (indeed, Britain) of any deserved reputation; as Forge pithily notes, both the Royal Academy Schools and the nationwide network of art schools anchored in South Kensington were all but rudderless, pedagogically.[15] This was very different from the situation in Paris, where the École des Beaux-Arts, increasingly prestigious but overcrowded, was being joined by the rapidly growing network of *académies libres*, fostering an environment buzzing with those 'busy-body thoughts' that so troubled Augustus. The significance of this for artistic innovation can be gauged by comparing John's early career with that of Louis Anquetin, whose similarly charismatic reputation at Cormon's studio we have encountered in an earlier chapter.[16] Both dominated their student cohorts, demonstrating enviable graphic gifts, and the lessons they took from a similar study of the Old Masters resulted in ambitious and impressive paintings (see overleaf, figs 3 and 4).

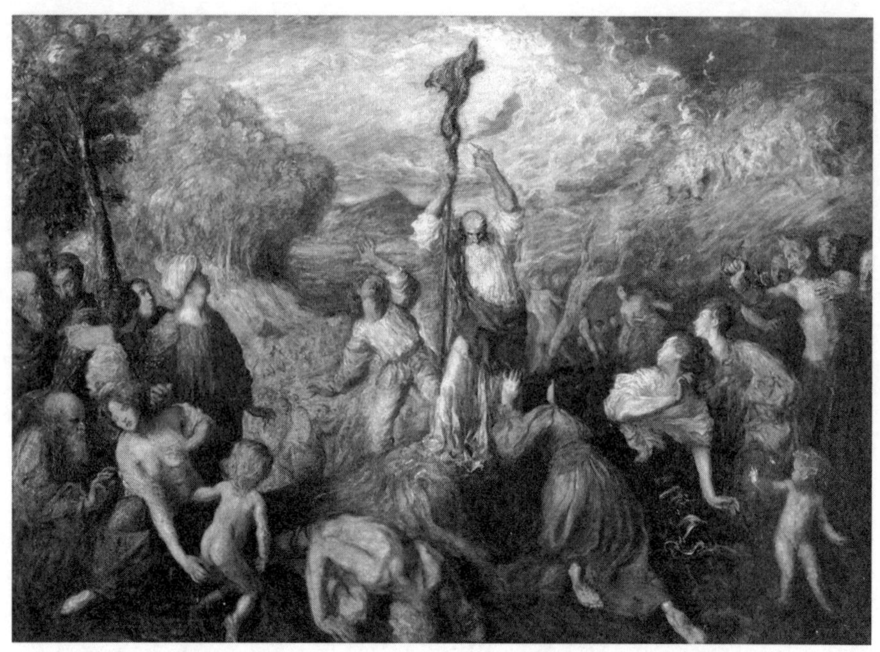

FIG. 3 Augustus John, *The Brazen Serpent*, 1898. Oil on canvas, 149.9 × 213.4 cm. UCL Art Museum, London

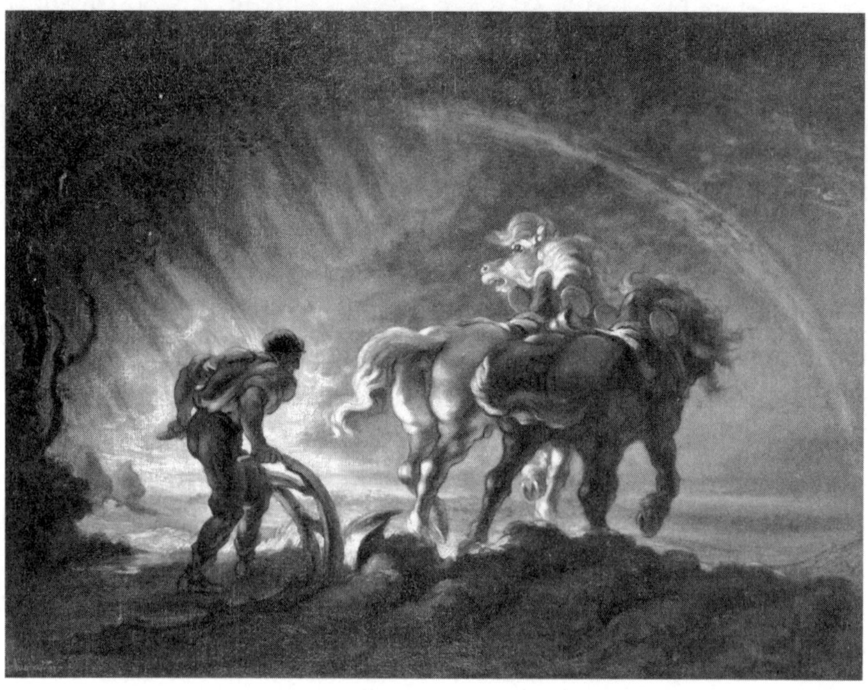

FIG. 4 Louis Anquetin, *Le Labour* (*Ploughing*), *c.* 1900. Oil on canvas, 91 × 119 cm. Private collection

Yet Cormon's unassertive, *laissez-faire* pedagogic style enabled Anquetin to lead the discussions in the studio, to draw on the new ideas buzzing round the *académies* network (and written about in the *petites revues*), thus to motivate also an aspiration to innovation, and lay claim to a new 'ism', that of *cloisonnisme* – and to have to contest this claim with others in that hive of *technie*-driven aesthetic experimentation. John, on the other hand, worked under the yoke of Tonks – who 'seemed to think I ought to take longer over my studies', he recalled ruefully – and remained, as Watney puts it, 'caught in the trap of his own much-acclaimed graphic dexterity', as well as inescapably tied to the inheritance that had been drummed into him by Tonks: 'I spent most of my spare time in the National Gallery, the British Museum, and other collections', he wrote much later in *Chiaroscuro* (1954), his autobiography, 'thus loading my mind with a confusion of ideas which a life-time hardly provides time to sort out.'[17]

The Slade thus arguably provided too narrow as well as too conservative a base for that contestation of a froth of new ideas, techniques and cultural precedents which, in the case of Paris, was a condition for the generation and development of new art. Its emphasis on traditional values and approaches as the foundation for personal expression also helped shape the emergent formation of progressive artists in London in other ways. As Forge observes,

> this devotion to the Old Masters can be seen as a reflection of Brown's and Tonks' intelligent academicism; but it can also be related to an attitude adopted by the whole group, that of a self-conscious posturing as artists.... We take self-consciousness for granted as an attribute of the twentieth-century artist: what is of special interest in John's attitude is its deliberately anachronistic character, reflected in his appearance, his subject-matter, his style. When he drew his wind-swept gypsies he was making a dramatic identification; when he etched a self-portrait in the manner of Rembrandt he was doing the same.[18]

This self-consciousness is noteworthy, and Forge's recognition of it not only in John's social as well as art-historical filiations but also in those of other artists is a critical one, for it begins to bring into focus that *performative* character of a contemporary artistic identity in London that would within a dozen years, as I shall argue, become a determining feature of London's emergent avant-garde formation.

Such self-consciousness of artistic status on the part of its students had perhaps other aspects. It was a feature of the Slade that thanks to its enlightened policy, relative to other art schools in Britain, in accepting female students and allowing them access to study of the nude model, there was a large cohort of them studying there at this time, a fact that has been widely remarked upon in scholarship of the last quarter of a century, often with the suggestion that it gave the Slade a progressive character.[19] As Catherine Heathcock suggests, however, the patriarchal attitudes then dominant in British society at large governed also the asymmetries between study facilities and teaching habits as between male and female students, despite such policies, with the consequence that women students were regarded as being more amateur than professional in their status – unlike the men, of course.[20] As she argues, this asymmetry was probably a factor in the rapid turn-of-the-century growth of the numbers of British women enrolling in the Parisian *académies libres*, which had a more liberal reputation.[21] She notes, however, that patriarchal attitudes to gender relations were much the same across the Channel and so they were little better than the Slade in this respect.[22]

Lastly, John's anti-professionalism – his antipathy both to its dominant version which prioritised artists' social status and commercially credible competence, and to the alternative version that privileged technical experimentation – was also, arguably, in part a product of Slade teaching. As Barnaby Wright has suggested, its traditionalism was on one level a strategy deployed to secure cultural authority for contemporary art against the rising tide of commercialism and the erosion of perceived higher artistic values. This was 'a resolutely anti-professional strategy', Wright argues, that stood in opposition to the 'professionalisation… behind government moves to standardise art education' via the system promoted by the South Kensington network, with its formulaic, anti-expressive emphasis on mechanistic design practices – epitomised by its 'elementary design' course that consisted, as Brown later summarised it, of 'fudging plant shapes into a geometrical framework'.[23] The Slade's answer to these professionalising pressures, Wright asserts pithily, was Augustus John, whose skills of life drawing together with his bohemian image epitomised the anti-professional expressiveness for which the school stood. 'If Poynter's work [as the Slade's first professor, in modelling its teaching on Parisian classical principles] spoke of an aspiration towards ideal form in ways that could go beyond the confines of art itself, then John's painting resolutely denies that possibility', Wright argues, adding: 'We can read this inward turn as symptomatic of the pressure felt at the Slade to defend the status of fine art, a reaffirmation of its traditions and its past heroes.'[24] John's artist-gypsy identity too was quickly harnessed to this defence of art's vital qualities, Wright notes, in an essay of 1907 on him by one of the Slade's teachers, the critic D.S. MacColl.[25] Yet the school's position was contradictory, Wright argues; for Slade draughtsmanship inscribed liberal educational values that were a bulwark against the negative associations of modern professionalisation – but this privileging of draughtsmanship can be seen as an extreme specialisation, and an articulation of a kind of professionalism of its own, one dependent on a professional discourse of art history that the school itself institutionalised.[26] Thus the Slade too was enmeshed in that wider culture of professionalisation against which it railed.[27]

WALTER SICKERT: PROFESSIONALISM AND CRAFT, FROM PARIS TO CAMDEN TOWN

If John's early career illustrates the anti-professionalist current within the dynamic of the rapidly evolving field of contemporary art in late nineteenth- and early twentieth-century London, that of Walter Sickert, in its turn, illustrates the complexities of its professionalism. For Sickert was uniquely and strategically positioned within this field in such a way that every aspect of his career before 1914 – his art education, painting practice, critical writing and entrepreneurial activities – contributed to the shaping and development of the field as a profession, to a degree unmatched by any other artist of the time. In addition, and crucially for the present analysis, close attention to each of these as registered in his voluminous if intermittent journalistic writings reveals, as we shall see, both the hybridity of his own position between the consolidating Secessionist and emergent avant-garde formations of London artists, and the fluidity of the relations between these, as each of them took account of the *technie*-driven 'alternative professionalism' that was burgeoning across the Channel.

From early adulthood, Sickert was unique among London's progressive late nineteenth-century artists through a combination of circumstances. Born in 1860, he had a polyglot upbringing, with a Danish father and Anglo-Irish mother, living his first decade in Munich before his family moved to London in 1869. After his schooling he was torn between the careers of acting and painting; it was the experience of encountering Whistler's painting, and then the artist himself, when still a teenager that tipped the balance towards the latter. At 21 he signed up for a year's course at the Slade, but within months had left to become Whistler's apprentice – a position in which he remained for nearly five years. The relationship gave him unparalleled access both to the new Parisian pictorial language of Impressionist painting, and to the ideas then developing in the Impressionist circle as how best to attract attention to their work via new exhibition initiatives and methods of display.[28] No one in London could match Whistler's acquaintance with either of these concerns (both of which the latter was assimilating and adapting for his own purposes in the years of Sickert's apprenticeship). As a result, Sickert was, early in his career, abreast of the newest art ideas, both technical and entrepreneurial, in Paris. More good fortune followed: thanks to an introduction from Whistler, in 1883 he met Degas, an encounter that began a friendship that was also an informal second apprenticeship, this time to perhaps the most technically accomplished and adventurous of all the Impressionists. Thus by his mid-twenties, Sickert had received an art education beyond anything the Slade might have offered, one grounded in the craft of painting as a set of techniques (and these the most innovative then available anywhere) and as a *métier* – a professionalism that was, crucially, artisanal rather than bourgeois. If this were not enough to position him advantageously in a London art field keenly aware of the pre-eminence of that of Paris, Sickert had by this time also become a close friend of Jacques-Émile Blanche, a Parisian *haut-bourgeois* of his own age, a bilingual Anglophile and an up-and-coming painter of society portraits, whose social circle, when added to the unrivalled Parisian cultural network to which Degas had given him access, opened many of the best doors in *le tout Paris*.[29]

These Parisian technical and social resources amounted to Sickert's *fonds de boutique*, the cultural capital on which he drew in the London art field for the rest of his life. Underpinning both was a fervent belief in Parisian art: its values, its methods, its rigour – and a very evident pride in his assimilation of these qualities that led him repeatedly to insist upon them. Thus, each nation had its own genius, he declared in 1908, noting somewhat mischievously that England's was for football and cricket, whereas 'the genius of painting still hovers over Paris, and must be wooed on the banks of the Seine'[30] – for this was a city, he declared two years later, 'where ideas count, where the town is stirred by a man, by an article, by a question of style, of wit! Paris, where *le snobisme* is still not paramount, where a man may still be "*fichu comme quatre sous, et être le grand Condé*"'.[31] The art ideas that counted, he insisted, were those of '"*La peinture*"', explaining that 'the phrase conveys a whole host of definite principles and associations in French.... An evocation, shall I say, produced in accordance with certain laws known to everyone, great and small, in Paris?'[32] These laws comprised, moreover, 'the traditional language of paint, learned in France, the sacred soil whence the art of painting first came to England in 1236, in the *entourage* of a French princess'.[33] Such an allegiance, so frequently declared, also made Sickert an ambassador, if (clearly) not always the most tactful or diplomatic one, for Parisian art, and the most significant bridge between the two cities, not only as a member of their liberal-bourgeois professional art formations but, more significantly, for a younger generation of aesthetically radical painters in London, as we shall shortly see.

As between the two components of his cultural capital, the technical and the social, it was the former that was of by far the greater importance to Sickert's sense of self as a professional artist. Although his friendship with Jacques-Émile Blanche led him always to temper his frequent critiques of the profession of portrait painter ('the portrait-painter… fills a useful and honourable place in a world of supply and demand') – and, indeed, for five years in the 1890s, when money was short, Sickert tried to add this string to his own bow[34] – it was 'because the portrait-painter is not free' and such painters are 'servants of their customers', 'every touch [of whose works] bespeaks them painted for the owners of the rooms', that, he wrote in 1910, 'I continue rather to draw attention to work outside these limitations'. 'Livery is an honourable wear', he declared, 'but liberty has a savour of its own.'[35] What counted for him was the nature and meaning of painting as a manual and intellectual practice, one whose essence he defined in several different ways, most insistently in a series of critical texts in the first half of 1910. What has become the best known of these definitions is placed in explicit opposition to fashionable 'drawing-room' painting: 'The more our art is serious', he argued, 'the more it will tend to avoid the drawing-room and stick to the kitchen. The plastic arts are gross arts, dealing joyously with gross material facts', he declared. 'They call, in their servants, for a robust stomach and a great power of endurance, and while they will flourish in the scullery, or on the dunghill, they fade at a breath from the drawing-room.'[36] Yet at other times the emphasis was different, and shaded towards a formalist essentialism: two weeks after the above declaration, made in May 1910, writing against art criticism by writers, he asserted that 'nothing of any value has been written on our art by writers not themselves craftsmen. I am convinced', he added, 'that it is impossible to approach art-criticism except from the core, from the material and its nature, outwards to its resulting message and to a consideration of the aims and effects moral, social, political, aesthetic or sentimental, of the work.'[37]

Early in the year he had already offered a medium-specific criterion of aesthetic value: for any medium, he wrote in January, 'a work executed in it is better or worse according as it brings out to greater or lesser advantage the special qualities that the particular instrument is fitted to bring out, and that another instrument cannot bring out as well'.[38] In July he developed this further, arguing:

> The real subject of a picture or drawing is the plastic facts it succeeds in expressing, and all the world of pathos, of poetry, of sentiment that it succeeds in conveying, is conveyed by means of the plastic facts expressed, by the suggestion of the three dimensions of space, the suggestion of weight, the prelude or the refrain of movement, the promise of movement to come, or the echo of movement past.[39]

This reads, to a modern eye, as being close to a Greenbergian medium-specific formalism, but to interpret it thus would be to remove it from its conjunctural context; its source, in that context, was not the connoisseurship of critics or collectors, but the craftsmanship of painters, that possessiveness towards their *métier* that was characteristic not only of Sickert but, more generally, of painters who, as writers turned increasingly to art criticism and presumed to speak for them (especially within the overlapping emergent literary and artistic formations of the Parisian avant-garde), found it necessary to insist on painterly criteria and concerns.[40] Sickert, indeed, followed his definition of painting in the May 'Spirit of the Hive' essay cited above by defining his own critical role as that of 'the craftsman as witness'.[41] At a moment when he was devoting increasing time and energy to painterly entrepreneurship on behalf of the Fitzroy Street Group and Camden Town Group circles, the need both to emphasise these technical allegiances and to proselytise for the shared interests of the painters of these groups in quotidian subjects as opposed to 'drawing-room' ones – to reiterate such an attachment to *métier* – was understandably at a premium.

It was also, however, being challenged from within the profession of painting itself, by the latest innovations from Paris. As news of the work of the Neo-Impressionists and then the Fauves, privileging, in their different ways, theory over painterly dexterity, filtered across the Channel, Sickert found himself obliged to make a stand in opposition to them. This was partly because of an evident exasperation with the promotional hyperbole that accompanied the showing of this new work (and was, indeed, increasingly a feature of the Parisian avant-garde's professionalised, competitive auto-promotion in a crowded market). Sickert was, from early in his career, attentive to this aspect of the Parisian manner, noting in a letter to *The Pall Mall Gazette* in 1889 that '[t]o paint in violet and green spots is popularly supposed to be the note of the French impressionism, or as it is now the fashion to call its latest development in Paris, "le vibrisme"'.[42] Twenty years later, he sounded this note somewhat more sharply. Writing in April 1910 of Camille Pissarro, one of his favourite painters, he distinguished him *as a painter* from his successors: 'Now this artist-impressionist, this painter-impressionist differs from the mass of theory-impressionists that the movement naturally bred';[43] and a few months later, in June, he admonished the latter sternly: 'I would invite the new French school, the Violentistes, the Tantpisistes, shall we say, to consider that intellectual evolutions take more than one generation to deploy.'[44] This was before Roger Fry's *Manet and the Post-Impressionists* exhibition at the Grafton Galleries in November; in response to this, Sickert was openly contemptuous of the *technie*-fuelled disregard of craftsmanship that he saw Matisse in particular as representing. 'Matisse has all the worst art-school tricks', he growled. 'Just a dashing hint of anatomy is obtruded; and you will find a line separating the light from the shade.... The instinct of self-preservation... must have dictated to him that this slickness of empty perfection, of a poor order, would never make its mark. So we have wilful deformations.'[45]

Yet exasperation was not the whole story; this rejection of avant-gardist *technie* in the name of craftsmanship also indexed a more complex attitude to painting, one that amounted to a hybrid position between the inheritances of both Paris and London, and an assimilation of key aspects of each. On the one hand, Sickert's attachment to *métier* countenanced an unwillingness, or inability, to see beyond it to the *conceptual* underpinnings of modernist painting in Paris. For all his assertion of the intellectual character of painting,[46] his frequent reiterations not only of its craft foundations but of the traditional character of these[47] reflect an antipathy to the Parisian avant-gardist project on an ideological level; experimentalism and rupture were not qualities he embraced. This is registered in his opinion of Manet, whom he saw, in the final analysis, as no more than 'the magnificent painter of the *morceau*',[48] 'a gifted pupil of the old Spanish school, a man honestly continuing sound traditions. *Bon peintre, et voilà tout.*'[49] Manet's touch was 'the touch of the born painter, doubled with that of the man who knows, almost too well, what painters like in painting. It is almost matinée painting, painting to a house filled with professionals.'[50] What passed unnoticed by Sickert, in his commitment to an artisanal craftsmanship that he opposed to such perceived professional glibness of manner, was the irony and semiotic play with which Manet reinvented painting for modernism – the pushing to the limit, in *Olympia* and *Un Bar aux Folies-Bergère*, for instance (see overleaf, figs 5 and 6), of both the provocation of the (putatively male) viewer's acquiescence in a sexual encounter and of the factitiousness of the illusion of this, and, against the incompatibility of such a juxtaposition, their straight-faced indexation to precedents set by the Old Masters (Titian's *Venus of Urbino* for the first of these, Diego Velázquez's *Las Meninas* for the second). If this was 'matinée painting', it was also subversive, driven by a critical conceptualism that led to Matisse, among others. (There is a further irony in this unnoticing itself on Sickert's part, since Manet's technical rule-breaking depended upon that very love of rules that the language historian Gilles Philippe has identified as both characteristically French and one source of turn-of-the-century English Francophilia,[51] and which, for all his own addiction to the latter, also passed Sickert by.)

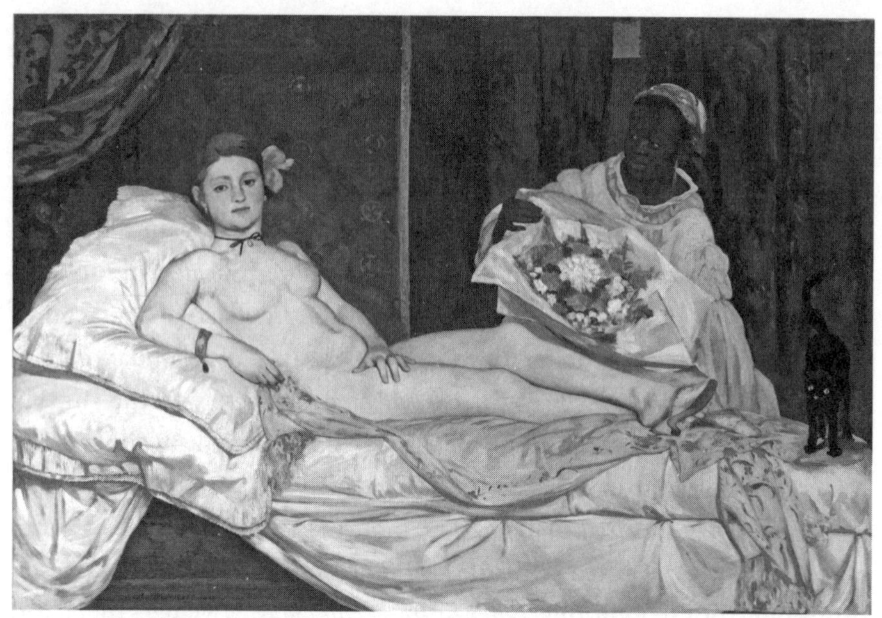

FIG. 5 Édouard Manet, *Olympia*, 1865. Oil on canvas, 130 × 190 cm. Musée d'Orsay, Paris

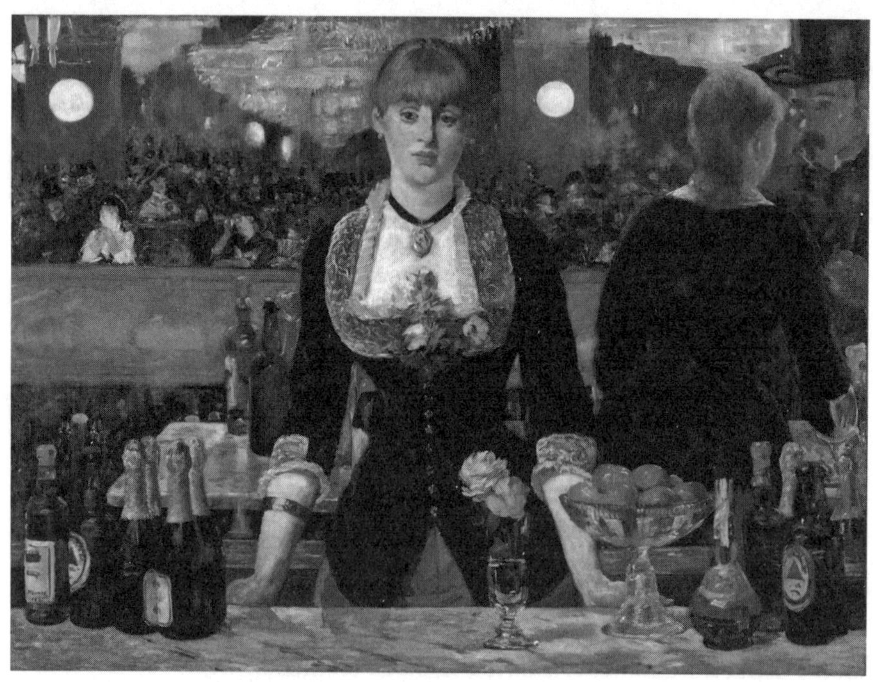

FIG. 6 Édouard Manet, *Un Bar aux Folies-Bergère*, 1882. Oil on canvas, 96 × 130 cm. Courtauld Gallery, London

On the other hand, his insistence not only on the material and formal properties of paint, but on its 'moral, social, political, aesthetic or sentimental' potential went beyond its capacity for capturing the surface of the visual world – his inheritance from Impressionism and Degas – to an engagement with the character of modern, urban experience that he saw as lying beneath these. The 'gross material facts' that, for Sickert, painting celebrated were not only those of the medium itself, or the look of things, but of that experience at large (and in particular its more tawdry, ordinary, everyday aspects). This, as David Peters Corbett has underlined, was his inheritance from recent London painting, from Watts to Whistler. Within a valuable insistence on the heterogeneity of English 'Symbolist' art, which encompassed both visionary and optical preoccupations, Corbett offers a reading of Sickert's work as 'expressing a wider dialectic in English painting at the end of the nineteenth century – that between what we might call Symbolist and Realist modes of representation', and suggests that 'the mutual influences and inheritances from these two intertwined strands in English art provided the material from which he constructed his own confrontation and analysis of modern experience'.[52]

For a while, he found this in music halls in particular: both the *déclassé* quality of the rough-and-tumble music halls and their vulgar theatricality suggested an authentic, unadulterated urban modernity. Such theatricality was not confined to the music hall; indeed, it was a quality that ran through a dynamic and conflicted metropolitan society and its classed, gendered and racialised cultures, both popular and elite, shaping habits of both sociality and consumption, as we shall see in the next chapter. Individuals and groups negotiated, adopted and enacted roles and identities shaped by such urban modernity and offered by popular media including mass-circulation newspapers and cinemas, which turned the experiences of city life into spectacle. Sickert addressed this role-play in paintings of subjects other than the music hall too, in particular in the series of paintings of naked women on iron-frame beds in shabby rooms, often accompanied by clothed men, works whose titles he repeatedly changed and interchanged for their presentation in different exhibitions.

Painted largely between 1905 and 1910, and now collectively known as the 'Camden Town Nudes',[53] their play with titles, variously and inconsistently offering and refusing alternative readings of their subjects, registers at once Sickert's mischievous enjoyment of 'bamboozling' his audience, his love of the tropes and protocols of popular media and culture, and a modernist insistence on problematising pictorial representation in an age in which these were destabilising and complicating its established conventions.[54]

As such, his modernism was shared with avant-garde artists across the Channel, and distinguished him from most of his London colleagues. That he should attain such a radical position, virtually alone among London painters before *c.* 1910, is a mark of his artistic intelligence, his reflexive engagement with his medium and his alertness to the attention currently being paid to both of these qualities in Paris. But his attachment to a representational paradigm that stems from Parisian optical realism and techniques of craftsmanship that privilege surface 'cuisine' in the manner of Degas ('the cooking side of painting', as he put it in 1910),[55] and that both reference and play against photography, marked out *his* interrogation of representation from that, yet more radical, of a younger generation of Parisian avant-garde artists (figs 7 and 8). He was in no position to understand Matisse's radical privileging of the holistic unity of a picture's surface in the interests of a reinvention of decorative painting, nor Picasso's equally radical foregrounding of the devices of pictorial illusionism. More generally, his lack of close contact with the post-1900 Parisian avant-garde formation prevented him from recognising the challenges, and the opportunities, posed to his own representational paradigm by the plethora of other newly available models from non-western and popular cultures and visual technologies which that formation was immersed in negotiating.

With his polyglot upbringing, personal charisma, artistic education that straddled the Channel, fondness for acting and complex engagement with the class-saturated tropes of popular culture, Sickert was thus not only aesthetically the most significant figure in the art field of Edwardian London, but also strategically its most influential agent. For he occupied

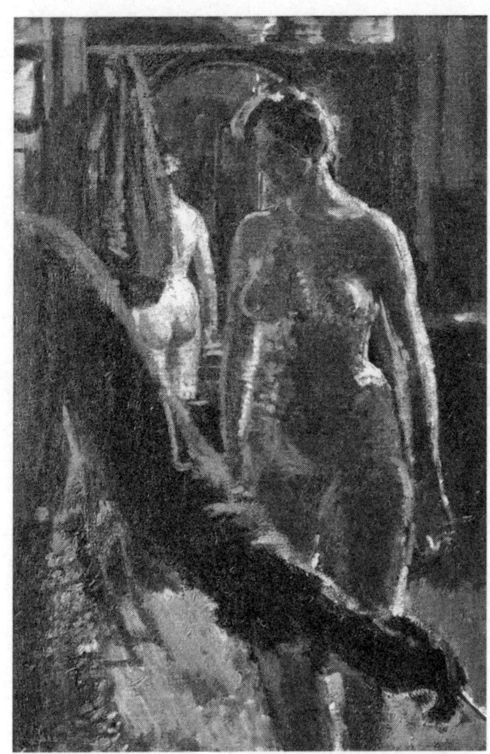

FIG. 7 Walter Sickert, *The Studio: The Painting of a Nude*, *c.* 1906. Oil on canvas, 75 × 49 cm. Private collection, London

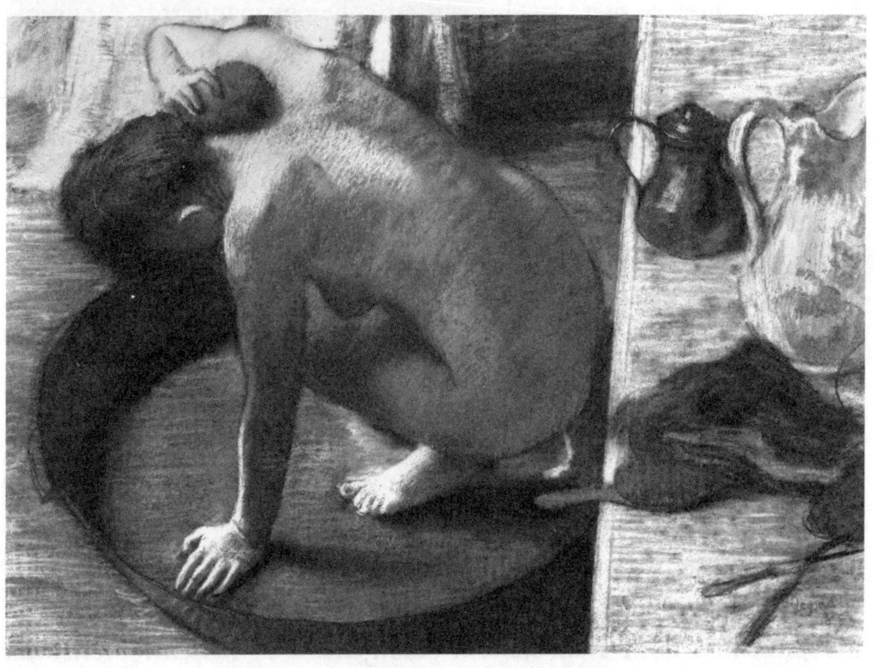

FIG. 8 Edgar Degas, *Le Tub*, 1886. Pastel on cardboard, 60 × 83 cm. Musée d'Orsay, Paris

an intermediary position within it, developing, as his art and ideas matured, into what we might see as a broker between the consolidating 'Secessionist' professionalism of some of its milieux, on the one hand, and, on the other, the emergent response in others to the gravitational pull of the Parisian avant-garde formation. It was a position that owed not a little to his youthful penchant for acting, and it gave him a quite unique authority and influence in that field.

This authority was further enhanced by his extra-pictorial entrepreneurial ambitions and predilections. From the start of his career, and following in this respect his initial mentor, Whistler, Sickert sought to play a role in the market. Upon his joining the NEAC in April 1888 he wasted little time in drawing together its more progressive members into a 'London Impressionist' coterie and mounting an exhibition of their work under this name at the Goupil Gallery in December 1889. Although the ten-strong group was (in the assessment of their leading historian, Wendy Baron) one of 'friends, sympathetic to each other's aims', rather than 'a common movement', let alone an Impressionist one, Sickert wrote for them a catalogue preface that was 'his earliest coherent manifesto'. Alongside the promotion of his own aesthetic ideas, he took to the politicking of the art world like a duck to water. 'Trained by his master Whistler in the arts of political manoeuvring and polemics', in Baron's succinct phrase, he had obtained by the mid-1890s a reputation as the *enfant terrible* of British art.[56] When he returned to London in 1905 after nearly a decade in Dieppe, persuaded by Spencer Gore's account of a rising generation of ex-Slade students in need of mentoring by an established but still-independent artist (who could in some measure stand in for, but also give access to, the infrastructural support provided in Paris by the *académies libres, petites revues* and adventurous dealers),[57] he immediately brought what Baron describes as his 'fierce professionalism' to bear on the management of their careers.

The first product of this was Sickert's foundation of the Fitzroy Street Group in the spring of 1907. Although it began modestly and informally, it represented both a substantial enlargement of his entrepreneurial activity and a significant structural development within the London art field: an initiative that, leading as it did to the Camden Town Group in 1911 and the London Group two years later – both large, formal, market-facing collectives – cemented that field's alignment with the pan-European Secessionist network. Unlike the proliferating contestatory and *technie*-led 'isms' of the Parisian avant-garde, this group of, initially, seven to nine artists was, as Baron observes, 'a co-operative commercial enterprise, run by a partnership of socially acceptable friends who broadly represented an offshoot of the NEAC', an initiative that 'was never intended to represent a movement or school'[58] but rather opened up a space in the market for art buyers of modest means yet progressive taste. It began with a suggestion by Sickert to Gore and other friends that they present their work at regular Saturday 'At Homes', with aims that he explained in a letter inviting his friend the painter Nan Hudson to join:

> I do it for 2 reasons. Because it is more interesting to people to see the work of 7 or 9 people than one and because I want to keep up an incessant proselytizing agency to accustom people to mine and other painters' work of a modern character. Every week we would put something different on the easels.

In this way, he hoped that he could '[a]ccustom people weekly to *see* work in a different notation from the current English one. Make it clear that we all have work for sale at prices that people of moderate means could afford. (That a picture costs less than a supper at the Savoy.)' Sickert had a specific kind of client in view:

> I want (and this we can all *understand* and never *say*) to get together a milieu rich or poor, refined or even to some extent vulgar, which is interested in painting and things of the intelligence, and which has not… an *aggressively* anti-moral attitude. To put it on the lowest grounds, it interferes with business.

Tellingly, he summarised it both in unambiguously commercial terms, and with reference to Parisian precedent, explaining, 'I want to create a Salon d'Automne milieu in London.'[59] In social terms, it apparently succeeded; as Baron observes in a remark I have already quoted, by the end of 1910 'a huge circle' of painters patronised the Fitzroy Street events: 'every progressive artist in London came, at least sometimes, to its Saturday Afternoons.' By this time the Fitzroy Street Group had changed: 'many of its original members had introduced their colleagues, friends, protégés and pupils' to the circle, as Baron notes, and this changed its character in two ways, which were less mutually exclusive than they might seem. The first was that, as it grew in number, the common denominator of its networking was, like that of the Nabis in Paris and the early years of the NEAC, an attachment to affective relations together with an occupational commitment to broadly defined criteria of 'quality' – in the recollection of one of their number, Charles Ginner, they sought 'a group which was to hold within a fixed and limited circle those painters whom they considered to be the best and most promising of the day'[60]. This was an aim that was not easy to achieve – Baron notes that its gatherings 'were composed of a cat's cradle of strands based on friendship and professional relations'[61] – and when, in 1911, the Fitzroy was superseded by the Camden Town Group, with a more explicit intention to rival and replace the increasingly moribund NEAC,[62] affective relations lost priority to a Secessionist professionalism for which standards of 'quality' were paramount. One register, as well as consequence, of this was the adoption of the sexist principle of the exclusion of women members: for despite the invited presence of Ethel Sands and Nan Hudson in the Fitzroy Street Group, they and all other female artists were excluded from its successor on the grounds that, as Ginner recalled Harold Gilman and Sickert in particular contending, 'some members might desire… to bring in their wives or lady friends, and this might make things rather uncomfortable between certain of the elect, for these… might not quite come up to the standard aimed at by the group'.[63] Sickert himself explained this more bluntly to his erstwhile colleagues: 'As a matter of fact, as you probably know, the Camden Town

Group is a male Club, and women are not eligible. There are lots of 2 sex clubs, and several one sex clubs, and this is one of them.'[64]

BLOOMSBURY: FRANCOPHILIA AND MISRECOGNITION

It was in the above respect especially that the masculinist professionalism of both the Secessionist network and the Parisian avant-garde did not apply to what was perhaps London's principal collective contribution to modernism before 1914. Whatever else may be said of it, the Bloomsbury group was certainly more liberal about questions of sexuality than those contemporary with it. Much has indeed been said; more ink has been spilled, I suspect, on discussions of this group – its character, achievements and significance, both cultural and beyond – than on any other British cultural formation of the twentieth century. The following pages will present a more selective focus, on the questions of Bloomsbury's position within the London contemporary art field, and of its relation, as a formation, to that of the Parisian avant-garde then in the process of consolidation. Specifically, this analysis returns, first, to my earlier characterisation of Bloomsbury as both more and less than an avant-garde formation on the Parisian model as I defined this; and, second, it builds on this to reveal Bloomsbury's artists as offering – accidentally, as it turned out – a further alternative to the 'alternative professionalism' of that model.

I introduced in Chapter 2 the reason why Bloomsbury was more than a reflection, or a reprise, of the Parisian avant-garde. The characterisation of it that I outlined, as founded primarily on a network of affective relations rather than, as in the case of the latter, on specific shared aesthetic doctrines, is beyond familiar to its historians: it is abundantly evident that Bloomsbury had other motivations for its coherence and longevity *as* a formation than those of professionalism and/or technical innovation alone, that were equal if not more telling in the view of its members. Its painterly practices were neither the origin of its existence as a collectivity, nor its primary interest; instead, they were only elements – however engrossing – of a way of working, the means (for Vanessa Bell and Duncan Grant in particular) of articulating their joy in human intercourse and the love of visual beauty. Yet among the foundations of Bloomsbury's way of living was a cultural Francophilia which, if it privileged the eighteenth century, also encompassed a disposition to look to Paris for leadership in matters of contemporary art. Being a collective of 'civilised individuals' meant acknowledging not only the high-cultural hegemony of that city, but also the gravitational pull of its recently emergent but now consolidated contemporary formation – and also that of its writers and intellectuals. In this respect, in its genuflection to its art discourse, achievements, technical radicalism and new heroes, Bloomsbury was thus, like most artists in London but more acutely, self-consciously subaltern to Parisian pre-eminence, and an orientation to the work and ideas generated by the avant-gardist professionalism of Paris was of cardinal importance for Bell, who paid close attention to French art ideas alongside her formal studies, as it was for Grant, who studied at the Académie de La Palette for nearly a year,[65] and even for Fry, a dozen and more years older than both, whose career as an art historian, critic and painter had already furnished him with connections in Paris.[66]

What needs to be acknowledged alongside this relation, however, is that, inevitably, London artists read this pre-eminence in terms of their own dominant cultural discourse, and looked within the Parisian formation for models that they could comprehend in these terms. In so doing, they misrecognised the concerns of the Parisian avant-garde. This acknowledgment complicates the concept of 'hierarchy' that they themselves appear to have internalised, and we therefore need to look in more detail at just *how* Bloomsbury in particular read Parisian *technie*. Within its class-inflected obeisance to all things French in the field of art and cultural taste, the Rococo revivalism that swept Paris in the last quarter of the nineteenth century confirmed Bloomsbury's predilection for art of that city's avant-garde that had an emphatically informal, domestic and often interior orientation, and that privileged decorative qualities, often at the expense of representational legibility. How was that art refracted through these predilections, and the amateurism that accompanied them?

The initial medium for this refraction was that discourse of late, Neo- and/or Post-Impressionist Parisian painting that was, as assimilated variously via the NEAC, the Slade and Sickert (and their respective networks), becoming increasingly naturalised as the studio-practice environment of progressive young artists in Edwardian London. Vanessa Stephen's foundation in 1905 of an informal, non-doctrinaire exhibiting group, the 'Friday Club', with the help of the emerging critic Clive Bell (whom she married in 1907), which met mostly at the Stephens' house in Gordon Square, provided a conduit for its absorption by the nascent Bloomsbury group;[67] it was enhanced from 1910 by the activities of Roger Fry, whose informed proselytising for what he termed 'Post-Impressionism' began that year and included the epochal exhibition *Manet and the Post-Impressionists* at the Grafton Galleries in London from early November that year until mid-January 1911.[68] As the historian of its painting Richard Shone observes, 'Fry galvanised Bloomsbury'; within two years he had organised not only the second of his two Post-Impressionism shows in London but also a show of modern British painting in Paris,[69] had taken Bell and Grant, whose work was 'still relatively conservative', to the studios in that city of Matisse and Picasso, and thereby both widened their horizons and raised their aspirations, and had established an international network that included dealers and collectors as well as artists and critics.[70] At the same time, he began to elaborate a theory of contemporary art that drew heavily upon these activities, privileging the Parisian avant-garde. This was conceptually shaped, however, in terms that, while they were often (and self-consciously) borrowed from Parisian avant-garde discourse, indicated that Fry substantially misunderstood that formation's professionalism, ignored its cultural politics and misrecognised its technical innovations – in ways that we need to understand, since they did much to guide and shape the distinctiveness of Bell's and Grant's achievement within modernism that *their* misrecognition of Parisian painting perhaps unwittingly secured, until and into the First World War.

Fry's first published iteration of this theory came with 'An Essay in Aesthetics' in *The New Quarterly* in April 1909. Starting from a definition of art by a certain [contemporary] painter as 'the art of imitating solid objects upon a flat surface by means of pigments'[71] which he dismissed as too simple, and surveying alternatives, Fry arrived at his own, of 'art as the expression of the imaginative life', which was 'separated from actual life by the absence of responsive action'; the 'various methods by which this [expression] is effected' he called 'the emotional elements of design', and comprised rhythm, the elements of mass and space, the effects of light and shade, and colour.[72] It is ironic, then, that the definition of the 'certain painter' was close to another by a Parisian avant-garde painter whom Fry regarded highly: 'It is well to remember that a picture – before being a battle horse, a nude woman, or some anecdote – is essentially a plane surface covered with colours assembled in a certain order.' This was the assertion with which Maurice Denis, theoretician of the Nabi group of painters, had opened his very first published essay in 1890, and which gave him notoriety at the age of 19.[73] The essay, provocatively entitled 'Définition du néo-traditionnisme', was a call to artists to reject the subjectivity of Impressionism's response to nature in favour of reconnecting with the great – and decorative – art of the past. As Denis grew older, its radical traditionalism gained an explicitly political colouration, such that by the time of his essay on Cézanne of 1907, the classicism that he celebrated in it had become inseparable from the right-wing politics of the monarchist *Action française*, which Denis joined in 1904.[74] In an article of 1909, 'De Gauguin et de Van Gogh au classicisme', after noting that '[today's] youth has become resolutely classical... in literature, in politics, young people have a passion for order. The return to tradition and discipline is as unanimous as was, in our youth, the cult of self and the spirit of revolt', Denis added: 'Finally the moment has come when one has had to choose... integral nationalism [i.e. that of the *Action française*] has the advantage of taking account... of the *successful* experiments of the past.'[75] All of this was lost on, or ignored by, Fry – unsurprisingly, perhaps, given that his commitment to the Bloomsbury values of 'civilised individualism' gave him little access to an avant-garde discourse of classicism that was, at the time, suffused with the politics, as well as aesthetics, of order to which Denis subscribed.[76] These values led him instead to emphasise, in the catalogue essay for the 1910 *Manet and the Post-Impressionists* exhibition, the subjective engagement (by individual viewers as well as individual artists) with 'the emotional significance which lies in things', and the efforts he saw in the paintings that he labelled Post-Impressionist 'to express emotions which the objects themselves evoked'.[77]

In a lecture he gave at the close of the exhibition in January 1911, Fry developed this idea into a comparison between the claims of representation and abstraction in painting that put more emphasis on the intentions of the artist than the experience of the viewer; and as his acquaintance with the art of the younger Parisian avant-gardists increased, he was drawn to the two who currently dominated their field, Matisse and Picasso. His predilections leant towards the first, and to an emphasis upon 'expression' above abstraction itself (perhaps as a result of reading Matisse's *Notes d'un peintre* of 1908, in which it was a key term),[78] and to associate it with 'decoration', which he came to value more highly as this acquaintance developed. Having dismissed the quality of the 'merely decorative' in his 1909 'Essay in Aesthetics', in the January 1911 lecture he declared that 'a painting of any kind is bound to be decorative, since by decorative we really mean conforming to the principles of artistic unity'. Taking this further 18 months later in the catalogue of the *Second Post-Impressionist Exhibition* of autumn 1912, he wrote that 'decorative unity of design... distinguishes all the artists of this school', and that Matisse's work possessed this 'to an extraordinary degree'.[79] Yet his several accounts of this work and that quality, as he defended the artist in the debate that greeted the second exhibition as it had the first, critically lacked any awareness of that theoretically informed pursuit of technical painterly innovation that, as we have noted, characterised Matisse's engagement with the problematic of decoration in fine art; Fry made no mention of colour theories or Signac's 1899 treatise, nor did he analyse any specific paintings very closely for their expressive or decorative qualities. In short, his recognition of the role of *technie* for the Parisian avant-garde was as minimal as that of its cultural politics. Instead, his use of the terms 'expression' and 'decoration' was shaped by the London art field's critical discourse; it owed much to his early participation in the Arts and Crafts movement, and to Bloomsbury's apperception and treatment of painting as an adjunct to its private-circle sociability.[80] A third term in particular registered this frame of reference; in turning to the concept of 'rhythm' to explain what he understood the Parisian artists to be about, Fry drew on (or possibly introduced into the London art-critical lexicon) one that was at once almost completely absent from the lexicon of Paris,[81] and yet, from the start of 1911, increasingly ubiquitous (although never defined) this side of the Channel. We shall explore how and why it was so in Chapter 10.[82]

A similar lack of engagement with the preoccupations of the new groupings in the Parisian avant-garde, as opposed to the appearance of their pictures, characterised Fry's interpretation of Picasso's Cubism – and also that of his fellow painters Bell and Grant. Predisposed as they were, along with many other artists in London, to admire the coming 'moderns' of Paris, they shared Frank Rutter's complete faith in whatever Picasso painted (especially when this seemed, as his Cubism did, so bizarre as to be beyond mere comprehension).[83] Rutter's was a brave admission by a leading London critic and curator; interestingly, however, it soon became a rhetorical gambit in art-critical discourse. Explaining Picasso's *Tête d'homme* (*Head of a Man*) of 1912 (pl. 27), shown in the *Second Post-Impressionist Exhibition*, to the readers of its catalogue at the end of that year, for instance, Fry confessed his inability to be sure what the artist was doing, and postponed judgment until 'our sensibilities to such abstract form have been more practised than they are at present'. As far as he could see, Picasso was seeking 'to create a purely abstract language of form – a visual music';[84] and this misrecognition of gallery Cubism's reflexive play with the devices of illusionism as 'pure abstraction' governed his understanding of the style from then on, with consequences for the ways in which Bloomsbury artists assimilated Cubism's innovations that were critical for their contribution to modernism.

Bell's written response to Picasso's innovations came in letters to friends and family, and was enthusiastic but unspecific. Reporting to Virginia from Paris late in 1911 on the purchase by Clive and herself of his *Pots et citron* (*Jars and Lemon*) of 1907 (pl. 28), she wrote, 'we're in a huge state of excitement having just bought a Picasso for £4.... I wonder how you'll like it. It's "cubist" and very beautiful colour.'[85] Just over two years later she was no clearer; despite having met Picasso in his studio (taken there by Gertrude Stein) in January 1914, and seen his latest *papiers collés* and constructions, she wrote to Grant: 'Some of the newest ones are very lovely I thought.... They are amazing arrangements of coloured papers and bits of wood which somehow do give me great satisfaction.... I came to the conclusion that he is probably one of the greatest geniuses that has ever lived.'[86]

Their painterly response to gallery Cubism, however, was more complex. On the one hand, it was acute but amateurish, assimilating Picasso's conceits bravely but unevenly and haphazardly, in a piecemeal manner. Examples are Grant's *The Tub* of *c.* 1913 (pl. 29) and Bell's *Seated Female Nude* of 1915 (pl. 31). The former work's borrowing of the stylistic hallmarks of Picasso's early *art nègre* Cubism, as in his *Nu à la draperie* (*Nude with Drapery*) of 1907 (pl. 30), is both uneven and tentative, the striations that so startlingly imbricate figure with ground in the latter reduced to rudimentary mimetic patterning by Grant, and the primitivism of his nude a pale, polite Anglicisation of the shocking alterity of Picasso's figure.[87] Less derivative and unrealised but correspondingly cautious, Bell's nude offers a similar homage, this time to Picasso's woodland nudes of 1908, such as the *Trois Femmes* (*Three Women*) (pl. 32) and the studies for it – but the radical distortions and interchanges of form in such works are tamed and domesticated into a decorative interplay between curves and rectangles in a conventional interior. In both cases, the assimilations visibly lack that commitment to the application of new techniques – the drive and focus to carry through an innovation across a whole painting – that characterised the professionalism of the Parisians.

On the other hand, the acuity with which both Bell and Grant registered new devices in gallery Cubism, and their readiness to experiment with them, is sometimes startling. Again, two examples will show this. In the late summer of 1914 Bell made a *papier collé* – a work made with pasted newsprint and other printed paper, subsequently entitled *Triple Alliance* – that appropriated the most recent, and revolutionary, pictorial innovations of Parisian gallery Cubism (pl. 33). Following the example of Picasso's series of works of late 1912–early 1913 which used newspaper accounts of the Balkan conflict of that moment, she combined newspaper cuttings reporting on the progress of the First World War, then only a month old, with papers of a more personal nature, to construct an image of a still life – a lamp, champagne bottle and siphon on a table. In its juxtaposition of background cuttings referencing the politics of the war with a foreground of objects alluding to her private life, *Triple Alliance* is closely comparable to Picasso's *Verre et bouteille de Suze* (*Glass with Bottle of Suze*) (pl. 34) – a fact that shows not only her awareness of the newest Cubist idioms and devices but, further, an empathy with Picasso's concern to juxtapose his everyday studio and social existence with the 'background of events' of that moment.[88] No artists other than Picasso, Georges Braque and Juan Gris, in Paris or anywhere else, had by that point adopted or experimented with pasted papers to make artworks, let alone adopted them in this way, and indeed many other Cubists (those in the salon Cubists' circle) were scornful of the initiative; given this, Bell's recognition of its significance seems extraordinary. Equally extraordinary is a *papier collé* begun by Grant at the same time, indeed, in the same place, as Bell's. They were staying with Virginia and Leonard Woolf at their rented Sussex home, Asheham House, and clearly were experimenting together with this new medium.[89] Grant's effort was, if anything, yet more alive to new avant-garde departures than Bell's: an abstract kinetic collage painting on a scroll of paper mounted on canvas 4.5 metres long by nearly 30 centimetres high, it consisted of 17 sections of pasted rectangles, each section in the same five colours but in different configurations (pl. 35). Grant intended it to be seen through slots in a box through which it would be spooled, lit from within and accompanied by the slow movement from one of J.S. Bach's Brandenburg Concertos.[90] Once again, the source for this idea was

Parisian; in Grant's case, however, it shows an impressive assiduousness in keeping *au courant* not only with the visual art ideas circulating in the avant-garde – as Simon Watney notes, Grant was 'familiar' with the experimental combinations of sound and colour of composer Alexander Scriabin, as well as the music-related abstract paintings of Parisian artist Léopold Survage, both of which were much discussed in Paris at the time – but also with their critical accompaniment: Watney cites an article on 'the possibility of installing a cinema screen on which a literary text would appear simultaneously with music'. It was written by the art critic Gabrielle Buffet in Apollinaire's *petite revue*, *Les Soirées de Paris*, published on 15 March 1914, which Grant bought and read.[91]

How to account for this extraordinary acuity of response by Bell and Grant to Parisian novelties? I would suggest it was due to several factors. One was the selection from the range of Parisian innovations – driven principally by a Cubist movement by then divided into two 'wings' – of the Cubism of those artists stabled in Kahnweiler's gallery, to which Fry would have been guided by his contacts among Parisian dealers (as opposed to those Cubists without dealers who were oriented to the Indépendants and Automne salons as their chief means of showing work).[92] His 1910 exhibition *Manet and the Post-Impressionists* owed much to the assistance of Eugène Druet,[93] and via this dealer and/or his Parisian poet-and-dealer friend Charles Vildrac, he made Kahnweiler's acquaintance; these intercessors would likely also have introduced Fry to gallery Cubism's collector and critic supporters, including Apollinaire and the Steins. Neither Bell nor Grant showed any interest in, or even awareness of, any other Cubist than those whose work was handled by Kahnweiler. Allied to such selectivity of sources of innovation was the growing notoriety of Picasso's Cubism as a 'scandalous' avant-garde phenomenon, which had by 1911–12 reached London, and which fuelled the Parisophilia of the Bloomsbury group in particular.[94] That Picasso could do no wrong we have already noted; it followed that his every innovation was worth adopting. Like their familiarity with Cubism as a style, however, the Bloomsbury artists' understanding of its significance was selective; hence the *Triple*

Alliance which, despite Bell's up-to-date deployment in it of pasted papers, presented them in a conventional spatial framework that showed no inkling of the semiotic play with signifiers of depth and flatness, foreground and background, upon which Picasso's *Glass with Bottle of Suze* turned. Third, such understanding leant heavily on Fry's interpretation of Cubism, which turned increasingly towards seeing the collage-related works of Picasso as decorative abstractions, even when the artist left clues to their representational character. In truth, Fry had no idea how to read either 'analytic' or 'synthetic' Cubism in Picasso's own terms, and hedged his bets. He bought from Kahnweiler in late 1913 a mock-*papier-collé* painting, *Tête d'homme* (*Head of a Man*) (pl. 36), which the artist had completed in Céret that summer, and which, when still unfinished, had been a part of the extraordinary (and short-lived) construction with a guitar player that he had put together out of newspaper, canvas, cardboard, string and a real guitar in his boulevard Raspail studio earlier that year;[95] Fry exhibited it with the same title in a London exhibition in January 1914, but was reported by a reviewer to have remarked that it ought rather to have been titled *A Design*.[96] Such an inclination to see abstraction as 'the logical extreme', as he had suggested in 1912,[97] of gallery Cubism would have given licence to Bell and Grant, who were equally puzzled by it but, schooled by Bloomsbury's self-conscious social and sexual iconoclasm to extend such iconoclasm to aesthetics, were nevertheless ready to experiment with the abandonment of representation.

In this departure, Bell and Grant were alone among London painters of the time in taking a step not only into abstraction, but one of a radical kind, that started from non-representation rather than arriving at it from representational origins: in late 1914 and early 1915 each of them experimented with geometric compositions of the former kind (pl. 37), albeit alongside others that had landscape or interior spatial clues (pl. 38).[98] Their engagement with such 'radical abstraction' did not last, but its relation to gallery Cubism's *papier collé* is evident, especially given that some of their experiments comprised geometric scraps of paper painted in different colours and pasted onto paper or canvas.[99] Part of their motivation – and a fourth factor enabling Bell and Grant's razor-sharp acuity – was, it has been persuasively suggested by Christopher Reed, the coexistence of their painting practices with their activities in designing for the Omega Workshops collective.[100] The two artists were, along with Fry whose project it was, the founder members of this strategically important, if short-lived (and too often dismissed) initiative in the history of British modernist design, which opened in July 1913 and closed six years later; from the start they contributed designs for domestic objects and materials of all kinds. Among these were rugs and textiles whose patterns were radically and inventively abstract in design, featuring intricate and dynamic arrangements of geometric planar forms – qualities that were unique to the Omega, and among the most adventurous and striking of the artists' visual works (pls 39 and 40). Reed suggests usefully that the requirement for starting from squares of gridded paper in order to indicate the patterns for the manufacturers of these items lay at the origin of this geometric abstraction, but he offers no explanation why this in itself entailed either stylistic feature, and other historians of the Omega have taken this no further.[101] The two painters would, however, have been reassured in elaborating their abstract geometry by the similar responses of other progressive artists in London to the initiatives not only of gallery Cubism but also of Futurist painting, which had arrived with much fanfare in early 1912; geometricised distortion of subject matter was in the air.[102]

Yet within this fevered atmosphere, Bell and Grant alone pursued this stylistic direction across both fronts of their art and design practices, bringing together in so doing their own responses to those several aspects of a nascent London avant-gardism noted above, to offer an inflection of that avant-gardism that was in keeping with their commitment to making art as an adjunct to (and an articulation of) their private family-and-friends sociability, rather than – as in the case of most of their modernist colleagues (in particular the emergent Vorticist group and its outriders) – as a vehicle for declaring an enthusiasm for the mechanised, public urbanism of the new century.[103] There were both gains and losses in this dismantling of the borders between fine art and design. Chief among the former, perhaps, was the licence it gave them to explore and develop the qualities of decorative design in a modern idiom; in this Bell's and Grant's achievements equalled (and preceded) those of artists working in design across the network of the European avant-garde, including those in the new Soviet Union and in eastern Europe, as well as at the Bauhaus and in Paris. In addition, it contributed to a revaluation of the role of decoration in art that not only (if briefly) distinguished Bloomsbury painting from its Parisian paradigm, but has in recent decades helped to dismantle the limiting binarism of an understanding of modernism as by definition excluding the decorative.[104] But these achievements came, perhaps, at the expense of a more sustained and reflexive engagement with the qualities and potential of *pictorial* abstraction that, too, could meet the now-international avant-garde criteria of criticality and innovation. If the purpose of paintings and rugs alike was to contribute visual pleasure to civilised sociability, what price the originality that *technie* stood for?

The experimentalism did not last; when Roger Fry came back from a 1916 trip to Paris to report that Picasso had returned to a more legible manner of figuration, he did so, in Richard Shone's words, 'with palpable relief', which was shared by his painter friends, who were quick to return, licensed by this, to literal subject matter.[105] In the same year Bell and Grant rented Charleston farmhouse in Sussex, which became the Bloomsbury circle's country seat for the next 60 years, and whose interiors offered the surfaces and spaces for the flourishing of their decorative predilections in less than avant-garde directions. And yet also – to return to my characterisation of it at the start of these pages on Bloomsbury – perhaps, more than. Christopher Reed makes an argument for an understanding of Bloomsbury's art as explicitly political, its formalism's reliance on subjective aesthetic response 'not just a vague utopian impulse, but a considered attempt to wrest art from the imperatives of capitalist consumerism and the control of the dominant classes served by conventional aesthetic judgement'; specifically, he insists, Fry's promotion of Post-Impressionism came 'at a moment when a rhetoric of individualism could be conceived as a radical act'.[106] While Reed provides little evidence for this claim, there is in it an insight that is significant in the broader context of that 'adversarial bourgeois' current of feeling that I have been tracing. Reed concludes his argument by noting: 'For Bloomsbury… the new art seemed to propel its viewers into a freer world, unconstrained by the insincerity and sanctimony of Victorian tradition.'[107] While the momentum of that utopian socialism, and its fellow travellers in the motley matrix of oppositional subcultures and affective communities that made up the adversarial bourgeois movement, was by 1910 no longer what it had been in the 1880s and 1890s – sidelined by the rise of 'scientific' socialism epitomised by the Labour Party – the emergence and consolidation of Bloomsbury as a group, on the terms we have noted, indicates that something of it was still alive.[108]

9

ARISTOCRATIC ASPIRATIONS: LONDON 'SOCIETY' BETWEEN THE BOURGEOISIE AND BOHEMIA

The dynamics of the London art field that I have been tracing became increasingly complex in the last years before the war, as awareness grew within it of the Secessionist network's significance, of the pre-eminence of the preoccupations of the Parisian avant-garde, and of the challenge of Futurism and its polemics. As this and the next chapter will show, these factors shaped in critical ways both the character of an emergent London avant-garde, and the manner of that emergence, in the two years before the First World War. They were, however, further embedded and implicated, to a degree proportionally greater than was the Parisian avant-garde dynamic I have traced, in broader social and cultural changes. In structural terms, we could say that the alternative professionalism which drove the emergence of the Parisian formation was a largely 'endogenous' phenomenon – that is to say, although it was a part of a broader movement of professionalisation common at the time to many middle-class occupations, it was, critically, formed in reaction to the particularities of that professionalisation within the Parisian fine art field. These included the growth of societies of artists based on status and career networks rather than specific aesthetic principles, the shared education of the École des Beaux-Arts, the privatisation of the Salon des Artistes Français and the challenge to it, from 1890, of the Société Nationale des Beaux-Arts, the growth of a *laissez-faire* hierarchy of dealers, their close relation to a cohort of critics, the rapidly increasing number of aspirant foreign artists seeking a Parisian art education, and the rising tension between artistic conservatives and innovators. The position of Paris as the acknowledged centre of contemporary European art underwrote this relative autonomy. The London contemporary art field, by contrast, was less institutionally developed, less comprehensive in the resources it held for supporting and shaping artists' careers, less authoritative and even certain in its aesthetic management – and, crucially, far smaller in its number of artists – and in consequence the emergence within it of an avant-garde formation was a substantially 'exogenous' affair, produced, in considerable part, by factors external to the field.

Primary among these, I argue in this chapter, was the role played by 'culture', and specifically contemporary artists' practices and dispositions, as stakes in the struggle between the hegemony of class and the challenge of consumerism in the shaping of British society and social attitudes in the pre-1914 decade. We have seen how the initiative of the Grosvenor Gallery, launched in 1877 by Sir Coutts and Lady Lindsay, entailed the 'raiding of Bohemia' for the cultural capital that it held, and which could be deployed to shore up the social pre-eminence of an aristocracy under siege from an industrial and entrepreneurial middle class and its materialistic values. This effort coincided, however, with the rapid rise of a consumerism, as that middle class grew and spent its wealth, for which the very values (of spirituality and beauty, of anti-bourgeois idealism and aestheticism) in pursuit of which 'Bohemia' was courted by 'Society' were seen to be within reach as adhering in *objets d'art*, which could be purchased and displayed for aspirational purposes – as Oscar Wilde famously underlined in confessing, 'I find it harder and harder every day to live up to my blue china.'[1] In response, and equally famously, Gilbert and Sullivan's operetta *Patience* and George du Maurier's cartoons (see fig. 2) ridiculed both the Aesthetic Movement and Wilde's pretensions. In the crudeness of his stereotype of an 'Aesthetic' couple, however, du Maurier not only missed, as Deborah Cohen has noted, the provocative materialism of Wilde's remark,[2] but also its ironically performative character. And in so doing, he missed what was, I shall argue, not only one of the key features of such middle-class shopping, but a defining feature of the relationship triangulated in this title's chapter: the centrality of performativity, of the staging of social identity, in the construction of these relations – and in the emergence, and character, of London's artistic avant-garde. For the years between the turn of the twentieth century and the outbreak of war marked, at one and the same time, the acme of the constitutive role, as it was then perceived, of class hierarchies in the shaping of British society and the first flourishing of a consumerism driven by rapid growth on both the demand and the supply side of the UK economy.[3] Thorsten Veblen published his *Theory of the Leisure Class* as the century turned, a book that laid bare the aspirations contained in (and generative of) this coincidence. 'The motive that lies at the root of ownership', he asserted,

> is emulation.... The members of each stratum accept as their ideal the scheme of life in vogue in the next higher stratum, and bend their energies to live up to that ideal.... No class of society, not even the most abjectly poor, foregoes all customary conspicuous consumption.... Very much of squalor and discomfort will be endured before the last trinket or the last pretence of pecuniary decency is put away.[4]

The Edwardian–Georgian period saw the first flowering of such a society, and it contributed centrally to the emergence of an avant-garde formation for which the *performance* of its avant-gardehood was, perhaps uniquely for such formations, of primary importance – of greater importance, indeed, than the aesthetic significance of the technical innovations and iconoclasms on which it was based.[5]

A DECLINING ARISTOCRACY: ANXIETY AND ASSIMILATION

The decline of the social hegemony of the British aristocracy in the last two decades of the nineteenth century is a fairly familiar chapter of its history,[6] but one whose salient features are worth recalling in the present context, for its effects on the field of contemporary art and design were far-reaching. By 1890 the agricultural depression of the last quarter of the century was being widely felt in the loss of rental income from landed property, and while the status of the old 'territorial' aristocracy[7] as leaders of Society remained unchallenged, this fall in rents did give substance to a common perception that while the new rich were getting richer, the old rich were not. Opportunities for new money to enter the magic circles of the highest 'sets' of Society became greater than ever before; the debuts in the London 'seasons' of 1881 and 1882 of the two Tennant sisters, daughters of a Glasgow industrialist with no aristocratic connections, were seen as scandalous by many in this elite but also opened the floodgates for other newcomers, and registered the beginnings of a shift in the balance of both social and, eventually, political power to the 'aristocracy of wealth'. It is true that this shift was not yet fully visible; the flourishing in the three decades before the First World War of the high-aristocratic coterie of the Souls, which was formed in 1889, is evidence of the continuing political and social pre-eminence of this tier.[8] It reached its political zenith at the turn of the century, with this coterie providing five members of Balfour's cabinet of 1902–05 and a viceroy of India. Yet even within this elite of the elite, the times were changing: one of the Tennant sisters, Margot, was a leading member, and in 1894 married another, Herbert Asquith, later Liberal prime minister (1908–16). As David Cannadine observes, 'At the very time that Society was becoming more plutocratic, the peerage was becoming more plebeian.'[9] Marriages of the daughters of the aristocracy with bankers became quite common: by the turn of the century, a quarter of bankers claimed an aristocrat for their fathers-in-law.[10] Many of these newcomers were foreigners, and of these most were Americans, both men and women, who brought industrial and commercial fortunes to 'the world metropolis' to trade for titles and, sometimes, political power: from four American peeresses in 1880, their number rose to over 50 in 1914.[11]

The changes wrought over these three and a half decades were assiduously analysed by members of Society's upper echelons and their chroniclers, some with consternation, others with approval.[12] The pages of Society magazines such as *The Pall Mall Magazine* (whose foundation in 1893 was a marker of the growth and depersonalisation of Society) were full of articles voicing their views, and as I have noted the 'Reminiscences' of titled women offering their valuations of the upheaval, and each seeking to secure her interpretation of its history, became numerous enough by the time of the First World War to constitute an identifiable writerly genre.[13] An example of the consternation is that of 'A Woman of the World', whose article 'Society in Retrospect', in *The Pall Mall Magazine* of August 1893, was laced with resentment, often explicitly anti-Semitic, of 'the two characteristics of English Society which have chiefly developed themselves during the last 20 years…: firstly, blatant vulgarity; second, undistinguishing, slavish and almost universal adoration of the Golden Calf'. The problem, as this author saw it, was class aspiration. In France class boundaries were clear, and people knew their places. 'In England, however, these broad lines of separation do not exist. Perhaps it is as a consequence of this that it is the desire of the great majority of Englishmen and Englishwomen to be mistaken for those of the classes immediately above them. The ingrained – I fear I must write the word – snobbishness of the English people', the anonymous author wrote with not a trace of irony, 'has during the last thirty years triumphantly asserted itself. The worship of the Golden Calf is, for better or worse, a *fait accompli*. Midas is king for the moment.'[14]

From others came approval of the changes, and of the contribution to them made by the newcomers. Writing in the same year, Lady St Helier (née Mary Jeune, and writing under that name) suggested that those of the past half-century were due

> to one cause – namely, the great facility of communication which is now enjoyed by everyone in Great Britain…. The effect of that change is to centralise everything in London, and to make Society much larger and more cosmopolitan, and to divide it up into many more sections or cliques, each increasing in size year by year.[15]

Jeune also noted that this had brought everyone nearer to London:

> In the days of the splendours of the Second Empire and the glories of the French court, the world went to Paris, the enterprising American getting more for his money there, both as regards amusement and Society, added to which, the Jewish portion of French Society was enormously rich and powerful.... Neither the Jews nor the Americans have altogether deserted Paris; but the latter come now to London in much larger numbers than formerly; for they find in London a society and welcome which they thoroughly appreciate.[16]

There is an implication here of a deliberate response to views such as those offered by the 'Woman of the World', a resolute liberalism of attitude that the same essay extended also in another direction. Writing of a 'set [of Society] which includes among its members the most brilliant, witty, and remarkable English men and women', Jeune identifies this grouping:

> for variety of ability, brilliancy of conversation, and a general concentration of the qualities which render people remarkable and original, there is nothing to be compared to that which exists in what is known as the Bohemian element of Society. There painters, poets, men of letters and science, musicians, journalists, actors, and very many remarkable women, meet in that debatable land, and while possessing the brilliancy of all other societies, it enjoys the particular privileges of being perfectly unconventional, and therefore simple and easy. Every member of that favoured set meet on common ground; position, wealth and rank count for nothing; every man and woman is accepted on his or her merits, quite irrespective of any exterior reasons.[17]

I noted in Chapter 7 the assimilation of bohemia by the aristocracy to support its own cultural – and thus also social – pre-eminence, for which the Grosvenor Gallery and its promotion of Aestheticism (and of Burne-Jones in particular) were vehicles; in the 1890s its initiative, and Lady Lindsay's programmatic encouragement of a 'higher Bohemia' within

Society, were taken up by a widening group of aristocratic hostesses, of whom Lady St Helier was one. Among its leaders, as Alice Comyns Carr (whose aspirations to membership of this social stratum on both counts we have already encountered) observed, was Lady Elizabeth Lewis: 'one of London's most notable hostesses in the latter years of the [nineteenth] century and the early years of [the twentieth]', Lady Lewis 'had a gift for entertaining which amounted almost to genius, and until quite recently… still maintained the traditions of a *salon*'. In Comyns Carr's opinion, she

> did much to break down the very definite barriers which still separated from each other the fashionable and Bohemian branches of London Society in the 'nineties. Lady Lewis, indeed, went farther in this direction than Lady Lindsay, for she opened her doors, not only to writers and painters, but also to actors and actresses, and the society to be met with at her house was always interesting and cosmopolitan in character.[18]

Such assimilation of bohemia was also taken up in a different way by another member of the Lindsay family, Sir Coutts's cousin Violet, who not only had a fairly successful practice as an amateur painter (and later sculptor), exhibiting at both the Grosvenor and the RA as well as in the USA and France, but who was also a prominent member of the Souls.[19] Described as its 'Queen' in the women's magazines, she was known as a Society beauty and painted by many other artists.[20] But the other half of this equation, that of her inheritance and aristocratic legacy, was equally significant: already a scion of one leading family, she married in 1882 into another; as Lady Manners and, after 1906, Duchess of Rutland, she raised, besides two male heirs, three daughters – Marjorie, Violet ('Letty') and Diana – who were in their turn the 'most outrageous and sought-after' of the second-generation coterie of the Souls, and were described by its historian as being 'central to the Coterie, as well as being the main reason that it earned the (handily alliterative) adjective "Corrupt"'.[21]

A social dynamic can be identified in this development of what might, without too much exaggeration of a conscious strategy, be called the project of the establishment of 'high Bohemia', one that was both diachronic, in the intergenerational character of its evolution, and synchronic, in its ongoing effort of social distinction from the middle class and its consumerist aspirations. As to the first: for all the initiative and achievements of its first generation, to which all of the above leading aristocratic women (all born in mid-century) belonged, the assimilation of what were perceived to be the highest social levels of London bohemia was, at the turn of the century, as yet incomplete. Partly for economic reasons (as one historian of aristocratic taste has noted, the 'new money' of the post-1900 generation was 'second-generation' in the sense of being inherited rather than earned, and sourced by parental wealth), and partly for social ones (the 'Corrupt Coterie' felt compelled as well as licensed, its historian has suggested, to 'outdo' their parents in outrageous behaviour),[22] the embrace of the most experimental art, the socialising with its creators, the cultivation of bohemian behaviours, was both the 'entitlement' and the social obligation of a younger generation of aristocrats for whom the political power and connections that had enticed their parents held less appeal. Hence (in part) the emergence, in the three years before August 1914, of a vogue for both social and cultural patronage of new art and artists, from Bloomsbury Post-Impressionism to Vorticism, among this younger generation of the titled and the monied, 'old' and 'new'.

The social patronage was referenced by (among others) the painter C.R.W. Nevinson. 'My work had attracted sufficient attention', Nevinson recalled a quarter of a century later,

> to get me into the Doré Gallery with Signac, Cézanne, Picasso, Derain… Severini, Matisse, Vlaminck, Delaunay…. Frank Rutter lectured in the evenings on modern art, and here I met Lady Muriel Paget, Lady Grosvenor, Lady Lavery, and through them pre-war Society…. I was now lunching and dining with all the rich and great of the land…. It was at Lady Cunard's I met Eddie Marsh, Lady Diana Manners, and one hundred and one Guardees and Guinnesses.[23]

Nevinson here namechecks only a few of the better-remembered Society participants in what was, as Lisa Tickner noted in a seminal article of 1997 on the 'popular culture of *Kermesse*' (Wyndham Lewis's lost-masterpiece painting of 1912–13), a brief moment of fashionability for London's avant-garde artists, a moment when 'wealthy, aristocratic, female patrons, some of them not averse to a certain butch allure... wanted dining rooms, fancy dresses, and party favours in avant-garde styles', when '[i]n the *Tatler* the avant-garde rubs shoulders with the aristocracy' (as well as 'with sportsmen and adventurers, popular entertainers, dancers and music-hall artists'); when, according to Wyndham Lewis, '[f]or a few months I was on constant exhibition.... Coronetted envelopes showered into my letter-box';[24] and when, in return, Tickner observed, 'a few aristocratic women' could acquire 'a celebrity based not on birth, wealth or attainment but on consumption and taste; an identity, indeed, derived from association with the avant-garde and from *being seen* as a consumer of outré commodities in the popular press'.[25] Her observation, more than 20 years ago, of this momentary alignment was acute and valuable, and contributed critically to the bringing into focus, for a subsequent cohort of historians of British modernist art, of a cultural moment when 'subjectivities, social relations, works of art, and aesthetic programmes were being constantly and reciprocally retuned'.[26] It is also, however, an observation tantalisingly undeveloped, glibly taking 'the avant-garde' as a familiar, 'given' collective rather than a construct in need of explanation, definition and delimitation, and begging the questions as to what 'butch allure' such a grouping could offer, and why, and what the consumption of 'outré commodities' signified in social, class terms in that pre-war moment in London. Yet in passing, it identifies two key features of that conjuncture: those of the crucial importance of 'being seen', of *performing* a desired identity; and of the ways in which 'a new fashionability both of popular forms like music-hall revue and of marginal forms like avant-garde art'[27] could be leveraged to this end. It is these features that we need to explore; but first, both Nevinson's and Tickner's brief references must be filled out.

PATRONAGE AND THE PERFORMANCE OF IDENTITY

The aristocratic vogue for the social and cultural embrace of experimental art and bohemian behaviours was sufficiently evident by 1911 to be identified by Roger Fry in that year: writing to Duncan Grant about his current correspondence with Lady Cunard, he revealed: 'I am cultivating her while the fit of art patronage lasts.'[28] It was taking several forms besides that (to which I shall return) of commissioning decorative schemes from modern artists, of which the attending of lectures on modern art and lunching and dining with artists in the news, to which Nevinson and Lewis gesture, were two. Others included the craze for fancy-dress 'artists' balls' (such as those of the Chelsea Arts Club, founded in 1891, which sought from 1908 to emulate the notorious Bal des Quat'z'Arts of Paris's Latin Quarter)[29] with ever more 'outrageous' costumes that included, besides the stock Old Master and *commedia dell'arte* characters, an enthusiasm for choosing outfits (or, more ambitiously, making up group tableaux) referencing Post-Impressionist or, after the Futurists' exhibition at the Sackville Gallery in March 1912, Futurist paintings.

One such event was the Albert Hall Picture Ball, held in December 1913, organised by Lady Muriel Paget, who commissioned costumes for two 'Futurist' tableaux for the event from Nevinson and Lewis, and persuaded a fellow arts patron, Sir Edward Marsh, to wear an outfit in one of them.[30] Lady Paget's purpose in convening the ball was to raise funds for the Invalid Kitchens movement, which she had founded in 1905 to provide meals for poor Londoners,[31] and as such indicates the breadth of reach of contemporary art's first flush of fashionability at the time. Other patrons had less selfless interests, of which two seem to have been paramount. The first, in that it followed a broadly applicable intergenerational rule, was that noted above: a wish on the part of this second generation of the 'aristocracy of wealth' to outdo its parents. As the historian of the 'Souls' coterie suggests:

> it is notoriously difficult to be a successful son [*sic*] of a famous father or a brilliant mother. It must have been even more difficult for the children

> of a whole group.... Reared in the nurseries of the great Souls houses, the [second-generation] Coterie grew into a clique determined to challenge the reputation of their too-powerful parents. Where the Souls had been mildly original (in allowing women to make intelligent conversation, to wear unstructured 'arts and crafts' dresses) the Coterie was wildly avant-garde. The Souls were vivacious; the Coterie must be frenetic. If the Souls had sometimes been controversial, the Coterie must frequently be outrageous.[32]

While this in itself was conventional, it was also understandable at a time when even *The Tatler* was acknowledging that '[n]obody can fail to notice that there is a wave of unrest passing all over the world.... It is as if the world were suddenly beginning to criticise all those traditions upon which our grandfathers were brought up.'[33] The second interest was, however, more specific to key features of this 'wave'. In her 'Popular Culture of *Kermesse*' article, Tickner notes that the Edwardian decade witnessed the rapid emergence of an illustrated press, whose use of the new photographic technologies helped to construct a 'new photographic hegemony [which]... marks a key moment in the consolidation of a spectacular society'.[34] It was this development, she argues, that fostered the ostentation of younger aristocrats. 'There was nothing new about pageants and fancy-dress parties', Tickner observes. 'What is new is the sense that they have an audience beyond their participants, that they provide copy and photographs for the press and can be restaged for new purposes.' She adds:

> These are no longer the more-or-less documentary images of the wealthy and influential en route to Parliament or Ascot or St Moritz or the local hunt. Here we have high society *arranging itself* in ordered tableaux for consumption by the readership of the illustrated press.[35]

This was a readership that Tickner does not seek to disaggregate. We do need to differentiate its components, however, for within this phenomenon lay a second, namely that growth and diversification of 'high society' that I noted earlier, swollen by the numbers of the newly monied, both

British and foreign, and increasingly scattered into 'sets'. When the elite had numbered little more than 400 people, as in the early nineteenth century, it was a 'set' itself, rather than a society; when it reached 6,000, as it did, on one careful estimate,[36] by the end of the century, it required the mediation of a section of the press that advertised its goings-on to itself as well as to a wider readership of those fascinated by the spectacle of it, and the decades around 1900 saw the appearance of a number of such publications: in 1893 *The Pall Mall Magazine* and *The Sketch*, in 1897 *Country Life*, in 1901 *The Tatler*, among others.

It is a moot question as to which section of their readership consumed this news of Society goings-on more voraciously; both the content and the tone of high-end journals such as *The Tatler* indicate that its pictured aristocrats were distinguishing (in Bourdieu's sense) their social identities primarily for admirers and rivals within Society, rather than for their social 'inferiors'. This is of a piece with the competitive commissioning of 'outré' decorative schemes for their London houses from the emergent artistic avant-garde, in which some of the leading aristocratic women indulged in the two years before the war. Although, as noted, Fry was from 1911 'cultivating' Lady Cunard in the hope of soliciting such a scheme,[37] this came to nothing. It would have been a coup for Fry, as the American-born Maud ('Emerald') Cunard was 'probably the most lavish hostess of her day';[38] instead, the first such commission came from another colourful aristocrat, the Countess of Drogheda, and it fell into the lap of Wyndham Lewis instead of Fry and the Omega Workshops. Kathleen Pelham Burn, the daughter of a Scottish mining heiress and a general in the Gordon Highlanders, had married the 10th Earl of Drogheda in 1909 (in what *The Tatler* noted was 'the most important' of that spring's Society weddings)[39] and had quickly moved to leverage her new position to her advantage, commissioning that same year a makeover of her dining room in black with curtains of gold, a 'pioneering' choice that made the commission 'famous in a fortnight', as *The Sketch* reported.[40] From this starting point the Countess opened the throttle of her social ambition: by 1914 she had gained a reputation, from her son's account of her, that matches well the characterisation offered earlier of the female members of the 'Corrupt Coterie' of the Souls' offspring: 'larger than life', a believer in the occult – and a celebrated hostess of spiritualist séances – she was also a lover of fast cars and aviation (and was nicknamed 'The Flying Countess' after she raised money during the First World War with an air exhibition), and she played in the Wimbledon tennis tournament in 1914.[41] At the same time she continued her art patronage, moving rapidly through the gears of this promotional vehicle from the conventional choice of a portrait of herself by John Singer Sargent in 1912, to sitting for a portrait bust by Jacob Epstein, and including the sculptor's copulating *Marble Doves* of 1913 in an exhibition of his work in her house in 1914.[42] In that year she returned to decorative schemes, commissioning Wyndham Lewis to design a new dining room on her ground floor (once again in black, but this time in velvet – perhaps to offset the silver-foil-walled drawing room on the first floor that she had already acquired, possibly from the Parisian *décorateur* to the aristocracy X. Marcel Boulestin, newly established in Belgravia) (pls 41 and 42).[43]

Lewis's scheme seems intended to shock (see pl. 56). It included a frieze running under the cornice around the entire room and consisting of a non-repeating sequence of abstract geometric shapes and suggested imagined objects, in garish reds, greens and other tints that assaulted the retina and clashed with the gold of the 'Renaissance' patterned cornice.[44] Separating what must have been, for dinner guests, an enveloping rich gloom were ten or twelve 7.5-centimetre-wide dado-to-cornice vertical panels of vermilion chevron shapes and silvered, bevelled glass, fragmentarily mirroring each other's flashing reflections as well as the glowing standard lamps across the darkness. The centrepiece was an overmantel mirror whose 37 panels were arranged in perspective recession to suggest a window, cage or cabinet, 'guarded' by twin flanking totemic larger-than-life figures reminiscent of African statues.

Whether the shock effect of this ensemble was intended by Lewis as primarily aesthetic or social is moot; we shall return to the question in the next chapter. But how the project came about, and how the Countess managed its presentation, are instructive. She had noticed Lewis's huge painting *Kermesse* (now lost), reworked from its initial iteration as a decorative feature in the Cave of the Golden Calf nightclub,[45] at a *Post-Impressionist and Futurist* exhibition curated by art critic Frank Rutter at the Doré Gallery, London, in October 1913. She was so impressed by it that she sent the artist an admiring note at the end of November. 'I adored your *Norwegian Dance* at the Doré Gallery, and gazed at it for ages', she wrote, giving *Kermesse* an alternative title; 'it moved before me – and I am gradually having my stupid old brain taught to appreciate the great cleverness of futurism.... *Do* please come and see me. I should so love you to do a frieze for me.... I will get the Decorator here at the same time.'[46] In late 1913 and early 1914, 'Futurism' was becoming a buzzword in the cultural discourse of the press, and thus in that of the public, and 'futurist' was soon to be an aesthetically unspecific catch-all adjective.[47] The Countess's acquaintance with genuinely Futurist art was probably equally vague, although she would probably have had more exposure to this than the general public; whether this led to her 'appreciation' of it is uncertain. But that her adventurousness in such decorative commissions was as much a matter of calculated self-presentation as of 'strong artistic feelings'[48] is evident in several respects. These include the boldness and provocativeness of the colour schemes and patterns in themselves;[49] the notoriety that Lewis's scheme gained on its unveiling in late February 1914, via a lavish 'private view' for a very select group of guests (the list of which was published in *The Times*); and a fulsome, well-illustrated account of its details in *The Sketch*, which included a flattering portrait of the 'Countess and Futurist: A Patron of the New Décor',[50] and which was followed by exposure in several other magazines. The 'ripples of controversy'[51] that these engendered and that spread rapidly through London Society as well as beyond were a testament to the audacity of both patron and decorator.

Who, then, was this performance – in all its aspects – for, to whom was the Countess (to consider her first) presenting herself as an *aficionada* of 'futurism'? And to what end? Two responses in particular suggest an answer to the first question. One was that of the American poet Ezra Pound, by

1914 well established as a strategic figure in London's loose formation of modernist writers, critics and their 'little magazines':[52] writing in the (then-fortnightly) literary magazine *The Egoist*, in the first issue after the private view, Pound suggested that 'one can only pause to compliment the Countess of Drogheda that she has set a good example to London', and followed this some months later with a private acknowledgment that the decoration had 'caused such a stir'.[53] 'London' for Pound meant, most immediately, not the city at large, nor the multi-class readership of its illustrated press, but its growing, and increasingly interrelated, milieux of aesthetically adventurous high-cultural producers, promoters and consumers; and as a close friend at that time of Lewis, he would perhaps have been aware of the Countess's confession of her appreciation of the latter's 'futurism'. That Pound should have been so impressed, on behalf of this cultural formation, not by Lewis's achievement but by his patron's, indicates how successful she had been, not only in assimilating its qualities – both for herself within her class, and for it – but also in demonstrating to that high-cultural field the reciprocal benefits to its members of such a liaison. We shall explore these further below.

The second response came, equally quickly, from within Society itself. In June of the previous year Fry had launched his project of the Omega Workshops, which sought not only to turn the decorative skills of his Bloomsbury coterie to commercial purpose, and thereby earn its members a modest living, but also to promote the decorative potential of Post-Impressionism.[54] Among its founding shareholders – presumably 'cultivated' by Fry into her purchase – was Lady Jean Hamilton, another prominent member of Society.[55] In March 1914 she commissioned the Omega to decorate no fewer than three rooms, including the entrance hall, of her house at 1 Hyde Park Gardens in Belgravia. She had hoped to offer the commission six months earlier, but had been unable to do so as she was then in the process of moving to the new address, and so she was beaten by the Countess of Drogheda to the distinction of pioneering the patronage of artists of the nascent London avant-garde. Not to be outdone, she not only followed the latter's example, within weeks, with a black-walled, 'Futurist'-friezed ballroom – which it is likely that Lady Hamilton herself devised, since, as Richard Cork notes, 'Fry and his fellow-artists would hardly have wanted to ape Lewis' scheme in so overt a manner' – but went further on her own decorative initiative. Drawing on her connections with (and surfing the current Society fashionability of) the Ballets Russes, where her niece was working, she sought to replicate its stage sets in her own home.[56] In thus planning her own decorative scheme, collaborating with the Omega artists on details (and purchasing furniture from them) but largely directing the commission, Lady Hamilton took such patronage beyond even that of the Countess; she was rewarded, if a little tardily, with a six-photo spread on the result in *The Sketch* in June 1915.[57]

Such competitive commissioning of decorations from the currently most notorious artists in London, and the associated self-promotion, indicates how patronage of bohemian activities and display of the results in the illustrated press could be used by aristocratic hostesses to present a cultural identity *within* Society as artistic, modern (in venturing beyond the tastes and traditions of their predecessors) and even themselves bohemian. Yet this patronage (both social and artistic) of bohemia was also an outward-facing gesture, of distinction vis-à-vis the 'wannabe' bohemians of the middle class.[58] For as the consumerism of the Aesthetic Movement had shown, the purchase of *objets d'art* such as items of Chinese blue-and-white porcelain could signify an appreciation of both their spiritual values and the social status that such activity conferred. As Deborah Cohen notes, the recognition of this route up the higher rungs of the late Victorian class ladder had enabled the emergence of 'art advisers' who published numerous handbooks on how to decorate the home, to dress, and to display the currently correct 'dominant' cultural tastes, for a (largely female) readership avid to climb that ladder.[59] One consequence of such advice, however, was to give a leg-up to aspirants lower down,[60] and thereby to compromise it as a vehicle for social ascent higher up. Three factors mitigated this threat to aristocratic distinction: the recourse that Society art patrons had to illustrated-press publicity for their purchases, which was beyond the reach of others; the self-confidence in their tastes to commission the most *outré* of decorations and decorators (where the middle-class aspiration was to *join* those with the dominant taste, not to challenge this); and the stage that Society afforded them to *perform* their bohemianism, rather than merely to buy it. Few outside this arena, after all, had the means or opportunity to decorate a ballroom. There were some from the middle class, admittedly, who managed to find a means to such performance, but the personal cost could be high. To return to a point and an example in an earlier chapter, the stakes of risking the artistic life were higher for women than for men, as Nina Hamnett's life showed.[61] As another example, that of Nancy Cunard (daughter of Lady Emerald) also shows, it was easier to be 'queen of Bohemia' if one were a princess (or at least a lady) already; 'high Bohemia' was then not so different from a finishing school. The distinction it afforded was succinctly captured in a recollection of this in 1914 by sometime Bloomsbury bohemian David Garnett, in a contribution to a posthumous homage to one of the few women who acquired the title without losing her art:

> It was in the early summer before the war started in August, 1914, that I first saw Nancy Cunard. I was with Francis Birrell talking, I think, to 'Saki', or to Geoffrey Fry, in the Café Royal when a party came in with one or two of Sir Herbert Beerbohm Tree's daughters and stopped to greet my companions. With them was a young girl – Nancy – who made a great impression on me. She was very slim with a skin as white as bleached almonds, the bluest eyes one has ever seen and very fair hair. She was marvellous. The world she inhabited was that of the rich and smart and the gulf between us seemed then unbridgeable. But the fact that she should appear in the Café Royal at all, even without her mother's knowledge, might have made me see that it was not.
>
> Some months later I saw her again with a young officer in uniform and was told that she was married and that he was in the Guards. I don't think I saw her again until after the war, unless peering down from the gallery at the people in the stalls or in the boxes I saw her at the Russian Ballet with her mother.[62]

If the performance of a bohemian identity was, however, a means for an embattled aristocracy to reassert its social distinctiveness via the harnessing of putatively anti-commercial values in the exercise of 'advanced' taste,[63] it was also a rearguard action, in that the momentum of the consumerism against which it set itself was one marker of a seemingly unstoppable 'modernity' then being driven by factors both social and technological. This modernity was, moreover, exciting – and the 'advanced' art patronised by 'high Bohemia' was inseparable from it. Thus aristocratic distinction was compromised by the demotic vitality of commercial-popular culture, as expressed and enjoyed by the mushrooming audiences for the cinema (as well as for the 'variety theatre', an embourgeoisement of music hall), the crazes for provocative popular dances such as the tango, the bunny hop and the turkey trot, the emergence of the illustrated press and the rapid growth of the advertising industry.[64] In response, and in a way that was also to become a hallmark, nearly a century later, of a *soi-disant* 'postmodern' sensibility (faced with a further expansion of this culture), 'advanced' taste was presented by its holders as that which embraced both 'low' and 'high' culture.[65] It was epitomised, in the two years immediately before the First World War, by the ubiquity and popularity of the term 'futurism' which, introduced in 1909–10 by Marinetti and his Italian artistic cohort, rapidly became a cliché of fashionable approbation, empty of specific reference, as we shall see in the next chapter.

STAGING AVANT-GARDEHOOD

It is readily apparent and frequently noted that the patronage of the Countess of Drogheda was of value for Lewis (and such aristocratic patronage in general for the nascent London avant-garde) both financially and in terms of the social and cultural kudos it brought.[66] What is less often considered is what its consequences were for that avant-garde's art practice, and aspirations for this. They were, I would argue, of two kinds, those concerning, on the one hand, bohemianism and, on the other, avant-gardehood; and they need to be distinguished carefully since they were closely related. As we have seen, the former has had, from its earliest assimilation as a cultural (and sometimes political) disposition by disaffected young men of the mid-nineteenth-century Parisian bourgeoisie, a performative character: for those who claimed a bohemian identity, art was a way of life, and as Elizabeth Wilson has observed, bohemianism 'brought into play all those aspects of daily life that were not central to the production of works of art'.[67] For progressive young artists in Edwardian London, it was just these ancillary components of a Parisian art education that were crucial to the allure that the city held as the centre of modern art, and that were so frequently reiterated in the souvenirs of its former Anglophone students that this became a sizeable writerly genre, whose standard tropes were the café discussions, cabaret entertainments, the penniless camaraderie and pop-up coteries, the iconoclasm and the horseplay of the *académies libres* to which they flocked. As London's commercial-popular cultural media proliferated after the turn of the century, their attractions, both social and spectacular, also offered new sites for a consumerist bohemianism in which class (but not gender or racial) barriers were temporarily dismantled, and to which the informal, unregulated nature of the 'artistic' life gave privileged access for its male adherents.[68] The embrace of the aristocracy, or part of it, gave this London bohemianism an added lustre, of which the centrality of the Café Royal to its sociality was a measure, and David Garnett's encounter there with the Cunard retinue an epitome.[69]

The allure of a bohemian identity had extended, as it crossed the Channel, into that of the artist *per se*, as the self-conscious posturing of Slade students in Augustus John's time there indicates, and John's own performance of bohemianism contributed to it; but the rapid growth of awareness in London of the Parisian avant-garde after Fry's 1910 *Manet and the Post-Impressionists* exhibition further enhanced its appeal. That avant-garde was a formation by then no longer merely emergent but consolidated, possessing within it a flourishing network of *petites revues* that meshed literary and artistic preoccupations in a way that galvanised London's writers and artists to do the same, and encouraged the careful construction, on the part of some of these, of highly self-conscious bohemian identities. It is no coincidence that those among them who together led the city's first self-consciously avant-garde grouping, that of Vorticism, in 1914 were conspicuous in this masquerade. For although they were among the first to recognise the avant-gardist potential of (above all Picasso's) Cubist *technie*, when it was encountered and keenly discussed within the nascent network of London's own 'little magazines' from around 1911–12, they did so – inevitably – in terms of the cultural discourse that prevailed there: a discourse in which aesthetics, class and consumerism were intricately interwoven, and where it was in the public arena of 'Society' that, even more than bohemianism, an 'avant-garde' identity counted most. Evelyn Silber, biographer of one of its members, the French sculptor Henri Gaudier-Brzeska, noted his 'need to live up to' such an identity after his arrival in London, and observed of his new milieu that 'posturing of one kind or another was common among those who defined themselves as leaders of the new poetry, painting and sculpture'.[70] This is corroborated for Lewis in particular by the contemporary observations or subsequent recollections of several who knew him well. One of them, Douglas Goldring, who knew both Pound and Lewis, recalled that '[b]oth of them, at that period, in clothes, hairdressing and manner, made no secret of their calling', adding that 'Pound contrived to look "every inch a poet", while I have never seen anyone so obvious a "genius" as Wyndham Lewis', while another of their circle, Edward Marsh, 'suspected him of pose' and Lewis's fellow Vorticist Frederick Etchells saw him as 'not an artist at all', but an impresario.[71] Lisa Tickner valuably captures one aspect of this performativity in an article of 1994, 'Men's Work? Masculinity and Modernism',[72] but avant-gardism itself, as well as its often 'butch' character, was at the centre of such staging of artistic identities, and in a further article exploring the historical and interpretative narratives that have positioned Gaudier-Brzeska's *Bust of Ezra Pound* in the history of art, Tickner asks: 'Is posturing a necessary condition for the avant-garde?'– borrowing the question from an account by the artist's companion, Sophie Brzeska, of the masculinist posturing that accompanied the commissioning of this work. It is an intriguing question, given this prevalence in that critical cultural (and, as we shall see, social) moment of the fascination for such a performative identity; but it is one that Tickner does not develop.[73]

It is worth doing so, however. My answer would be: both 'yes', and 'no', it depends on the conjuncture. In this immediately pre-First World War moment, and in a manner comparable to my earlier assessment of Bloomsbury's character, but for different reasons, the Vorticists were both less than an avant-garde in the Parisian sense I have discussed, and more than one. Explanation and elaboration of this apparent paradox must wait for the next chapter; in the present context it suffices to establish the distinction on which it is based, which is the difference between the performance of bohemianism and that of 'avant-gardehood': between, that is, enacting the disposition, qualities and behaviours of the former, and presenting in the work of art itself visual and technical innovations whose primary signification is of their innovative character *per se* – *technie* for *technie*'s sake, as this might be termed. As we have seen, this technicism was at that time the predominant concern of the Parisian avant-garde,[74] and in the Cubism of Picasso in particular. In an analysis of this, art historian T.J. Clark argues that at times this artist's concern for 'putting pictorial illusionism through its paces' took his painting practice beyond coherent (if reflexive) representation into a kind of pretence, a Mallarméan play of signifiers.[75] It was this pretence that, I would argue, was *misrecognised* by the emergent Vorticist avant-garde, viewed through the lens of its performed identities as a signifier, not of such poetic potentialities of painting but of the avant-gardehood of their author.

As such, this misrecognition turned their practice away from the 'alternative professionalism' of the Parisian avant-garde's technicist self-absorption towards the larger world of cultural consumption and spectacle. In terms of that binarism with which this chapter began, it reinforced the exogenous character of their avant-gardism – its openness, that is to say, to the broader social dynamics of the London pre-war conjuncture. More than this: it is arguable that – to return to that more fundamental binarism which has run through this book – it thus belonged rather to that ideology of 'affective relations' than to the dynamic of professionalism, because the behavioural informalities and anti-bourgeois attitudes that, for these London artists, avant-gardehood inscribed mattered more to them, in their performance of it, than did the forging of means to modernist aesthetic advance. And yet: in that moment of the consolidation of monopoly capitalism, this ideology was as assimilable to the consumerism that was driving the opening-up of personal relations to the cash nexus as was the aspiration to 'live up to' blue-and-white porcelain.[76] These assimilations and dynamics are the subject of the next chapter.

10

LONDON'S AVANT-GARDE MOMENT: PARIS, AVANT-GARDEHOOD AND 'FUTURISM', 1912–15

We are the first men of a Future that has not materialized

WYNDHAM LEWIS
Blasting and Bombardiering (1937)[1]

Hyberbolic as Wyndham Lewis may have been in his recollection of Vorticism's moment, as an assertion of its status as Britain's first artistic avant-garde grouping it was accurate. A rich historiography of British modernist art in the pre-First World War decade has fairly comprehensively shown how, in the years bracketed by this chapter's title, London at last caught up with and joined the continental avant-garde network with an 'ism' of its own, and one that was as combative and provocative as any. However, we still need to understand better than we presently do the discursive factors that shaped the character both of this moment and of the infant formation to which it gave birth. If the 'exogenous' dynamics of aristocratic social anxieties, middle-class cultural aspirations and consumerist bohemianism were primary among these, they were so largely indirectly in the role of midwives. More intimately determinant were the 'endogenous' features of the London art field (and as such, indicative of a new complexity adequate to its generative role), as it was brought into closer relation to roughly parallel developments in the city's literary field by writers who saw in it equivalents with their own modernism, and as awareness grew within it both of the pre-eminence of the preoccupations of the Parisian avant-garde, and of the challenge of 'futurism' and its polemic. How these several factors interacted to produce the distinctive qualities of the London avant-garde is the subject of this final chapter.

LONDON'S LITTLE MAGAZINES: ON ART AND THE ASSIMILATION OF PARIS

London had no equivalent before *c.* 1910 for the substantial, multifarious role played in Paris by the *petites revues* that I discussed earlier. Those artistic collectivities that, as we saw in Chapter 8, grew in number and significance for the former's contemporary art field after the turn of the century were largely market-led and oriented towards the proliferating pan-European Secessionist network, and there was little engagement in and through them with a literary field that was much bigger, had greater status and was of more cultural consequence; above all, there was nothing in London to match the seething, proliferating milieux of the *petites revues*. Of course, there were parallels, to a degree, between the two capitals as regards the rapid expansion of the field of what became known in London as the 'little magazines', for much the same broad reasons: the growth and diversification of the newspaper and periodical press, as the skills of, on the one hand, reading, and, on the other, advertising developed rapidly in the quarter-century before the First World War; the progress of printing and paper-making technologies, which made older presses cheaper and more available as they were replaced; the growth of the literary field, and emergence of milieux within it oriented to experimentation and innovation. But in comparison with the size, cultural status, infrastructural support for and innovative preoccupations of the diverse field of cultural production in Paris, that of London was small, and the difference was reflected in the number of little literary magazines published in each: as against the nearly 200 that circulated in Paris between 1900 and 1914, of which around 50 were founded after 1910, London generated fewer than five a year.[2] Very few of these gave sustained, serious and informed consideration to contemporary art; as Rebecca Beasley observes, for their editors 'contemporary visual art and design signalled their publication's modernity and provided an avant-garde frame for literary material that was often less secure in its experimentation'. She adds: 'these magazines provide no theoretical account of the relationship between literature and the visual arts in their pages, no interrogation of the visual content's unstable status as stand-alone artwork, illustration, or decoration, no acknowledgement of its difference from the verbal matter that surrounded it.'[3]

A second difference from Paris lies in the readership orientation of the little literary magazines of London as opposed to the *petites revues*. While it would be foolish to generalise too categorically about such a heteronomous field, there is agreement upon, in Mark Morrison's words, an 'important impulse in early British modernism to enter into what we now call the public sphere, rather than to create magazines to cater to a small élite'; thus 'modernist authors often saw their earliest publications in Alfred Orage's *New Age* (founded 1907), Ford Madox Ford's *English Review* (founded 1908), and other magazines that seemed much more recognizably like the established Edwardian journals'.[4] This contrasted with the Parisian *petites revues*' participation in the emergence of its literary and artistic avant-gardes: as Michel Leymarie notes, these amounted to 'microsocieties that gathered around common values and a collective project', and 'place[d] themselves under the sign of eclecticism and rupture in relation to their elders, the *grandes revues* of the [political and social] élites'. '*Par excellence*', Leymarie summarises, they were 'the site of debate and of manifestos, where one's colours and values [were] held aloft'.[5]

The little magazines of Edwardian London were not, in other words, an avant-garde formation. They were too few in number; they were too eclectic to be combative on behalf of a declared aesthetic position – indeed, little inclined to it: as poet and critic Laurence Binyon remarked approvingly in 1910 at the moment of Fry's first Post-Impressionist show, 'we in England don't have movements if we can help it', while editor and critic John Middleton Murry in 1913 criticised 'the preposterous cargo of "ismes" under which French poetry has laboured for twenty years'.[6] They were also too implicated with the larger world of the established journals, and the border with those was too blurred: an example of this is the career of Holbrook Jackson, who was the first patron of *The New Age*, yet became acting editor of the popular *T.P.'s Weekly* in 1911 (and official editor in 1914)[7]. Lastly, they were committed to bringing 'high' cultural topics to a popular readership. As Faith Binckes notes of the latter journal: 'Under Jackson's editorship, it discussed distinctly highbrow topics such as Bergsonian philosophy, the state of publishing in Paris, and the revival of poetry in London.'[8] When the painter J.D. Fergusson agreed to join the new little magazine *Rhythm* as art editor in 1911, it was, he demanded, on condition that the magazine 'would be cheap, not a deluxe magazine. I wanted any herd-boy to be able to have the latest information about modern painting', he recalled.[9] This was not a concern, by and large, of the *petites revues*.

Yet the example of Paris was soon acknowledged. Coincident with the rise of Cubism there, and the *succès de scandale* of Fry's winter 1910–11 Post-Impressionism exhibition, came a step up in the London literary field's awareness of Parisian avant-gardism that was registered in the foundation of the aforementioned magazine *Rhythm* in the spring of 1911. Joining the heightened cross-Channel traffic of young British artists heading to the *académies libres* in the wake of the exhibition, Oxford undergraduate and aspirant literary critic John Middleton Murry visited Paris for some weeks in the winter of 1910–11 seeking to learn about Bergsonism; he instead encountered a cosmopolitan 'republic of art' which 'had no counterpart in London',[10] and decided to risk everything in starting his own magazine, which would challenge the 'abysmal ignorance of French literature' he saw as then prevailing in England, bringing to its readers an informed acquaintance with contemporary currents in Paris.[11] These were to include fine art as well as literature, an ambition that *Rhythm* signalled with Fergusson's appointment and the reproduction in its first issue of a Picasso drawing – the first appearance of this artist's work in an English magazine.[12] It was followed over the two years of *Rhythm*'s existence by reproductions of other Parisian and/or avant-gardist painters, including André Derain, Auguste Herbin, Dunoyer de Segonzac, Wassily Kandinsky and Natalia Goncharova. The interdisciplinarity was a significant innovation in the

London 'little magazine' field and, together with the debates in its pages that such reproductions provoked, contributed crucially to that raising of awareness of Parisian and European avant-garde developments that was cemented jointly by Fry's second Post-Impressionist exhibition of late 1912, and by the extraordinary notoriety of Futurism which arrived in London the same year.[13]

The character both of this interdisciplinarity and of those debates, however, betrays not only the magazine's uncertain and unreflective engagement with Parisian aesthetics – *Rhythm* fits so well Beasley's critical assessment of the inclusion of such visual material, cited above, that she might have had it in mind – it is also indicative of the London literary and artistic fields' lack of acquaintance with developments within that city's avant-garde. As such this engagement is worthy of closer scrutiny, for it registers a consequent misrecognition of these developments which helped to differentiate London's emergent contemporary cultural discourse from that of Paris. It was grounded, reasonably enough, in Murry's own acquaintance (on the strength of his one visit) with Parisian avant-garde milieux; this, however, was inevitably limited. Again reasonably, not speaking much French,[14] he gravitated towards Anglophone circles, in particular a group of painters that included the Americans Anne Estelle Rice, Jo Davidson, Marguerite Thompson and William Zorach, the Scots Fergusson and Samuel Peploe, the Englishwoman Jessica Dismorr and a sole Frenchman, André Dunoyer de Segonzac.

Significantly, this group occupied a liminal position with regard to the boundaries of the avant-garde in Paris. It was centred substantially on the role of Fergusson who, although largely self-taught, was self-confident, ambitious and apparently charismatic, and had been visiting France since the mid-1890s on painting holidays with his friend Peploe. He had settled in Paris (with a studio in Montparnasse) in 1907 and frequented the Académie de La Palette, whose director between 1902 and 1911 was the Anglophile portraitist (and friend of Sickert) Jacques-Émile Blanche and which attracted many Anglophone students, as well as many from elsewhere in Europe.[15] Fergusson established himself quickly there, and was teaching for it part-time within a matter of months; at the same time he climbed the mainstream professional ladder, exhibiting at the Salon d'Automne as early as 1907, becoming a *sociétaire* (society member) in 1909 and a member of its jury from 1911. Stylistically, and in the company of his friends (Rice and Peploe in particular), his painting steadily assimilated the hallmarks, first of Post-Impressionism, and then – rather tardily, after the circus-wagon of its notoriety had passed – of Fauvism. Their main artist of reference was Matisse (as Fergusson made clear),[16] yet their work was some distance from Matisse's concerns, untheorised and eclectic, resembling the spontaneity, loose brushwork and decorative non-mimetic palette of that 'ism' three years earlier.[17] Current avant-garde preoccupations with *technie* had moved on by then, and classicism, primitivism, Cubism and, increasingly, Simultanism were instead *en vogue*.[18]

A possible exception to the group's liminality rests on the claim made by its London supporters[19] and by subsequent art historians[20] for its allegiance to Bergsonism, since this was an affiliation then common to many within the Parisian avant-garde. The evidence for the group's familiarity with Bergson beyond its currency in café-based discussion is largely conjectural, however, and their application of his concepts in their paintings is moot. What is not in doubt is that those in the London 'little magazines' milieux who knew of the work of this group assumed this degree of familiarity and, since it was congruent with their own infatuation with Bergsonism, interpreted their work in its terms. For the philosopher's celebrity in the five years before the First World War reached far beyond Paris: he was almost as much a *mondain* figure in Britain as in France; his most influential books, written between 1889 and 1907, were all first translated into English between 1910 and 1912; he lectured at Oxford and Birmingham in May 1911, and gave four lectures in London that October.[21] While London's Bergsonist discourse was as varied in its preoccupations as that of Paris, within the field of the little literary magazines it was his concept of intuition that stirred the most interest; perhaps inevitably, since it gave a privileged place to artists as having access, through this faculty, to the inner reality of their objects of attention, and at a moment when modernist writers were grappling with the threats and opportunities presented by the flourishing of popular culture, the sense of distinction that Bergson appeared to offer was appealing.[22]

Thus it was as an aspirant Bergsonian that Murry first visited Paris, for several weeks in 1910–11, to sit at the *maître*'s feet; however, distracted (by his own account) by pretty seamstresses in a boulevard Saint-Michel café as much as by the artists whom he met, he never reached the Collège de France where Bergson was lecturing.[23] In default of this he acquired, presumably from these artists, a degree of familiarity with the philosopher's concerns, as a letter of that time to a friend in London attempting a summary of his intellectual enthusiasms suggests:

> Modernism means, when I use it, Bergsonism in philosophy – that is a really *Creative* Evolution with only in the end an Intuition to put the individual at its heart roots; an Intuition which is the raising of Personality to the nth degree, a conscious concentration of vision.... Now Bergsonism stands for post Impressionism in its essential meaning – and not in the sense of the Grafton Exhibition:[24] it stands for a certain symbolism in poetry on the one hand; and a definite rejection of suggestion on the other. It stands equally for Debussy and Mahler in music; for Fantaisisme in Modern French literature, and generally if you like for 'guts' and bloodiness.[25]

While the broad gestures of his references in this account of Bergson's ideas betray Murry's uncertainties over them, there was one term on which he fastened more than on others. As we have seen, describing his passionate discussions on art with his new artist friend there, Fergusson, he recalled: 'One word was recurrent in all our strange discussions – the word 'rhythm'.... Assuredly it was a very potent word.' But he added: 'We never made any attempt to define it; nor even took any precaution to discover whether it had the same significance for us both.'[26]

This vagueness was not unique to Murry among London cultural commentators; despite 'rhythm' acquiring a currency among them from

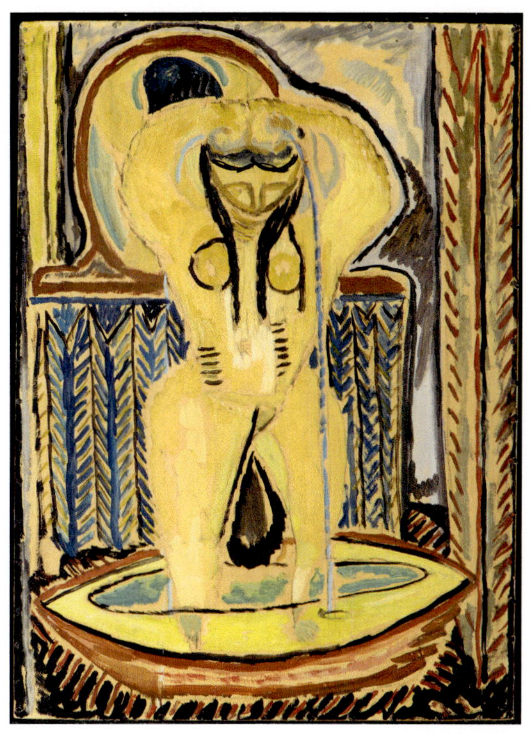

PL. 29 Duncan Grant, *The Tub*, *c.* 1913. Watercolour and wax on paper on canvas, 76.2 × 55.9 cm. Tate Britain, London

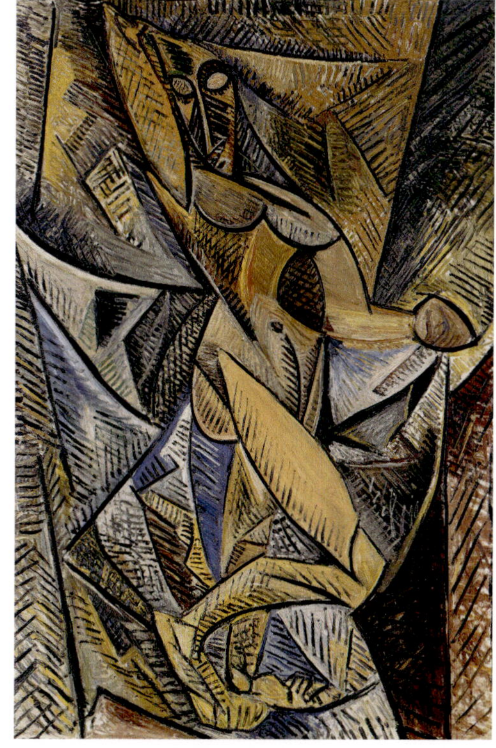

PL. 30 Pablo Picasso, *Nu à la draperie* (*Nude with Drapery*), 1907. Oil on canvas, 152 × 101 cm. State Hermitage Museum, St Petersburg

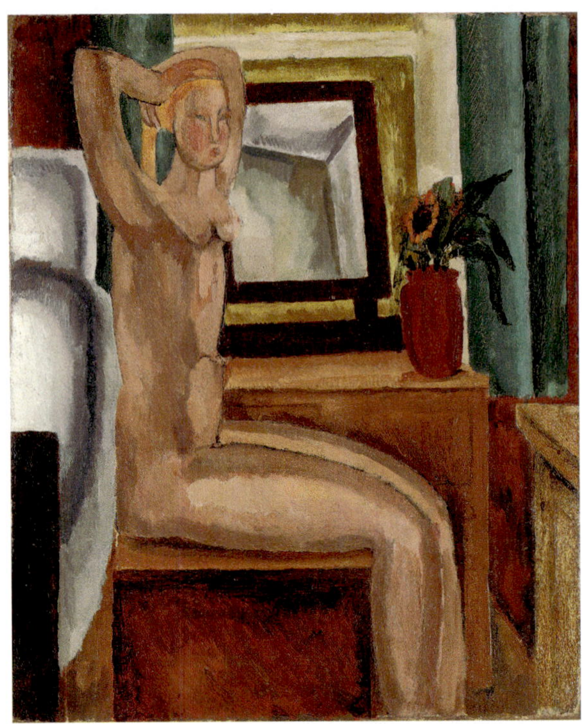

PL. 31 Vanessa Bell, *Seated Female Nude*, 1915. Oil on canvas, 62.2 × 50.8 cm. Private collection

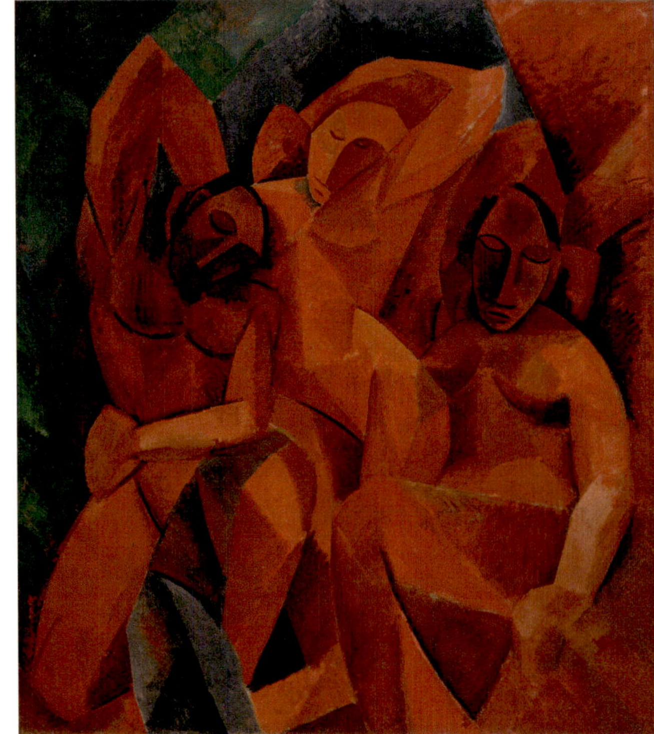

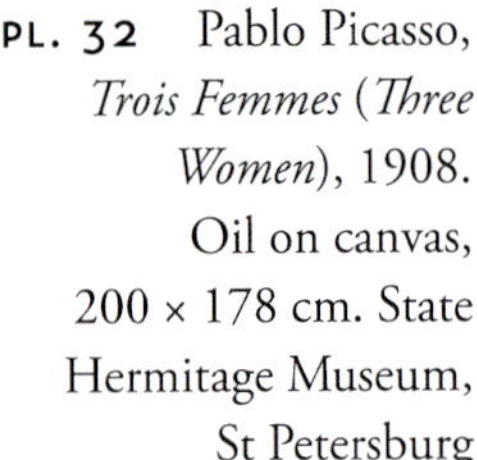

PL. 32 Pablo Picasso, *Trois Femmes* (*Three Women*), 1908. Oil on canvas, 200 × 178 cm. State Hermitage Museum, St Petersburg

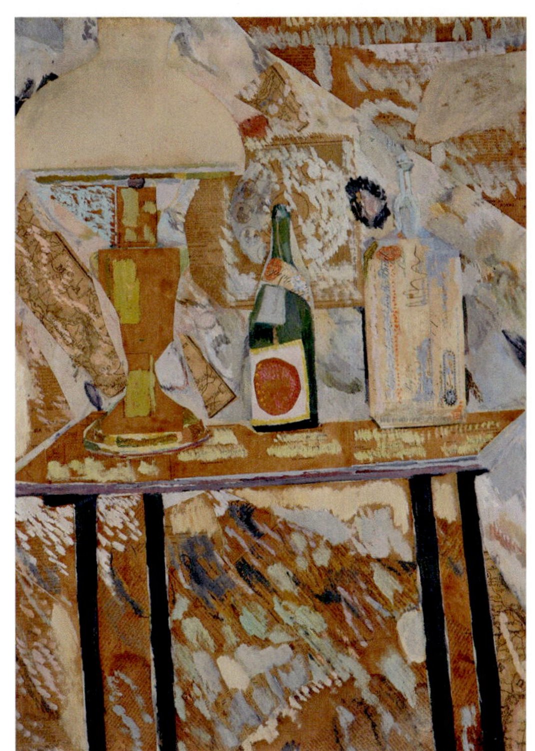

PL. 33 Vanessa Bell, *Triple Alliance*, 1914. Collage, newsprint, oil, pastel on canvas, 101.5 × 82.8 cm. Leeds University Art Collection

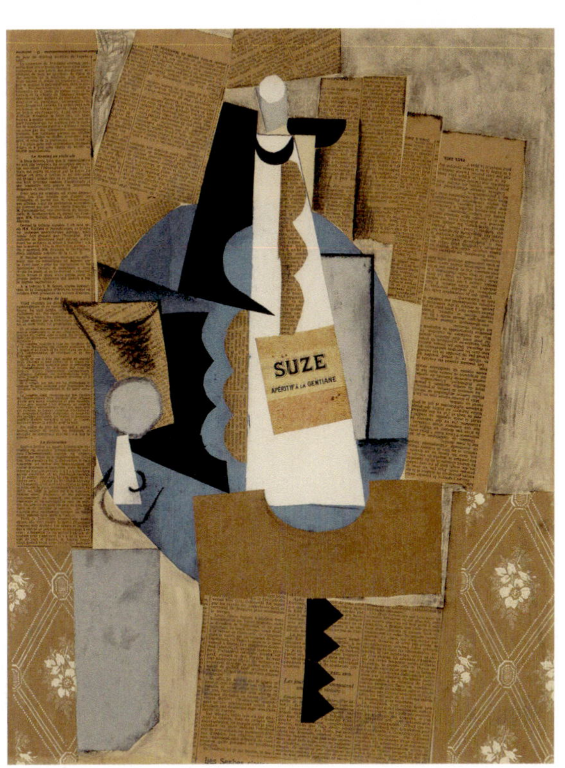

PL. 34 Pablo Picasso, *Verre et bouteille de Suze* (*Glass with Bottle of Suze*), 1912–13. Pasted papers, gouache and charcoal, 65.4 × 50.1 cm. Kemper Art Museum, Washington University, St. Louis

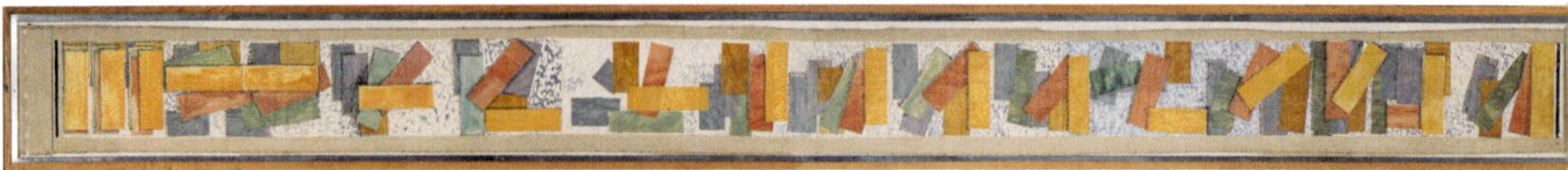

PL. 35 Duncan Grant, *Abstract Kinetic Collage Painting with Sound*, 1914–15. Gouache and watercolour on paper on canvas, 28 × 450 cm. Tate Britain, London

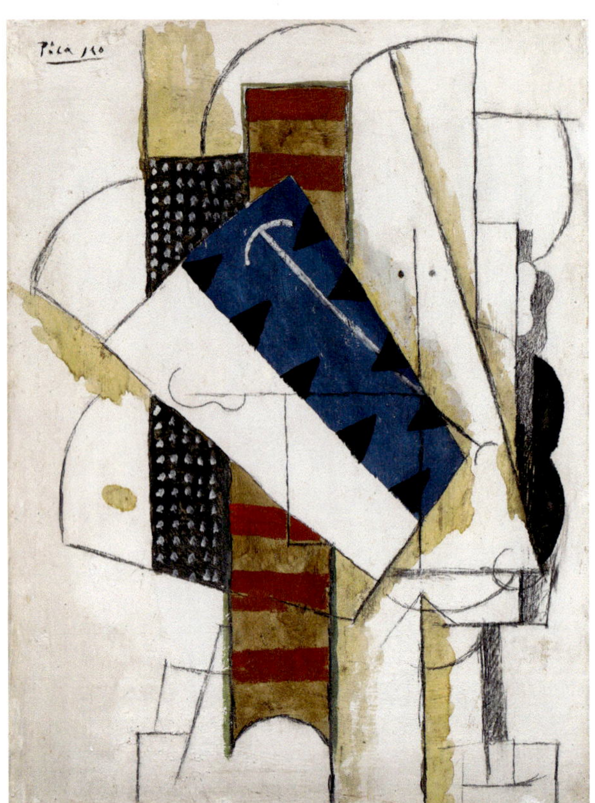

PL. 36 Pablo Picasso, *Tête d'homme* (*Head of a Man*), 1913. Oil, gouache, varnish, ink, charcoal and pencil on paper, 61.6 × 46.4 cm. Museum of Modern Art, New York

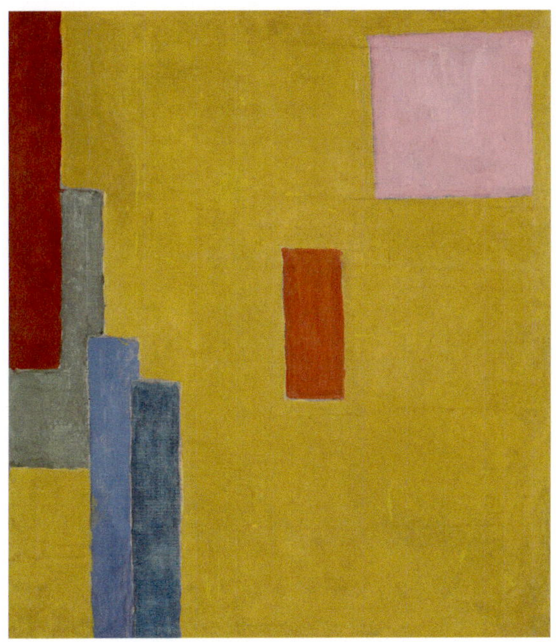

PL. 37 Vanessa Bell, *Abstract Painting*, *c.* 1914. Gouache and oil on canvas, 44.2 × 38.8 cm. Tate Britain, London

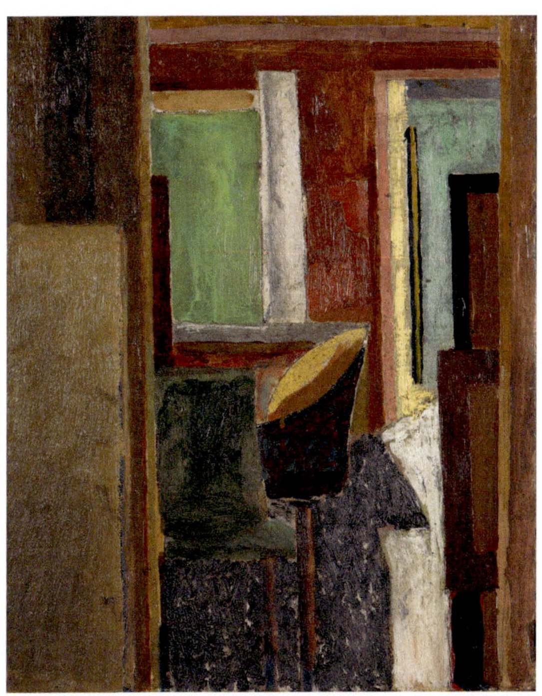

PL. 38 Duncan Grant, *Interior at Gordon Square*, 1914–15. Oil on wood panel, 40 × 32.1 cm. Tate Britain, London

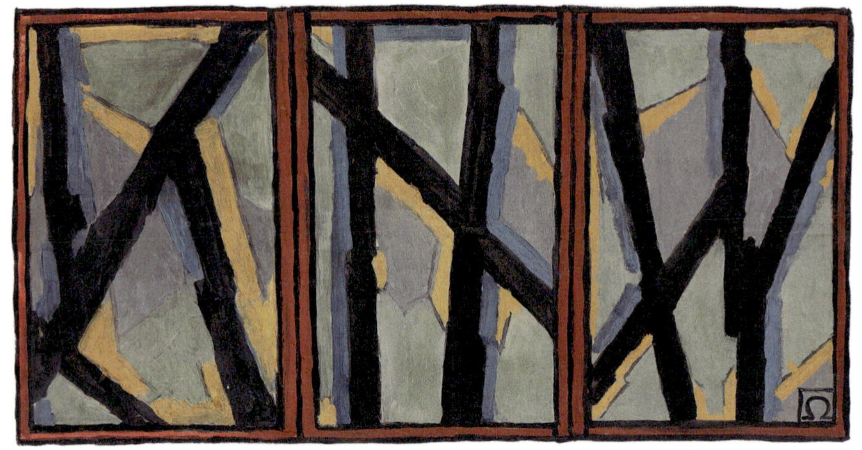

PL. 39 Vanessa Bell, *Design for Omega Rug*, 1914. Oil on paper, 30.5 × 58.5 cm. Anthony d'Offay, London. Estate of Vanessa Bell

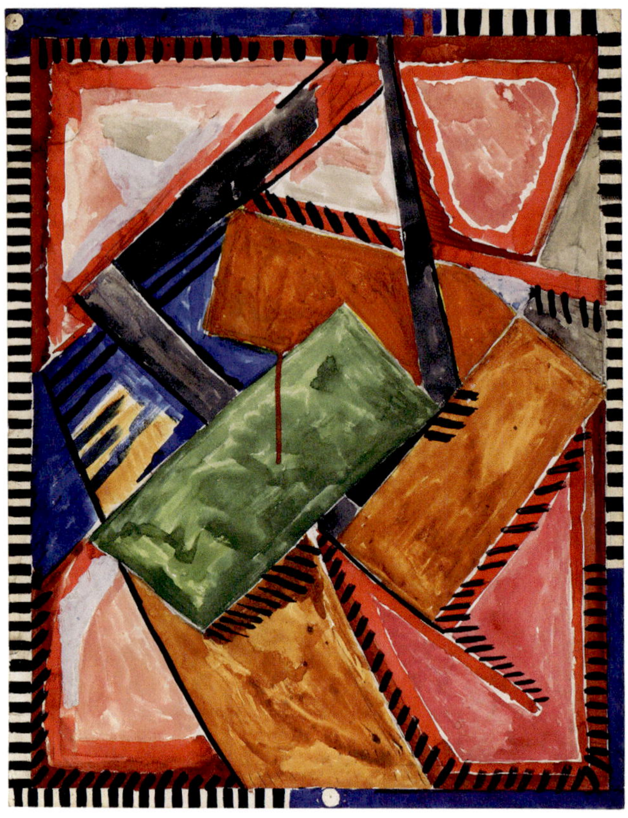

PL. 40 Duncan Grant, *Rug Design*, 1913–15. Gouache and pencil on paper, 60.8 × 48.3 cm. Courtauld Gallery, London

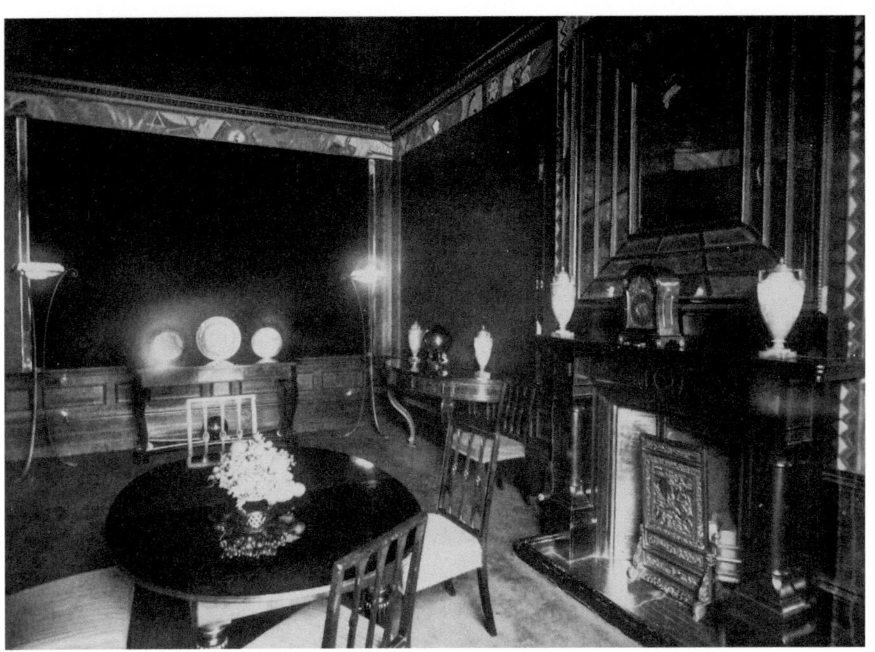

PL. 41 Wyndham Lewis, decorative scheme for the Countess of Drogheda's dining room, 1913–14. No longer extant

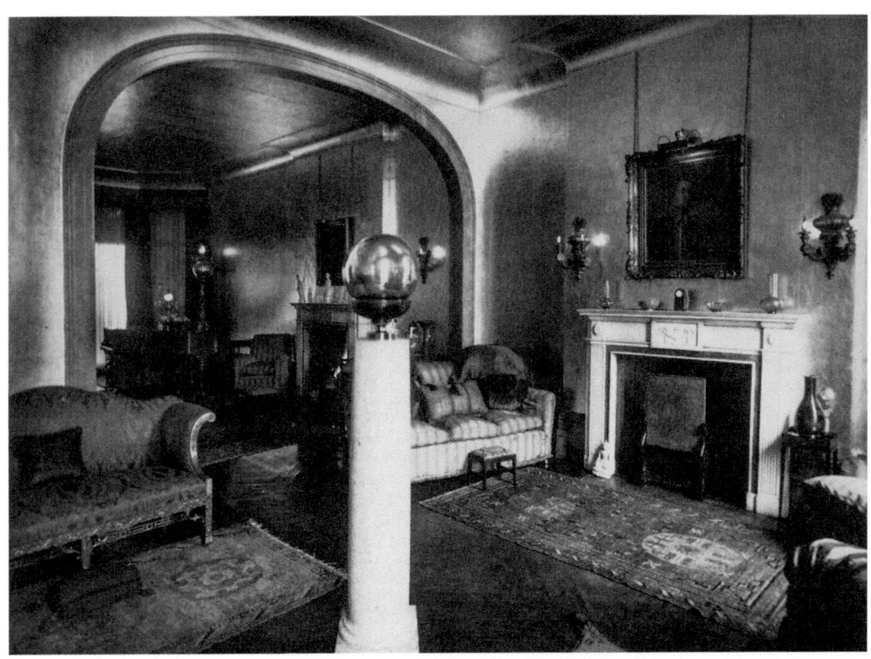

PL. 42 X. Marcel Boulestin, decorative scheme for the Countess of Drogheda's drawing room, 1913. No longer extant

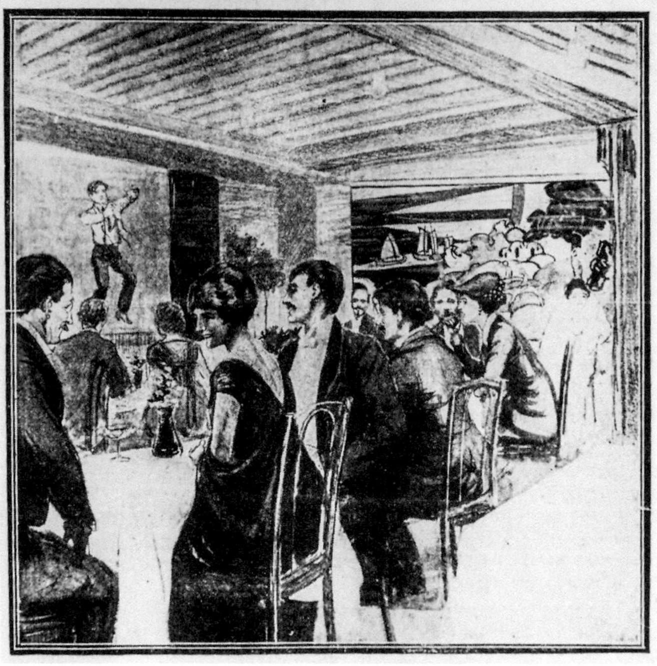

PL. 43 'A Night in the Cave of the Golden Calf', 1912. Drawing, published in *The Daily Mirror*, 4 July 1912

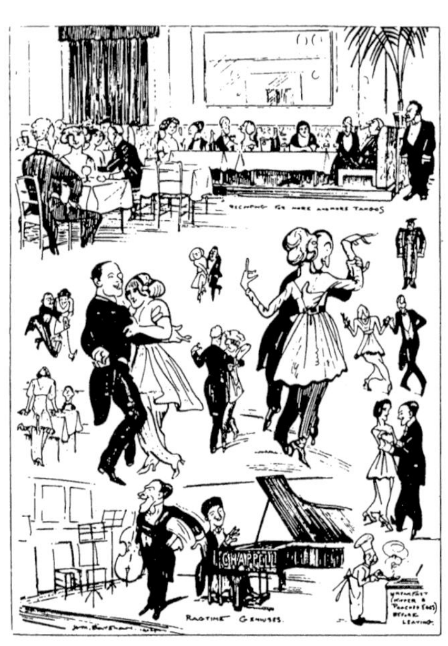

PL. 44 'The Four Hundred Club', 1914. Drawing, published in *The Sketch*, 14 January 1914

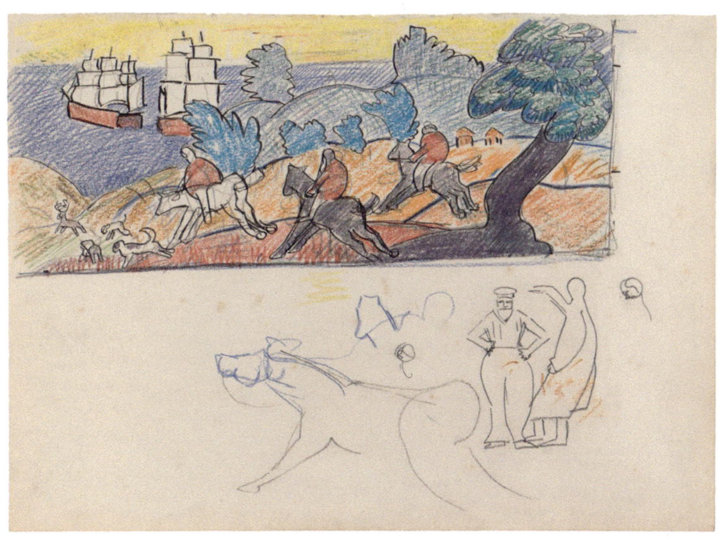

PL. 45 Spencer Frederick Gore, *Study for Deer-Hunting Mural, Cave of the Golden Calf*, 1912. Oil on paper, 28 × 61 cm. Yale Center for British Art, New Haven

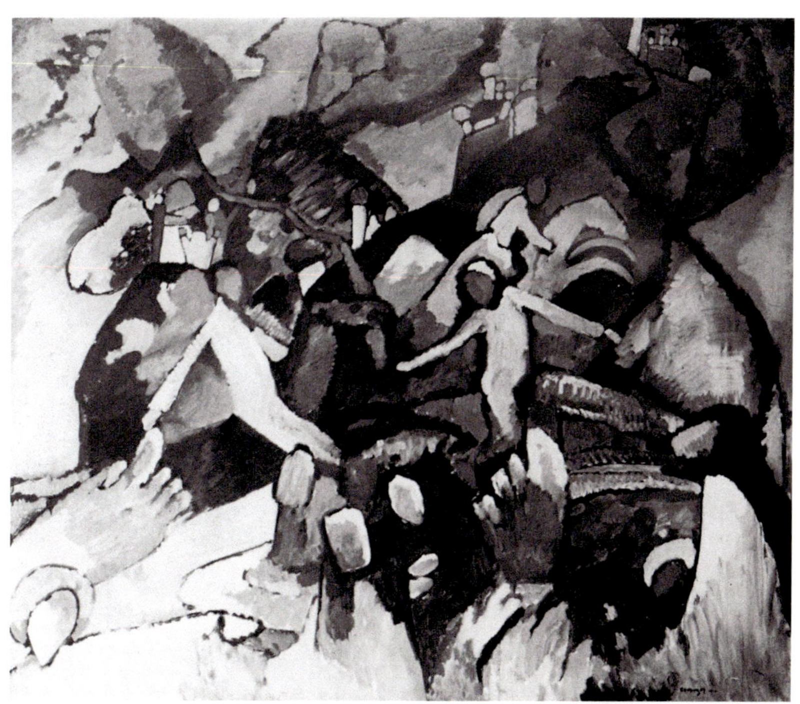

PL. 46 Wassily Kandinsky, *Composition I*, 1910. Oil on canvas, 120 × 140 cm. Destroyed

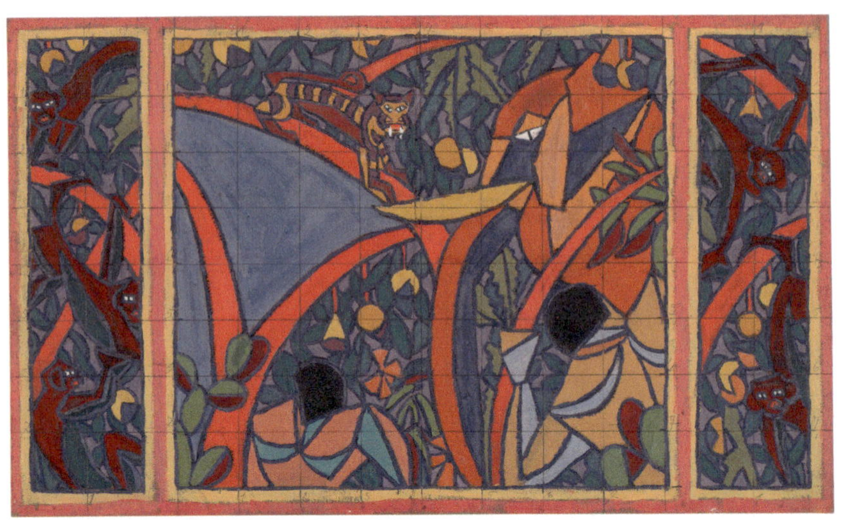

PL. 47 Charles Ginner, *Study for Tiger-Hunting Mural, Cave of the Golden Calf,* 1912. Oil on board, 34.3 × 57.5 cm. Yale Center for British Art, New Haven

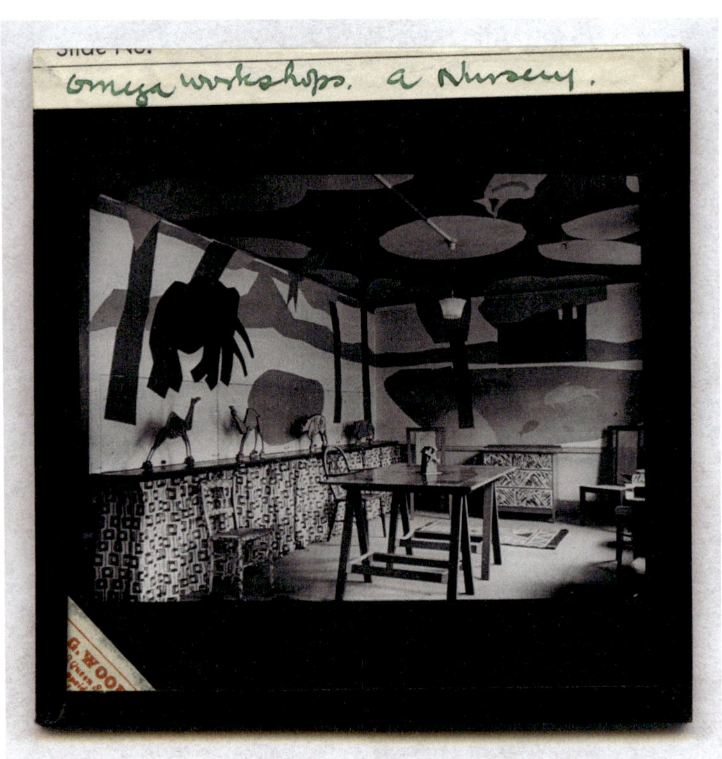

PL. 48 Vanessa Bell, Nursery mural design for Omega, 1913. No longer extant

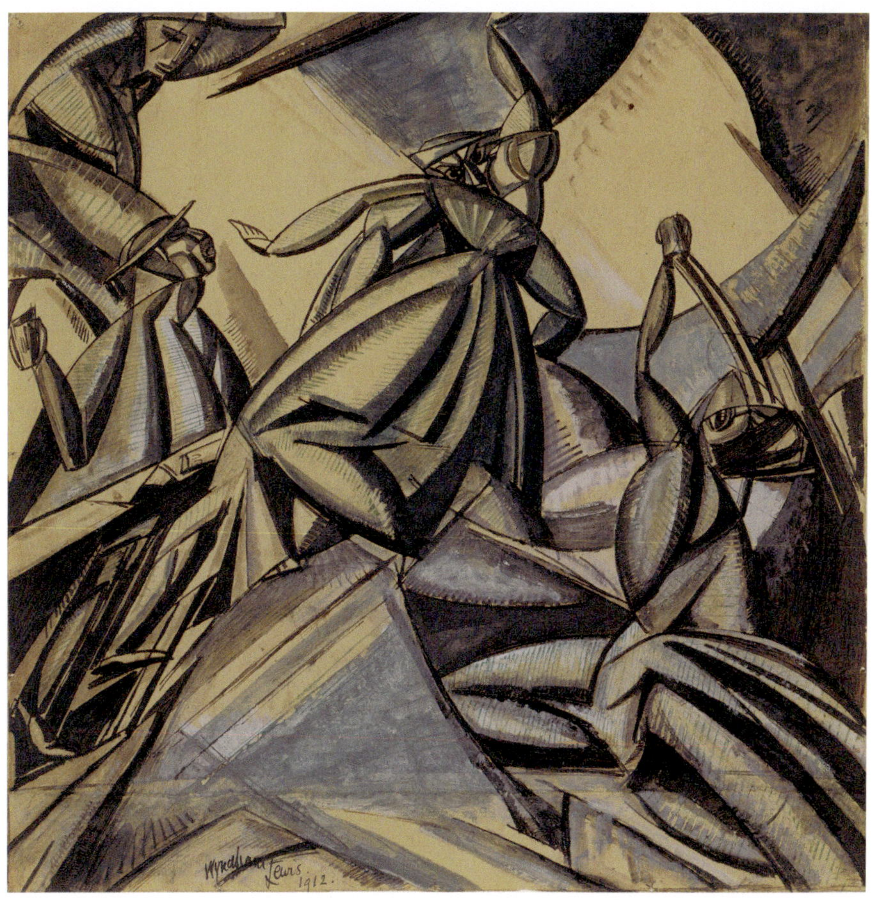

PL. 49 Wyndham Lewis, *Kermesse* (study), 1912. Ink, wash and gouache, 35 × 35.1 cm. Yale Center for British Art, New Haven

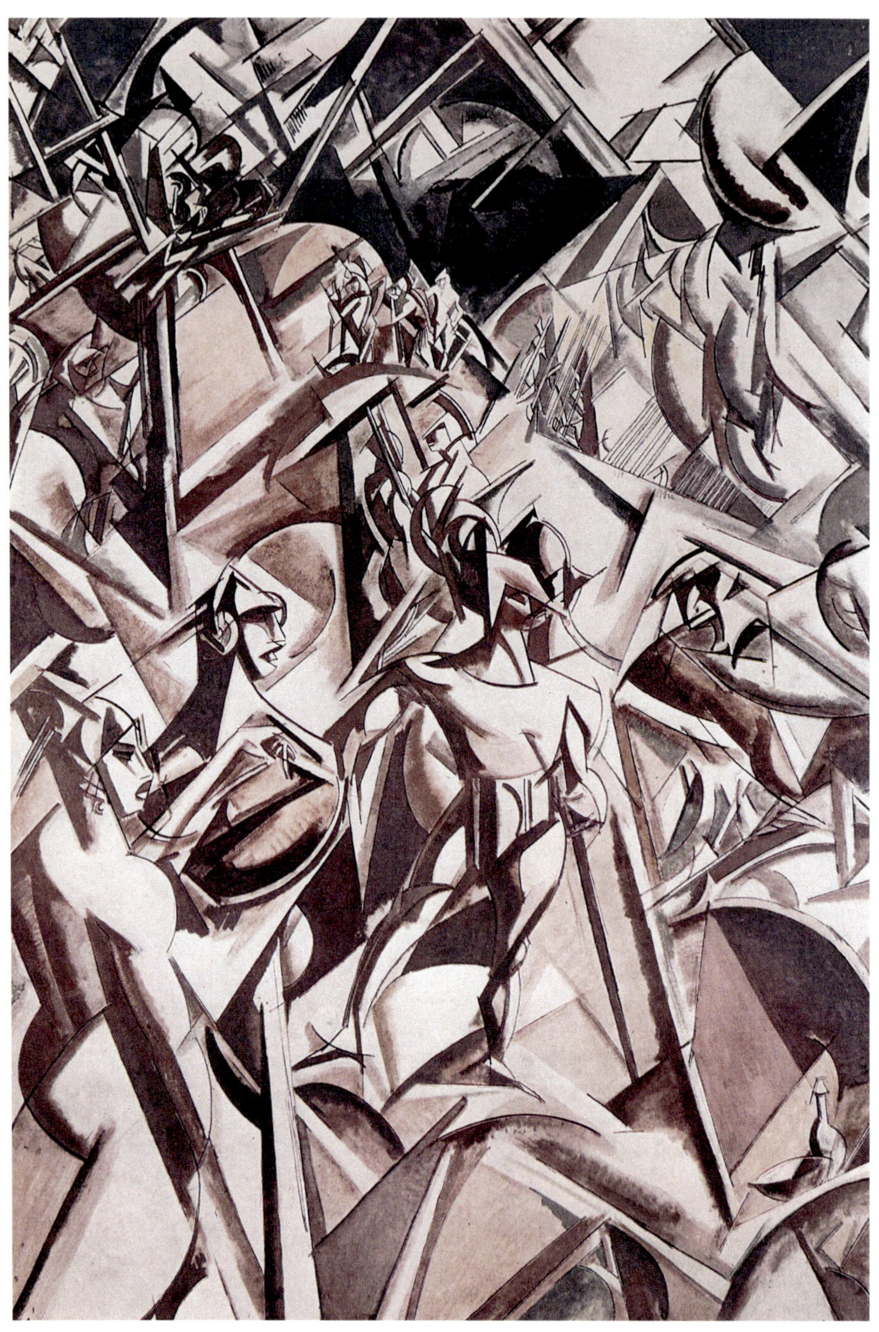

PL. 50 Wyndham Lewis, *Timon of Athens: The Thébaïde*, 1912. Watercolour and bodycolour, 49.5 × 34.3 cm, portfolio. Private collection

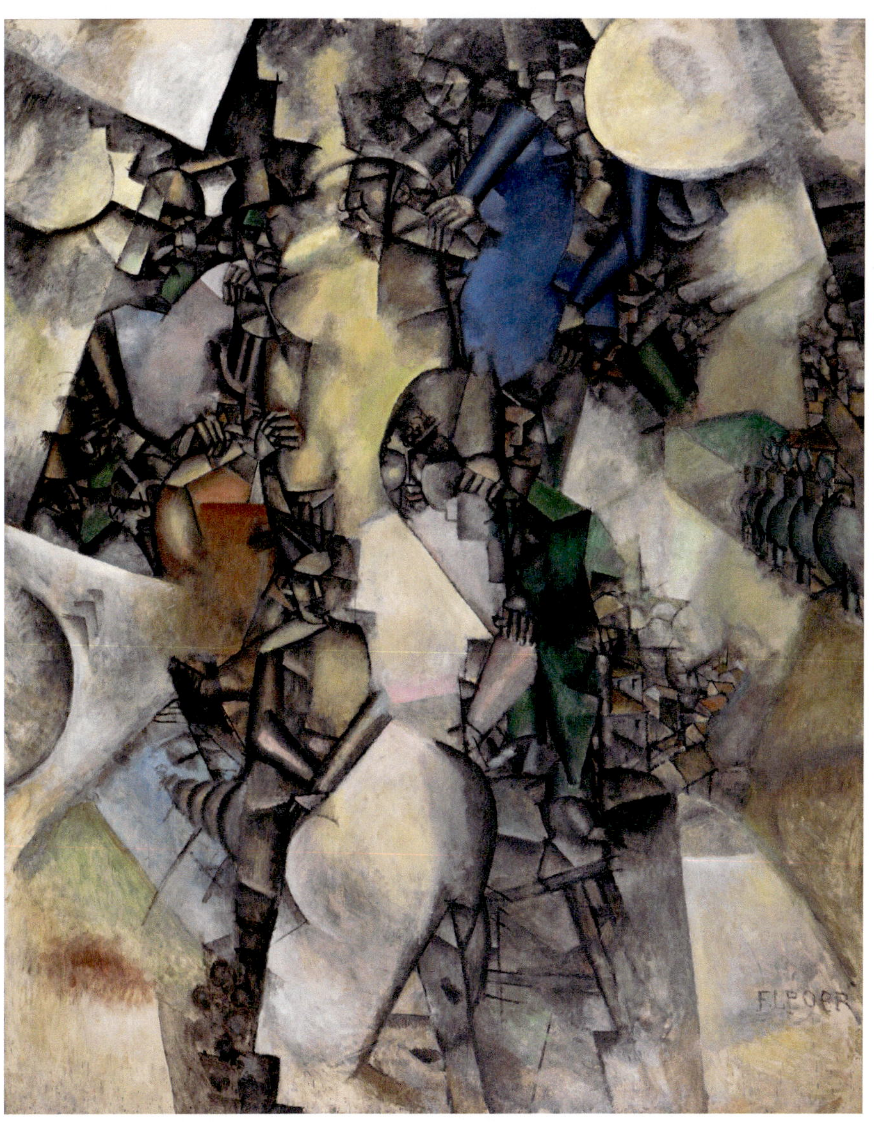

PL. 51 Fernand Léger, *La Noce* (*The Wedding*), 1911–12. Oil on canvas, 257 × 206 cm. Musée National d'Art Moderne, Paris

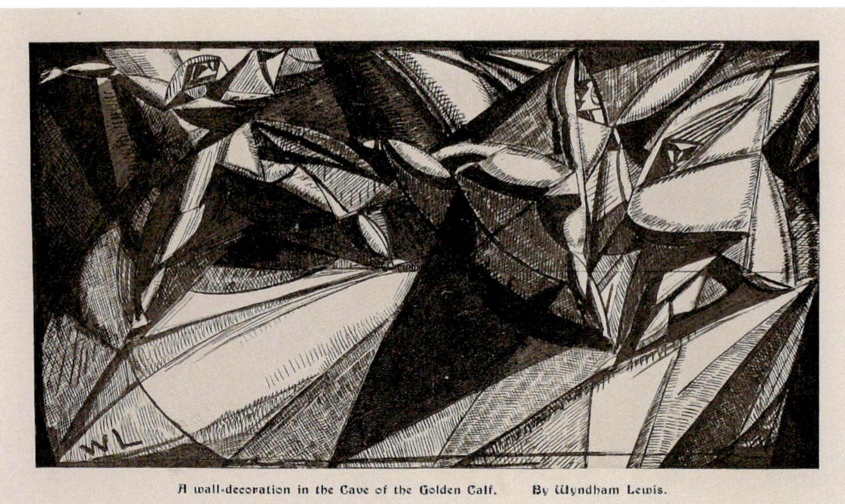

PL. 52 Wyndham Lewis, *Study for a Wall Decoration in the Cave of the Golden Calf*, 1912. Ink, dimensions and whereabouts unknown

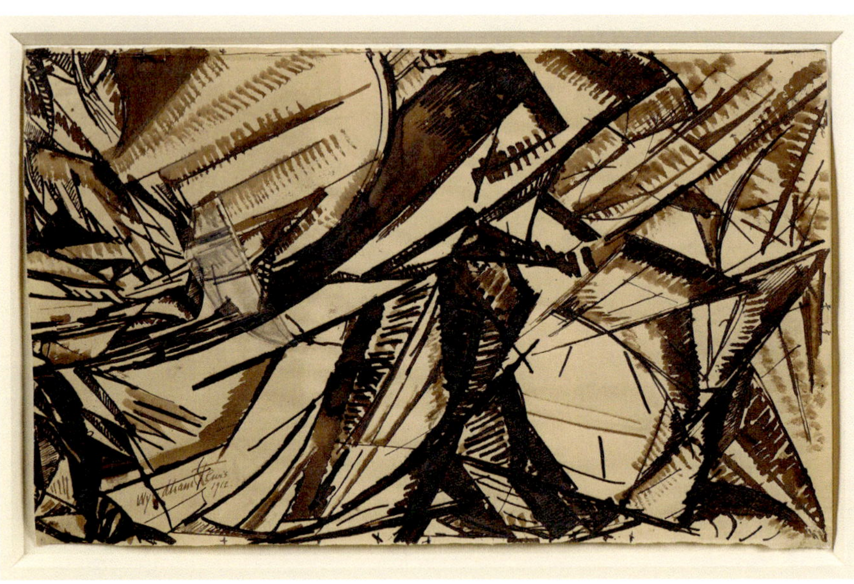

PL. 53 Wyndham Lewis, *Abstract Design*, 1912. Ink and watercolour, 24 × 38.5 cm. British Council, London

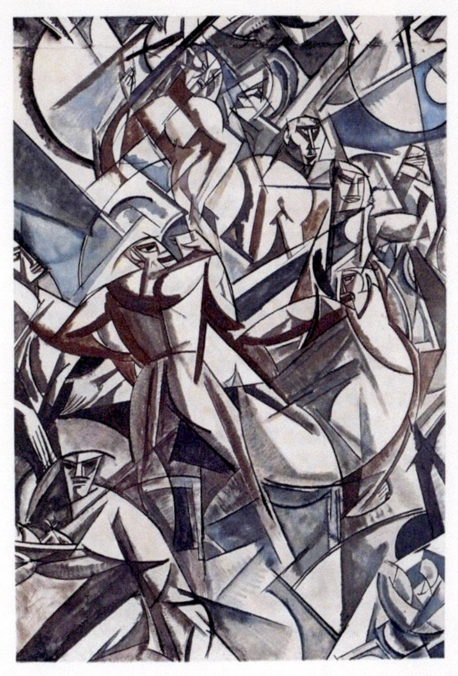

PL. 54 Wyndham Lewis, *Timon of Athens: A Feast of Overmen*, 1912. Watercolour and bodycolour, 49.5 × 34.3 cm, portfolio. Private collection

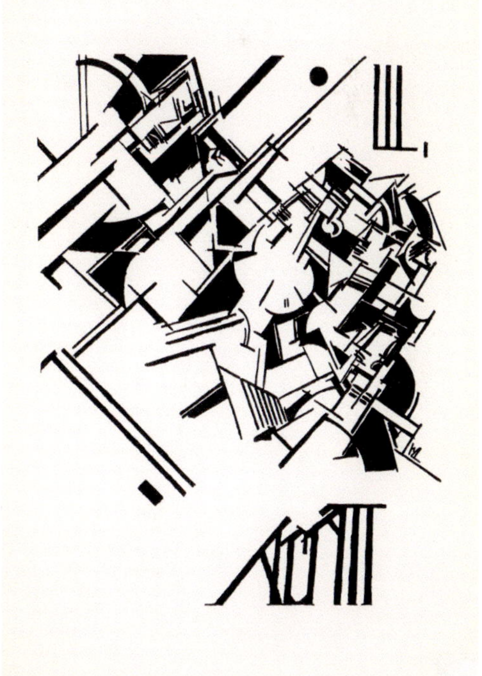

PL. 55 Wyndham Lewis, *Timon of Athens: Act III*, 1912. Watercolour and bodycolour, 49.5 × 34.3 cm, portfolio. Private collection

MARCH 4, 1914 THE SKETCH. 265

LADY DROGHEDA'S FUTURIST DINING-ROOM: DECORATIONS.

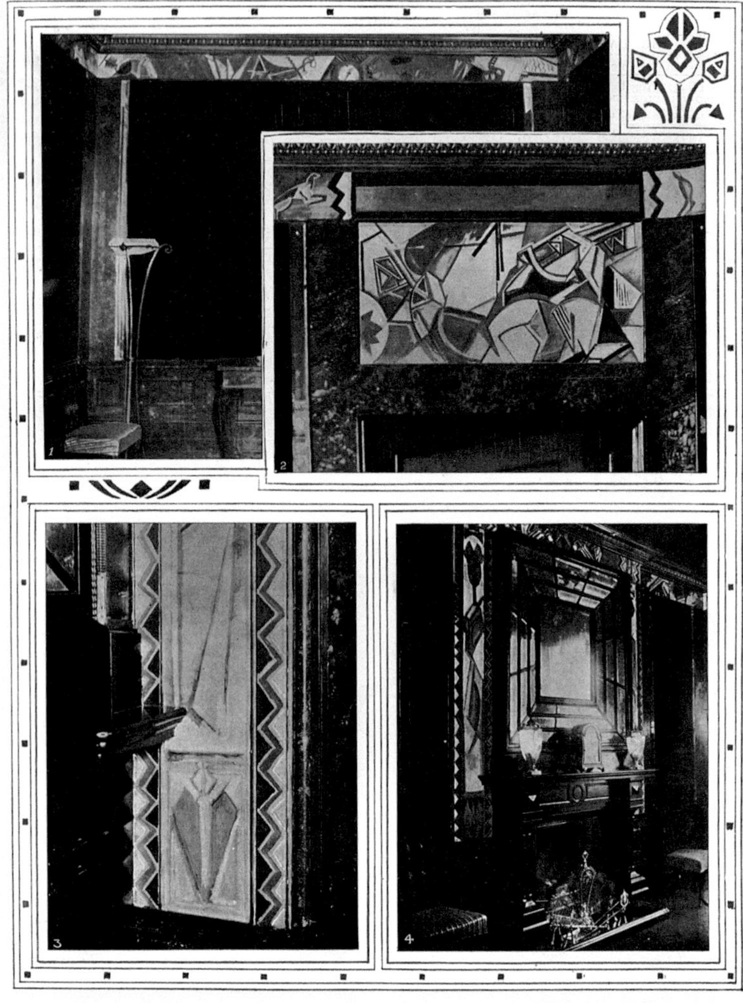

1. MULTI-COLOURED FUTURIST FRIEZE; REDDISH-BROWN PANELLING; A "BOWL OF FIRE" LIGHT.

2. THE FUTURIST PICTURE AND FRIEZE OVER THE DOOR.

3. A FUTURIST BORDER TO THE MANTELPIECE.

4. THE FUTURIST FIREPLACE; WITH BLACK-BEADED GLASS, COLOURED FUTURISTIC PANELS, AND TWO RED-GLASS VASES LIGHTED INSIDE.

As we note under our page portrait of the Countess, Lady Drogheda has had her dining-room at 40, Wilton Crescent decorated in the Futurist manner by Mr. Wyndham Lewis. These photographs were taken by special permission.

Photographs specially taken for "The Sketch."

PL. 56 Wyndham Lewis, Decorative motifs in the Countess of Drogheda's dining room, 1913–14. Published in *The Sketch*, 3 March 1914. No longer extant around 1910 until the war sufficient to warrant both the naming of a magazine with it and the use of it as a catch-all term for contemporary cultural innovations across the arts, none of them ever managed to define it. The failure to do so is striking, and was acknowledged as such by some at the time. With regard to the latter usage, critic and curator Frank Rutter later recalled that in that pre-war moment, 'RHYTHM was the magic word':

> What it meant *exactly* nobody knew, and the numerous attempts made at defining it were not very convincing. But it sounded well, one accepted it; one 'knew what it meant', and did not press the matter further. When we liked the design in a painting or drawing, we said it had Rhythm.[27]

The uncertainty was corroborated at the time: even Roger Fry, who probably introduced the term into British art-critical discourse in 1909, found it hard to define, as we have seen.[28] Writing in the *The Fortnightly Review* in May 1911, he could only manage: 'Rhythm is the fundamental and vital quality of painting, as of all the arts – representation is secondary to that, and must never encroach upon the more ultimate and fundamental demands of rhythm.'[29] He was more analytical than most in attempting to explain the reliance of Post-Impressionist artists on rhythm rather than representation, however: 'Particular rhythms of line and particular harmonies of colour have their spiritual correspondences.... The artist plays upon us by the rhythm of line, by colour, by abstract form, and by the quality of the matter he employs.'[30] A year later, he had refined his account of the term, but not by much: reviewing the Allied Artists Association's summer exhibition in July 1912, he praised the entry of Wyndham Lewis, *Kermesse*, for its 'rhythmic disposition of abstract units of form' and 'elementary geometric forms based on the rhythm of the human figure'; the definition remained implicit and vague.[31]

As regards the titling of his magazine, Murry never did explain this. Even his statement, in the first issue, of its 'Aims and Ideals', eschewed a definition: 'to find art in the strong things of life, is the meaning of

RHYTHM' is the closest he came to one, in a declaration of purpose that was otherwise couched in more elevated than technical, or even aesthetic, terms. A year later, in 'The Meaning of Rhythm' – an article whose title might have led a reader finally to expect one – Murry and his co-author of it, Katherine Mansfield, avoided the word entirely until their last sentence, offering there the closing peroration:

> Art and the artist are perfectly at one. Art is free; the artist is free. Art is real; the artist is real. Art is individual; the artist is individual. Their unity is ultimate and unassailable. It is the essential movement of Life. It is the splendid adventure, the eternal quest for rhythm.[32]

Such avoidance of precision, indeed of clarity, in the critical apparatus brought to bear on contemporary art by London commentators would seem unhelpful, since these writers – in particular Murry and his associates in the *Rhythm* circle such as O. Raymond Drey, who wrote about the Paris avant-garde for the magazine – had an investment both in their own discernment regarding Parisian developments and in supporting Anglophone participation in these (Drey married 'Rhythmist' painter Rice in 1913), and greater specificity of analytical insight would have furthered the cause of both. The concept of rhythm was not, however, widely taken up by the artistic avant-garde, for whom the appeal of the newest current of technicist innovations, those of Cubism, lay elsewhere;[33] it is a term hardly ever to be found, moreover, either in the art reviews of the *petites revues*, or in the writings of avant-garde artists themselves.[34] It seems likely that it was of most interest to those concerned with time-based media, such as music, dance and poetry, and that as an interest in dance spread rapidly across western societies in the pre-war decade, taking in not only the Ballets Russes but also Isadora Duncan and popular crazes such as for the 'Apache' dance and the tango, 'rhythm' became a useful (and usefully vague) connotative concept, applicable across cultural practices as a means of exploring their non-mimetic aspects, as these increasingly gained salience within modernism.[35]

The aesthetic vagueness of London art critics was especially true of their response to Cubism – and to the work of Picasso in particular – which was as uncertain as that of Rutter and Fry, which I noted earlier, and made in much the same terms.[36] In the first place, the reliance that these two placed on Picasso's prior (and Parisian) reputation as a guarantor of the profundity of his unreadable paintings from 1911 on was shared broadly; Murry spoke for more than himself when he acknowledged in his first essay on the artist:

> At the outset, modernist, ultra-modernist as I am in my artistic sympathies, I frankly disclaim any pretension to an understanding or even appreciation of Picasso. I am awed by him.... Picasso has done everything.... He has made drawings with a magical line that leaves one amazed by its sheer and simple beauty – and yet he has reached a point where none have explained and none, so far as I know, have truly understood.[37]

Such incomprehension did not daunt every critic (even when coupled with vagueness about 'rhythm'): reviewing the Salon d'Automne of 1912, Drey declared: 'It is difficult to understand why such a fuss should be made about cubism. The theory, in its simplest form, is comprehensible enough', he added, explaining: 'The cubists, like good Fauves, are trying to rid Art of the incubus of preconceived mental associations which have tied it so long to mere representation.'[38]

The following spring, in a review of the Salon des Indépendants entitled 'Indépendants and the Cubist Muddle', Drey developed this with (loose) reference to 'rhythm': 'Picasso, then, has come from contemplation of form and substance to an abstract rhythmic statement.' He added: 'Rhythmic statement is not new in paint. Rhythmic statement independent of concrete representation, abstract rhythmic statement, is.'[39] The condescending title of Drey's piece suggests his awareness of the recent (March 1912) weighty article on Cubism by the leading conservative Parisian literary and art critic Jacques Rivière which I noted in Chapter 6, and which displayed just the same quality. If Drey did know of this substantial critique – it was likely to have been well known in Paris by the time he wrote his review – his account of Cubism did not reveal the fact, beyond the borrowing of Rivière's curl of the lip for his title. Where the Parisian's emphasis is on stripping away all of those interrogations of the devices of pictorial illusionism that, in retrospect, made Cubist reflexivity so central for subsequent modernist painting, with the neo-Kantian aim of distinguishing, in painting that was unquestionably representational, between things 'as they appear' and their 'essence' independent of perception, it is clear from Drey's remark about rhythm quoted above that he assumed, as did Fry, that – as the latter wrote in explanation of the painter's *Tête d'homme* (*Head of a Man*) of 1912 (see pl. 27) shown in the *Second Post-Impressionist Exhibition* – Picasso was seeking 'to create a purely abstract language of form; a visual music'.[40] Drey, in his turn, wrote of Picasso's Cubism in his Indépendants review that

> never before has painting appealed directly to the emotions without enlisting the aid of the intellect. People complain when music becomes representative, realistic. It is no longer music, we are told. Yet who can say what music is, or what is painting? It is a poor game to try to confine the human spirit, to temper creation, to put our own blinkers on the visionary.[41]

The contrast within critical discourse between, on the one hand, this vagueness of analytical language and misreading of paintings and, on the other, the specificities of Parisian avant-garde theorising and criticism, as represented by Rivière's essay – as well as by many other texts from within that avant-garde, from Signac's 1899 treatise on Neo-Impressionism to Cubism in 1912[42] – could hardly be greater, and it prompts the question as to the reason for such disparity. It is possible to argue that it reflects London's position as a peripheral satellite to Paris's centre, that its critics simply did not possess the professional acumen or familiarity with current *technie* that was deployed there, and indeed there is a note of amateurism in the confessions of bewilderment in the face of, say, Picasso's hermetic

Cubism. But to hear only this note, to read this criticism only in the terms of Parisian avant-garde professionalism, would be to take the latter as an objective standard, rather than the narrow specialisation that, *inter alia*, it also was. For the London art-critical discourse was elaborated in the pre-war half-decade not only in default of the conditions that produced those of Paris, but also from alternative principles, circumstances and traditions that provided their own interpretative context. These were principally three: one literary, the second broadly cultural, even implicitly political, the third indicative of a fundamental departure from the Parisian aesthetic paradigm of representation. The literary context was an understanding of 'rhythm' as, if far from precise, yet already well grounded in an Anglophone discourse – in, primarily, Arthur Symons's Symbolist literary theorising and W.B. Yeats's poetry as well as his love of Symbolist theatre, which were influential points of reference for an emergent modernist literary formation.[43] As Frank Kermode observed in a seminal book and subsequent article on the former, Symons brought a Symbolist, anti-naturalistic idea of popular dance (principally that of Loïe Fuller) to bear on contemporary literary practice, including his own poetry. Fuller's art of illuminated drapes in motion, which used masses of flowing silk to evoke a dream-like ambience in which the perception of geometrical space was abolished, in Symons's view created visual rhythms that had transcendental implications;[44] these, as literary historian Alan Robinson argues, Symons broadened into an animistic aesthetic which governed all contemporary art, including that of composer Richard Wagner and sculptor Auguste Rodin.[45] Symons's infatuation with Fuller's dancing was paralleled by Yeats's enthusiasm for the anti-naturalistic theatre of Edward Gordon Craig, the performances of West End leading actor Florence Farr and those of Parisian star Sarah Bernhardt, the last of which Yeats characterised as a 'rhythmic progression' of gestures, 'the nobler movements that the heart sees, the rhythmical movements that seem to flow up into the imagination from some deeper life than that of the individual soul'.[46]

This literary inheritance provided London's emergent cohort of little-magazine art critics with an adaptable understanding of 'rhythm' as 'the very rhythm of the world', as Robinson suggests – enabling them to elide, pragmatically, the Bergson of *Creative Evolution* that they recognised as paradigmatic with congruent connotations of 'a Neoplatonic *Anima Mundi* or *nous* [and] Schopenhauerian "will"'.[47] A second, broader inheritance was of that 'adversarial bourgeois' ideology of affective relations that we have seen running through British culture from the mid-nineteenth century, articulating the motley responses to dominant capitalist social and cultural values. This could comprehend, as we have seen, both the egalitarian, socialistic emphases and allegiances of affective communities and relations, and the elitism of notions of (masculinist) brotherhood, such as that idea of the artist as 'angel' proposed by Allen Upward and readily adopted by Ezra Pound.[48] In the London art field of 1912–14, for an emergent avant-garde formation that lacked either the critical mass or the self-conscious professionalism of its Parisian equivalent – indeed, that spurned professionalism, as it understood the term – the assimilation, and adaptation to the requirements of its self-identity, of whatever was driving innovation beyond the Channel was easier, perhaps only possible, in terms of this broad and tacitly anti-capitalist ideology. The language reached for reflected these terms. Thus Murry's declaration of *Rhythm*'s 'Aims and Ideals': 'Aestheticism has had its day', he asserted,

> It has been inevitably submerged by the surge of the life that lay beyond its sphere. We need an art that strikes deeper, that touches a profounder reality.... To treat what is being done today as something vital in the progress of art, which cannot fix its eyes on yesterday and live... in creation to give expression to an art that seeks out the strong things of life; in criticism to seek out the strong things of that art – such is the aim of RHYTHM.[49]

There was little room in such rhetoric for the consideration of Rivière's arguments as to 'why lighting should be replaced' in painting, and with what, or even for the recognition of any need for such technical precision; such narrow professional criteria were not at issue. What *was* at issue was the perceived need to furnish aesthetic criteria that brought contemporary technical radicalism into relation with *extra*-aesthetic concerns – in particular, those that were adequate to the roles both of the new art, whatever it was, of the new century, and of the artist in this century's new society.

The third inheritance of the London art-critical discourse offered one alternative avenue of cultural discourse to the *technie*-driven professionalism of Paris that amounted to a paradigm departure from it. This was the legacy of the Aesthetic Movement that saw beauty and, within this, a decorative purpose as fundamental to art. The Parisian engagement with technical issues around representation and the pictorial (and less often sculptural) devices that enabled this was, by *c.* 1910, already generations old and deeply embedded in studio practices and assumptions. In consequence, the possibilities offered by *non*-representation were considered by very few French artists at that time, and the exploration of them was left to foreigners either in Paris for a time, such as Piet Mondrian, Frank Kupka and, a little later, Liubov Popova and Kazimir Malevich, or independent of it, such as Wassily Kandinsky. No French artist, even in the *technie*-obsessed avant-garde of that pre-war decade, experimented with abstraction, except Robert Delaunay, whose aesthetic allegiances, once he had broken with Cubism in 1912, were closer to (besides his Russian artistic partner and wife, Sonia) German Expressionists and the Swiss painter Paul Klee than to French colleagues. Arguably, it was the very *lack* of having been steeped in the close engagement with Parisian questions of pictorial representation that gave those artists who absorbed its ideas from the distance of their 'peripheral' cities the relative freedom from its potential constraints (the blissful ignorance, one might say) to innovate in ways unthinkable to its Paris-trained adepts.[50] This was as true of London artists as of those elsewhere, and given their Aestheticist inheritance, they were predisposed to misrecognise Parisian representational radicalisms as a step into a discourse of abstraction whose decorative implications blurred the lines between fine and applied art, and opened the way to that harnessing of avant-garde *technie* for the embellishment of opulent interiors that was more noticeable in London than anywhere else in Europe. The theoretical articulation – such as it was – of this elision was grounded, unsurprisingly, in the concept of rhythm.

THE CAVE OF THE GOLDEN CALF: CONSUMERISM, CLASS AND PERFORMANCE

Until Richard Cork's pioneering study of 1985, whose meticulous research and detailed reconstruction of its brief existence opened up a veritable treasure trove of documentation and insights,[51] the Cabaret Theatre Club, as it was formally named, was seen as a marginal feature of London's pre-First World War art field, little written about and even less considered. The measure of Cork's achievement is that the Cave of the Golden Calf, as it was popularly known after its entrance signboard, has since and as a consequence become recognised as, on the contrary, a key site within that field and a significant focus for any history of British modernist art, and has acquired a substantial historiography within both this and that of the history of cabaret.[52] What follows both draws and comments upon some of the analyses that have been presented, in the tracing of the threads of the argument of the present study through the history, character and context of this nightclub as a cultural (ad)venture. A preliminary summary of these would, however, be germane and, it is to be hoped, useful.

The Cabaret Theatre Club was a nightclub launched in London in the spring of 1912 by Frida Uhl Strindberg, an Austrian writer who had been, in the mid-1890s, the second wife of Swedish playwright August Strindberg. She was a member of the Young Vienna circle of *fin-de-siècle* writers that met in the cafés of that city, where she started a cabaret in 1900.[53] Coming to live in London from 1908, and familiar with the Cabaret Fledermaus, opened in Vienna by the Wiener Werkstätte the previous year, she was well positioned to answer the call made in the spring of 1911 by theatre impresario and critic J.T. Grein for a cabaret to be founded in London, to exploit the vogue for commercial popular evening entertainment that was then sweeping Europe. A model of informal, often small-scale (the preferred term was 'intimate'), late-night dining, dancing and/or variety performance spaces, often in low-rent basements, that originated in 1880s Paris with Rodolphe Salis's Chat Noir,[54] by 1910 cabarets could be found in most of the continent's major cities, and Grein was 'certain' that such a venue in London 'would be more than a nine days' wonder'.[55] Mme Strindberg immediately responded, calling him the next day with an offer of funds if he would take up his own suggestion and start one; when he declined, she stepped in herself.[56]

The Cave was opened on 26 June 1912 in the basement of a clothing warehouse at 9 Heddon Street off Regent Street, W1, and closed less than two years later in February 1914. It was an enormous oblong room reached by an outside staircase, 'capable of housing, perhaps, two hundred persons in atmospheric comfort' (pl. 43),[57] seated at small tables at which food and drink were served, and at the side of which a small, low, curtained stage was set, on which, from the outset, what was for London an adventurous selection of dancers, singers, *diseuses*, musicians and actors – *inter alia* – performed. It was enlivened by strikingly colourful, dynamic and (for the most part) decorative murals of, among others, jungle and hunting scenes that drew on early Kandinsky, the Douanier Rousseau and Cubism (see pls 45–47 and 49). These were painted by a team of three artists, recruited with the help of Mme Strindberg's former lover Augustus John and led by Spencer Frederick Gore, accompanied by Wyndham Lewis and Charles Ginner, together with sculptors Jacob Epstein (for the 'primitivist' caryatids that lined the basement's pillars) and Eric Gill (who made the gilded priapic calf that stood on a pedestal inside the entrance, and the signboard depicting it). Several press reviews upon its opening testified that it was an exotic and even unsettling space; the *Times* critic, noting the 'small stage and mural decorations representing we should not care to say what precise stage beyond impressionism', added that the latter were likely to 'turn into appalling goblins after a little too much supper'.[58]

The Cave's commercial prospects were decidedly uncertain. As cabaret historian Lisa Appignanesi observed, 'the cabaret form had never really taken hold in England, either as a meeting and performance place for writers and artists, or as a centre for satirical dissent.'[59] The Café Royal held a virtual monopoly on such fashionable hospitality in culturally conservative London; poet and editor Douglas Goldring later recalled that 'if a "new movement" was started on the Continent, the Café Royal was always the first place to hear of it and to "produce" it in England'.[60] Yet the mushrooming of the cabaret model across Europe, together with the momentum of the appetite for cultural consumerism, and specifically for that ostentatious aspect of it, on the part of London's well-to-do, that I explored in the last chapter, offered grounds for Grein's optimism, and in the wake of his appeal and shortly before the Golden Calf opened, a number of other 'European-style' venues sprang up in London, including the Moonshine Cabaret and the Theatre Cabaret, both namechecked by the illustrated weekly *The Sphere*.[61] The momentum for new nightlife venues grew steadily until the war; *The Sketch* reported in January 1914 that 'there have arisen three Supper Clubs – with, it is rumoured, more to come'. The reason, it suggested, was that 'London is in the midst of another new movement.... It is evident that she desires to keep later hours or, at all events, she is growing resentful at the fact that the authorities ring the curfew at night at so early an hour.'[62] Yet as the concept of 'supper club' itself suggests – and as an illustration in the same paper a week earlier shows (pl. 44) – these were conventionally decorated, in no way comparable to the Golden Calf, and added nothing to the lustre which it had briefly bestowed on the city's cultural entertainment scene. This conventionality was significant, as we shall see.

Mme Strindberg's was thus an audacious and an innovative venture. Typically, as it appears from accounts of her, she came out fighting for her vision, and from the start threw down a gauntlet to London's entertainment industry and its clientele, with advance publicity boldly declaring her intentions. A 'Preliminary Prospectus' published in March 1912 promised a 'varied programme... a return of art to intuition and simplicity.... On one hand such art as we owe to the genius of the people, the dance, folk lore – on the other offering free development to the youngest and best of our contemporaries and – "Futurists".' The last reference was thoroughly – and combatively – up-to-date, as the Futurist painters' first exhibition in London, fresh from its debut in Paris, was currently to be seen at the Sackville Gallery, and Mme Strindberg's determination to match it with local talent was clear: 'the decoration will be entirely and exclusively the work of leading young British artists', the Prospectus declared.[63] A month later a press announcement from the 'Preliminary Committee' declared the Cabaret Theatre Club to be 'the first English artists' cabaret'.[64] It was the decoration that was perhaps its most innovative feature, for, as Cork notes: 'Although cabarets had already proved an uninhibited stimulus to avant-garde movements elsewhere in Europe, none of them had attempted to carry out a programme of decorations as elaborate and ambitious as the wall-paintings, sculptural installations and stage scenery in this extraordinary interior.'[65] But the boldness of the assertions about its Englishness was equally striking, for it directly challenged the imperialistic complacency and implicit xenophobia that coloured several of the press reviews, as well as the insularity of their expectations: upon entry to the Cave, 'the world of London seems to have completely disappeared. It is not English; nothing is English',[66] wrote one; another, that '[y]ou might be in Cairo or Vienna, in Brussels or in Amsterdam, in Madrid or in Stockholm; you are surely not in England', and noted 'a babel of tongues – French predominating; but you also hear Spanish and Russian, and German also, and... Swedish', adding, 'at one table are seated four East Indians, wearing turbans, brilliant robes, costly beads'.[67] The challenge ran through all of the project, from the primitivism of the murals and pillar caryatids that put in the shade the Post-Impressionism that had shocked so many at Roger Fry's Grafton Gallery exhibition only months earlier,[68] by way of the demonic dancers of Lewis's illustrations for the publicity material, the cave-painting quality of his drop-curtain for the stage, and his huge (2.7 metres square), disturbingly aggressive, near-abstract painting *Kermesse* (pl. 49), that hung above the entrance stairs (to welcome, or warn, the arriving guests), to the juxtaposition of popular culture and experimental art. 'The variety performance, with its concentration on one personality, with its bright, vivid scenes and "impressions", is in a sense, if not the natural form of art, at least a perennial expression of artistic temperament', declared the publicity. 'To give art in this spontaneous and flexible form will be the aim of the new cabaret', it promised.[69]

And from the outset, as a venture it succeeded. As *The Sunday Times* noted, on opening night it was 'besieged by customers'; as Augustus John later recalled, 'one look at the seething mob outside its doors, on opening night, was enough for me. I passed on.'[70] Inside, *The Times* noted a few weeks later, the audience 'talked and laughed as loud when the stage was occupied as when it was empty.... So there was plenty of that cheerful din which means that people are at their ease, and the performers took their chance against the buzzing talk and the whirring electric fans.'[71] The clientele in those early weeks was also cosmopolitan. As one reviewer reported:

> You discover that the woman talking so volubly to the Spanish dancer is the widow of a famous German professor, and the shy-looking girl is the wife of a Danish poet, who later recites an English translation of his poems. Three or four well-groomed men have arrived, and they are trying their French on a dark-haired, dark-eyed woman to whom they have been presented – the men are all soldiers, officers from one of the Guards regiments, and the woman is a prima donna from Milan. Presently she sings an aria from a French opera, and you listen entranced. She is followed – the performer always rising from among the audience – by a girl dancer of the cult which Maud Allan made familiar to us, and with bared feet and limbs she endeavours to convey the motions of a grasshopper.... It does not strike one at all as astonishing to hear that the dancer is one of the attractions of grand opera and that she has just been borrowed for a cabaret evening.[72]

The intoxication of it all is palpable, and the enthusiasm of this fashion-conscious London clientele for the exoticism of Mme Strindberg's cultural cocktail – of Englishness with foreignness, of music hall, variety-style entertainment and commercial-popular culture with opera – is clearly evident. Yet there are two implications of this account that I wish to draw out as significant for the present study. The first is that the Golden Calf was an expensive venue, as the culturally omnivorous, and thus well-to-do, character of this clientele suggests, and as several reviews and recollections of it noted;[73] the fashionability of the Cave was, as such, inseparable from those class aspirations and cultural-consumerist dynamics that I explored in Chapter 9. The second – and closely related – is the presence of Guards officers among those attending this opening night: these are not the usual consumers of such a cocktail, and they represent an anomalous element; indeed, a Trojan horse, as it were, within this crowd. For as those who have discussed it agree, the social make-up of the Cave's clientele changed quite rapidly, as the initiative was assimilated to the requirements of those more likely to be found at the Café Royal and the Four Hundred Club (see pl. 44).[74] Journalist Ashley Gibson, one of the Club's habitués from the beginning, later recalled:

> On such later occasions as I explored the Cave it seemed to be doing good business.... Madame's flair for recruiting impeccable artists secured her a chef beyond criticism, nor did the establishment's cellar give ground for complaint. While these remained, and the cabaret turns maintained their novelty, supper parties in those subterranean alcoves continued popular with those who could afford them, for the fun was fast and furious. There lay the rub, however. The clientèle whom it was intended to attract could not afford to keep it up.... The vulgarer stockbroking element soon preponderated... their notions of fun were a little too fast and furious, and the Cave... met the common fate of such institutions in the West End of London.[75]

Gibson's recollections and assessments, like all such memoirs, may be partial (in both senses of the term), but they are corroborated by two other accounts, this time fictitious, one of them written and published in 1913, at the exact moment of the Cave's comet-like trajectory through the night culture of London, the other within three years of its demise. The first, novelist and art critic Charles Marriott's *Subsoil*, a novel about the subterranean layers of its art world of the time, devotes its second chapter to a scene in a nightclub called the Rocking Horse, a thinly disguised reference to the Golden Calf, the topicality and identifiability of which must have been striking on its appearance, probably late in 1913. Central to this chapter is a view shared by the main character, an artist named Sutherland, and his friends, also all artists, of the club as having become 'too prosperous' and having sold out to affluent 'philistine' respectability. This is hinted at in the opening chapter's first mention of the venue:

> The 'Rocking Horse', now… famous in art circles… had been adopted as a war-cry by the younger and more experimental painters and writers in London. The club had been started under wealthy patronage as their rallying-place. Sutherland had lent his name in support of its origin, and had even assisted in its decoration, but a disbelief in transplanted atmospheres had kept him from taking it very seriously. The immediate support of the newspapers, with an insistence on the possibility of a Bohemia in evening dress, had further shaken his belief. He had only been to the club once since its opening about a year ago.[76]

This disquiet is quickly established as the chapter's theme, from Sutherland's entrance with a friend under the Golden Calf-like provocation of its eponymous rocking horse sign – 'Below the sign stood a very solid commissionaire, and Sutherland observed in passing the discrepancy between the symbol of adventure and that of social stability. "Getting too prosperous, eh?" he said to Beresford'[77] – via the initial notations of its modernity: it was 'freakishly decorated', the atmosphere was 'cooled by an electric fan [and] charged with the odour of superior cooking' – to the alienation the artist feels immediately on entering:

> Already, thought Sutherland,… the original purpose of the room, as hinted at by the decorations and the stage, was ignored. There were about fifty people there, the greater number being men in evening-dress, so that Sutherland in his tweeds looked, though he was too interested to feel, a conspicuous figure.[78]

The theme is largely carried by the conversational observations of the group of artist friends he joins:

> One of the painters, an excessively polite young man named Jenner, began apologetically to explain the ideas of the management. 'Things have to be done gradually', he said. 'You have to get people used to the idea that artistic pleasure is not necessarily disreputable, and if the place is to be a success, the prosperous Philistine must be encouraged even at the cost of some tameness in the entertainment.'[79]

Marriott indicates whom Jenner (and he himself) has in mind, and suggests the disaffection of the artists, in a few caricatural strokes:

> 'I can tell you a few of them', said Beale.... 'The pink party with sandy hair and no chin... is Archibald Hay, the Cattle King from Argentina.... Two tables nearer the stage you'll see Asher Bernstein, of Gordon and Bernstein, the print publishers. Up against the piano, with his bald head bobbing up and down to a dirty story, is Colonel Constantine, the hero of a frontier-accident. He's brought a party of nice boys with him to show them life, and... they're disappointed because we don't make beasts of ourselves.'[80]

If Marriott's was, as it appears, the only novelistic appropriation of the Cabaret Theatre Club contemporary with its brief existence, it was followed shortly after its demise by Gilbert Cannan's *Mendel*, a novel published in 1916 about artists based on the life of painter Mark Gertler, which also features a recognisably Golden Calf-like nightclub, this time called Merlin's Cave; in its only, and brief, appearance, this venue is similarly, if more pithily, characterised in terms of the contrast between 'common and shabby' artistic bohemianism and the 'wealth and cleanliness' of its majority clientele of evening-dressed 'swells'. 'What do you think of this place?' asks Mendel's girlfriend, in one exchange; 'I suppose if the swells come it'll be a success, but they do spoil it.' To which Mendel replies. 'Yes.... They spoil everything.'[81]

Clearly the caveats against taking fiction as documentary truth need to be observed in making use of such material as corroboration, but there are reasons for taking account of these two novels. A first is that, together with a number of memoirs from the interwar period, such as those by Ashley Gibson and Edgar Jepson, they have been so frequently cited by most of the Golden Calf's historians in evidence for their own characterisations of it as to have become legitimised in the historiography. A second is that, unlike later fiction as well as the memoirs, they fasten exclusively upon the contrast between its intended (and initial) clientele and its eventual one – its vulgarisation by 'swells' – and in so doing are congruent with the more detailed recollections of it. A third reason is that – also unlike the later testimony and fictional reconstructions – they were written when memory of this club was fresh, not the other side of the cataclysm of the First World War. Marriott's from 1913 seems quite intentionally a *roman à clef* in respect of the nightclub, and would surely have been read as such at the time by its familiars, among others. By contrast, the post-war representations of the Cabaret Theatre Club have, in their summary accounts, a distinctly tropological character. The reiterated recollections and imaginings of it by novelist and serial memoirist Ford Madox Ford from the early 1920s, like the souvenirs of fellow writers Osbert Sitwell and Violet Hunt (Ford's partner) – all referenced repeatedly in the historiography – share an emphasis on aspects of an atmosphere of hedonistic excess in which intoxicating aesthetic experiment, frenzied dancing and sensory overload together teetered on the brink of nightmare: in Ford's 1923 novel *The Marsden Case* the Night Club has a 'foreign' and 'oriental' space of 'orgies', where even the vol-au-vents are 'gilded' and its interior, a 'vast cellar' and 'cavern', is accessed by a flight of 'yawning, black stairs', and where by 'half past one… the place [is] dreadful; the thin air tight in the lungs; the lights too bright; the dreadful white pillars leering'.[82] In his 1948 volume of memoirs Sitwell echoed this, recalling a 'low-ceilinged night-club, appropriately sunk below the pavement… and hideously but appropriately frescoed, [which] appeared in the small hours to be a super-heated Vorticist garden of gesticulating figures, dancing and talking while the rhythm of the primitive forms of ragtime throbbed through the wide room'.[83] In her memoirs, published in 1926, Hunt took this over the top: 'we were poised on the point of a needle, trembling in space', she wrote, 'and all the *rémue-ménage*, this nervous gaiety, this singing of German lieder and performing of amateur plays at the Cabaret Club, under the walls covered with Wyndham Lewis's raw meat designs… Bismarckian images, severings, disembowellings, mixed pell-mell with the iron shards that did it, splashed with the pale blood of exhausted heroes'.[84] The last image in particular reminds us that, for Ford and Hunt at least, the war was not far in the past. Indeed, *The Marsden Case*, literary historian Nathan Waddell argues,

> might be described, at least in the context of its relation to the artistic avant-gardism and social cultures associated with the Cabaret Theatre Club, as an impassioned, nostalgic reconstruction of a pre-war climate that Ford still clearly viewed as desirable in an early 1920s moment marked by bad 'omens' and 'groans'.[85]

Much of the characterisation of Mme Strindberg's club offered by its historians draws heavily on such reimaginings – at the expense, I would argue, of those qualities that, as I have noted, are found in contemporary accounts, both fictional and journalistic. We need to make this distinction, because whatever functions the emphasis on its transgressive qualities served for novelists and memoirists in the interwar context of a cultural avant-gardist formation then in the ascendant across Europe and beyond, in this *pre*-First World War moment of its emergence in London the dynamic of its shaping by the vectors of class, aspirant cultural consumerism and 'evening-dress' bohemianism (to borrow Marriott's designation) should be recognised, and was acknowledged at the time.

I am arguing, then, that the Cabaret Theatre Club, which Frida Strindberg hoped would shake up London with its cosmopolitan avant-gardism, and make money doing so, was instead assimilated to, and eventually compromised by, this dynamic. Yet the significance of the

Golden Calf is not only that it is a register of the co-option of an unruly and cosmopolitan bohemianism, but further that it both assisted the emergence – finally – in London of an avant-garde nucleus of visual artists ('formation' is perhaps too ambitious a description for so few), and conditioned the terms of this. It did so specifically in the programme of decorative murals, and of illustrations and other decorations that Lewis in particular contributed to this. Ironically, it was Sickert, for whom avant-gardist iconoclasm and *technie* were usually anathema, who alone appears to have recognised this at the time. Giving a speech at the opening, in December 1913, of a *Post-Impressionists, Cubists and Others* exhibition at Brighton Art Gallery, Sickert is reported to have declared that he 'looked upon Mr Wyndham Lewis as a man of extraordinary talent', adding: 'To understand the real value of his work one should see the decoration he has done for a night club called the Cabaret. For a club where you go to dance the tango or to have other amusement, this is just the right form of decoration.' Perhaps Sickert's response was conditioned by his fondness, noted earlier, for the overlaps between art and popular urban cultural performance.[86] Noting this response, Richard Cork comments: 'He may have been influenced by the infectious gaiety of the Club's ambience, and have decided that it legitimized a degree of stylistic radicalism he would have found unacceptable in a gallery exhibition.'[87] These two comments, one contemporary with the club, the other a historian's retrospection, together offer the insight that it was the decorative purpose of the paintings – their performative character, as signifiers of the Golden Calf's avant-garde modernity and bohemian transgression – that gave licence to their creators each to surpass his previous work in technicist boldness. For Gore and Ginner this enabled their breaking the limitations of their Camden Town Post-Impressionism in murals whose stylistic references were, for the first time, contemporary in continental terms rather than a generation old – not only Gauguin, but Kandinsky and Henri Rousseau. For Lewis, it enabled him to confront both the bravura *technie* of current (gallery and salon) Cubism and the *braggadocio* of the Futurist painters' ostentatious 'modernolatry'.

Yet for all of them, this licence came with limiting conditions. While the decorative agenda fostered Gore and Ginner's engagement with an emerging new 'continental' art of experimentation and abstraction,[88] it resulted in what might be called a 'nursery' primitivism whose flat patterning, childish simplifications of form and bright colours in no way disturbed the imperialistic tropes of orientalism and exoticness, instead 'unwittingly serv[ing] to aestheticise the Other towards stereotype'.[89] Thus, on the one hand, Gore's hunting scene nodded unmistakably to Kandinsky (pls 45 and 46), whose *Composition I* of 1910 he had helped to hang at the Allied Artists exhibition that summer, while Ginner's jungle indexed not only those of Henri Rousseau but perhaps also Picasso's early (1907) Cubism;[90] on the other hand, both opened up decorative possibilities that, far from provoking hallucinations of 'appalling goblins', appear to have been picked up by Vanessa Bell for her own children's nursery in 1913 (pls 47 and 48).[91] For both artists, the commission enabled them briefly to acknowledge the potential for non-representational painting that was contained in contemporary concepts of 'the decorative', but not to develop this. Gore died before he could, but had shown little evidence of building upon the startling abstraction of the background to his *Deer-Hunting* mural beyond the semi-abstract patterning of some easel landscapes painted in the summer of 1912, when he was also at work on the mural; Ginner reverted, with few exceptions, to the referential framework of late nineteenth-century realisms. In other words, neither secured an avant-gardehood that lasted beyond their Golden Calf work.

Lewis was a different matter. A more substantial artist, he profited more significantly from the commission for the Golden Calf decorations and illustrations and the experience of undertaking them, and was also more profoundly affected by the project of the Cave itself: the commission was his first, and as Cork notes, the work he did for it 'was instrumental in defining his identity as an artist'.[92] In early 1912 he was already free of any London parochialism by virtue of his upbringing, of his expulsion from the Slade after two years in mid-1901, and of having spent most of 1903–08 in Europe, visiting Spain, the Netherlands and Munich for months at a time, and living much of the rest of the period in Paris. By the time he returned to London at the end of 1908 he had, in Paul Edwards's words, 'converted himself… into an educated European',[93] in the process acquiring a better acquaintance with Paris's avant-garde of that decade, and its preoccupations, than any other London-based artist. Back in London he kept up with these and, as Edwards suggests, 'by 1909 he already appears to have had some knowledge… of Picasso's recent work [prior to that year]'.[94] By 1911 he was, arguably, assimilating the latter's 1909 Cubism, although there is little visual (or any other) evidence for Edwards's assertion that he 'seems to have been aware of the epistemological premises inherent in cubist practice' (by which I take Edwards to be referring to its reflexive character – its interrogation of its own pictorial illusionism – in the Cubism of Picasso and Braque from 1910); instead Lewis remained more attached to the expressive (indeed, expressionist) potential of Picasso's 1907–09 early Cubism – the period of the *Demoiselles d'Avignon* and its initial progeny – than did Picasso himself.[95]

The Golden Calf commission came at a crucial, and decisive, time: the spring of 1912 saw not only the arrival, with much fanfare and critical hullabaloo, of Futurist paintings in London, but also the consolidation of the reputation of the salon Cubists at the Paris Salon des Indépendants, with Fernand Léger, Robert Delaunay, Henri Le Fauconnier, Albert Gleizes and Jean Metzinger all showing large, ambitious, technically innovative paintings.[96] Together these events declared both an explicit aesthetic technicism and an embrace of urban, technology-driven modernity – 'simultaneity', to use the *mot du jour* – as integral to claims for artistic avant-gardehood. For an artist as ambitious as Lewis by then was, determined to seize and assert an avant-garde identity on Parisian terms, this combined challenge was unignorable.

His first response was a self-consciously public aesthetic statement, a staging of an equivalent avant-gardehood with a painting even bigger than all but Delaunay's huge *City of Paris*: the *c.* 2.7 × 2.7 metre *Kermesse* (pl. 49). Its performative character was recognised by Frida Strindberg, who immediately rented it for the entrance stairway of the Cave before it was even finished:[97] an appropriation and elaboration of the expressionistic Africanism of Picasso's *Nu à la draperie* (*Nude with Drapery*) (see pl. 30) into an image of what Cork appositely summarises as 'ecstatic conflict'[98] that was ideal for the Golden Calf, both in its subject of popular dance and in the ecstasy of this, which (together with the priapic-calf signboard hanging above it) it promised via the apparent conflict of its protagonists. But it was more than this, and surely intended as such. It seized the frenzy of those new dance crazes, for the Apache dance, the tango, the bunny hop and the turkey trot, which infatuated all sections of London society, as Lisa Tickner has comprehensively shown – thereby, as she argues, '*staging* an encounter between violence and sexuality, refusing absolutely the coy fleshiness of the salon nude in favour of something more imperious but mechanical', by means of 'a newly expressive formal vocabulary allied to a keen sensibility toward the textures and experience of everyday life'.[99] At the same time it joined that philosophical understanding of dance, stemming from Romanticism, that Frank Kermode explored in the essay noted earlier in this chapter. Kermode argues that dance was regarded as 'the most primitive, non-discursive art, offering a pre-scientific image of life, an intuitive truth.... [It] belongs to a period before the self and the world were divided, and so achieves... "original unity".'[100] It was a work that picked up the 'continental' gauntlet on all of these levels.

His second response was to confront, while in France for some weeks in the summer of 1912, the stylistic innovations of the salon Cubists' paintings that had been in the Indépendants, and to do so with a perhaps deliberate engagement, not with 'simultaneity', contemporaneity or even ostensibly with visual art, but with literature: specifically Shakespeare's play *Timon of Athens*, for a folio edition of which he was informally commissioned by an obscure London publisher to produce a series of illustrations.[101] As a theme, a Shakespeare play about a foolishly generous ruler whose harsh treatment by supposed friends leads him to misanthropy enabled Lewis to adapt the latest, publicly displayed examples of Cubist *technie* to his own purposes and intermedia strengths, and to distinguish these clearly from the competition. Much has been written about this magnificent set of drawings in relation to Lewis's evolving ideas about his art and writing, the relation between them and to the world.[102] Less considered, however, is their staging of avant-gardehood itself. The key innovation of the salon Cubists that spring was their use of isolated, spatially disconnected components of a scene, inserted montage-fashion into a composition, to indicate at once its several visual components and the perception of them by its participants and the beholder.[103] Léger, Delaunay and Le Fauconnier in particular deployed this device, and in some of the half-dozen colour plates of his *Timon* portfolio Lewis directly adopted it from them: a comparison of the *Thébaïde* plate with Léger's *La Noce* (*The Wedding*) (pls 50 and 51) shows that Lewis's composition borrows not only (as do other plates) the latter's juxtapositions across its canvas of curves, angles, lines and volumes, representational with apparently non-representational forms, which were part of the Frenchman's emerging expressive Cubist syntax of 'contrasts of forms', but specifically the sequence of curves (in the Léger representing a view of a line of poplar trees) at its right side. That Lewis should, moreover, locate this device in precisely the same place in his illustration suggests an intention to signal, if in a coded and private way, his awareness of its avant-garde modishness.

A third response was another technicist appropriation, this time of the conceit of 'lines of force' introduced by some of the Futurist painters into their newest pictures. This device, a means by which the Italians sought to convey pictorially the temporal interpenetration of people and their ambience, which their Sackville Gallery March 1912 exhibition catalogue manifesto, 'The Exhibitors to the Public', had asserted as intrinsic to the dynamism of modern (urban) experience, had been displayed in many of the works included in the exhibition.[104] Lewis applied it immediately, and even more broadly, in paintings that, in their turn, developed the dynamic qualities of the dancers in *Kermesse*. Edwards describes this appropriation as a means of enhancement of the 'expression of [the] latent explosive power' of Picasso's *Demoiselles* and its immediate progeny 'so that they project the energies of the figures across the picture plane'; the result, he suggests in a close formal analysis, was that '[t]he formal design of the picture and the animation of the picture surface as a whole then become referable to its content'.[105]

There were, I would argue, two consequences of this adoption by Lewis of these last two technical innovations. One was a greater formal complexity and hence ambiguity in his paintings. If *Kermesse* was already hard to read, the *Timon* series was more so, and in the decorative images for the Golden Calf that he worked on (few of which survive, even as studies) he took his designs to the brink of non-representation: the *Study for a Wall Decoration in the Cave of the Golden Calf* (pl. 52) can – just – be read through the lines and planes 'of force' as a couple dancing, but the (later titled) *Abstract Design* (pl. 53) offers the merest, most schematic hint of a similar subject. Both, if they were ever installed, would have stood out sharply from the Gore and Ginner murals, as both darker in mood and far less legible – as forceful a pair of declarations of avant-gardehood as could then be seen in London. They were more than this, however, and – to return to the rhetorical question of Tickner's mentioned in the last chapter, as to whether posturing was 'a necessary condition for the avant-garde' – more too than simply 'postures', necessary or not. Yet in the context of the Cave, and the cultural conjuncture of that year on both sides of the Channel,[106] postures are what, *inter alia*, they were, for Lewis and for his audience; and the prioritising, by both, of such a performative understanding of avant-gardehood distinguished that of London from those of elsewhere in 1912–15.

One of those, of course, and influentially, was that of Futurism, to whose significance for London we shall shortly turn. But there was a second consequence of Lewis's adoption and performance of Parisian avant-gardehood that I have already touched on in general terms earlier in this chapter, as being of equal significance for London avant-gardism. In the context of the formalist theories of painting that were emerging in a London art and art-critical field increasingly aware, since Fry's 1910 Grafton Gallery exhibition, of European developments – in particular the theories of Fry (and their vulgarisation by Bell), Kandinsky (as interpreted and translated by Michael Sadleir) and Wilhelm Worringer (introduced by T.E. Hulme)[107] – the question of the options for non-representational painting, and the relation to these of the concept of decoration, was of pressing topical concern. And decoration, as we have repeatedly seen, had 'exogenous' as well as 'endogenous' connotations. The emergence of an artistic avant-garde in London, I have been arguing, is inseparable from the former; the consumerist inheritance of the Aesthetic Movement, the competitive patronage of aristocrats and the establishment of the Omega Workshops with the aim of catering to both are evidence. With respect to these options for painting, Edwards notes that 'the formalist theories of the period [that were accessed in London] tended to confuse the decorative or design dimension of form and the capacity of line and colour to represent shapes, space and volume', and that Lewis's work of the period alternates between decoration and representation.[108] Ironically, it was in his *Timon* drawings, rather than the works intended for the Golden Calf (whose explicit functionally decorative role freed Lewis to use them instead to foreground their avant-gardehood), that this alternation is most evident: in the above comparison between Lewis's *Thébaïde* and Léger's *La Noce*, the former is clearly more pattern-like in its juxtapositions of curves, angles, lines and volumes, representational and non-representational forms, and their distribution across its surface than the latter's more holistic, centrally focused composition, and this quality is even more evident in the other main plates, such as *A Feast of Overmen* (pl. 54) and *Timon*;[109] indeed, some of the functionally decorative half-titles for each Act of the play seem as much studies for possible abstract patterns as integrated compositions (pl. 55).[110] It was a short step from these to the explicitly decorative friezes Lewis designed for the Countess of Drogheda's dining room (pl. 56), which were discussed in the previous chapter. As I suggested, whether the shock effect of this ensemble was intended by Lewis as primarily aesthetic or social is moot; in avant-gardist, technicist terms it was a spectacular challenge to the *technie*-for-*technie*'s-sake of the Cubists and a riposte to the thrown gauntlet of Futurism's claim to 'place the spectator in the centre of the picture'; in social terms it was equally spectacular in its ostentation and unconventionality, a gratifying return (as the press and Society responses demonstrated) for the Countess on her cultural investment and self-promotional nous. But in truth it was both, and inextricably so: the bravura performativity of Lewis's scheme, its decorative éclat and high-bohemian aristocratic context consolidated that new front for avant-gardist contestation which the decorations for the Cave had opened, one that further fostered the staging of avant-gardehood as opposed to epistemic play.

THE CHALLENGE OF FUTURISM

If the dynamics (both exogenous and endogenous) of the English discourse of decoration thus tended to give the technical preoccupations of the emergent London artistic avant-garde a performative character that met the requirements of cultural consumerism, the spectacular appearances in London of Italian Futurism from 1912 until the war presented the challenge of a rival performance on different terms. Futurism, however, was much more than simply another avant-garde artistic movement. As one of its leading recent historians, Günter Berghaus, observes, from its inception its founder Marinetti 'made it quite clear that he saw in it not only an artistic, but also a social and political force of innovation', adding: 'His project of renewal encompassed all aspects of human existence, and was conceived as a total and permanent revolution.'[111] Marinetti's notorious energy, commitment and astute entrepreneurialism, moreover, enabled him both to surf and to shape the zeitgeist of a pan-European infatuation with the technologies of urban modernisation, and their consequences for city living, that swept the continent in that dawn of the new century. His founding Futurism manifesto, published in late February 1909 nearly simultaneously in several cities across Europe from Paris to Sofia,[112] was followed before August 1914 by a further 11 manifestos on different arts, most of them written by Marinetti himself or with his assistance. By the start of the war these had spawned multiple futurisms pursued by other cultural avant-gardists throughout the continent.[113] What concerns the pages that follow, however, is a more narrowly focused set of questions: those of the reception in London of 'futurism' as a cultural and consumerist fashion by the press and public at large; of Futurism as an avant-gardist 'ism' within its contemporary art field, by Lewis and his Vorticist colleagues in particular; and the relation between these two receptions. Although Marinetti worked hard to recruit a cohort of contributors to Futurism, it was overwhelmingly 'his' movement, and recognised as such, in particular by the press and public, who were greatly entertained by his *braggadocio*; both the momentum and the meaning of 'futurism' in London, as at once a cultural novelty and an exemplar of artistic avant-gardism, owed a great deal to his promotional visits to the city. Hence my focus will be primarily on him, and on these visits.

Marinetti came to London to give lectures on Futurism on four separate occasions between the publication of his manifesto and August 1914; it is worth noting that almost all of his lectures, as well as the promotional razzmatazz that increasingly accompanied them, were addressed to the general public, as opposed to a specifically artistic audience.[114] The first followed a two-year campaign by him, begun even before the launch of the founding manifesto, in which he showered the press with publications and announcements to promote his project and its principles across Europe, including in London where, in the words of a recent analysis, these 'were given a somewhat bemused airing in the English press before 1910'. The response seems to have been laughter rather than shock.[115] Perhaps as an effort to reverse this, Marinetti came to London himself at the end of 1910.[116] On 13 December, at the Lyceum Club for Women on Piccadilly, he gave a lecture to an audience of suffragettes that seems to have been 'an amalgam of all the early Futurist manifestos', including an essay, 'Contempt for Women', which attacked the idea of romantic love and the cliché of 'woman conceived as the reservoir of love' and which attempted awkwardly to befriend the suffragettes, whose current fight for political rights made them the 'best allies' of Futurism.[117] Coming at the end of an intense marketing campaign that appeared to have so far failed, his lecture seems to have sought to stir controversy with the help of this provocative and perceivably ambiguous reference to the highly topical issue of gender politics; accounts of the event, however, suggest that his subsequent claims of 'continuous cheers' on the part of the audience and 'violent riot' by suffragettes were inaccurate.[118]

By the time of Marinetti's second visit, in the spring of 1912, both Futurist cultural activities and the movement's reception had hugely expanded, with artistic manifestos, the orchestrated chaos of Futurist *serate* (literally, 'evenings' of staged actions in which the performers provoked their audiences into active and usually hostile responses) and the appetite of the press for reporting the spectacle together giving them a Europe-wide notoriety.[119] In the first half of 1912 a debut exhibition of work by Futurist painters toured the continent, arriving in London in mid-March after an initial showing in Paris the month before, and continuing to Berlin, Brussels and elsewhere.[120] It was greeted in the London press with the reader-pleasing mockery and ridicule, and lack of any analysis, that had become conventional in the popular reception of modern art since Fry's 1910 *Manet and the Post-Impressionists* exhibition.[121] Marinetti caught up with the show on 19 March, lecturing not only on Futurism but also, more controversially, on his audience itself, castigating England as 'a nation of sycophants and snobs, enslaved by old worm-eaten traditions, social conventions, and romanticism'. The event was avidly reviewed in *The Times*, *The Daily Chronicle* and *The Morning Leader*, among other papers, and in mid-April he reported to a fellow Futurist that after only six weeks in England, the Futurists had elicited 350 articles in newspapers and reviews and had earned more than 11,000 French francs in sales of paintings.[122] Already, too, the journalistic convention that linked avant-garde innovation with anarchism (and, this time, the suffragettes too) was being made about Futurism, and over the course of the next two years, this expanded to become a standard trope; as Lawrence Rainey notes: 'By a kind of metonymy facilitated by the modern newspaper's juxtaposition of disparate events, futurism [became] the cipher of contemporary crisis.'[123]

By the time of Marinetti's third visit in mid-November 1913, the topic of 'Futurist painting' had become more familiar to the public, as a result of further exposure.[124] Marinetti himself, by then a cultural celebrity, blitzed London with six lectures in six days that attracted substantial audiences and press attention. In these he shifted his position from the still-Symbolist view, evident in his 1909 manifesto, of art as superior to popular culture even as it drew upon the latter's vitality, to a populism that denied this hierarchy, insisting (as *The Times* reported after one lecture) that 'art should not be worshipped', but 'should express all the intensity of life – its beauty… its sordidness', indeed, 'the very complex of our life today'.[125] If this itself did not distinguish art from that view of Sickert's that we encountered earlier, of painting as a 'gross material' practice, his embrace of the music hall (or variety theatre, as that exemplar of commercial popular culture had by then become)[126] certainly did so; his manifesto on this medium, which *The Daily Mail* published during his visit, declared that the 'Variety Theatre, born as we are from electricity, is lucky in having no tradition, no masters, no dogma, and it is fed by swift actuality', that it 'is naturally anti-academical, primitive, and ingenuous, and therefore all the more significant by reason of the unforeseen nature of all its fumbling efforts and the coarse simplicity of its resources', and that it 'destroys all that is solemn, sacred, earnest and pure in Art – with a big A'.[127]

Marinetti's fourth visit came as the press-and-public vogue for Futurism was reaching its height, in the spring and early summer of 1914, heightened by a second Futurist painters' group exhibition at the Doré Gallery from late April to early June. Arriving for the opening, Marinetti appears to have stayed more than six weeks in London, giving lectures on Futurism and/or performances of his onomatopoeic poems on four occasions in May.[128] On this visit, his cultural populism was taken further: Marinetti put his art where his mouth was, as it were, by performing at a music hall, for a full week, twice a day, between 15 and 21 June. The venue was both ambitious and telling: the Coliseum, the biggest and most lavish of all music halls in London, with a seating capacity of 4,000. Built a stone's throw from Charing Cross Station in 1904 to catch the crowds of shoppers flocking into London for the day, described by its historian as 'middle-class people for whom a serious play might seem too ambitious and a visit to a music hall far too racy',[129] the Coliseum gave them 'a sanitized version of the music hall – a "Palace of Variety" that offered, in the words of its programme, "the social advantages of the refined and elegant surroundings of a Club".'[130] The Coliseum show was keenly anticipated, with newspapers competing against each other with advance publicity. By all contemporary accounts, as well as the judgment of cultural historian Rainey, however, it failed: at the premiere, despite the inclusion of Luigi Russolo's diverting *intonarumori* (noise machines),[131] after 15 minutes of Marinetti lecturing the audience in Italian – which was met by sustained booing – the curtain was lowered by the management, afraid that 'people would start throwing things'. For the next performances it demanded that Marinetti include some gramophone recordings of music by Edward Elgar; this new ingredient was met by stony silence.[132] Nevertheless, by the summer of 1914, as Rainey has observed, Marinetti 'had acquired an extraordinary stature in the life of the British commercial press. Mass circulation weeklies such as the *Sketch* and the *Graphic* assiduously reported his sayings and doings.... His views on "Futurist" clothes made headlines and his every lecture was reported with warm good humour or respectful earnestness.'[133] By this time any pretence on the part of press or public to retain any artistic specificity in the use of the term 'futurist' had been abandoned and, as art historian Jonathan Black has noted, it could refer to anything – especially any sellable lifestyle accessory, such as items of clothing, interior design, food, even kitschy knick-knacks.[134]

While 'futurism' was thus, as most of its historians have assumed, by 1914 an overused generalisation devoid of any precision, arguably it yet also had an ironic edge. For in so far as 'the future', after all, was recognised by the public as the territory claimed by the avant-garde – by definition – by means of its unreadable pictures and incomprehensible manifestos, then as a derisive catch-all label for anything that it could offer (as well as a sanction for all of the novelty merchandise), 'futurism' could hardly be bettered. And in a sense it was accurate – as we have seen, the avant-garde *did* claim a specialist expertise, as professionals, as arbiters of what was valuably new in art. What distinguished Marinetti from other avant-gardists was his embrace of modern, technologically sophisticated, communications and entertainment industries – all driven by advertising – as both the proper subject and the appropriate media for art in the new century. As art historian Walter Adamson cogently summarises, faced by the rapid rise of these industries, there were three options for the recently emergent avant-garde: 'to join the mass-entertainment frenzy, even if that meant debasing art to the level of kitsch'; 'to split the world of art such that the masses would be entertained by the new industries, while genuine art would continue to prevail in a separate, small élite-cultural refuge' (the Symbolist option, from which Marinetti was detaching himself in 1913); or 'to blend kitsch and art' in a way that satisfied both its popular audiences and the artists who would create it.

The last, suggests Adamson, was Marinetti's choice, and he saw such creative work as the role of the avant-garde – and himself (as an avant-gardist) as 'both a new taste professional specialising in mass-cultural entrepreneurship who knew how to retain control of the artistic product, *and* as the leader of a pocket of resistance to the bourgeoisie and its sacralised culture'.[135] To this role he brought formidable organisational skills, a love of these new media and, above all, an astute awareness of the potential of advertising. His chosen option, however, was a difficult balancing act between democracy – or, more realistically, the mass market – and elitism; the nearest Marinetti (and Futurism) came to balancing these was in the medium of Futurist *serate* that he developed from the start of 1910.[136] These were revues (the informal, often cabaret-based, variety entertainments of the kind that the Golden Calf offered, as we have seen) but with a difference, in that they drew upon the culture and large audiences of the music hall, yet developed the form significantly (Marinetti summarised their principles in his 'Variety Theatre' manifesto of 1913). Artfully promoted in advance not only with posters, like a commercial-popular performance, but also with the staged arrival of the artists hours early and hired crowds milling around the theatre, each performance provoked the audience by starting late, insulting it, 'seeding' it with provocateurs who began pelting the stage with rotten vegetables and goading it into noisy hostility. The point was to elicit a 'performance' in which the audience was an active participant rather than a passive crowd; although the Futurists included declarations of their poems and manifestos, made on stages presenting their paintings, these were not the 'art'; this, rather, was the spontaneous event itself, the 'collaboration' between Futurists and audience. Marinetti valued the *serate* greatly, seeing them as having the most immediate significance for Futurism;[137] between 1910 and 1914 he led the performance of dozens of them in theatres up and down the length of Italy. And, indeed, they were perhaps his most radical contribution to Futurism (indeed, to modernism *tout court*; it is arguable that in its radical anti-mimesis this new, hybrid medium was a dramatic equivalent of the rejection of illusionism in other avant-garde work of the 1910s, such as Vladimir Tatlin's corner reliefs of 1914–15).

The Coliseum audience participated in the collaborative artworks of the London *serate* in its British fashion – that is, not very rowdily by all accounts, but with alternated boos and stubborn silence. To judge this response as a mark of the failure of Marinetti's performance, however, as the London press reviewers and Rainey agree it was, is to miss the point of its author's intentions for it. Marinetti himself was recorded as seeing it as a 'succès fou',[138] and in his terms – those of the Futurist theories of theatre, including variety theatre, that he had already published – it was. In 1911 he had included a manifesto, 'The Pleasure of Being Booed', in an anthology of Futurist declarations, asserting in it Futurism's 'contempt for the audience' and 'horror of the immediate success that normally crowns dull and mediocre works', and insisting that 'authors should have no preoccupation except innovative originality'.[139] If one participant in the Coliseum performances can be faulted in Futurist terms, then, it is the audience, which was perhaps not rowdy *enough* (although had the management not brought the curtain down, it might have 'started throwing things'). Those for the Futurists' Italian *serate* had been, consistently, socially mixed, with a preponderance of the bourgeoisie who, according to one commentator of the time, 'took great pleasure in not understanding a thing of what these madmen were doing and saying on stage'.[140] This was probably also true of the Coliseum audience, who would have known by mid-1914 what they might expect from a Futurist event. More to the point, Marinetti would not have cared, since he would not have seen them as fit to judge it; this he would have seen as his prerogative, as the (avant-garde) artist. Although he was committed to bringing art to the general public, he was not interested in 'entertaining' his audience; his interest was, one could say, doctrinal rather than pragmatic.[141] The problem was, there was no audience for the avant-gardism of the Futurist *serate* other than the performers themselves; in Bourdieu's terms, there *was* no intermediate space in which the heteronomous and autonomous principles – kitsch and art – could be brought into balance.

Underneath Marinetti's obsession with bringing art to a public audience, then, was an elitist avant-gardism, a commitment to the difference and superiority that his (alternative) professional identity as a Futurist gave him vis-à-vis that public. Yet he understood, too, that the future of modern art lay in the fusion of artistic imagination and innovation with the exuberance and iconoclasm of popular culture. The comparison with the view of Wyndham Lewis on this relation is instructive. 'The Press in 1914', Lewis later recalled,

> had no Cinema, no Radio, and no Politics: so the painter could really become a 'star'.... Anybody could become one, who did anything funny. And Vorticism was replete with humour, of course; it was acclaimed the best joke ever. Pictures, I mean oil-paintings, were 'news'. Exhibitions were reviewed in column after column, and no illustrated paper worth its salt but carried a photograph of some picture of mine or of my 'school', as I have said, or one of myself, smiling insinuatingly from its pages.[142]

Apart from the wilful ignoring of the flourishing entertainment media of the time, the slippage in this remark from ironic social observation to implicit self-regard is evident; equally evident, in another recollection that I have already quoted, is his disdain for the art public in particular: 'From about the beginning of 1914,' Lewis writes,

> I saw a great deal of what is called 'society'. Everyone by way of being fashionably interested in art… wanted to look at this new oddity, thrown up by that amusing spook, the Zeitgeist… these good people of the British *beau monde* looked upon the artist as an oddity, to be lion-hunted for expensive howdahs.[143]

This kind of elitism, in which an enjoyment of a public dimension to his avant-gardism was combined with a contempt for it, is crucially different from that of Marinetti. In an article of the mid-1990s, Paul Edwards suggested a trajectory in Lewis's idea of the artist over the initial, pre-First World War phase of his career, in which this ambivalence became more marked. Edwards traces a shift on Lewis's part from a Romantic idea of the artist as possessor of 'an authentic spirit which is that of the people' (whose 'inert semi-conscious[ness]' is given expression by the 'universal egoism' of the poet', who writes 'new scripts for the masses') to a recognition of the economic determination of this role (Lewis is very funny in his 1909 essay 'The Pole' about Breton peasants recognising the value of hiding their undiscovered Gauguins from the 'constant stream of breathless gentlemen' whose pursuit of these was pushing up their price).[144] As his first novel, *Tarr*, evolved over the decade of his writing it,[145] this recognition was strengthened – the novel satirises the myth of artistic bohemia as much as 'The Pole' does that of the authentic, 'primitive' peasant; in 1911 Lewis coined the term 'bourgeois-bohemians' to describe its true character. He also developed the idea of the 'man of the world' to describe a social actor who, as Edwards suggests, 'knows his way around, and is able, by means of social strategies, to flourish and gain power', who 'cleverly presents himself as a real creator'. Eventually Lewis assimilated the strategising, and 'having excused himself from the [Romantic artist's] dangerous duty of having to live the authentic, non-bourgeois life… became free to role-play', becoming 'as much of a strategist as the "Man of the World" whom he considered to be his enemy.'[146] Among the roles performed, as I have noted, was that of the avant-gardehood of his painterly *technie*.

It was this amalgam of idealism and pragmatism that was congruent with the elitism of Pound and Upward as expressed in the latter's notion of an 'Angel Club' which the American embraced, and which we encountered in Chapter 1. While Pound's essay 'The New Sculpture' of February 1914 remained attached to the Romantic idea of the artist as 'born to rule', and Upward similarly saw the role of artists as like that of 'bees from a hive… [who] should pass to and fro among the nations whithersoever they are sent in the service of Humanity', the purpose of such collectivities was also practical, as Pound noted in his suggestion of an order named 'The Brothers Minor', as an 'accomplice' to Upward's, 'to foster the arts as the church orders fostered painting' for the purpose of 'subsidising artists, that is, artists of recognisable value'.[147] None of these three shared Marinetti's commitment to an avant-gardism that saw art as public practice, even if they saw it as having a role in offering imaginative revaluations of life for that public's benefit.

It was thus, in London, not in the public arena of commercial-popular culture that Marinetti's Futurist movement gained any aesthetic purchase, but within the field of its contemporary art. While Lewis, Pound and their 'little gang' that drew together in the nine months before the First World War to form 'Vorticism' did not endorse the Italian's version of avant-gardism, they responded to the gauntlet that he threw down to the Parisian formation's pre-eminence and hegemony, and thus to its satellites across Europe; and they did so by following his promotional strategy.[148] Indeed, they had to, if their fledgling 'ism' were to avoid being subsumed as the English branch of Futurism. It was a close-run thing, given C.R.W. Nevinson's position both of acolyte of Marinetti and near-imitator of Futurist painting styles, and of his continued membership of the group even as Lewis distanced it progressively from the Italian movement.[149] Those nine months, between the autumn of 1913 and the outbreak of war in August 1914, represented a difficult gestation and birth for Vorticism: a period of hectic jockeying by Lewis for a space for his nascent coterie between Bloomsbury Post-Impressionism, Cubism and Futurism. From the acrimonious break with Fry's Omega Workshops in the 'Ideal Home Rumpus' of October 1913, by way of the 'welcome dinner' for Marinetti that Lewis and Nevinson organised the following month, the group participation in two exhibitions curated by Frank Rutter that positioned them first as Cubists and then as Futurists – with press statements, catalogue essays, public posturing and private intergroup invective – to the eventual launch of Vorticism with its own magazine, *Blast*, in July 1914, its crowded sequence of stages has been narrated repeatedly by historians. What has been less remarked has been the *character* of these events. For it is significant that, unlike all previous such initiatives in London, these were motivated not by market considerations, nor by affective relations, but by 'formational' ambitions – that is, they were not about sales and friendships but concern for positioning and differentiating Vorticism in *professional* terms, and the enactment of that gesture of 'rupture' that, for a generation, had driven the alternative professionalism of the Parisian avant-garde formation.

It was, then, I am arguing, in directly addressing, and meeting, the criteria for avant-gardehood on the Parisian terms on which Marinetti had, with such éclat, built his Futurist project that the Vorticists represented the first British art grouping to acknowledge the hegemony of this formation and to join its network. Lewis and Pound, in particular, recognised its cultural significance and potential, and sought to develop it with ambitious schemes for seizing the initiative within the emergent London formation on an institutional level – and in so doing, matching and surpassing the salon Cubists' success in securing Cubism's lineage with the appointment of Le Fauconnier and Metzinger to the faculty of the *académie libre* of La Palette in Paris in 1912. This included a pedagogic direction of development that even Marinetti had not exploited. With encouragement and substantial funding from his painter friend Kate Lechmere, Lewis established the Rebel Art Centre in March 1914 in Great Ormond Street, with a name that ostentatiously declared its avant-gardehood and a prospectus that went beyond the Omega Workshops (which he also sought to rival) in offering not only schemes for interior decoration but a programme of lectures on, and classes in, the newest art styles. Perhaps one model for this was Pound's scheme, which he had been gestating since 1908, had detailed in *The New Age* in May 1913 and had surely discussed with Lewis, for a 'College of the Arts', aimed primarily but not exclusively at American students, with a comparably ambitious programme of multi-departmental teaching. Clearly such an institutional strategy was on their promotional agenda. Pound's scheme came to nothing, however, and, despite the kudos of a lecture by Marinetti on 6 May 1914, the Rebel Art Centre folded after three months.[150]

And yet. In the last analysis, for all the frantic avant-gardism in London – and to return to my equation of the end of the last chapter – in this immediately pre-First World War moment, and in a manner comparable to my earlier assessment of Bloomsbury's character, but for different reasons, the Vorticists were both less than an avant-garde (in the paradigmatic Parisian sense I have discussed), and also more than one. On the one hand, Vorticism was decked out as an 'ism' with all the promotional and positional accoutrements of such a status, yet committed for reasons other than modernist aesthetic innovation alone to the advanced *technie* that underwrote it. On the other, it was open by virtue of these *social* aspirations to considerations of *extra*-aesthetic status that played little part in the professionalism of the Parisian formation. For the London avant-garde of the summer of 1914, even within aesthetic terms, the 'Mallarméan play of signifiers', as I termed it in the last chapter, that characterised Picasso's Cubist *technie*, was of less interest than, for some, such as Bell and Grant, the decorative potential of abstract painting, for others, above all Lewis, the misanthropic anti-humanism that ran through both *Tarr* and *Timon*. And both were increasingly attracted by the gravitational pull of aspirational cultural consumerism and commodified popular culture. If the war had not brought the curtain down on it prematurely, what would have become of this performance?

CODA: INTO THE FUTURE

When I was researching an earlier project some years ago, I came upon the front page of a leading Paris newspaper from the end of June 1914. One of its headlined items was about plans for an international exhibition of modern decorative arts to be held in the city in the following year. It was a major story, since the recent fortunes of the French decorative arts industries, the challenge to their erstwhile pre-eminence launched by other European countries including Germany and Britain, and how this affected the French economy and national self-image, had been the object of sustained press and governmental attention for some years, and the exhibition was anticipated with great interest, not to say apprehension; hence the prominence of its coverage in the paper. On the same page, buried in the lower right-hand corner, was a small paragraph reporting the assassination the previous day of Archduke Ferdinand of Austria in Sarajevo.

The incongruity of this juxtaposition, its reversal of that order of importance of these two news items which hindsight has imposed, was a valuable reminder to me of the myth-making power of history, and the need to recognise the chance character of events at the same time as seeking to understand their causes and consequences. August 1914 did not represent that ending dividing an Edenic 'before the Fall' from its aftermath which history has bequeathed us in the conventional narrative, but a caesura, in that the outbreak of war severed some, but not all, and strengthened others, of the threads that this account has drawn through the cultural history of the first avant-garde groupings of Paris and London. In that last summer of peace the new formation encompassed, in these two cities, a diverse set of positions and orientations, offering between them alternative possible futures for art and artists. Which of these futures would happen was uncertain, a roll of the dice.

But the dice of history are always loaded, if inexpertly, and I hope that the analysis that this book has offered, and the tools it has used, suggest how they were loaded in 1914. To summarise severely, I have argued, first, that the Parisian avant-garde, the perceived centre of the new avant-garde network, was caught, in that decade before the war, between the currents of a professionalism whose market-led imperatives narrowed its radicalism to concerns with technicist innovation, or *technie*, and an ideology of rupture with everything this market stood for. Second, that the emergent avant-garde in London, one of its perceived satellites, was shaped not only by the gravitational pull of these art-field pressures and tensions across the Channel but also, beyond them, by the pressures of cultural consumerism and its assimilation to the social struggle between classes and genders, and the inheritance of an ideology of affective relations that was opposed to those pressures. These endogenous and exogenous factors, and the relations between them, are complex, and it has taken ten chapters of close analysis to account for them. A step back from their detail, however, allows the discerning of two underlying dynamics that have threaded their way between the lines of this narrative.

One was that of the discourse of decoration, to which repeated reference has been made throughout it. The flourishing and elaboration of this over the course of the cultural conjuncture of the 30 years around the turn of the twentieth century happened because it had several different, and potent, meanings. 'Decoration' was at once a vehicle for the pursuit by the Parisian avant-garde of the many varied and competing technical innovations *du jour*; a gathering hegemony of anti-avant-garde forces in that *avant-guerre* that produced the triumph of cultural consumerism; and an echo, in its love of useless splendour, of that utopianism of which the latter was a distortion. Thus – to take these in turn – for Gauguin, the Nabis, Matisse and their acolytes within the avant-garde, *le décoratif* referred to non-mimetic qualities or emphases in painting, which both drew upon cognate connotations of symbolism and/or ornament and enabled the assertion of painting's medium specificities, while for the Cubists it was a means of assimilating and yet mediating the advert-saturated visual environment of the commercial everyday. At the same time, for many artists and critics, most of them outside the avant-garde, on both sides of the Channel the category of 'decoration' challenged the boundaries between fine art and *objets d'art*; moreover, if 'decoration' was the purpose of both, it opened the floodgates of cultural consumerism and turned that avant-garde's art practices into instruments of economic and/or nationalistic interest. And for those for whom both technicist innovation and the 'creative industries' smacked of a professionalisation of art that was anathema, decoration stood for that amateurism of the best kind that characterised affective community, as both the Arts and Crafts movement and Bloomsbury's interiors testified.

Yet even the radical utopianism, if such it was, of Bloomsbury's decorations could be co-opted for consumerism, and indeed was, via Fry's Omega Workshops and their branding of Post-Impressionist sociability; and this was perhaps how the dice were loaded, for ultimately the exogenous economic and social factors I have discussed stood for interests that played for larger stakes than the endogenous forces of the avant-garde, and had more resources. That of commodification was among the most powerful, and by 1915 even the ultra-technicism of Cubism's reflexive styles had succumbed to the seductions of decoration for consumption's sake,[1] and likewise – as we have seen – Vorticism's rebarbative geometries to the requirements of aristocratic fashion.

The second underlying dynamic was that within the avant-garde of the instrumental logic of a professionalism, albeit alternative to that of the artistic mainstream, whose focus on technical expertise and innovation not only imposed its terms on an emergent London formation already disposed to defer to Parisian initiatives in the cultural field but, arguably, paralleled the growing counter-hegemony of 'scientific' socialism in the political. For just as the narrowing of the focus of leftist political activism in Britain to the requirements of electoral success sidelined the perceived amateurish dilettantism of utopian socialism, so avant-garde artistic professionalism disbarred the alternatives still grounded in affective relations, and in similar terms. If this logic was partly driven by market imperatives internal to the field of contemporary art, it was also, and more fundamentally, that of developments that would, over the following half-century, make of the avant-garde the research and development arm of the culture industry, its aesthetic innovations a means of uncovering new cultural energies in marginal social communities and co-opting them for 'high' art.[2]

Yet as Raymond Williams observed, no hegemony is ever total,[3] and among the possible futures for the avant-garde in August 1914 were also two that offered a challenge to the dominant one, if only temporarily. One was already under way. For in so far as all foreign artists drawn to Paris in the five years before the war by the very status of its avant-garde and its technicism brought with them their own cultural agendas, assumptions and expectations, they returned home after a few months (as they mostly did) with a technical repertoire understood in terms of the latter. They were thus instrumental in beginning the dismantling of Parisian hegemony at the height of its ascendancy, of turning the language of *technie* from French into a *lingua franca*, with as many dialects as there were nodes in the pan-European avant-garde network. London artists, from Sickert to Lewis, were participants in this. From this we can see not only that, as Piotr Piotrowski noted in a seminal essay to which I referred in this book's Introduction,[4] 'peripheral' sites of cultural practices are often richer in their creativity than the 'centre' to which they defer, precisely because this deference obliges them to negotiate between the initiatives stemming from that centre and their own local agendas, which can result in greater innovation. More than this, they are often well placed to provoke, over time, a shift in these relations. For a time, indeed, this shift happened, in ways that are, however, beyond the remit of this book. It was assisted, of course, by the calamity of the war, which both indirectly brought New York into the network of the avant-garde, with profound consequences, and directly placed politics once again at the centre of its agenda. It also brought several of the combatant countries, by its end, to the brink of revolution, in which process members of that avant-garde participated. Those who joined or supported the one (temporarily) successful of these, the Bolshevik Revolution in Russia, constructed in the five years after

1917 an alternative to Parisian 'alternative professionalism', a fusing of its technicism with social engagement, the radicalism of whose brief challenge to dominant culture, before it was swept off the board by the roll of history's loaded dice, remains relevant a century later. What lessons for the present are found in the avant-garde's first flowering depends, however, on how the conjunctures of then and now, and the relation of that avant-garde to the dynamic of its own historical moment, are configured. As I explained at the start of this analysis of that relation, my choice, for a comparison with Paris, of London (still the 'world metropolis' at that turn-of-the twentieth-century, yet perceived, then and now, as one of the more 'peripheral' satellites of Paris in cultural terms) was deliberate. It has allowed me to make visible the complexity of the relations between endogenous and exogenous factors – between socio-economic and cultural dynamics – in each capital, in the closest, but also the most polarised pairing of cities, in this sense, that the pre-First World War conjuncture presented. It has thereby offered a chance to better understand the choice of directions taken and not taken into the new century, by radical artists in both capitals. I hope that the tools it has presented and deployed have furnished a more historically adequate understanding of the avant-garde as a concept and formation than has been available until now, and that they will be of use in future conjunctural analyses beyond Paris and London, across its networks.

NOTES

INTRODUCTION

1 It underlined this semantically, in keeping with the 'Tate' branding itself, by dispensing with definite articles as a mark of these qualities.

2 Tim Barringer et al., *Pre-Raphaelites: Victorian Avant-Garde*, exh. cat., London: Tate Publishing, 2012; 9, 12, 36–8, 231–2 for instances of this assertion.

3 Examples include Dianne Sachko Macleod, *Art and the Victorian Middle Class: Money and the Making of Cultural Identity*, Cambridge: Cambridge University Press, 1996, especially ch. 3, 'Pre-Raphaelitism: Progressive or Regressive?'; Cordula Grewe, *The Nazarenes: Romantic Avant-Garde and the Art of the Concept*, Pennsylvania: Pennsylvania State University Press, 2015; and Wendy Graham, *Critics, Coteries and Pre-Raphaelite Celebrity*, New York: Columbia University Press, 2017.

4 This model builds upon previous explorations of the concept and formation that I have made; see, in particular, David Cottington, 'The Formation of the Avant-Garde in Paris and London, c. 1880–1915', *Art History*, vol. 35, no. 3, June 2012, 596–621; idem, *The Avant-Garde: A Very Short Introduction*, Oxford: Oxford University Press, 2013; idem, 'The Transnational Hierarchies and Networks of the Artistic Avant-Garde, ca. 1885–1915', in Marja Jalava, Stefan Nygård and Johan Strang, eds, *Decentering European Intellectual Space*, Leiden and Boston, M.A.: Brill, 2018, 65–87. On Williams's seminal groundwork see n. 9 below.

5 On this early history see Matei Calinescu, *Five Faces of Modernity: Modernism, Avant-Garde, Decadence, Kitsch, Postmodernism*, Durham, N.C.: Duke University Press, 1987, and Cottington, *The Avant-Garde*.

6 In his private notebook of the early 1860s (published posthumously as *Mon Coeur mis à nu*) Baudelaire wrote bitterly of 'the Frenchman's passionate predilection for military metaphors': 'the poets of combat. The littérateurs of the avant-garde.' Ironically, this usage was derogatory: 'This weakness for military metaphors', he noted, 'is a sign of natures that are not themselves militarist, but are made for discipline – that is to say, for conformity.' Charles Baudelaire, *My Heart Laid Bare*, trans. Norman Cameron, London: Weidenfeld and Nicolson, 1950, 188–9.

7 See Chapter 5.

8 See Chapter 3.

9 Raymond Williams, 'The Uses of Cultural Theory', in Tony Pinkney, ed., *The Politics of Modernism: Against the New Conformists*, London: Verso, 1989, 163–76.

10 Raymond Williams, 'The Significance of "Bloomsbury" as a Social and Cultural Group', in D. Crabtree and A.P. Thirlwell, eds, *Keynes and the Bloomsbury Group*, London: Macmillan, 1980. See Chapters 2 and 8.

11 A previous and invaluable consideration and application of Williams's theory was offered nearly 30 years ago by David Peters Corbett and Andrew Thacker, to which I am greatly

indebted: 'Raymond Williams and Cultural Formations: Movements and Magazines', *Prose Studies*, vol. 16, no. 2, August 1993, 84–106. It was, however, as they explicitly advised, a 'tentative reading' of its two sample objects of analysis, those of the group around Charles Ricketts and the magazine *The Dial* in the 1890s and of the Vorticist group and its magazine *Blast* in 1914, 'intended to be indicative of the way a formational analysis might proceed rather than an exhaustive account' (ibid., 86). Three decades later, in another conjuncture but with an equally pressing need for the clarifications it promises, the present study picks up this baton and, I hope, takes that analysis further.

12 Piotr Piotrowski, 'Toward a Horizontal History of the European Avant-Garde', in Sascha Bru et al., eds, *Europa! Europa? The Avant-Garde, Modernism, and the Fate of a Continent*, Berlin: De Gruyter, 2009, 49–58.

13 On this multiplicity see Okwui Enwezor, 'Specious Modernity: Speculations on the End of Postcolonial Utopia', in Nicolas Bourriaud, ed., *Altermodern: Tate Triennial*, exh. cat., London: Tate, 2009.

14 An excellent recent introduction, Sascha Bru's *The European Avant-Gardes, 1905–1935: A Portable Guide*, Edinburgh: Edinburgh University Press, 2018, describes English art of the period as 'remarkably provincial' (113).

CHAPTER 1

1 Mary Anne Clawson, *Constructing Brotherhood: Class, Gender, and Fraternalism*, Princeton, N.J.: Princeton University Press, 1989, 13. It should be noted from the outset that, given the historically patriarchal character of western society, there is no equivalent recorded history, nor any social salience, of secular sisterhoods, and that the association of women for purposes of sociability, mutual aid, career advancement or gender solidarity has been marginalised both by historians and society at large, until the rise of the women's movement from the late nineteenth century onwards. There were no equivalents before then, as far as I am aware, for the artistic brotherhoods discussed in this chapter.

2 Ibid., 146.

3 Kurt H. Wolff, ed. and trans., *The Sociology of Georg Simmel*, New York: Free Press of Glencoe, 1950, esp. part IV, 'The Secret and the Secret Society'.

4 Examples include M.L. Kennedy, *The Jacobin Clubs in the French Revolution*, Princeton, N.J.: Princeton University Press, 1982; Jan Marsh, *The Pre-Raphaelite Sisterhood*, New York: St Martin's Press, 1985; Claire Frèches-Thory and Antoine Terrasse, *The Nabis: Bonnard, Vuillard and their Circle*, New York: Abrams, 1991; Laura Morowitz and William Vaughan, eds, *Artistic Brotherhoods in the Nineteenth Century*, Aldershot: Ashgate, 2000 (this is the most substantial contribution, and I am indebted to this collection of essays for much of the information, and some key ideas, offered in this section); and, most recently, Bridget Alsdorf, *Fellow Men: Fantin-Latour and the Problem of the Group in Nineteenth-Century French Painting*, Princeton, N.J.: Princeton University Press, 2013.

5 George Levitine, *The Dawn of Bohemianism: The 'Barbu' Rebellion and Primitivism in Neoclassical France*, University Park and London: Pennsylvania State University Press, 1978, ch. 1 passim. 'Barbu', French for 'bearded', referred to their common adoption of this facial feature; see below.

6 William Vaughan, 'The First Artistic Brotherhood: *Fraternité* in the Age of Revolution', in Morowitz and Vaughan, eds, *Artistic Brotherhoods*, 34–5.

7 Ibid., where Vaughan suggests that Quay (or Quai as he spells it) was one of the 'children of the nation' whom from 1792, out of Revolutionary fervour, David had accepted and taught for free.

8 This was later described by a former group member, the dissident novelist Charles Nodier, as 'a question of nothing less than of a reform of society based on a plan, not precisely that of St Simonians but of the same type'. Quoted in Levitine, *The Dawn of Bohemianism*, 63.

9 Ibid., 62.

10 Ibid., 67–8. Vaughan notes that this 'cognitive dressing', as he terms it, 'was an important [means] in the 1790s for signalling political affiliations'. Vaughan, 'The First Artistic Brotherhood', 41.

11 'Bohemia' and 'bohemianism', in the modern sense as inclusive of – even driven by – an oppositional cultural politics, were phenomena (and concepts) that emerged, first in Paris in the 1820s, in the context of Romanticism; their first major cultural marker was the notorious 'battle of Hernani' that greeted the opening performance, at the Comédie-Française in February 1830, of Victor Hugo's play of that name.

12 Levitine, *The Dawn of Bohemianism*, 79. The descriptions of Chaillot are those of Peter Walch, reviewing Levitine's book in *The Art Bulletin*, vol. 62, no. 4, December 1980, 671.

13 Levitine, *The Dawn of Bohemianism*, 70.

14 On such symbolism see Warren Roberts, *Jacques-Louis David and Jean-Louis Prieur, Revolutionary Artists: the Public, the Populace, and Images of the French Revolution*, New York: State University of New York Press, 2000; Lynn Hunt, *Politics, Culture, and Class in the French Revolution*, Los Angeles: University of California Press, 2004.

15 Joachim Le Breton, *Rapport sur les Beaux-Arts*, Fine Arts Section of the Institut de France, 1808, 113, quoted in Levitine, *The Dawn of Bohemianism*, 128.

16 Wolff, ed. and trans., *The Sociology of Georg Simmel*, esp. part IV, 'The Secret and the Secret Society'. Cited by Levitine, ibid., 2.

17 Levitine, *The Dawn of Bohemianism*, 132.

18 See Chapter 7.

19 Morowitz and Vaughan, eds, *Artistic Brotherhoods*, 40. See also Kennedy, *The Jacobin Clubs in the French Revolution*.

20 Charles Nodier eulogised her in superlatives a year after her death (*Essai d'un jeune barde*, 1804, cited in Levitine, *The Dawn of Bohemianism*, 47).

21 The origin of this name is uncertain; Keith Andrews suggests 'the sharp tongue of Johann Christian Reinhardt, a German painter of the old school'. Keith Andrews, *The Nazarenes: A Brotherhood of German Painters in Rome*, Oxford: The Clarendon Press, 1964, 29.

22 The linking is Levitine's, in *The Dawn of Bohemianism*, 131.

23 Andrews, *The Nazarenes*, 23.

24 Jason Rosenfeld, 'The Pre-Raphaelite "Otherhood" and Group Identity in Victorian Britain', in Morowitz and Vaughan, eds, *Artistic Brotherhoods*, 69.

25 Johann Friedrich Overbeck, the dominant member of the group, and co-leader of it with Franz Pforr in its early years (1808–12), wrote to his father in 1810: 'Now we thus become monks!' Letter of 29 September 1810, cited in Mitchell B. Frank, 'The Nazarene *Gemeinschaft*: Overbeck and Cornelius', in Morowitz and Vaughan, eds, *Artistic Brotherhoods*, 52.

26 In October 1811 Overbeck wrote in his diary: 'How pure the soul of the pious Fiesole [Fra Angelico] must have been, how so entirely without longing, entirely devoted to the heavenly, that is Christian love! How strict and regulated his monastic way of life!' Cited ibid., 52.

27 Cited ibid., 53.

28 Overbeck wrote of his friendship with his fellow commune member Franz Pforr: 'We were separated from everyone and lived only for ourselves and for art; we were shut away from all others, only we both were one. We always began our pictures together and tried to finish them at the same time.' Letter of March 1810, cited ibid., 54.

29 This term, and its distinction from that of 'sociality', should be clarified, since both are used throughout this book: whereas sociality is the character of being social, sociability is the skill or disposition of being sociable, of interacting well with others. See https://wikidiff.com/sociality/sociability.

30 As Frank notes, 'in such male friendships, as Mosse explains, eroticism "was difficult to banish", but more often than not "it was combined with a quest for sexual purity"'. Frank, 'The Nazarene *Gemeinschaft*', citing George Mosse, *Nationalism and Sexuality*, New York: Howard Fertig, 1985, 76.

31 On the lack of equivalence between 'brotherhoods' and 'sisterhoods' (indeed, the almost complete absence of the latter from the history of mid-nineteenth-century European artistic groupings), see for London, Deborah Cherry, *Painting Women: Victorian Women Artists*, London: Routledge, 1993, and for Paris, Tamar Garb, *Sisters of the Brush: Women's Artistic Culture in Late Nineteenth-Century Paris*, New Haven, C.T., and London: Yale University Press, 1994.

32 In Tönnies' words, 'All intimate, private and exclusive living together… is understood as life in Gemeinschaft. Gesellschaft is public life – it is the world itself.' Tönnies understood that the latter was the dominant social structure of the nineteenth century and that its succeeding of the former was a matter of inevitability – 'a period of Gesellschaft follows a period of Gemeinschaft' – hence, it represented modernisation. Ferdinand Tönnies, *Community and Association*, trans. Charles P. Loomis, London: Routledge & Kegan Paul, 1974, 37.

33 Frank cites both Pevsner and Lankheit in his 'Nazarene *Gemeinschaft*' article in Morowitz and Vaughan, eds, *Artistic Brotherhoods*, and develops his analysis in his *German Romantic Painting Redefined: Nazarene Tradition and the Narratives of Romanticism*, Aldershot: Ashgate, 2001; republished by Routledge, 2017.

34 Andrews, *The Nazarenes*, 34.

35 On this post-Revolutionary moment of the market see Francis Haskell, *Rediscoveries in Art: Some Aspects of Taste, Fashion and Collecting in England and France*, London: Phaidon, 1980.

36 Jean Hamilton, *The Sketching Society, 1799–1851*, London: Victoria and Albert Museum, 1971, 1–13. The terms 'emergent' and 'residual' are those usefully suggested by Raymond Williams; see his *Marxism and Literature*, Oxford: Oxford University Press, 1977.

37 Rosenfeld, 'The Pre-Raphaelite "Otherhood"', 70, who cites Paul Barlow, '"The Backside of Nature", The Clique, Hogarthianism, and the Problem of Style in Victorian Painting', PhD dissertation, University of Sussex, 1989.

38 William Vaughan, '"Brothers in Art, Brothers in Love": The Ancients as an Artistic

Community', in William Vaughan, Elizabeth E. Barker and Colin Harrison, eds, *Samuel Palmer 1805–1881: Vision and Landscape*, exh. cat., London: British Museum, 2005, 17–21.

39 Ibid., 18.

40 Ibid. Both their communal life and their Nazarenesque dress were adopted half-heartedly: only Palmer actually lived at Shoreham full-time, and only he appears to have dressed eccentrically.

41 The term 'homosociality' was coined and theorised by Eve Kosofski Sedgwick in *Between Men: English Literature and Male Homosocial Desire*, New York and London: Columbia University Press, 1985. The quotation in the title of Vaughan's essay on the Ancients comes from a recollection by one member of the group, Edward Calvert, which in full reads: 'We were brothers in art, brothers in love, and brothers in that for which art and love subsist – the Ideal – the Kingdom within.' [Samuel Calvert], *A Memoir of Edward Calvert by his Third Son*, London: Sampson & Low, 1893, 17.

42 Vaughan observes that Palmer's son later destroyed works by his father that, as he recalled in his biography of him, suggested a 'mental condition… full of danger, and neither sufficiently masculine nor sufficiently reticent'. A.H. Palmer, *The Life and Letters of Samuel Palmer, Painter and Etcher*, London: Seeley & Co., 1892, 18; cited in Vaughan, '"Brothers in Art, Brothers in Love"', 20.

43 Andrews notes that while Ruskin's precepts on the relation between art and morality in his writings on the Pre-Raphaelites were 'entirely in harmony with those the St Luke Brothers had formulated in Vienna almost fifty years earlier', 'his comments on their art, whenever they occur in his writings and letters' exhibit a startlingly 'vituperative, almost pathological violence' with 'repeated use of such words as "imbecile", "unspeakable", "sickening"'. He suggests that this may have resulted from the critic's 'insanely anti-Catholic prejudice'. Andrews, *The Nazarenes*, 76–7.

44 Amelia Yeates and Serena Trowbridge, eds, *Pre-Raphaelite Masculinities: Constructions of Masculinity in Art and Literature*, Farnham: Ashgate, 2014, 3. More broadly, see also James Eli Adams, *Dandies and Desert Saints: Styles of Victorian Manhood*, Ithaca, N.Y.: Cornell University Press, 1995; Herbert Sussman, *Victorian Masculinities: Manhood and Masculine Poetics in Early Victorian Literature and Art*, Cambridge: Cambridge University Press, 1995; James Eli Adams and Andrew H. Miller, eds, *Sexualities in Victorian Britain*, Bloomington: Indiana University Press, 1996.

45 Thus the penis-like shadow projected from the groin of the aggressive brother of Isabella on the left, whose tip is overlaid by a pile of salt spilled from a cellar, which was a recognised metaphor for ejaculation (and a conceit in keeping with the adolescent prurience of the group's secret alternative 'Penis Rather Better' decoding of the already secret 'PRB'). This detail was first noted and discussed in a keynote article by Carol Jacobi of 2012, which builds upon a considerable and growing bibliography of recent research into such PRB preoccupations. Carol Jacobi, 'Sugar, Salt and Curdled Milk: Millais and the Synthetic Subject', *Tate Papers*, 18, autumn 2012, https://www.tate.org.uk/research/publications/tate-papers/18/sugar-salt-and-curdled-milk-millais-and-the-synthetic-subject, accessed 8 September 2021.

46 These included the poet Christina Rossetti and artists Elizabeth Siddall, Fanny Cornforth and Jane Morris. See Jan Marsh, ed., *Pre-Raphaelite Sisters*, exh. cat., London: National Portrait Gallery, 2019.

47 Marsh, *Pre-Raphaelite Sisterhood*, 1.
48 Rosenfeld, 'The Pre-Raphaelite "Otherhood"', 72.
49 See Chapter 2, 65.
50 Yeates and Trowbridge, *Pre-Raphaelite Masculinities*, 6–7. On this patronage see Dianne Sachko Macleod, *Art and the Victorian Middle Class: Money and the Making of Cultural Identity*, Cambridge: Cambridge University Press, 1996.
51 Martha Ward, 'Impressionist Installations and Private Exhibitions', *The Art Bulletin*, vol. 73, no. 4, December 1991, 599–622; Patricia Mainardi, *Art and Politics of the Second Empire: The Universal Expositions of 1855 and 1867*, New Haven, C.T.: Yale University Press, 1987, esp. 49–61; see also Chapter 4.
52 Raymond Williams, 'The Politics of the Avant-Garde', in Tony Pinkney, ed., *The Politics of Modernism, Against the New Conformists*, London: Verso, 1989, 50–1.
53 Nina Lübbren, *Rural Artists' Colonies in Europe, 1870–1910*, Manchester: Manchester University Press, 2001, 1–3.
54 See Chapter 3.
55 Lübbren, *Rural Artists' Colonies in Europe*, 6–7.
56 See Chapters 3 and 4.
57 For the details of these given here see Alsdorf, *Fellow Men*, 33.
58 See Chapter 7.
59 See Chapter 4.
60 See ibid.
61 '[Un] nom, vis-à-vis des ateliers, [qui] faisait de nous des initiés, une sorte de société secrète d'allure mystique, et proclamait que l'état d'enthousiasme prophétique nous était habituel.' Maurice Denis, 'L'Époque du symbolisme', *Gazette des Beaux-Arts*, March 1934. Cited in Anthony Glinoer and Vincent Laisney, *L'Âge des cénacles. Confraternités littéraires et artistiques au XIXe siècle*, Paris: Fayard, 2013, 178.
62 Cited in Claire Frèches-Thory and Antoine Terrasse, *The Nabis: Bonnard, Vuillard and their Circle*, trans. Mary Pordoe, New York: Abrams, 1991, 24 (no source given). (Originally published in French as *Les Nabis*, Paris: Flammarion 1990.)
63 Glinoer and Laisney, *L'Âge des cénacles*, 16–17.
64 'Their friendship was a joy', wrote Octave Mirbeau in his preface to the catalogue of the exhibition *Félix Vallotton*, Galerie Druet, January 1911. Cited in Frèches-Thory and Terrasse, *The Nabis*, 24. Glinoer and Laisney note that it was 'thanks to solid friendships, underpinned by regular correspondence and frequent get-togethers, [that] the Nabi group lasted until 1899'. *L'Âge des cénacles*, 179.
65 Glinoer and Laisney, *L'Âge des cénacles*, 178.
66 Morowitz and Vaughan, eds, 'Introduction', *Artistic Brotherhoods,* 17 and 29 n. 60. On one such realised decoration see Michael Marlais, 'Conservative Style/Conservative Politics: Maurice Denis in Le Vésinet', *Art History*, vol. 16, no. 1, March 1993, 125–46.
67 Laura Morowitz, 'Anonymity, Artistic Brotherhoods and the Art Market in the *Fin de Siècle*', in Morowitz and Vaughan, eds, *Artistic Brotherhoods*, 185–96; also Pierre Lenz, *L'Esthétique de Beuron*, translated from the German by Paul Sérusier, Introduction by Maurice Denis, Paris: Bibliothèque de l'Occident, 1905.
68 Morowitz, 'Anonymity, Artistic Brotherhoods', 192.
69 'Le but de ce groupe, dit des Anonymes, est donc l'art pour l'art. Pas de gloriole, pas de commerce, pas de réputation: l'édification d'une idée, d'une oeuvre. Chaque membre

y apporte ses efforts, concourt à l'édifice. On ne peut pas plus être enlevé du groupe qu'une pierre d'une maison.... Donc c'est à l'appréciation d'ensemble que nous faisons appel et non à des distinctions individuelles.' Bernard, letter to Émile Schuffenecker, 19 January 1891. Paris, Bibliothèque Nationale de France, n.a. fr.14277; quoted ibid., 185.

70 'Pas de popularité, pas de jalousies, pas plagiats malhonnêtes.' 'Il renonce à l'ensemble d'un édifice qui sera la synthèse des efforts de chacun.' Ibid., 189.

71 Ibid., 193.

72 Presumably Van Gogh was thinking of Christ's Apostles.

73 Cited in Wladyslawa Jaworska, *Gauguin and the Pont-Aven School*, London: Thames & Hudson, 1972, 59.

74 Ibid., 60. The 'Guild of St Luke' ('Lukasbund') was the formal name that the Nazarenes gave themselves.

75 An example is Louis Anquetin's role for fellow students at Cormon's *académie libre* in the launch of *cloisonnisme* in the late 1880s; see Chapter 4.

76 On these conjunctural dynamics see Chapter 5.

77 Glinoer and Laisney, *L'Âge des cénacles*, 212, who note that '[c]ette ultime tentative de "faire cénacle" signe symboliquement, par son échec, l'acte de décès de cette forme de sociabilité'. ('This final attempt to make a cenacle registers symbolically, by its very failure, the moment of decease of this form of sociability.') (See below, however, on Action d'Art.)

78 Reprinted in Christian Sénéchal, *L'Abbaye de Créteil*, Paris: Delpeuch, 1930, 138–47, under the title 'L'Appel de 1906'. It consists of a four-page preamble followed by 'Statutes' itemised into 28 articles.

79 Published in his novel *Gargantua* in 1535, Rabelais's imaginary Abbaye was the first utopia in French literature. Its guiding principle was the reverse of that experienced in existing abbeys, whose monks were subject to obedience to discipline and hierarchy; the motto of Rabelais's abbey was 'fais ce que tu voudras': ('Do what you wish'). The name was given in Article 3; Sénéchal, *L'Abbaye de Créteil*, 142.

80 '[I]ls réalisent, toutes proportions gardées, une sorte de LIBRE VILLA MÉDICIS, dont les hôtes, sans le joug d'une erreur officielle, travailleraient en toute paix, communiant dans leurs enthousiasmes, unissant leurs besoins, associant leurs ressources.' 'Statuts. Article Premier'. Reprinted in ibid., capitalisation in original. From 1576 the Villa was the principal Medici property in Rome, with its decoration and contents intended to assert the ascendancy of the family. In 1803 Napoleon made it the home of the French Academy in Rome.

81 '[*C*]*ette demeure trop haute et trop escarpée pour tous les impurs*, et par laquelle nous échapperons aux *bas-fonds*.' Sénéchal, *L'Abbaye de Créteil*, 139, italics in original.

82 '[I]ls seront eux-mêmes les artisans, donnant ainsi à leurs labeurs intellectuels le nécessaire complément du travail manuel.' Ibid., 142.

83 Their histories were recovered and recorded assiduously by Jean Maitron in his *Histoire du mouvement anarchiste* of 1951 (reprinted Paris: Maspero, 1975).

84 On Barzun see Chapter 6. He was the secretary to a leading Radical-Socialist government minister, Joseph-Paul Boncour.

85 Glinoer and Laisney, *L'Âge des cénacles*, 610. See also Sénéchal, *L'Abbaye de Créteil*, 99–102 on the number printed at Créteil.

86 See Sénéchal, *L'Abbaye de Créteil*, ch. 7, 'Hôtes et visiteurs', for details.

87 They seem to have been chosen (or sought out) quite cannily: Jules Romains's *La Vie unanime* of 1908, for instance, made significant waves and the 'ism' that it launched, Unanimism, gained much attention, while Mécislas Golberg's *Cahiers* was a precious volume, published posthumously, by an author whose subversive career and aestheticist anarchism gave him cult status both before and (especially) after his early death in 1907.

88 On these developments see Chapter 5, which in turn draws on David Cottington, *Cubism in the Shadow of War: The Avant-Garde and Politics in Paris, 1905–1914*, New Haven, C.T., and London: Yale University Press, 1998.

89 For an exhaustive and invaluable survey of this moment in Parisian poetry see Michel Décaudin, *La Crise des valeurs symbolistes. Vingt ans de poésie française, 1895–1914*, Toulouse: Privat, 1960.

90 On this milieu see Mark Antliff, 'Cubism, Futurism, Anarchism: The "Aestheticism" of the "Action d'Art" Group, 1906–1920', *Oxford Art Journal*, vol. 21, no. 2, 1998, 101–20; Paul Desanges, 'Chronique d'une communauté militante: Les Forgerons 1911–1920', *Le Mouvement social*, 91, April–June 1975, 35–58. The retrospective character of the names chosen for these groupings should be noted: both consciously connote medieval occupational (craft) collectivities. See Cynthia Maris Truant, *The Rites of Labor: Brotherhoods of Compagnonnage in Old and New Régime France*, Ithaca, N.Y., and London: Cornell University Press, 1993; Clawson, *Constructing Brotherhood.*

91 On this milieu, which was the midwife, as it were, to the birth of London's artistic avant-garde, see Chapter 10. *The New Age*, which was a weekly, published 'upwards of eighty' articles on Nietzsche from 1907 until 1913. Suzanne Hobson, *Angels of Modernism: Religion, Culture, Aesthetics 1910–1960*, Basingstoke: Palgrave Macmillan, 2011, 81.

92 Michael Levenson gives a brief biography, noting that Upward was a scholar, a barrister, a volunteer soldier, a scoutmaster, and an author of detective stories, plays and poems, as well as of two books before 1914, *The New Word* (1907) and *The Divine Mystery* (1913), and the articles referenced below. Levenson, *A Genealogy of Modernism: A Study of English Literary Doctrine 1908–1922*, Cambridge: Cambridge University Press, 1984, 71.

93 Sarah Victoria Turner, '"Spiritual Rhythm" and "Material Things": Art, Cultural Networks and Modernity in Britain, c.1900–1914', unpublished PhD thesis, Courtauld Institute of Art, 2009, 201. See also Levenson, *A Genealogy of Modernism*, 72–4; Hobson, *Angels of Modernism*, 94–5.

94 Upward's articles were published over three months in *The New Age* as 'The Order of the Seraphim' I (10 February 1910, 349–50), II (10 March 1910, 445–6) and III (21 April 1910, 590–91).

95 'The Angel Club', *The New Freewoman*, 1 October 1913. Although anonymous, it seems accepted that the author of this article was Upward; see Hobson, *Angels of Modernism*, 90–93.

96 Ezra Pound, 'The Order of the Brothers Minor', in 'Correspondence', *The New Freewoman*, 15 October 1913, 176; 'The New Sculpture', *The Egoist*, vol. 1, no. 4, 16 February 1914. For further consideration of these texts, see Chapter 10.

97 Ezra Pound, 'The New Sculpture', *The Egoist*, vol. 1, no. 4, 16 February 1914, 221–2.

98 On utopian socialism, its conjuncture and its collectivist significance see Chapter 2.

99 I return to these points and the history to which they gesture in the next and the last chapter.

CHAPTER 2

1 Sarah Cole, *Modernism, Male Friendship, and the First World War*, Cambridge: Cambridge University Press, 2003, 4.

2 Terry Eagleton, 'The Flight to the Real', in Sally Ledger and Scott McCracken, eds, *Cultural Politics at the 'Fin de Siècle'*, Cambridge: Cambridge University Press, 1995, 11–21.

3 Pater's declaration from the 'Conclusion' to his 1873 *Studies in the History of the Renaissance*, that 'to burn always with this hard, gem-like flame, to maintain this ecstasy, is success in life', has long been regarded as the epitome of Aestheticism.

4 On Carpenter see below.

5 Eagleton, 'The Flight to the Real', 11, 12, 13–14.

6 This crisis and its consequences were closely tracked and documented in a seminal article by Stephen Yeo of nearly 50 years ago, '"A New Life": The Religion of Socialism in Britain, 1883–1896', *History Workshop Journal*, vol. 4, no. 1, autumn 1977, 5–56. It has recently been revised and reprinted as *A New Life: The Religion of Socialism in Britain, 1883–1896: Alternatives to State Socialism,* Brighton: Edward Everett Root, 2018.

7 H.W. Nevinson, *Changes and Chances*, London: Nesbit, 1923; Beatrice Webb, *My Apprenticeship* (1926), 2nd edn, London: Longmans, 1946, 154–5; cited ibid., 10.

8 Ibid.

9 The dichotomy led immediately to a split in the group in January 1884 and the foundation by some of its members of the more pragmatic Fabian Society. From the minutes of the group's meeting of 7 December 1883, cited in Sheila Rowbotham, *Edward Carpenter: A Life of Liberty and Love*, London: Verso, 2008, 89.

10 Carpenter wrote over three dozen books across all of these fields. For a list see ibid., 535–6. On his network of friendships see ibid., 1–8.

11 Ibid., 8.

12 'Nunquam' (Robert Blatchford), *Merrie England*, London: 'Clarion', 1894. The book sold over 2 million copies worldwide. Margaret Drabble, ed., *The Oxford Companion to English Literature*, Oxford: Oxford University Press, 2006, 109.

13 This was the title of a lecture delivered to the Hammersmith Branch of the Socialist Democratic Federation (S.D.F.) at Kelmscott House on 30 November 1884. It was first published in Morris's newspaper *The Commonweal* in 1887.

14 *News from Nowhere* was first serialised in *The Commonweal* in 1890, and then published as a book by his Kelmscott Press in 1892. The quotation is from the facsimile edition, London: Victoria and Albert Museum with Thames & Hudson, 2017, 189–90.

15 From the memoirs of engineering trade unionist-turned-Labour minister G.N. Barnes, *From Workshop to War Cabinet* (1924): 'we were passing through a fanatical time.... Those were indeed exciting times. They were in fact too exciting to last.' Cited in Yeo, '"A New Life"', 31.

16 This marginalisation has been theorised, in a different perspective, by the anti-colonialist historian Leela Gandhi in her *Affective Communities: Anticolonial Thought, Fin-de-Siècle Radicalism, and the Politics of Friendship*, Durham, N.C., and London: Duke University Press, 2006.

17 Ibid., 177–8.

18 George Orwell, *The Road to Wigan Pier*, London: Gollancz, 1937, 206. For two more recent analyses of the constellation of discourses that made up this field, and its demise, see Ruth Livesey, *Socialism, Sex, and the Culture of Aestheticism in Britain, 1880–1914*, Oxford: Oxford University Press, 2007; Stanley Pierson, *British Socialists: The Journey from Fantasy to Politics*, Cambridge, M.A., and London: Harvard University Press, 1979.
19 Gandhi, *Affective Communities*, 178.
20 Ibid., 183.
21 Deborah Cherry, 'The Hogarth Club: 1858–1861', *Burlington Magazine*, 122, April 1980, 237–44. It had been preceded by two earlier attempts, in 1852 and 1855, both initiated by Rossetti, together with Ford Madox Brown; ibid., 237 n. 3.
22 Jason Rosenfeld, 'The Pre-Raphaelite "Otherhood" and Group Identity in Victorian Britain', in Laura Morowitz and William Vaughan, eds, *Artistic Brotherhoods in the Nineteenth Century*, Aldershot: Ashgate, 2000, 80 n. 32.
23 Ibid., 72.
24 A view that he entrenched in later life, in a series of retrospective articles in 1886 stressing his own role in forging the style, entitled 'The Pre-Raphaelite Brotherhood: A Fight for Art': *The Contemporary Review*, 49, April 1886, 471–83; May 1886, 737–50; June 1886, 820–33.
25 On this emerging field see Elizabeth Prettejohn, 'Aesthetic Value and the Professionalization of Victorian Art Criticism 1837–78', *Journal of Victorian Culture*, vol. 2, no. 1, spring 1997, 71–94.
26 Deborah Lutz, *Pleasure Bound: Victorian Sex Rebels and the New Eroticism*, New York and London: W.W. Norton, 2011, 156–7.
27 Ibid., 154.
28 Elizabeth Prettejohn, *Art for Art's Sake: Aestheticism in Victorian Painting*, New Haven, C.T., and London: Yale University Press, 2007, 29. The leading 'other such grouping' was that of Holland House: see Chapter 7.
29 The phrase 'art for art's sake' first appeared in Swinburne's book on William Blake, published early in 1868; the book also presents a developed account of his theoretical position on the radical autonomy of art.
30 Rikky Rooksby, *A.C. Swinburne: A Poet's Life*, London: Scolar Press, 1997, 141.
31 Richard Dellamora, *Masculine Desire: The Sexual Politics of Victorian Aestheticism*, Chapel Hill: University of North Carolina Press, 1990, 69.
32 Lutz, *Pleasure Bound*, 13.
33 Dellamora, *Masculine Desire*, 17–18.
34 The Leonardo essay contains Pater's celebrated reverie on the *Mona Lisa*, described in 1978 by his biographer, with Carlsbergian hyperbole, as 'probably still the most famous piece of writing about any picture in the world'. Michael Levey, *The Case of Walter Pater*, London: Thames & Hudson, 1978, 125.
35 Dellamora, *Masculine Desire*, 18.
36 Cole, *Modernism, Male Friendship, and the First World War*, 31, citing Peter Parker, *The Old Lie: The Great War and the Public-School Ethos*, London: Constable, 1987, 53.
37 E.M. Forster, *Abinger Harvest*, San Diego, C.A.: Harcourt, 1936, 4. Cited ibid., 32.
38 Cole, *Modernism, Male Friendship, and the First World War*, 34–5.
39 On these see Paul R. Deslandes, *Oxbridge Men: British Masculinity and the Undergraduate Experience, 1850–1920*, Bloomington: Indiana University Press, 2005.

40 W.C. Lubenow, *The Cambridge Apostles, 1820–1914: Liberalism, Imagination and Friendship in British Intellectual and Professional Life*, Cambridge: Cambridge University Press, 1998, 29.
41 Ibid., 26.
42 Ibid., 30. On 'angels' as a term for an elite see Allen Upward at the end of the last chapter.
43 Ibid., 26.
44 Adam Kuper, *Incest and Influence: The Private Life of Bourgeois England*, Cambridge, M.A., and London: Harvard University Press, 2009, 253–6.
45 Leonard Woolf, *An Autobiography*, vol. 2: *1911–1969*, Oxford: The Clarendon Press, 1980, 11–13.
46 G.E. Moore, *Principia Ethica* (1903), Cambridge: Cambridge University Press, 1968, 188–9.
47 Both comments quoted by Michael Holroyd, *Lytton Strachey: The New Biography*, New York: Farrar, Straus and Giroux, 1995, 89–90.
48 Kuper, *Incest and Influence*, 201.
49 Ceri Crossley, 'Rediscovering the French Eighteenth Century', in Ceri Crossley and Ian Small, eds, *Studies in Anglo-French Cultural Relations: Imagining France*, Basingstoke: Macmillan, 1988, 107.
50 Lytton Strachey, 'Madame du Deffand', in *Books and Characters, French and English*, London: Chatto & Windus, 1922, 83, 85.
51 Christophe Campos, *The View of France: From Arnold to Bloomsbury*, London: Oxford University Press, 1965, 211–22.
52 Raymond Williams, 'The Significance of "Bloomsbury" as a Social and Cultural Group', in Derek Crabtree and A.P. Thirlwell, eds, *Keynes and the Bloomsbury Group*, London: Macmillan, 1980, 40–67; 58–9.
53 Ibid., 58–9.
54 Grace Brockington, *Above the Battlefield: Modernism and the Peace Movement in Britain, 1900–1918*, New Haven, C.T., and London: Yale University Press, 2010; Mark Hussey, *Clive Bell and the Making of Modernism*, London: Bloomsbury, 2021, Part III.
55 The phrase is Leonard Woolf's, from the first volume of his autobiography, *Sowing* (1960), quoted in Williams, 'The Significance of "Bloomsbury"', 47.
56 The launch of the *Dreadnought* in 1906 marked the start in earnest of the competition with Germany to rearm. See Robert Massie, *Castles of Steel: Britain, Germany, and the Winning of the Great War at Sea*, London: Pimlico, 2003. On the concept of *blague*, a term borrowed from French, see Chapter 3.
57 Clive Bell, *Art*, London: Chatto & Windus, 1914, 291. See Chapter 1 on the culture of amateurism that spanned the class hierarchy of late Victorian and Edwardian Britain, and Chapter 8 for its aristocratic connotations in particular.
58 Kuper, *Incest and Influence*, 218.
59 On the patronage and the commercialism (via the Omega), see Chapter 9.
60 On 'civilised individuals' as a concept see Williams, 'The Significance of "Bloomsbury"', 62–7.
61 Writing had become a profession for women, but had only fairly recently emerged from the status of genteel female accomplishment. Art was less advanced in this direction. See Deborah Cherry, *Painting Women: Victorian Women Artists*, London: Routledge, 1993.

62 See Chapters 3 and, especially, 5 for a development of this point. For examples of such work see Richard Shone, ed., *The Art of Bloomsbury*, exh. cat., London: Tate Gallery, 1999, esp. 73–130 and 136–59.
63 See Chapter 7.
64 See Jose Harris, *Private Lives, Public Spirit: Britain 1870–1914*, Harmondsworth: Penguin, 1994, ch. 5.
65 Stephen Knott, *Amateur Craft: History and Theory*, London: Bloomsbury, 2015.
66 See Robin Gilmour, *The Idea of the Gentleman in the Victorian Novel*, London: George Allen & Unwin, 1981.
67 Crossley and Small, eds, *Studies in Anglo-French Cultural Relations*; Campos, *The View of France*.
68 Jeffrey Merrick and Bryant T. Ragan, eds, *Homosexuality in Modern France*, Oxford: Oxford University Press, 1996, 4. 'Nevertheless, police continued to arrest men suspected of sodomitic solicitation under Article 330 of the Napoleonic Penal Code of 1810 (which condemned "public offences against decency") and under Article 331 concerning the age of consent (11, until it was raised to 13 in 1863).' Vernon A. Rosario II, 'Pointy Penises, Fashion Crimes, and Hysterical Mollies: The Pederasts' Inversions', in ibid., 148.
69 William A. Peniston, 'Love and Death in Gay Paris: Homosexuality and Criminality in the 1870s', in Merrick and Ragan, eds, *Homosexuality in Modern France*, 142.
70 Harris, *Private Lives, Public Spirit*, 220–21.
71 Carol E. Harrison, *The Bourgeois Citizen in Nineteenth-Century France: Gender, Sociability, and the Uses of Emulation*, Oxford: Oxford University Press, 1999, 23; Bridget Alsdorf, *Fellow Men: Fantin-Latour and the Problem of the Group in Nineteenth-Century French Painting*, Princeton, N.J.: Princeton University Press, 2013, 8.
72 Harrison, *The Bourgeois Citizen in Nineteenth-Century France*, 27, 33.
73 Ibid., 222.
74 Ibid., 226.
75 Ibid., 88.
76 Ibid., 7. *Cercles* (circles) were formally constituted collectivities, often modelled on English 'clubs'; on their numbers see Maurice Agulhon, *Le Cercle dans la France bourgeoise 1810–1848*, Paris: Armand Colin, 31.
77 Harrison, *The Bourgeois Citizen in Nineteenth-Century France*, 90–91.
78 Ibid., 223.
79 Peter H. Amman, *Revolution and Mass Democracy: The Paris Club Movement of 1848*, Princeton, N.J.: Princeton University Press, 34–5.
80 W. Scott Haine, *The World of the Paris Café: Sociability among the French Working Class, 1789–1914*, Baltimore, M.D., and London: Johns Hopkins University Press, 1996, 207, 223.
81 Ibid., 237.
82 Ibid., 207. On the relation between art and anarchist politics in the Parisian *fin de siècle* see Chapter 5.
83 Ibid., 230–1.
84 Ibid., 228. See also Harold B. Segel, *Turn-of-the-Century Cabaret: Paris, Barcelona, Berlin, Munich, Vienna, Cracow, Moscow, St Petersburg, Zurich*, New York: Columbia University Press, 1987, 48–50; Jerrold Seigel, *Bohemian Paris: Culture, Politics and the Boundaries of Bourgeois Life, 1830–1930*, New York: Viking, 1986, 288–95.

CHAPTER 3

1 Mary Gluck, 'Theorizing the Cultural Roots of the Bohemian Artist', *Modernism/Modernity*, vol. 7, no. 3, 2000, 351–78; 351.
2 See, e.g., T.J. Clark, *Image of the People: Gustave Courbet and the 1848 Revolution*, London and New York: Thames & Hudson, 1973; George Levitine, *The Dawn of Bohemianism: The 'Barbu' Rebellion and Primitivism in Neo-classical France*, University Park, P.A., and London: Pennsylvania State University Press, 1978; Marilyn Brown, *Gypsies and Other Bohemians: The Myth of the Artist in Nineteenth-Century France*, Ann Arbor, M.I.: UMI Research Press, 1985; Jerrold Seigel, *Bohemian Paris: Culture, Politics and the Boundaries of Bourgeois Life, 1830–1930*, New York: Viking, 1986; Elizabeth Wilson, *Bohemians: The Glamorous Outcasts*, London and New York: I.B. Tauris, 2000.
3 Robert Darnton, 'Introduction', in Anne Gédéon Lafitte, Marquis de Pelleport, *The Bohemians: A Novel*, Philadelphia: University of Philadelphia Press, 2010, iv and 149, nn. 1, 2.
4 Brown, *Gypsies and Other Bohemians*, 1.
5 Ibid., 7.
6 Clark, *Image of the People*, 33.
7 Seigel, *Bohemian Paris*, 3, 5.
8 Mary Gluck, *Popular Bohemia: Modernism and Urban Culture in Nineteenth-Century Paris*, Cambridge, M.A., and London: Harvard University Press, 2005, 16.
9 Ibid., 15–19, 117–19.
10 Brown, *Gypsies and Other Bohemians*, 3.
11 See David Cottington, *Cubism in the Shadow of War: The Avant-Garde and Politics in Paris, 1905–1914*, New Haven, C.T., and London: Yale University Press, 1998, 39; also Seigel, *Bohemian Paris*, 295, with whom I agree on the distinction, but for different reasons.
12 Seigel, *Bohemian Paris*, 295.
13 See Chapter 2.
14 There is now a rich and substantial body of scholarship on this engagement, among the seminal contributions to which are T.J. Clark, *The Painting of Modern Life: Paris in the Art of Manet and his Followers*, London and New York: Thames & Hudson, 1985; and Thomas Crow, 'Modernism and Mass Culture in the Visual Arts' (1982), in Francis Frascina, ed., *Pollock and After: The Critical Debate*, New York and London: Harper & Row, 1985.
15 See, e.g., Émile Goudeau, *Dix Ans de Bohème*, Paris: La Librairie Illustrée, 1888; Daniel Grojnowski, 'Une Avant-garde sans avancée: Les "Arts Incohérents", 1882–1889', *Actes de Recherche en Sciences Sociales,* November 1981, 73–86; Catherine Charpin, *Les Arts incohérents (1882–1893)*, Paris: Syros, 1990; Phillip Dennis Cate and Mary Shaw, eds, *The Spirit of Montmartre: Cabarets, Humour and the Avant-Garde, 1875–1905*, New Brunswick, N.J.: Zimmerli Art Museum, Rutgers University, 1996; Gluck, *Popular Bohemia*, 108–31; Jorgelina Orfila, '*Blague,* Nationalism and Incohérence', in June Hargrove and Neil McWilliam, eds, *Nationalism and French Visual Culture, 1870–1914*, Washington, D.C., New Haven, C.T., and London: Yale University Press, 2005, 173–93.
16 Francisque Sarcey (1913), cited in Jeffrey Weiss, *The Popular Culture of Modern Art: Picasso, Duchamp and Avant-Gardism*, New Haven, C.T., and London: Yale University Press, 1994, 120, 294, n. 53.
17 Ibid.

18 Daniel Grojnowski and Denys Riout, *Les Arts incohérents et le rire dans les arts plastiques*, Paris: Corti, 2015, 47. This mutual animosity is the more understandable in light of that sharpening distinction between bourgeois and working class that was noted in the last chapter with respect to associations in France.

19 Ibid., 48–9.

20 *Zutisme* was a short-lived poetic movement that expressed its members' disgust at the new bourgeois republic's combined effacement of that uprising and cherrypicking of its policies, via the publication of parodies of Parnassian poetry's ideal beauty that transformed its high-cultural idioms into obscene hymns to female genitalia. See Orfila, '*Blague*, Nationalism and Incohérence', 179.

21 Cate and Shaw, eds, *The Spirit of Montmartre*, 20.

22 Ibid., 27.

23 Charpin, *Les Arts incohérents*, 15.

24 Cate and Shaw, eds, *The Spirit of Montmartre*, 1. For details of this and the following exhibitions in Lévy's series see, besides Cate, Charpin, *Les Arts incohérents*, 15–45.

25 Cate and Shaw, eds, *The Spirit of Montmartre*, 31. The casual racism underpinning this humour was in keeping with contemporary racial prejudice both within and beyond bohemia – a feature shared, it may be noted, with the humour of Bloomsbury black-face charades noted in the last chapter.

26 'Nous ne faisons point de l'Art… et jamais nous n'avons voulu en faire. Nous nous amusons et nous voulons amuser les autres.' Jules Lévy, 'Les Incohérents', *Le Chat Noir*, 30 October 1886, 2. Quoted in Orfila, '*Blague*, Nationalism and Incohérence', 189 n. 7.

27 'L'Incohérence est la rigolade sans méchanceté… ce divertissement parisien'. Lévy, 'Les Incohérents', *Le Chat Noir*, 30 October 1886, 3. Quoted in Orfila, '*Blague*, Nationalism and Incohérence', 193 n. 89.

28 'La gaieté et l'esprit français ont été souillés.… Il faut réhabiliter cette gloire nationale qu'on nomme l'esprit français, c'est pourquoi les incohérents sont venus.' Lévy, 'Les Incohérents', 3. Quoted in Orfila, '*Blague*, Nationalism and Incohérence', 193 n. 90.

29 Orfila, '*Blague*, Nationalism and Incohérence', 187–8.

30 Ibid, 189 n. 9.

31 Ernest Raynaud, *La Bohème sous le Second Empire: Charles Cros et Nina*, Paris: L'Artisan du Livre, 1930, 15; Orfila, '*Blague*, Nationalism and Incohérence', 181. See also Lionel Richard, *Cabaret, cabarets: Origines et décadence*, Paris: Plon, 1991.

32 Charpin, *Les Arts incohérents*, 23.

33 Cate and Shaw, eds, *The Spirit of Montmartre*, 29.

34 The existence of such an appreciative audience does not imply, however, that it shared the subversive aims of the practitioners of *fumisme*; we can infer from it only that plenty of people enjoyed the jokes. On the publicity techniques see, e.g., Rosalind Williams, *Dream Worlds: Mass Consumption in Late Nineteenth-Century France*, Berkeley: University of California Press, 1982; Weiss, *The Popular Culture of Modern Art*.

35 On this community see Daniel Grojnowski and Bernard Sarrazin, *L'Esprit fumiste et les rires fin-de-siècle*, Paris: Corti, 1990; Cate and Shaw, eds, *The Spirit of Montmartre*.

36 Grojnowski and Sarrazin, *L'Esprit fumiste*, 15.

37 Goudeau, cited in Gluck, *Popular Bohemia,* 124–5. See also G.G. Lemaire, *Les Cafés littéraires*, Paris: Henri Veyrier, 1987.

38 Grojnowski, 'Une Avant-garde sans avancée', 74.

39 For an overview of its history see Christophe Charle, *La Crise des sociétés impériales*, Paris: Seuil, 2001. For Britain see Harold Perkin, *The Rise of Professional Society: England since 1880*, London: Routledge, 1989; for France, Gerald L. Geison, ed., *Professions and the French State, 1700–1900*, Philadelphia: University of Pennsylvania Press, 1984; for Germany, Geoffrey Cocks and Karl Jarausch, eds, *German Professions 1800–1950*, Oxford: Oxford University Press, 1990.

40 Significant theorisations of professions and professionalisation include: Magali Sarfatti Larson, *The Rise of Professionalism: A Sociological Analysis*, Berkeley: University of California Press, 1977; Eliot Freidson, *Professional Powers: A Study of the Institutionalization of Formal Knowledge*, Chicago, I.L.: University of Chicago Press, 1986; M. Burrage and R. Torstendahl, eds, *Professions in Theory and History*, London: Sage, 1990. For a summary of present positions and methodologies see Karl H. Jarausch, *The Unfree Professions: German Lawyers, Teachers and Engineers, 1900–1930*, Oxford: Oxford University Press, 1990, 3–26.

41 Raymonde Moulin, 'De l'Artisan au professionnel: l'artiste', in R. Moulin, *De la Valeur de l'art. Recueil d'articles*, Paris: Flammarion, 1995, 91–106; Robert Jensen, *Marketing Modernism in Fin-de-Siècle Europe*, Princeton, N.J.: Princeton University Press, 1994; Béatrice Joyeux-Prunel, *Nul n'est prophète en son pays? L'internationalisation de la peinture des avant-gardes parisiennes 1855–1914*, Paris: Musée d'Orsay/Nicolas Chaudun, 2009.

42 Jensen, *Marketing Modernism*, 167.

43 Ibid., 10.

44 Ibid., 11.

45 As Jensen acknowledges, it was first borrowed for art history by Albert Boime, in his *The Academy and French Painting in the Nineteenth Century*, London: Phaidon, 1971. Jensen, *Marketing Modernism*, 139.

46 Jensen, *Marketing Modernism*, 10; Joyeux-Prunel, *Nul n'est prophète en son pays?*, 16. Neither pays much attention to the British context. On this see Elizabeth Prettejohn, 'Aesthetic Value and the Professionalization of Victorian Art Criticism 1837–78', *Journal of Victorian Culture*, vol. 2, no. 1, spring 1997, 71–94.

47 See the Introduction.

48 Robert Estivals, Jean-Charles Gaudy and Gabrielle Vergez, *L'Avant-garde. Étude historique et sociologique des publications ayant pour titre 'l'avant-garde'*, Paris: Bibliothèque Nationale, 1968.

49 Denys Riout, 'Théodore Duret, Gentleman de la critique (1838–1927)', introduction to Théodore Duret, *Critique d'avant-garde* (1885), Paris: ENS des Beaux-Arts, 1998, 21.

50 Joyeux-Prunel, *Nul n'est prophète en son pays?*, 6, who records also the following: '"trouble-fêtes"… "impressionnistes", "intransigeants", "peintres de la modernité" chez Joris Karl Huysmans ("Le Salon de 1879", repris dans [J.-K.] Huysmans, [*Oeuvres complètes*, vol. 6: *L'Art moderne*, Paris], 1928, 10–11)'. Ibid., 242 n. 20.

51 Martha Ward, *Pissarro, Neo-Impressionism and the Spaces of the Avant-Garde*, Chicago, I.L.: University of Chicago Press, 1996, 58. Griselda Pollock has made a similar set of distinctions, if more schematically. Griselda Pollock, *Avant-Garde Gambits 1888–1893: Gender and the Colour of Art History*, London and New York: Thames & Hudson, 1993, 12–16.

52 Ward, *Pissarro, Neo-Impressionism*, ch. 2.

53 Félix Fénéon, *Oeuvres plus que complètes,* textes réunis et présentés par Joan U. Halperin, tome I, *Chroniques d'art,* Geneva–Paris: Droz, 1970, 46–9; Joan U. Halperin, *Félix Fénéon, Aesthete and Anarchist in Fin-de-Siècle Paris,* New Haven, C.T., and London: Yale University Press, 1988, 92. On Fénéon's role both in coining this term and in furnishing a key criterion of avant-garde status, see Chapter 5.

54 Joyeux-Prunel, *Nul n'est prophète en son pays?,* 96–9.

55 Ibid., 58.

56 On the Nabis in their cultural context see Paul-Henri Bourrelier, *La Revue blanche: une génération dans l'engagement 1890–1905*, Paris: Fayard, 2007; Clément Dessy, *Les Écrivains et les Nabis. La littérature au défi de la peinture*, Rennes: Presses Universitaires de Rennes, 2015; Claire Frèches-Thory and Antoine Terrasse, *The Nabis: Bonnard, Vuillard and their Circle,* New York: Abrams, 1991.

57 See, e.g., Robyn Roslak, *Neo-Impressionism and Anarchism in Fin-de-Siècle France: Painting, Politics and Landscape*, Aldershot: Ashgate, 2007; Michael Marlais, 'Conservative Style/Conservative Politics: Maurice Denis in Le Vésinet', *Art History*, vol. 16, no. 1, March 1993, 125–46.

58 Pierre Bourdieu, 'The Field of Cultural Production, or: The Economic World Reversed', in Pierre Bourdieu, *The Field of Cultural Production: Essays on Art and Literature*, ed. Randal Johnson, Cambridge: Polity, 1993, 29–73; 30.

59 Louis Vauxcelles, *Gil Blas*, 1 September 1909, 1: 'ces soi-disant coloristes d'avant-garde'; Roger Allard, 'Sur quelques peintres', *Les Marches du sud-ouest*, June 1911, 58: 'des peintres dits "d'avant-garde" par une métaphore puérilement belliqueuse'; Allard, 'Les Arts plastiques. Futurisme, simultanéisme et autres métachories', *Les Écrits français*, 3, 5 February 1914, 255–6: 'L'avant-gardisme n'est pas seulement un ridicule, c'est une plaie.' For more examples, and analysis of them, see Cottington, *Cubism in the Shadow of War*, 49–53.

60 Williams, *Dream Worlds*, 64–5; Weiss, *The Popular Culture of Modern Art*; Michael B. Miller, *The Bon Marché: Bourgeois Culture and the Department Store 1869–1920*, Princeton, N.J.: Princeton University Press, 1981. France's first advertising trade magazine, *La Publicité*, was founded in 1903; see Daniel Pope, 'French Advertising Men and the American "Promised Land"', *Historical Reflections*, 5, summer 1978, 118.

61 See Chapter 4.

62 See ibid.

63 Michael C. Fitzgerald, *Making Modernism: Picasso and the Creation of the Market for Twentieth-Century Art*, New York: Farrar, Straus and Giroux, 1995, 15–46; Jensen, *Marketing Modernism.*

64 The number of foreign exhibitors at the Salon d'Automne almost doubled from 21 per cent of the total in 1904 to 37 per cent in 1907; by 1912 this had reached 45 per cent. For detailed figures see Béatrice Joyeux-Prunel, 'L'Art de la mesure. Le Salon d'Automne (1903–1914), l'avant-garde, ses étrangers et la nation française', *Histoire et mesure*, 1, 2007, 22, who notes that, since it took two years from arrival in Paris to acceptance at the Automne, there were probably many more trying to get in. See also Antoine Marès, 'Pourquoi des étrangers à Paris?', in *L'École de Paris 1904–1929, la part de l'Autre*, exh. cat., Paris: Musée d'Art Moderne de la Ville de Paris, 2000, 138–47.

65 On all of the above developments see David Cottington, *Cubism and its Histories*, Manchester and New York: Manchester University Press, 2004, 7–14.

66 This criterion departs from the tripartite model of the development of the avant-garde suggested by Raymond Williams and noted in previous chapters.

67 Freidson, *Professional Powers*, 35. Freidson elaborates usefully: 'we cannot realistically assume that there is a holistic folk that produces only one folk concept of profession in societies as complex as ours. What a profession is phenomenologically, then, is not determined solely by any single group – neither by members of an occupation, nor by those of the other occupations they deal with in the course of their work, nor by their clients or employers, nor by sociologists or the state.' Ibid., 36. Lawrence Haworth offers a related definition of 'profession' (and its derivatives), similarly broader in its reference than that of 'liberal-bourgeois' professionalism, as referring to 'a distinctive competence' possessed by 'people… who instinctively define themselves by reference to the occupation in which this competence can be expressed'. *Decadence and Objectivity: Ideals for Work in the Post-Consumer Society*, Toronto: University of Toronto Press, 1979, xi.

68 Between 1903 and 1914 participation in the Salon d'Automne and the Indépendants together averaged around three thousand artists. See Joyeux-Prunel, 'L'Art de la mesure', 152; René Huyghe, André Parinaud, eds, *Un siècle d'art moderne. L'histoire du Salon des Indépendants*, Paris: Denoël, 1984; Henri Bidou, 'Les Salons de 1910', *Gazette des Beaux-Arts*, May 1910, 361. On the rise in the number of artists in Paris between the early 1870s and the first decade of the new century see Chapter 4, n. 8.

69 Edwin H. Sutherland, ed., *The Professional Thief, by a Professional Thief*, Chicago, I.L.: University of Chicago Press, 1937.

70 Ibid., 198.

71 Ibid.

72 Ibid., 198, n. 2.

73 Ibid., 200.

74 Ibid., 202.

75 Ibid., 204.

76 Ibid., 207.

77 Ibid.

78 Orfila, '*Blague*, Nationalism and Incohérence'.

79 'The fact that France was generally a source of Filth was common English knowledge by the time of the Wilde trials [of 1895]', writes Julian Barnes in his portrait of Belle Époque Paris, *The Man in the Red Coat*, London: Jonathan Cape, 2019, 17.

80 Jean-Paul Crespelle, *La Vie quotidienne à Montmartre au temps de Picasso 1900–1910*, Paris: Hachette, 1978.

81 Roland Dorgelès, *Bouquet de Bohème*, Paris: Albin Michel, 1947, 228–44; Bruce Altshuler, *The Avant-Garde in Exhibition: New Art in the Twentieth Century*, Berkeley: University of California Press, 1998.

82 Picasso once remarked to the photographer Brassaï that his former lover Fernande Olivier 'was very gifted, but she didn't possess that sacred fire of work'. Cited in Wilson, *Bohemians: The Glamorous Outcasts*, 103.

83 Ibid., 3.

84 Peter Brooker, *Bohemia in London: The Social Scene of Early Modernism*, Basingstoke: Palgrave Macmillan, 2007, 2–3.

85 Wilson, *Bohemians: The Glamorous Outcasts*, 24.

86 Lisa Tickner, 'Bohemianism and the Cultural Field: *Trilby* and *Tarr*', *Art History*, vol. 34, no. 5, November 2011, 2–34.

87 On the novel and the vogue it created see Hugh David, *The Fitzrovians: A Portrait of Bohemian Society 1900–1955*, London: Sceptre, 1989, 21–4.

88 Tickner, 'Bohemianism and the Cultural Field', 5–6.

89 Theresa Ann Gronberg, 'Femmes de Brasserie', *Art History*, vol. 7, no. 3, September 1994, 329–44; Carol Duncan, 'Virility and Domination in Early Twentieth-Century Vanguard Painting' (1973), repr. in Norma Broude and Mary D. Garrard, eds, *Feminism and Art History: Questioning the Litany*, New York: Harper & Row, 1982, 293–313.

90 Brooker, *Bohemia in London*, 107.

91 Cottington, *Cubism in the Shadow of War*; Cottington, *Cubism and its Histories*.

92 Brooker, *Bohemia in London*, 108.

93 Ibid., 106.

94 Ibid., 108. Hamnett's autobiography, *Laughing Torso*, London: Constable, 1932, is an enjoyably breathless yet artfully disingenuous narrative of her apparently outrageous adventures as a 'bohémienne'. However, Brooker's conventional view of her work has been convincingly challenged recently: see the essays on her, and illustrations of her work, in Nathaniel Hepburn, ed., *Nina Hamnett/Lisa Brice*, exh. cat., Charleston Press No. 4, Charleston, Sussex: Charleston Trust, 2021.

95 On what became known as 'High Bohemia', and Nancy Cunard at the Café Royal, see Chapter 9.

96 Brooker, *Bohemia in London*, 112. On this art see Lisa Tickner, *The Spectacle of Women: Imagery of the Suffrage Campaign 1907–1914*, London: Chatto & Windus, 1987.

CHAPTER 4

1 Béatrice Joyeux-Prunel, *Nul n'est prophète en son pays? L'internationalisation de la peinture des avant-gardes parisiennes 1855–1914*, Paris: Musée d'Orsay/Nicolas Chaudun, 2009, 32, 78, 97–9.

2 See Chapter 3.

3 Joyeux-Prunel, *Nul n'est prophète en son pays?*, 78.

4 Juliet Simpson, 'The Société Nationale: The Politics of Innovation in Late Nineteenth-Century France', *Apollo*, vol. 149, no. 444, February 1999, 49–55; Jean-Paul Bouillon, 'Sociétés d'artistes et institutions officielles dans la seconde moitié du XIXe siècle', *Romantisme*, 54, 1986, 89–113. The management of the Salon had been delegated to the Artistes Français in 1881 by Gambetta's government, before when it had been run by the Académie des Beaux-Arts, one of the five académies of the Institut de France.

5 Joyeux-Prunel, *Nul n'est prophète en son pays?*, 'ce système était dominé par des artistes surdotés socialement', 11; 'L'art moderne était parvenu à rejoindre la haute société cosmopolite, et à lui emprunter ses pratiques', 78.

6 An exact number is hard to ascertain, as so much of the information on them is in the form of recollections published by former students, for which there was a vogue around the turn of the century (part of that broader vogue for 'bohemiana' that the last chapter noted and *Trilby* epitomised). Such recollections are often vague and inconsistent, and as often use different names for the same *académie*.

7 'The paste, the painting on the first try.' George Moore, *Confessions of a Young Man*, written 1886 but not published until 1918. Quoted in John Milner, *The Studios of Paris: The Capital of Art in the Late Nineteenth Century*, New Haven, C.T., and London: Yale University Press, 1988, 11. This book's few pages on the *académies libres* are an invaluable summation of primary sources.

8 On the rise in the number of artists in Paris between the early 1870s and the first decade of the new century see Christophe Charle, *Naissance des 'Intellectuels' 1880–1900*, Paris: Minuit, 41 and annexe 1. On the expansion of that city's artistic field see C. and H. White, *Canvases and Careers: Institutional Change in the French Painting World*, New York: Wiley and Sons, 1965; M.-C. Genet-Delacroix, 'Esthétique officielle et art national sous la Troisième République', *Le Mouvement social*, 131, April–June 1985, 118–19; Bouillon, 'Sociétés d'artistes et institutions officielles', 89–113; Milner, *The Studios of Paris.*

9 Clive Holland, 'Lady Art Students' Life in Paris', *The Studio*, 30, 1904, 225–33.

10 'L'atelier libre de Cormon n'avait rien d'académique: chacun y travaillait comme il l'entendait, s'esquivant les jours de la correction du "patron".' Émile Bernard, 'Louis Anquetin artiste peintre', *Mercure de France*, 1 November 1932, 590–607, quoted in Anne Rivière, ed., *Émile Bernard, Propos sur l'art*, 2 vols, Paris: Séguier, 1994, 1:260–61.

11 '[s]on goût du grand et sa façon délibérée de construire la forme'; 'inquiet toujours de monter vers le plus fort et le mieux'; 'Anquetin était pris par l'idée d'être le grand peintre de la vie moderne, et rêvait de fonder dans son art Manet et Daumier.' Ibid., 260, 261.

12 Bernard recalled that the technique was baptised 'cloisonnisme' by the then-director of the 'little magazine' *La Revue indépendante*, Édouard Dujardin, who was a close friend of, and influence on, Anquetin. Ibid., 261–2.

13 Clément Dessy, *Les Écrivains et les Nabis. La littérature au défi de la peinture*, Rennes: Presses Universitaires de Rennes, 2015, 21–2, 44.

14 The initiative was that of one of their number, Paul Ranson, who had himself studied at the Académie Julian, and was named after him when he died the following year. Milner, *The Studios of Paris,* 218.

15 For a searching analysis of these exhibiting societies in the context of the evolving Parisian art market see Bouillon, 'Sociétés d'artistes et institutions officielles'.

16 The Mirlitons brought together aristocrats with musicians, painters and writers; the musicians predominated, and the society's nickname derives from the 'Danse des Mirlitons' (Dance of the Pipe Flutes) in Tchaikovsky's *Nutcracker* ballet. There were 150 members, and the subscription was 3,000 francs, a sum prohibitive for all but the wealthiest artists; its clubhouse was in the Place Vendôme. See James Ross, 'Music in the French Salon', in R. Langham Smith and C. Potter, eds, *French Music since Berlioz*, Aldershot: Ashgate, 2006, 101. Society portraitist Jacques-Émile Blanche recalled the Mirlitons (which later became known as L'Épatant), and its rival and 'facsimile' Le Volney, in his *La Pêche aux souvenirs*, ed. Armand Pierhal, Paris: Flammarion, 1949, 153–8.

17 Bouillon, 'Sociétés d'artistes et institutions officielles', 93.

18 The frame of reference for the assessment that follows, of Impressionism in relation to the emergence and consolidation of an avant-garde formation in Paris, is provided largely by Charles S. Moffett, ed., *The New Painting: Impressionism 1874–1886*, exh. cat., Geneva: Burton with Fine Arts Museums of San Francisco and the National Gallery of Art, Washington, D.C., 1986; Martha Ward, 'Impressionist Installations and Private Exhibitions', *The Art Bulletin*, vol. 73, no. 4, December 1991, 599–622; Patricia Mainardi,

Art and Politics of the Second Empire: The Universal Expositions of 1855 and 1867, New Haven, C.T.: Yale University Press, 1987, esp. 49–61.

19 For a detailed assessment of the market-based motivation for the Impressionist exhibitions, see Bouillon, 'Sociétés d'artistes et institutions officielles', 95–6ff.

20 Ward, 'Impressionist Installations', 600.

21 Moffett, 'Introduction', in *The New Painting*, 17.

22 Cited and translated in John Rewald, *The History of Impressionism* (1973), 4th rev. edn, New York: Secker & Warburg, 1980, 309.

23 *The New Painting* offers no specific analysis of the avant-garde status itself of the Impressionist group; this remains assumed and undefined. See, e.g., the 'Introduction' by the exhibition's director, Charles S. Moffett.

24 Reprinted in *The New Painting*, 37–49.

25 'The Impressionists and Édouard Manet', *The Art Monthly Review and Photographic Portfolio*, London, vol. 1, no. 9, 30 September 1876, 117–22.

26 Moffett, 'Introduction', in *The New Painting*, 19. On 'position-taking' see Chapter 3, pages 88–89 and n. 58.

27 Stephen F. Eisenman, 'The Intransigent Artist or How the Impressionists Got their Name', in *The New Painting*, 50–59.

28 Bouillon, 'Sociétés d'artistes et institutions officielles', 95.

29 'Il faut faire un pas de plus et arriver à la grande notoriété. Vous n'y arriverez point par des expositions de sociétés particulières. Le public ne va pas à ces expositions, il n'y a que le même noyau d'artistes et d'amateurs qui vous connaît d'avance.' Ibid., 95–6.

30 Ibid., 96. On the economic condition of France in the last quarter of the nineteenth century see F. Capie and G. Wood, eds, 'Great Depression of 1873–1896', in D. Glasner and T.F. Cooley, *Business Cycles and Depressions: An Encyclopedia*. New York: Garland Publishing, 1997, 148–49. The French economy suffered worse than most others, its GNP growing only 10 per cent between 1875 and 1905, against that of Germany (113 per cent) and that of Britain (60 per cent); see Y. Breton, A. Broder and M. Lutfalla, eds, *La Longue Stagnation en France: l'autre grande dépression, 1873–1897*, Paris: Economica, 1997, esp. 460.

31 Bouillon, 'Sociétés d'artistes et institutions officielles', 96.

32 Letter from Sisley to Duret, 14 March 1879, quoted in Ronald Pickvance, 'Contemporary Popularity and Posthumous Neglect', in *The New Painting*, 246; English translation from Rewald, *The History of Impressionism*, 421.

33 'Il y a à Paris à peine quinze amateurs capables d'aimer un peintre sans le Salon. Il y en a 80,000 qui n'achèteront même pas un nez si un peintre n'est pas au Salon. Voilà pourquoi je les envoie tous les ans deux portraits.' Lionello Venturi, *Les Archives de l'impressionnisme. Lettres de Renoir, Monet, Pissarro, Sisley et autres. Mémoires de Paul Durand-Ruel, Documents*, 2 vols, Paris and New York: Durand-Ruel, 1939, 1: 115.

34 Jean Des Cars and Pierre Pinon, *Paris-Haussmann: 'le pari d'Haussmann'*, exh. cat, Paris: Pavillon de l'Arsenal, 1991.

35 On this new middle class see Chloé Gaboriaux, 'Fonder la République sur les "nouvelles couches sociales" (Gambetta): description du monde social et préférences institutionnelles dans la France des années 1870', *Histoire@Politique*, vol. 25, no. 1, 2015, 12–23.

36 On the relation between the rising middle class and Impressionist painting see Meyer Schapiro's two seminal essays of the 1930s, 'The Social Bases of Art' (1936) and 'The

Nature of Abstract Art' (1937), reprinted in Schapiro, *Modern Art: The Nineteenth and Twentieth Centuries*, London: Chatto & Windus, 1978, 185–211; also Albert Boime, 'Entrepreneurial Patronage in Nineteenth-Century France', in E.C. Carter, R. Forster and J.N. Moody, eds, *Enterprise and Entrepreneurs in Nineteenth and Twentieth Century France*, Baltimore, M.D., and London: Johns Hopkins University Press, 1976, 137–201.

37 Nicholas Watkins, 'The Genesis of a Decorative Aesthetic', in Gloria Groom, ed., *Beyond the Easel: Decorative Painting by Bonnard, Vuillard, Denis and Roussel*, New Haven, C.T., and London: Yale University Press, 2001, 1–28.

38 On the blurring of the distinction between Salon and industrial fair consequent upon the sharing of a venue after 1855, see P. Mainardi, 'The Eviction of the Salon from the Louvre', *Gazette des beaux-arts*, ser. 6, no. 112, July–August 1988, 31–40.

39 See Chapter 7.

40 Ward, 'Impressionist Installations', 599–622.

41 Ibid., 617.

42 Ibid., 618.

43 Joyeux-Prunel, *Nul n'est prophète en son pays?*, 76–7.

44 Martha Ward, 'The Rhetoric of Independence and Innovation', in Moffett, ed., *The New Painting*, 422.

45 'La prise en charge de quelques carrières impressionnistes par la galerie Petit constituait donc une valorisation symbolique sans précédent.' Joyeux-Prunel, *Nul n'est prophète en son pays?*, 54.

46 On this shift of gravity see C. and H. White, *Canvases and Careers*; Robert Jensen, *Marketing Modernism in Fin-de-Siècle Europe*, Princeton, N.J.: Princeton University Press, 1994; Nicholas Green, 'Circuits of Production, Circuits of Consumption: The Case of Mid-Nineteenth-Century Art Dealing', *Art Journal*, vol. 48, no. 1, spring 1989, 29–34; Joyeux-Prunel, *Nul n'est prophète en son pays?*, ch. 2, 48–55.

47 Jennifer A. Thompson, 'Durand-Ruel and America', in Sylvie Patry, ed., *Inventing Impressionism: Paul Durand-Ruel and the Modern Art Market*, exh. cat., London: National Gallery/Yale University Press, 2015, 134–51.

48 Anne Distel, 'Durand-Ruel and Impressionist Collectors in France', in ibid., 120–33. Distel notes that in the 1890s 'Durand-Ruel's position was strengthened: Degas, Monet and Renoir were selling well and American collectors were highly receptive; the dealer's financial situation had improved and, in 1893, he reformed the family company as "Durand-Ruel and Sons" to take advantage of a stock that was increasing in value'. Ibid., 132.

49 Jensen, *Marketing Modernism*, ch. 2, esp. 49–51.

50 In his memoirs Vollard himself used the term 'marchand-découvreur'. Cited in Ann Dumas, 'Ambroise Vollard, Patron of the Avant-Garde', in Rebecca A. Rabinow, ed., *Cézanne to Picasso: Ambroise Vollard, Patron of the Avant-Garde*, New York, New Haven, C.T., and London: Metropolitan Museum of Art with Yale University Press, 2006, 9.

51 Perhaps exaggerating a little, Vollard recalled that the 'gallery' was merely a lock-up stall only 3 metres wide. Ibid., 7.

52 Ibid., 6.

53 Ibid., 9.

54 Ambroise Vollard, *Recollections of a Picture Dealer*, trans. Violet M. MacDonald, New York: Hacker Art Books, 1978, ch. 7.

55 Francis Jourdain, *Né en '76*, Paris: Éditions du Pavillon, 1951, 150.

56 'Le Barc de Boutteville se renseigna sur cette bande hétéroclite, n'en comprit pas toujours le comportement, et, finalement, se laissa volontiers convaincre qu'il y avait, non pas une fructueuse opération à réaliser, mais un joli rôle à jouer en facilitant les débuts de ces jeunes gens.' Ibid., 130.

57 The classic historical account of Montmartre is Louis Chevalier, *Montmartre du plaisir et du crime*, Paris: Laffont, 1980. For a more anecdotal approach see Jean-Paul Crespelle, *La Vie quotidienne à Montmartre au temps de Picasso 1900–1910*, Paris: Hachette, 1978.

58 'La constitution pendant une période de 10 ans d'une collection de tableaux, principalement d'oeuvres importantes de peintres jeunes ou commençant à peine à arriver à leur notoriété… leur revente aux enchères publiques.' Excerpt from the statutes of the Society, registered in February 1904 and cited in Guy Habasque, 'Quand on vendait La Peau de l'Ours', *L'Oeil*, March 1956, 17. See also Michael Fitzgerald, 'Skin Games', *Art in America*, vol. 80, no. 2, February 1992, 71–82 and 139–41; and on this sector of the market in general, Malcolm Gee's indispensable 'Dealers, Critics and Collectors of Modern Painting: Aspects of the Parisian Art Market 1910–30', unpublished PhD thesis, University of London, 1977. The value of 250 francs in 1910 is roughly equal to £1250 today.

59 The term *dénicheur* was coined by André Level, the instigator of the Peau de l'Ours initiative, to whom the responsibility for acquiring items for its collection was given by the other members. This independence of judgment, which led the *dénicheurs* to reject the Impressionist and decorative conventions that then dominated public taste, was, however, grounded in a profound attachment to tradition. See David Cottington, *Cubism and its Histories*, Manchester and New York: Manchester University Press, 2004, 14–15.

60 See Chapter 5; also Jeanine Warnod, *La Ruche et Montparnasse*, Paris and Geneva: Weber, 1978; Jean-Paul Crespelle, *La Vie quotidienne à Montparnasse à la Grande Époque 1905–1930*, Paris: Hachette, 1976.

61 This was Marie Laurencin. See Michael C. Fitzgerald, *Making Modernism: Picasso and the Creation of the Market for Twentieth-Century Art,* New York: Farrar, Straus and Giroux, 1995, 37. Although she was not a member of the Peau de l'Ours, Gertrude Stein can be counted among the *dénicheurs*, and appears to have been the only woman in this category, although her brother Leo, who shared her enthusiasm for this activity, prided himself more ostentatiously on his discernment. On the Peau de l'Ours and the *dénicheurs* see David Cottington, 'Cubism and the Politics of Culture in France 1905–1914', unpublished PhD thesis, University of London, 1985, and Fitzgerald, *Making Modernism*, ch. 1.

62 Weill began with the derisory sum of 50 francs as capital (roughly £250 today). Marianne Le Morvan, *Berthe Weill 1865–1951. La petite galeriste des grandes artistes*, Paris: L'Harmattan, 2011, 22.

63 The gender imbalance was maintained also on the supply side: even Weill, more sympathetic than most to women artists and always supportive of new talent, showed the work of only ten women, as against 110 men, in these 60 exhibitions. Gillian Perry, *Women Artists and the Parisian Avant-Garde: Modernism and 'Feminine' Art, 1900 to the Late 1920s*, Manchester and New York: Manchester University Press, 1995, Appendix 2, 160–63. The value of 25 francs in 1910 is roughly equal to £125 today.

64 Thus Signac was given such a contract by Bernheim-Jeune in 1907, and Matisse in 1909.

65 See (in chronological order): Rémy de Gourmont, *Les Petites Revues. Essai de bibliographie,* Paris: Mercure de France, 1900; Maurice Caillard and Charles Forot, 'Les Revues

d'avant-garde', *Belles Lettres,* 65–6, December 1924, republished by Ent'revues and J.-M. Place, 1990; Roméo Arbour, *Les Revues littéraires éphémères paraissant à Paris entre 1900 et 1914,* Paris: Corti, 1956; Hans Brill, 'The Fin de Siècle', in Trevor Fawcett and Clive Phillpot, eds, *The Art Press: Two Centuries of Art Magazines,* London: The Art Book Company, 1976, 23–32; Yves Chevrefils-Desbiolles, *Les Revues d'art à Paris, 1905–1940,* Paris: Ent'revues, 1993, republished in 2014 by the Presses Universitaires de Provence; Jacqueline Pluet-Despatin, Michel Leymarie and Jean-Yves Mollier, eds, *La Belle Époque des revues, 1880–1914,* Paris: L'IMEC, 2002; and Yves Chevrefils-Desbiolles and Rossella Froissart Pezone, eds, *Les Revues d'art. Formes, stratégies et réseaux au XXe siècle,* Rennes: Presses Universitaires de Rennes, 2011. For a historiography of studies of little magazines in London see Chapter 10, n. 2.

66 Obvious exceptions are the works already noted by Jensen, Ward and Joyeux-Prunel, whose contributions have been invaluable – but none of these considers the impact of the *petites revues littéraires* on the artistic avant-garde as a formation.

67 Thomas Loué, *La Revue des Deux Mondes de Buloz à Brunetière. De la belle époque de la revue à la revue de la Belle Époque,* PhD thesis, Université de Paris 1, 2 vols, 1998, 1:267.

68 Michel Leymarie, 'Introduction. La belle époque des revues?', in Pluet-Despatin et al., eds, *La Belle Époque des revues,* 10.

69 Christophe Charle, 'Le Champ de la production littéraire', in Henri-Jean Martin and Roger Chartier, eds, *Histoire de l'édition française,* 4 vols, Paris: Promodis, 3, 1983, 128.

70 Ibid., 3:129.

71 Christophe Charle, *Naissance des 'Intellectuels' 1880–1900,* Paris: Minuit, 1990, ch. 1 and annexe 1.

72 'Oui, je soutiens (et ceci pour moi doit être un dogme pratique dans la vie d'artiste) qu'il faut faire dans sa vie deux parts: vivre en bourgeois et penser en demi-dieu.' Gustave Flaubert, letter to Louise Colet, 21 August 1853, in *Correspondance,* ed. J. Bruneau, 6 vols, Paris: Gallimard, Pléiade, 2, 1973, 402.

73 On the cultural-political context of the literary *petites revues* see Pamela A. Genova, *Symbolist Journals: A Culture of Correspondence,* Aldershot: Ashgate, 2002. On the technological context, see Richard R. Brettell, *Modern Art, 1851–1929,* Oxford: Oxford University Press, 1999.

74 It must be noted, however, that the understanding of 'politics' within the milieu of these revues was often extra-parliamentary, and that they often dismissed parliamentary politics while espousing more radical political activities and causes. See Richard Shryock, 'Becoming Political: Symbolist Literature and the Third Republic', *Nineteenth-Century French Studies* 33, nos 3–4, spring–summer 2005, 385–98. On the *revues d'art* in particular see Chevrefils-Desbiolles, *Les Revues d'art à Paris, 1905–1940,* and Chapter 5 below.

75 Brill, 'The Fin de Siècle', 23. On the latter he stresses the 'strong contrast' between the support of the writers in the *petites revues* for radical art from Impressionism on, and the conservatism of most art periodicals. Ibid., 25.

76 Sorel, 'Les Journaux font du journalisme; les revues font de la culture; il ne faut pas se laisser aller à confondre les rôles' (in a letter of 1907); Edmond and Jules Goncourt, 'Le livre est un honnête homme, le journal est une fille' (1860, in their *Journal*); Blum, 'Les Revues ne sont pas des livres. Il ne serait pas juste de reprocher à un article de revue sa facture trop rapide et trop légère. Il n'y a pas de caractère d'éternité. Ce n'est pas la pensée sous sa forme definitive. Mais ce n'est pas non plus la chronique de journal qu'on lit en

buvant son chocolat' (*La Revue blanche*, 27, January 1894, 91); all cited in Leymarie, 'Introduction. La belle époque des revues?', 11–12.

77 Ibid.

78 Janis Bergman-Carton, 'La Revue Blanche: Art, Commerce and Culture in the French Fin-de-Siècle,' *Nineteenth-Century Contexts*, vol. 30, no. 2, June 2008, 167–89. For a comprehensive account of the *Revue blanche* milieu see Paul-Henry Bourrelier, *La Revue blanche: une génération dans l'engagement 1890–1905*, Paris: Fayard, 2007.

79 On the interdependence of the avant-garde and the dealer-based market see n. 46 above.

80 Bergman-Carton, 'La Revue Blanche', 177. She notes also that 'for a brief period, Paul Fort's Théâtre d'Art actually mounted an "exhibition" on stage as the epilogue to several Symbolist plays. After the final act, the curtain would rise one more time for a three-minute meditation on a single painting by an unknown artist accompanied by a musical selection and a scent chosen specially for the occasion.' Ibid.

81 Bergman-Carton's main concern, it should be noted, is with the *Revue blanche*'s characterisation – and condemnation – by such critics of the anti-Semitic right as Camille Mauclair and Charles Maurras as a Jewish publication. While her searching analysis of this characterisation and its implications makes a valuable contribution to current understanding of the reach and prejudices of this poisonous discourse in *fin-de-siècle* Paris, it is not of direct relevance to the present study.

82 Ibid., 178. On Vollard's term, see Vollard, *Recollections of a Picture Dealer*.

83 I am indebted to Francesca Berry for this point, as for many other details on Nabi social and professional networks; see also Chapter 5. On 'The Annexe' as a nickname see Bergman-Carton, 181.

84 Among these were 'Le Don de contredire', *La Revue blanche*, vol. 3, no. 13, November 1892, 225–34, and 'Des Peintres intelligents', *La Revue blanche*, 22, 1 May 1900, 53. On these articles, and this relationship, see Chapter 5.

CHAPTER 5

1 Martha Ward, *Pissarro, Neo-Impressionism and the Spaces of the Avant-Garde*, Chicago, I.L.: University of Chicago Press, 1996. See especially ch. 2, 'The Neo-Impressionist Avant-Garde: Critics, Spaces, Histories'.

2 These circumstances were not confined to those French factors I have noted here; in the same period, 'rupture' was in play across Europe: viz. Bismarck's unification of Germany, Garibaldi's comparable achievements in Italy and, in another register, the catastrophes (for France) of the Franco-Prussian War and the subsequent Commune and its suppression, to name but four seismic events.

3 A key role in this naming was played by Félix Fénéon, a critic and editor, friend of psychophysicist Charles Henry and Symbolist poet Gustave Kahn, and anarchist, who was a close supporter of the group. His use of 'avant-garde' as a neologism, writing of the group in June 1886 as 'the avant-garde of impressionism' (only the second use of the term in a contemporary art context, after that of Duret, see n. 14) set the cat among the pigeons in this milieu. See Ward, *Pissarro, Neo-Impressionism*, 57–8.

4 See Chapter 3.

5 See, e.g., Robyn Roslak, *Neo-Impressionism and Anarchism in Fin-de-Siècle France: Painting, Politics and Landscape*, Aldershot: Ashgate, 2007; Michael Marlais, 'Conservative Style/

Conservative Politics: Maurice Denis in Le Vésinet', *Art History*, vol. 16, no. 1, March 1993, 125–46. See Chapter 8, 218 and nn. 74–5.

6 Clément Dessy, *Les Écrivains et les Nabis. La littérature au défi de la peinture*, Rennes: Presses Universitaires de Rennes, 2015, chs 2 and 3.

7 Ibid.; also Béatrice Joyeux-Prunel, *Nul n'est prophète en son pays? L'internationalisation de la peinture des avant-gardes parisiennes 1855–1914*, Paris: Musée d'Orsay/Nicolas Chaudun, 2009; Francesca Berry and Mathias Chivot, *Maman: Vuillard and Madame Vuillard*, exh. cat., Birmingham: Barber Institute of Fine Arts, 2018.

8 See Ward, *Pissarro, Neo-Impressionism*, ch. 5, 'Avant-Gardism and "The Advance"'.

9 Published in *Art et critique*, nos 65 and 66, 23 and 30 August 1890, 540–42 and 556–8, reprinted in Maurice Denis, *Du Symbolisme au classicisme. Théories*, ed. Olivier Revault d'Allonnes, Paris: Hermann, 1964, 33–46, and in Maurice Denis, *Le Ciel et l'Arcadie*, ed. Jean-Paul Bouillon, Paris: Hermann, 1993, 5–21. See David Cottington, 'Back to the Future? Avant-Gardes, Classicisms and the Idea of an Arrière-Garde', in Hiromi Matsui, ed., *Avant-Garde Art and 'Classicism'*, Tokyo: Chuo-Koron Bijutsu Shuppan-sha, 2020, 27–56.

10 Joyeux-Prunel, *Nul n'est prophète en son pays?*, chs 1–3.

11 Ernest Florian-Parmentier, *La Littérature et l'époque. Histoire de la littérature française de 1885 à nos jours*, Paris: Figuière, n.d., and Serge Diaghilev, *Comoedia*, 1913; both quoted in Alain and Odette Virmaux, *Dictionnaire des mouvements artistiques et littéraires (1870–2010)*, Paris: Félin, 2012, 15–16. Diaghilev declared: 'Vingt écoles naissent en un mois. Le Futurisme, le Cubisme, c'est bientôt l'Antiquité, la Préhistoire. À trois jours près, on est Pompier. Le Mototisme détrône l'Automototisme pour être surpassé par le Trépidisme et le Vibrisme qui bientôt n'existent plus parce que surgissent le Planisme, le Sérénisme, l'Exacerbisme, l'Omnisme et le Séisme.'

12 Daniel Pope, 'French Advertising Men and the American "Promised Land"', *Historical Reflections*, 5, summer 1978, 117–38.

13 Gabriel-Albert Aurier, 'Choses d'art', *Mercure de France*, vol. 4, no. 26, February 1892, 185–6, cited in Dessy, *Les Écrivains et les Nabis*, 62.

14 In 1885 critic Théodore Duret gathered together his essays of the 1870s; his entitling the collection *Critique d'avant-garde* (a reference to his own qualities as a critic rather than to the art with which they were concerned) – an isolated neologism that was not repeated until Fénéon's in 1886, noted earlier – registered the widening currency of this discourse.

15 'J'ai expliqué autrefois à propos de littérateurs la valeur de l'artiste novateur et qu'on est artiste dans la mesure où l'on est novateur. À propos des peintres de la venue la plus récente, une seule question se pose: sont-ils vraiment novateurs? (Inutile de s'adjoindre ce problème: "Et leurs nouveautés sont-elles préférables?", car tous les pires ont été faits, et le nouveau sera forcément du mieux.)' Mühlfeld, 'À Propos de Peintures', *La Revue blanche*, vol. 4, no. 20, June 1893, 458. Cited in Dessy, *Les Écrivains et les Nabis*, 61.

16 '[I]ls semblent en effet mériter ce nom par leur louable soin de s'affranchir des tyranniques conventions, de s'évader de la geôle des épouvantables formules courantes pour, en toute probité d'artiste, oeuvrer selon leur seul instinct, et sans autres règles que cette probité et le souci de faire oeuvre d'art.' Maurice Cremnitz, 'Beaux-Arts. Exposition de quelques peintres chez le Barc de Boutteville', *Essais d'art libre*, vol. 4, no. 23, December 1893, 231–3. Cited in Dessy, *Les Écrivains et les Nabis*, 61–2.

17 '[R]ejettent avec une sérénité inconsciente perspective et modelé et croient affirmer une fière volonté en déformant jusqu'à la laideur.' 'Qu'ils apprennent donc d'abord les arcanes de leur art, ces novateurs de vingt ans… des jeunes gens qui ne savent pas construire une tête.' Alphonse Germain, *Pour le Beau. Essai de kallistique*, Paris: Girard, 1893, 37. Cited in Dessy, *Les Écrivains et les Nabis*, 61–2.

18 '[L]'effroyable appareil de l'éducation… soumet de pauvres cerveaux, tendres, sans défense'; 'don précieux, don dangereux, don glorieux de contredire'. Thadée Natanson, 'Le Don de contredire', *La Revue blanche*, vol. 3, no. 13, November 1892, 225–34. Cited in Dessy, *Les Écrivains et les Nabis*, 63 and 79 nn. 45–6.

19 Ward, *Pissarro, Neo-Impressionism*, 105–8.

20 'Cette affiche est la première application de la polychromie rationnelle établie sur des principes rigoureusement mathématiques par l'auteur du *Cercle*… cette production du jeune polychromiste laisse prévoir quels effets de complexité et de nouveauté d'impressions saura atteindre une *technie* servie par d'habiles lithographes et des chimistes suffisants.' 'Thérèse' (a pseudonym used by Fénéon), 'Une Affiche', *La Cravache*, 15 September 1888, reprinted in Félix Fénéon, *Oeuvres plus que complètes*, textes réunis et présentés par Joan U. Halperin, tome I, *Chroniques d'art*, Geneva–Paris: Droz, 1970, 1:132.

21 'Je dis *technie* et non *technique*, suivant un néologisme de Wronski qui habille une idée absolument nouvelle et incomprise. La poychromie est aussi vieille que l'humanité; et les *techniques* polychromes ont commencé avec les premières civilisations…. Mais la *technie polychrome* est née avec la théorie de la sensation de couleur et ne pouvait naître avant.' Ibid. In its stress on innovation or originality the term is also distinct from 'techne', the Greek word in modern parlance meaning 'technique' or 'craft', which has no such connotations.

22 For a close visual analysis of Signac's application of colour theories in this work see Starr Figura, 'Signac's *Portrait of M. Félix Fénéon in 1890*', in Starr Figura, Isabelle Cahn and Philippe Peltier, eds, *Félix Fénéon: The Anarchist and the Avant-Garde*, exh. cat., New York: The Museum of Modern Art, 2020, 59–65.

23 Ward, *Pissarro, Neo-Impressionism*, 106–7. On the relevance to avant-gardism of mainstream indifference see Pierre Bourdieu, 'The Field of Cultural Production, or: The Economic World Reversed', in his *The Field of Cultural Production: Essays on Art and Literature*, ed. Randal Johnson, Cambridge: Polity, 1993, 29–73.

24 'La religion d'un procédé immuable n'est pas un signe de progrès et de révolution artistique. Que le mélange des tons se fasse dans notre oeil ou qu'il existe sur la toile regardée, voilà qui est bien indifférent.' Gustave Geffroy, 'Pointillé-cloisonnisme', *La Justice*, 11 April 1888, cited and translated in Ward, *Pissarro, Neo-Impressionism,* 106, 294 n. 4.

25 Dessy, *Les Écrivains et les Nabis*, 59–61.

26 Ward, *Pissarro, Neo-Impressionism*, 108.

27 Richard Shiff, *Cézanne and the End of Impressionism: A Study of the Theory, Technique, and Critical Evaluation of Modern Art,* Chicago, I.L., and London: University of Chicago Press, 1984; Edward Fry, 'Picasso, Cubism and Reflexivity', *Art Journal*, vol. 47, no. 4, winter 1988, 296–310.

28 As reported by Maurice Denis, who declared in his 1907 article on him: 'Quelques mois avant sa mort, Cézanne nous disait: "J'ai voulu faire de l'impressionnisme quelque chose de solide et de durable comme l'art des musées".' Denis, 'Cézanne', *L'Occident*, 70, September 1907, 118–33; reprinted in Revault d'Allonnes, ed., *Théories*, 155–72; 160.

29 Shiff, *Cézanne and the End of Impressionism*, 125.
30 See especially ibid., 100–21.
31 Responses to Charles Morice's 1905 *enquête* on the currently preferred fountainhead of contemporary art showed Cézanne to be the first choice by a comfortable margin. Philippe Dagen, *La peinture en 1905: l'"Enquête sur les tendances actuelles des arts plastiques' de Charles Morice*, Paris: Lettres Modernes, 1986.
32 Fry, 'Picasso, Cubism and Reflexivity', 296.
33 Ibid.
34 In particular, Pepe Karmel's painstaking formal analyses in his *Picasso and the Invention of Cubism*, New Haven, C.T., and London: Yale University Press, 2003, and Hiromi Matsui's more recent meticulous comparison of the artist's early notebook drawings with models of classical anatomical schemas, 'L'Architectonique cubiste du corps: les schémas anatomiques chez Picasso et Raymond Duchamp-Villon, 1907–1918', unpublished doctoral thesis, Université Paris Ouest Nanterre La Défense, 2015.
35 On the distinction between 'gallery' Cubism, i.e., that of the stable of Cubists sponsored exclusively by Daniel-Henry Kahnweiler's gallery from 1909, and the 'salon' Cubism of those whose exposure was primarily in the annual salons, see David Cottington, *Cubism and its Histories*, Manchester and New York: Manchester University Press, 2004, ch. 2.
36 Ward, *Pissarro, Neo-Impressionism*, 105–23; Catherine Bock, *Henri Matisse and Neo-Impressionism 1898–1908*, Ann Arbor, M.I.: UMI Research Press, 1981.
37 Guillaume Apollinaire, 'Le Salon des Indépendants', *L'Intransigeant*, 22 March 1913, translation in Leroy C. Breunig, *Apollinaire on Art: Essays and Reviews 1902–1918*, trans. Susan Suleiman, London and New York: Thames & Hudson, 1972, 283.
38 Paul Signac, *D'Eugène Delacroix au néo-impressionnisme*, Paris: Revue blanche, 1899.
39 Bock, *Henri Matisse and Neo-Impressionism*, 14.
40 Ibid, 16. In light of the subsequent research of Jensen, Joyeux-Prunel and others noted above, Bock's 1981 use of the term 'Symbolist' can be substituted by 'juste milieu' or 'Secessionist'.
41 Qualities that were noted, and sharply critiqued, by Nabi theoretician Maurice Denis, in his essay 'De Gauguin, de Whistler et de l'excès des théories', *L'Ermitage*, 11, 15 November 1905, 309–19, reprinted in Denis, *Le Ciel et l'Arcadie*, 84–99. See Chapter 6 on this.
42 Translations of parts of Signac's treatise were published almost immediately in the Berlin magazine *Pan* and in Vienna's *Ver Sacrum*. The book in its entirety was published in German in 1903. Bock notes that 'collections of neo-impressionist paintings were begun in Hagen, Weimar, and Berlin. New adherents to the movement sprang up in these countries, as well as in Italy and Finland, usually where impressionism itself was still only beginning to make some headway.' Bock, *Henri Matisse and Neo-Impressionism*, 57.
43 See Chapter 4.
44 On this see Richard Thomson, in A.G. Robins and R. Thomson, *Degas, Sickert and Toulouse-Lautrec: London and Paris, 1870–1910*, exh. cat., London: Tate Publishing, 2005, 100, 111. For a theorisation of this style, see Mécislas Golberg's *La Morale des lignes*, Paris: Éditions Allia, 2017, an instant cult classic upon its posthumous publication in 1907, and the illustrations for it provided by André Rouveyre. On Golberg see Pierre Aubéry, *Anarchiste et décadent: Mécislas Golberg, 1868–1907*, Paris: Lettres Modernes,

1978; David Cottington, *Cubism in the Shadow of War: The Avant-Garde and Politics in Paris, 1905–1914*, New Haven, C.T., and London: Yale University Press, 1998.

45 Claire Frèches-Thory and Antoine Terrasse, *The Nabis: Bonnard, Vuillard and their Circle*, New York: Abrams, 1991.

46 See Chapter 3, n. 59.

47 See Chapter 3, n. 68.

48 See n. 64 below.

49 Jean Maitron, *Le Mouvement anarchiste en France des origins à 1914*, 2 vols, Paris: Maspero, 1983, 9.

50 Richard Shryock, 'Becoming Political: Symbolist Literature and the Third Republic', *Nineteenth-Century French Studies* 33, nos 3–4, spring–summer 2005, 385. Boulanger's eclectic movement drew its support as much from the right as the left.

51 Ibid., 386.

52 Ibid., 388.

53 Miriam R. Levin, *Republican Art and Ideology in Late Nineteenth-Century France*, Ann Arbor, M.I.: UMI Research Press, 1986, 1.

54 'Véritable tranquillisant social… qui unit les pauvres aux riches, les illettrés aux savants.' Annie Stora-Lamarre, *L'Enfer de la IIIe République. Censeurs et pornographes 1881–1914*, Paris: Imago, 1990, 129.

55 Among the most influential articulations of this ideology was a book, *Solidarité*, published in 1896 by the then premier, Léon Bourgeois (Villeneuve-d'Ascq: Presses Universitaires de Septentrion, 1998).

56 Shryock, 'Becoming Political', 392.

57 Ibid, 394.

58 Patrick McGuinness, *Poetry and Radical Politics in Fin de Siècle France. From Anarchism to 'Action Française'*, Oxford: Oxford University Press, 2015, 76–7.

59 Ibid., 93.

60 Ibid., 100.

61 Mike Davis, 'Artisans of Terror', in *In Praise of Barbarians: Essays against Empire*, Chicago, I.L.: Haymarket Books, 2008, 168.

62 McGuinness, *Poetry and Radical Politics*, 101.

63 Pierre Quillard, review of Édouard Dubus, *Quand les Violons sont partis* (1892), in *L'En-Dehors*, 53, April 1892, 3; cited in McGuinness, *Poetry and Radical Politics*, 95.

64 See especially the pioneering study by Robert and Eugenia Herbert, 'Artists and Anarchism: Unpublished Letters of Pissarro, Signac, and Others', parts 1 and 2, *Burlington Magazine*, 102, November, 472–82, and December 1960, 517–22; Eugenia Herbert, *The Artist and Social Reform in France and Belgium, 1850–1898*, New Haven, C.T.: Yale University Press, 1961; Maitron, *Le Mouvement anarchiste en France*; Madeleine Rebérioux, 'Culture et militantisme', *Le Mouvement social*, 91, April–June 1975, 3–12; Richard D. Sonn, *Anarchism and Cultural Politics in Fin de Siècle France*, Lincoln: University of Nebraska Press, 1989; John D. Hutton, *Neo-Impressionism and the Search for Solid Ground: Art, Science and Anarchism in Fin-de-Siècle France*, Baton Rouge: Louisiana State University Press, 1994; Robyn Roslak, *Neo-Impressionism and Anarchism in Fin-de-Siècle France: Painting, Politics and Landscape*, Aldershot: Ashgate, 2007.

65 McGuinness, *Poetry and Radical Politics*, 86.

66 Paul Signac, 'Impressionnistes et révolutionnaires', *La Révolte*, 4, 13–19 June 1891, 4.

67 Translated by Alan Astro, in Hutton, *Neo-Impressionism and the Search for Solid Ground*, Appendix, 249–52.
68 Pierre Bourdieu, 'The Field of Cultural Production, or: The Economic World Reversed', in Pierre Bourdieu, *The Field of Cultural Production: Essays on Art and Literature*, ed. Randal Johnson, Cambridge: Polity, 1993, 29–73.
69 For a detailed assessment of Signac's text in relation to anarchism see Katherine Brion, 'Paul Signac's Decorative Propaganda of the 1890s', *RIHA Journal*, 44, July 2012, https://www.riha-journal.org/articles/2012/2012-jul-sep/special-issue-neo-impressionism/brion-signacs-decorative-propaganda.
70 Some recent examples from a huge historiography: Alain Pages, *L'Affaire Dreyfus: vérités et légendes*, Paris: Perrin, 2019; Tom Conner, *The Dreyfus Affair and the Rise of the French Public Intellectual*, Jefferson, N.C.: McFarland, 2014; Bertrand Tillier, *Les Artistes et l'affaire Dreyfus: 1898–1908*, Seyssel: Champ Vallon, 2009.
71 J.-M. Mayeur and M. Rebérioux, *The Third Republic from its Origins to the Great War 1871–1914*, Cambridge: Cambridge University Press, 1984; Catherine Meneux, ed., *Regards de critiques d'art. Autour de Roger Marx (1859–1913)*, Rennes: Presses Universitaires de Rennes, 2009.
72 Mayeur and Rebérioux, *The Third Republic from its Origins to the Great War 1871–1914*, 145.
73 '[D]évoiler les mensonges sociaux, dire comment et pourquoi ont été crées les religions, imaginé le culte patriotique, construite la famille sur le modèle du gouvernement.' Fernand Pelloutier, *L'Art et la révolte*, Paris: Bibliothèque de l''Art Social', 1897, 7.
74 See Chapter 6.
75 L. Mercier, *Les Universités populaires, 1899–1914. Éducation populaire et mouvement ouvrier au début du siècle*, Paris: Ouvrières, 1986. See also Cottington, *Cubism in the Shadow of War*, 20–26.

CHAPTER 6

1 Yve-Alain Bois, 'On Matisse: The Blinding: For Leo Steinberg' (trans. Greg Sims), *October*, 68, spring 1994, 60–121; 70, citing Matisse's interview with Pierre Courthion in 'Autres propos de Matisse', ed. Dominique Fourcade, *Macula*, 1, 1976, 102. See also Bois, 'Matisse and "Arche-drawing"', in his collection of essays *Painting as Model*, Cambridge, M.A.: MIT Press, 1990, 3–63 and 262–79.
2 'Se rappeler qu'un tableau – avant d'être un cheval de bataille, une femme nue, ou une quelconque anecdote – est essentiellement une surface plane recouverte de couleurs en un certain ordre assemblées.' Maurice Denis, 'Définition du néo-traditionnisme', *Art et critique*, 23 August 1890, reprinted in Maurice Denis, *Du Symbolisme au classicisme. Théories*, ed. Olivier Revault d'Allonnes, Paris: Hermann, 1964, 33–46; 33.
3 'Il ne sera pas découragé par cette première expérience; mais elle l'avertira des dangers de l'abstraction. *Luxe, calme et volupté* est le schéma d'une théorie. C'est dans la réalité qu'il développera le mieux ses dons, très rares, de peintre. Il retrouvera, dans la tradition française, le sentiment du possible.' Denis, 'La Réaction nationaliste', *L'Ermitage*, 15 May 1905, quoted in Maurice Denis, *Le Ciel et l'Arcadie*, ed. Jean-Paul Bouillon, Paris: Hermann, 1993, 95 n. 57.
4 See Catherine Bock, *Henri Matisse and Neo-Impressionism 1898–1908*, Ann Arbor, M.I.: UMI Research Press, 1981; Bois, 'On Matisse: The Blinding', who builds on insights offered by Leo Steinberg's 'Contemporary Art and the Plight of its Public' (reprinted in

Steinberg, *Other Criteria*, Oxford and New York: Oxford University Press, 1972); and John Elderfield, especially his 'Describing Matisse', in MoMA New York's *Henri Matisse: A Retrospective* exhibition catalogue of 1992. An important critique of this narrative is offered by Todd Cronan's *Against Affective Formalism: Matisse, Bergson, Modernism*, Princeton, N.J.: Princeton University Press, 2013.

5 Bock, *Henri Matisse and Neo-Impressionism*, 3–4.

6 Raymond Escholier, interview with Matisse, *Matisse ce vivant*, Paris, 1956, 18; cited in Bock, *Henri Matisse and Neo-Impressionism*, 117.

7 For details of these sources see the prefatory note in Bois, 'On Matisse: The Blinding', 60, and Bois, 'Matisse and "Arche-drawing"', 262 n. 1.

8 Bois makes a slip of the pen in dating this to 1894. This encounter with Neo-Impressionist technique – not that of 1904, as Denis assumed – was Matisse's first.

9 Matisse, 'On Modernism and Tradition', *The Studio*, 1935, reprinted in Jack Flam, *Matisse on Art*, New York: Phaidon, 1973, 72.

10 Ibid.

11 Bois, 'On Matisse: The Blinding', 85.

12 At Signac's villa he also met the critic Félix Fénéon, anarchist intellectual, Neo-Impressionist supporter and friend of Signac, and until the previous year editor of *La Revue blanche*, whose familiarity with colour theory would have underwritten Matisse's increasing engagement with it. In 1907, soon after Fénéon's appointment to the Galerie Bernheim-Jeune to lead its engagements with contemporary art, the gallery became his dealer. See Claudine Grammont, 'Fénéon and Matisse', in Starr Figura, Isabelle Cahn and Philippe Peltier, eds, *Félix Fénéon: The Anarchist and the Avant-Garde*, exh. cat., New York: The Museum of Modern Art, 2020, 148, 149.

13 Bois, 'On Matisse: The Blinding', 91–2, citing Dominique Fourcade, *Matisse: Écrits et propos sur l'art*, Paris: Hermann, 1972, 129.

14 Matisse, *Notes of a Painter* (1908), quoted ibid., 84 n. 75.

15 '[C]e qu'on trouve surtout en particulier chez Matisse, c'est de l'artificiel; non pas de l'artificiel littéraire, comme serait une recherche d'expression idéaliste; ni de l'artificiel décoratif, comme en ont imaginé les tapissiers turcs et persans; non, c'est quelque chose de plus abstrait encore; c'est la peinture hors de toute contingence, la peinture en soi, l'acte pur de peindre. Toutes les qualités du tableau autres que celles du contraste des tons et des lignes, tout ce que la raison du peintre n'a pas déterminé, tout ce qui vient de notre instinct et de la nature, enfin toutes les qualités de représentation et de sensibilité sont exclues de l'oeuvre d'art.' Denis, *Le Ciel et l'Arcadie*, 96.

16 On this multiplicity see Chapter 5, n. 11.

17 This was a rivalry famously remarked upon by Gertrude Stein as creating two camps, 'the Picassoites and the Matisseites', within the Parisian avant-garde. Gertrude Stein, *The Autobiography of Alice B. Toklas* (1933), New York: The Modern Library, 1993, 79.

18 In this context, to Fry's insights should be added those of Adam Gopnik on the role of cartoons in the shaping of Picasso's Cubist reflexivity as, in Gopnik's words, 'a working representational code that comments on the way representational codes work'. Adam Gopnik, 'High and Low: Caricature, Primitivism, and the Cubist Portrait', *Art Journal*, vol. 43, no. 4, winter 1983, 371–6.

19 'Les cénacliers s'encouragent, se stimulent, s'entraident, en un mot: *fraternisent*. En temps de paix, ils se serrent les coudes; en temps de guerre, ils serrent les rangs. La règle non

écrite du cénacle, c'est le soutien mutuel.' Anthony Glinoer and Vincent Laisney, *L'Âge des cénacles. Confraternités littéraires et artistiques au XIXe siècle*, Paris: Fayard, 2013, 17.

20 Ibid., 209. They offer 25 specific 'isms', and gesture towards more.

21 Albert Gleizes, *Souvenirs. Le Cubisme 1908–1914*, Paris: Cahiers Albert Gleizes, 1957, 19–20.

22 Georges Ribemont-Dessaignes, *Déjà jadis*, Paris: Juillard, 1958, 30 and 38.

23 Pierre Cabanne, *Entretiens avec Marcel Duchamp*, Paris: Belfond, 1967, 21–2 and 51.

24 See Béatrice Joyeux-Prunel, 'Fénéon at Galerie Bernheim-Jeune', in Figura, Cahn and Peltier, eds, *Félix Fénéon: The Anarchist and the Avant-Garde*, 139–47; see also Chapter 4.

25 The *Figaro* publication was on 20 February. In a blatantly hyperbolic promotional tactic, the manifesto was published almost simultaneously by numerous dailies across the continent, from Bologna to Bucharest (London, however, was not included). On the challenge of Futurism to Parisian hegemony see Chapter 10.

26 On Marinetti's formation and emergence see Günter Berghaus, *The Genesis of Futurism: Marinetti's Early Career and Writings 1899–1909*, Leeds: Society for Italian Studies, 1995. See also Luca Somigli, *Legitimizing the Artist: Manifesto Writing and European Modernism 1885–1915*, Toronto: University of Toronto Press, 2003, ch. 2.

27 On Futurism as an avant-garde movement, see also Chapter 10.

28 Gino Severini, *The Life of a Painter* (*Tutta Vita di un Pittore*) (1983), trans. Jennifer Franchina, Princeton, N.J.: Princeton University Press, 1995, chs 2–6.

29 Umberto Boccioni, Carlo Carrà, Luigi Russolo, Giacomo Balla and Gino Severini, *Manifesto of the Futurist Painters*, 11 February 1910; idem, *Futurist Painting: Technical Manifesto*, 11 October 1910; idem, 'The Exhibitors to the Public', in *Exhibition of Works by the Italian Futurist Painters*, London: Sackville Gallery, March 1912; Umberto Boccioni, *Technical Manifesto of Futurist Sculpture*, 11 April 1912. All reprinted in English translation in Umbro Apollonio, ed., *Futurist Manifestos*, London and New York: Thames & Hudson, 1973, 24–7, 27–31, 45–50, 51–65.

30 Camille Mauclair, 'Le Préjugé de la nouveauté dans l'art moderne', *La Revue*, 1 April 1909, 289–302; for Vauxcelles and Allard see Chapter 3, 89 and n. 59.

31 See Chapter 5; also Jeffrey Weiss, *The Popular Culture of Modern Art: Picasso, Duchamp and Avant-Gardism*, New Haven, C.T., and London: Yale University Press, 1994.

32 For a roll-call of *littérateurs* who contributed substantial interpretations (whether supportive or critical) of Cubism between 1911 and 1914 see Mark Antliff and Patricia Leighten, eds, *A Cubism Reader: Documents and Criticism, 1906–1914*, Chicago, I.L., and London: University of Chicago Press, 2008.

33 Jean Metzinger, '"Cubisme" et tradition', *Paris-Journal*, 16 August 1911, 5; Albert Gleizes, 'Les Beaux-Arts. À propos du Salon d'Automne', *Les Bandeaux d'or*, November 1911, 42–51; Gleizes, 'Le Cubisme et la tradition', *Montjoie!*, 1, 10 February 1913, 4, and 2, 25 February, 2–3.

34 'Donc aimer l'oeuvre vivante, à cause des forces de vie qui sont en elle, c'est comprendre et posséder la nature, puisque par le fait du génie, une pensée humaine a su la contenir toute entière.' Roger Allard, 'Les Beaux-Arts', *La Revue indépendante*, August 1911, 138.

35 'Ainsi naît, aux antipodes de l'impressionnisme, un art qui… offre dans leur plénitude picturale, à l'intelligence du spectateur, les éléments essentiels d'une synthèse située dans

la durée.' Roger Allard, 'Au Salon d'Automne de Paris', *L'Art libre* (Lyon), vol. 2, no. 12, November 1910, 441–3.

36 'Mon intention est de rendre aux cubistes un peu plus de liberté et d'aplomb, en leur fournissant les raisons profondes de ce qu'ils font. Il est vrai que ce ne pourra pas être sans leur montrer combien jusqu'ici ils l'ont fait mal.' Jacques Rivière, 'Sur les Tendances actuelles de la peinture', *La Revue d'Europe et d'Amérique*, 1 March 1912, 384–406; 385. See David Cottington, 'Cubism, Law and Order: The Criticism of Jacques Rivière', *Burlington Magazine*, vol. 126, no. 981, December 1984, 744–50.

37 Linda Goddard, *Aesthetic Rivalries: Word and Image in France, 1880–1926*, Oxford: Oxford University Press, 2012; James Kearns, *Symbolist Landscapes: The place of Painting in the Poetry and Criticism of Mallarmé and his Circle*, London: Modern Humanities Research Association, 1989.

38 The theoretical issues raised by this question of the structural relations between different cultural practices within formations in a given node of an avant-garde network are complex, and there is unfortunately no space for them in the present work. They will be explored in a future article.

39 Nicholas Watkins, 'The Genesis of a Decorative Aesthetic', in Gloria Groom, ed., *Beyond the Easel: Decorative Painting by Bonnard, Vuillard, Denis and Roussel*, New Haven, C.T., and London: Yale University Press, 2001, 1–28; Maurice Denis, 'L'Influence de Paul Gauguin', in Denis, *Le Ciel et l'Arcadie*, 73–81.

40 Watkins, 'The Genesis of a Decorative Aesthetic'; Nancy J. Troy, *Modernism and the Decorative Arts in France: Art Nouveau to Le Corbusier*, New Haven, C.T., and London: Yale University Press, 1991.

41 I have discussed elsewhere this discourse and its consequences for the Cubist groups: see David Cottington, *Cubism in the Shadow of War: The Avant-Garde and Politics in Paris, 1905–1914*, New Haven, C.T., and London: Yale University Press, 1998, 67–84; idem, '"Une audace tranquille": La Fresnaye, le cubisme et l'avant-garde avant 1914', in Françoise Lucbert and Yves Chevrefils-Desbiolles, eds, *Par-delà le Cubisme. Études sur Roger de La Fresnaye, suivis de correspondances de l'artiste*, Rennes: Presses Universitaires de Rennes, 2017, 71–87.

42 The analysis offered below is a re-engagement with, and development of, that presented at much greater length in my *Cubism in the Shadow of War* in 1998.

43 Madeleine Rebérioux, in J.-M. Mayeur and M. Rebérioux, *The Third Republic from its Origins to the Great War 1871–1914*, Cambridge, England: Cambridge University Press, 1984, 205.

44 Sanford F. Elwitt, *The Third Republic Defended: Bourgeois Reform in France, 1880–1914*, Baton Rouge and London: Louisiana State University Press, 1986, 2.

45 Ibid., 7.

46 On the number of foreign artists exhibiting at the Salon d'Automne in 1912 see Chapter 3. There were some high-profile foreign avant-gardists, however, who were enthusiastic Francophiles, notably Guillaume Apollinaire and Ricciotto Canudo.

47 '[L]'organe de la littérature jeune… le soutien d'une politique réformatrice.' H.-M. Barzun, *L'Action intellectuelle: notations d'esthétique*', Paris: Rey, 1908, 18. The magazine failed to appear, through lack of funds.

48 Christian Sénéchal, *L'Abbaye de Créteil*, Paris: Delpeuch, 1930, 119–20. On the Abbaye see Chapter 1.

49 'Fédérer intellectuellement les jeunes élites créatrices du monde entier.' H.-M. Barzun, *Poème et drame*, vol. 1, no. 1, November 1912, inside back cover.

50 '[D]es "révolutionnaires" malheureusement égarés en paroles sociales, qui confondent la recherche esthétique avec la lutte des partis'; 'la seule force créatrice *en avant* ne peut surgir que de l'instinct poétique'. Barzun, 'Après le Symbolisme: l'art poétique d'un idéal nouveau: voix, rythmes et chants simultanées', *Poème et drame*, vol. 1, no. 4, May 1913, 13–14. '[P]ar les angoisses, les privations, les dangers de leur aventure, par l'hostilité des cités grasses qui les exilent, par la dureté de la conquête qui sera plus tard le patrimoine de tous.' Barzun, *Poème et drame*, vol. 1, no. 2, January 1913, 38.

51 See Chapters 1 and 10.

52 It became *L'Effort libre* after the issue of March 1912, as a result of a court action challenging Bloch's choice of name.

53 Madeleine Rebérioux, 'Avant-garde esthétique et avant-garde politique: le Socialisme français entre 1890 et 1914', *Raison présente*, 6 (1968), 73–82.

CHAPTER 7

1 Béatrice Joyeux-Prunel, *Nul n'est prophète en son pays? L'internationalisation de la peinture des avant-gardes parisiennes 1855–1914*, Paris: Musée d'Orsay/Nicolas Chaudun, 2009. See also Christophe Charle, ed., *Le Temps des capitales culturelles, XVIIIe–XXe siècles*, Paris: Champ Vallon, 2009.

2 Edward Morris, *French Art in Nineteenth-Century Britain*, New Haven, C.T., and London: Yale University Press, 2005, 261–2. On Fantin-Latour's membership of multiple groups, see Chapter 1.

3 Apparently these still lifes 'sold so well that they were practically unknown in France during his lifetime'. Anne L. Poulet and A.R. Murphy, *Corot to Braque: French Paintings from the Museum of Fine Arts, Boston*, Boston, M.A.: The Museum, 1979, 73.

4 See Chapter 10.

5 Poynter subsequently became director of the National Gallery, as well as president of the Royal Academy. The South Kensington school became the hub of a network of art schools across the country that provided most of the national art-education system.

6 'Lorrimer… did not share in the amusements of the Quartier Latin, but spent his evenings at home with Handel, Michaelangelo and Dante, on the respectable side of the river.' George du Maurier, *Trilby* (1894), Oxford: Oxford University Press, 1995, 94–5. The identification is made in both Caroline Dakers, *The Holland Park Circle: Artists and Victorian Society*, New Haven, C.T., and London: Yale University Press, 1999, and Morris, *French Art in Nineteenth-Century Britain*.

7 The 'square brush' technique, pioneered by the then-famous Jules Bastien-Lepage, who had died in 1884. On his influence see Kenneth McConkey, *British Impressionism*, London: Phaidon, 1989, 28–9.

8 For an overview see Pamela Fletcher, 'Shopping for Art: The Rise of the Commercial Art Gallery, 1850s–90s', in Pamela Fletcher and Anne Helmreich, eds, *The Rise of the Modern Art Market in London, 1850–1939*, Manchester: Manchester University Press, 2011, 47–64.

9 Morris, *French Art in Nineteenth-Century Century Britain*, 136.

10 Kenneth McConkey, *The New English: A History of the New English Art Club*, London: Royal Academy, 2006, 25.

11 Morris, *French Art in Nineteenth-Century Britain*, 139. Morris notes, as the only such gallery, that of Georges Petit, on which see further in this chapter. There were two significant exceptions: that of Whistler, whose familiarity with Paris enabled him to find exposure there, and that of Burne-Jones, for whom see further in this chapter.

12 Henry James, *The Painter's Eye*, ed. John L. Sweeney, London: Rupert Hart-Davis, 1956, 148, 167–8. On the Grosvenor Gallery see the following section of this chapter.

13 Richard Thomson, 'Introduction', in Anna Gruetzner Robins and Richard Thomson, *Degas, Sickert and Toulouse-Lautrec: London and Paris 1870–1910*, exh. cat, London: Tate Publishing, 2005, 18.

14 Petra ten-Doesschate Chu, 'The Lu(c)re of London: French Artists and Art Dealers in the British Capital, 1859–1914', in John House, Petra ten-Doesschate Chu and Jennifer Hardin, eds., *Monet's London: Artists' Reflections on the Thames, 1859–1914*, exh. cat., St Petersburg, F.L.: Museum of Fine Art, 2005, 39–54.

15 By this means Durand-Ruel sought to join the network of art clubs and exhibition societies that were beginning to flourish in London and across the UK. Ibid., 39.

16 Richard Thomson, 'Exporting Style and Decadence: The Exchanges of the 1890s', in Robins and Thomson, *Degas, Sickert and Toulouse-Lautrec*, 96–151; 96–9.

17 These were mostly ballet and rehearsal scenes, but included *Dans un Café* of 1875–76, which became notorious, as *L'Absinthe*, for its apparently low-life subject matter when it was eventually shown in London nearly 20 years later. On Hill see Alice Meynell, 'A Brighton Treasure House', *Magazine of* Art, 5, 1882, 1–7, and Ronald Pickvance, 'Henry Hill: An Untypical Victorian Collector', *Apollo*, 76, 1962, 789–91. On the *Absinthe* affair, see Pickvance, '*L'Absinthe* in England', *Apollo*, 77, 1963, 395–8. On Degas's reputation in England see Anna Greutzner Robins, 'The Greatest Artist the World Has Ever Seen', in Robins and Thomson, *Degas, Sickert and Toulouse-Lautrec*, 61–92.

18 Anne Helmreich, 'The Socio-Geography of Art Dealers and Commercial Galleries in Early Twentieth-Century London', in Helena Bonett, Ysanne Holt and Jennifer Mundy, eds, *The Camden Town Group in Context*, Tate Research Publication, May 2012, https://www.tate.org.uk/art/research-publications/camden-town-group/anne-helmreich-the-socio-geography-of-art-dealers-and-commercial-galleries-in-early-r1105658, accessed 8 September 2021, citing Youssef Cassis, 'Introduction: Comparative Perspectives on London and Paris as International Financial Centres in the Twentieth Century', in Youssef Cassis and Éric Bussière, eds, *London and Paris as International Financial Centres in the Twentieth Century*, Oxford: Oxford University Press, 2005, 2.

19 Fletcher, 'Shopping for Art', 47.

20 Dakers, *The Holland Park Circle*, and Chapter 1.

21 It should be noted in passing that while the Grosvenor Gallery was perhaps the pre-eminent late Victorian institutional expression of this dynamic in the cultural sphere, it was not alone in this in the broader context of London 'Society', its limits and its status. It was joined in the late 1880s, and surpassed in the 1890s in terms of rank and influence, by an elite upper-aristocratic 'set', The Souls, which emerged into prominence as that Society fragmented into cliques with the influx of 'new money' gained from industrial and financial activities rather than landed inheritance. The Souls,

who numbered about 40 of the leading younger aristocratic men and women (about half of each), almost all had landed fortunes and pedigrees. On this 'set' see Nancy W. Ellenberger, 'The Souls and London "Society" at the End of the Nineteenth Century', *Victorian Studies*, vol. 25, no. 2, winter 1982, 133–60; Angela Lambert, *Unquiet Souls: The Indian Summer of the British Aristocracy, 1880–1918*, Basingstoke: Macmillan, 1984.

22 'The Grosvenor Gallery', *Art Journal*, 16, 1877, 244. See also 'The Grosvenor Gallery', *The Times*, 12 March 1877, 4.

23 *The Times*, 10 May 1877; cited in Susan P. Casteras and Colleen Denney, eds, *The Grosvenor Gallery: A Palace of Art in Victorian England*, New Haven, C.T. and London: Yale University Press, 1996, 15.

24 Charles Hallé, *Notes from a Painter's Life, Including the Founding of Two Galleries*, London: John Murray, 1909, 108–9.

25 'The Grosvenor Gallery', *Art Journal*, 16, 1877, 244, cited in Casteras and Denney, eds, *The Grosvenor Gallery*, 15. Lindsay's predilections were underlined by Henry James a few weeks later, as 'the product of a theory that there is a demand for a place of exhibition exempted both from the exclusiveness and the promiscuity of Burlington House, in which painters may communicate with the public more directly than under the academic dispensation, and in which the more "peculiar" ones in especial may have a chance to get popular.' Henry James, 'The Picture Season in London, 1877', *The Galaxy*, August 1877, reprinted in James, *The Painter's Eye*, 139.

26 'The Grosvenor Gallery', *The Times*, 12 March 1877, 4, cited in Casteras and Denney, eds, *The Grosvenor Gallery*, 15.

27 Letter in the manuscript collection of the University of British Columbia, Vancouver, quoted in Susan P. Casteras, 'Burne-Jones and the Pre-Raphaelites at the Palace of the Aesthetes', in Casteras and Denney, eds, *The Grosvenor Gallery*, 76. Carr failed to persuade the notoriously anti-exhibitionist Rossetti to accept his invitation, apparently because Lindsay's unwillingness to ruffle the RA's feathers had led him also to invite six Academicians, which was a conciliatory gesture too far for this artist.

28 Hallé's figure was £100,000 to £150,000; Hallé, *Notes From a Painter's Life*, 102. For the equivalent, see https://www.nationalarchives.gov.uk/currency-converter/.

29 Colleen Denney, 'The Grosvenor Gallery as Palace of Art: An Exhibition Model', in Casteras and Denney, eds, *The Grosvenor Gallery*, 17. The takings from ticket sales should not be underestimated, however: the Grosvenor's launch was successful enough to attract 7,000 visitors on its first day in 1877, and the first five weeks of its 1879 season netted £2,000 in admission charges, at a shilling a head (approximately £140,000 in today's terms). Christopher Newall, *The Grosvenor Gallery Exhibitions: Change and Continuity in the Victorian Art World*, Cambridge and New York: Cambridge University Press, 1995, 14, 34.

30 Including the purchase and installation as the Bond Street entrance doorway to the Gallery of the former portico, designed by Palladio, of the Church of Santa Lucia in Venice. Denney, 'The Grosvenor Gallery as Palace of Art: An Exhibition Model', 17.

31 Youssef Cassis, 'Bankers in English Society in the Late Nineteenth Century', *Economic History Review*, 2nd ser., 38 (1985), 217–19. See also David Cannadine, *The Decline and Fall of the British Aristocracy*, New Haven, C.T., and London: Yale University Press, 1990, ch. 8; Harold Perkin, *The Rise of Professional Society: England since 1880*, London: Routledge, 1989, 62–75.

32 Denney, 'The Grosvenor Gallery as Palace of Art: An Exhibition Model', 9.
33 Colleen Denney, 'Introduction', in Casteras and Denney, eds, *The Grosvenor Gallery*, 3.
34 Henry James again provided testimony of this, describing the Grosvenor project as 'an artistic enterprise of an unusually brilliant sort', and emphasising that it was 'primarily an artistic enterprise; for it has had its origin, on the part of its distinguished proprietor… rather in the love of pictures than in the love of money'. James, *The Painter's Eye*, 139.
35 Casteras and Denney, eds, *The Grosvenor Gallery*, 1–7. See also Virginia Surtees, *Coutts Lindsay 1824–1913*, Norwich: Michael Russell, 1993.
36 Paula Gillett, 'Art Audiences at the Grosvenor Gallery', in Casteras and Denney, eds, *The Grosvenor Gallery*, 40.
37 Denney, 'Introduction', 159 n. 7.
38 Gillett, 'Art Audiences at the Grosvenor Gallery', 45, 55.
39 Pamela Horn, *High Society: The English Social Elite 1880–1914*, Stroud: Alan Sutton, 1992.
40 Gillett, 'Art Audiences at the Grosvenor Gallery', 45.
41 Elizabeth Wilson, *Bohemians: The Glamorous Outcasts*, London and New York: I.B. Tauris, 2000, 93, 110.
42 Gillett, 'Art Audiences at the Grosvenor Gallery', 44. Princess Louise, Queen Victoria's fourth daughter, was an artist (trained at the South Kensington Schools), who, as well as attending Grosvenor functions, also socialised with artists of Oscar Wilde's circle. Ibid., 41–2. See also Eve Adam, ed., *Mrs J. Comyns Carr's Reminiscences*, London: Hutchinson, 2nd edn, 1926, 117–18 (and below) for the testimony of a Grosvenor 'bohemian'.
43 The parallel was no coincidence, for the commitment to artists' interests shown by the Lindsays, although motivated by their identification with art practice as amateurs, was congruent with the seizing by artists of the management of their own careers that, as I have argued, was constitutive of their professionalisation. On the relation between these motives, see below in this chapter.
44 Denney, 'Introduction', 3.
45 Hallé, *Notes from a Painter's Life*, 109–10.
46 Gillett, 'Art Audiences at the Grosvenor Gallery', 43.
47 See Dakers, *The Holland Park Circle*. On the Lindsays in this circle see Denney, 'Introduction', 2.
48 Liz Prettejohn, *Art for Art's Sake: Aestheticism in Victorian Painting*, New Haven, C.T., and London: Yale University Press, 2007, 29–30. On the Tudor House circle see Chapter 1.
49 Adam, ed., *Mrs J. Comyns Carr's Reminiscences*, 57–8. The note of condescension towards her upper-aristocratic hostess, on the one hand, and the toe-curling ingratiation with Whistler, on the other, speak volumes about the class-and-culture dynamic in play in this alliance – a dynamic underlined by the pretentiousness of the memoirs' title itself: for '*Reminiscences*' was a genre of memoir both much in fashion and particular to aristocratic women in the early twentieth century, as the influx of 'parvenu(e)s' to Society threatened its standards and required their reassertion. Examples include Ralph Nevill, ed., *The Reminiscences of Lady Dorothy Nevill*, London: Edward Arnold, 1907; Jenny Churchill, *The Reminiscences of Lady Randolph Churchill*, London: Edward Arnold, 1908; Lady St Helier, *Memories of Fifty Years*, London: Edward Arnold, 1909.
50 Denney, 'The Grosvenor Gallery as Palace of Art: An Exhibition Model', 32.

51 That of Comyns Carr, in particular, who had written more than one highly appreciative critical article on Burne-Jones before the Grosvenor's establishment.

52 Having withdrawn in 1870, out of disillusionment with critical response to his work, from exhibiting anywhere. The two paintings were *Love among the Ruins* of 1870–73 and *The Beguiling of Merlin* of 1872–77.

53 The term is that of Alison Smith, 'Burne-Jones on Show: Exhibition Pictures, 1877–98', in Alison Smith, ed., *Edward Burne-Jones*, London: Tate Publishing, 2018, 126.

54 Andrzej Szczerski, *Views of Albion: The Reception of British Art and Design in Central Europe, 1890–1918*, Berne: Peter Lang, 2015, 83.

55 Ibid.

56 Denney, 'The Grosvenor Gallery as Palace of Art: An Exhibition Model', 36.

57 Martha Ward, 'Impressionist Installations and Private Exhibitions', *The Art Bulletin*, vol. 73, no. 4, December 1991, 599–622. See Chapter 4.

58 On 'Les Vingt, as it was familiarly called, and its strategy see Joyeux-Prunel, *Nul n'est prophète en son pays?*, esp. 63–4.

59 On the clans of nineteenth-century English society see Adam Kuper, *Incest and Influence: The Private Life of Bourgeois England*, Cambridge, M.A. and London: Harvard University Press, 2009.

60 Helmreich, 'The Socio-Geography of Art Dealers and Commercial Galleries in Early Twentieth-Century London'.

61 As I noted in Chapter 4, n. 59, it was one such collector, André Level, who coined the term *dénicheur* for his ilk, and in 1904 set up a vehicle for their speculative activities, the Société de la Peau de l'Ours.

62 This was recognised by at least one London observer at the time: art critic Huntly Carter, writing in response to the 1911 exhibition of the Salon des Indépendants (at which the 'salon Cubist' group debuted) in *The New Age*, noted that in the Paris contemporary art market, '[e]ach dealer or private speculator makes a corner in an extremist or group of extremists, writes up the work, and waits patiently for the absent-minded millionaires'; 'this system of subsidising extremists is both good and bad', he added. 'It allows artists to produce their best work freely; and it also encourages some to exceed the limit of extravagance. But though the system is open to endless abuse, it affords the new tendencies a sanctuary and it enables artists to be themselves. We have nothing of the kind in England. Hence the reason why art is valet to the dealer.' Huntly Carter, 'The Indépendants and the New Intuition in Paris', *The New Age*, 25 May 1911, 83.

63 Anne Helmreich and Ysanne Holt, 'Marketing Bohemia: The Chenil Gallery in Chelsea, 1905–1926', *Oxford Art Journal*, vol. 33, no. 1, March 2010, 47, citing William Roberts, 'Dealers and Galleries', in *Five Posthumous Essays and Other Writings*, Valencia: Artes Graficas Soler, 1990.

64 Helmreich and Holt, 'Marketing Bohemia', 48, citing Samuel Shaw, 'The Chenil Gallery, 1905–1927', unpublished MA dissertation, University of York, 2008.

65 Helmreich and Holt, 'Marketing Bohemia', 43.

66 Roberts, 'Dealers and Galleries', cited ibid., 48.

67 This equivalence was commonly and popularly drawn; see, e.g., the 1917 revue *The Chelsea Matinée* at the Chelsea Palace Theatre, which included an item titled 'Montmartre in Chelsea', featuring, in the words of the critic of *The Sketch*, 'the uncontrolled revels of the gamins [*sic*] from SW3'. *The Sketch Supplement*, 28 March 1917, 4–5.

68 Helmreich and Holt, 'Marketing Bohemia', 46.

69 For a classic mythification of this character see Arthur Ransome's *Bohemia in London*, published in 1907 when he was 23. See also 'Chelsea' in Findlay Muirhead, ed., '*London and its Environs*, 2nd edn, London: Macmillan, 1922, and Simon Knowles, 'Suburban Identity in Paul Maitland's Paintings of Cheyne Walk', *Journal of Victorian Culture*, vol. 19, no. 1, 1 March 2014, 43–62.

70 Helmreich and Holt, 'Marketing Bohemia', 48.

71 Roberts, 'Dealers and Galleries', cited ibid.

72 Charles Rearick, *Pleasures of the Belle Époque: Entertainment and Festivity in Turn of the Century France*, New Haven, C.T., and London: Yale University Press, 1985; Roger Shattuck, *The Banquet Years: The Origins of the Avant-Garde in France: 1885 to World War I* (1955), London: Jonathan Cape, 1969.

73 Cecily Mackworth, *English Interludes: Mallarmé, Verlaine, Paul Valéry, Valery Larbaud in England, 1860–1912*, London: Routledge, 1974, 40 and 41. See also, among many others, especially Hugh David, *The Fitzrovians: A Portrait of Bohemian Society 1900– 1955*, London: Sceptre, 1989; Arthur Ransome, *Bohemia in London*, London: Chapman and Hall, 1907; and Peter Brooker, *Bohemia in London: The Social Scene of Early Modernism*, Basingstoke: Palgrave Macmillan, 2007.

74 Arthur Symons, *The Symbolist Movement in Literature* (1899), New York: Dutton, 1958. The observation should be extended to cabarets, a more recent phenomenon (in their modern form; they have a long pre-modern history). The vogue for these, begun in the 1880s with Rodolphe Salis's *Chat Noir* in Paris (see Chapter 3), swept across Europe in the next 50 years. Lisa Appignanesi, one of their historians, notes that 'the cabaret form had never really taken hold in England, either as a meeting and performance place for writers and artists, or as a centre for satirical dissent'. Lisa Appignanesi, *The Cabaret* (1975), New Haven, C.T., and London: Yale University Press, 2004, 208. See also Chapter 10.

75 Much of the following paragraph is indebted to Guy Deghy and Keith Waterhouse, *Café Royal: Ninety Years of Bohemia*, London: Hutchinson, 1955, which, for all its evident myth-making, offers a detailed and fairly reliable anecdotal history.

76 Douglas Goldring later recalled that 'if a "new movement" was started on the Continent, the Café Royal was always the first place to hear of it and to "produce" it in England'. Douglas Goldring, *Reputations: Essays in Criticism*, London: Chapman and Hall, 1920, 138.

77 Deghy and Waterhouse, *Café Royal*, 58.

78 Ibid., 70–77.

79 Ibid., 61.

80 On The Apostles see Chapter 2. On English coteries more generally see N.G. Annan, 'The Intellectual Aristocracy', in J.H. Plumb, ed., *Studies in Social History*, London: Longmans, Green & Co., 1955, 256–83.

81 Edgar Jepson, *Memories of an Edwardian and Neo-Georgian*, London: Richards, 1937, 70.

82 Brooker, *Bohemia in London*, 96, citing Alun R. Jones, *The Life and Opinions of T.E. Hulme*, London: Victor Gollancz, 1960.

83 Wendy Baron, *Perfect Moderns: A History of the Camden Town Group*, Aldershot: Ashgate, 2000, 39.

84 Anthony Glinoer and Vincent Laisney, *L'Âge des cénacles. Confraternités littéraires et artistiques au XIXe siècle*, Paris: Fayard, 2013, 208–9.

CHAPTER 8

1 I am indebted for help in clarifying the positioning of John that is proposed in the following paragraphs particularly to Lisa Tickner's analysis of the artist in her *Modern Life and Modern Subjects: British Art in the Early Twentieth Century*, New Haven, C.T., and London: Yale University Press, 2000, esp. 49–65, and to Michael Holroyd's *Augustus John: The New Biography*, London: Vintage, 1987, esp. chs 5 and 6.

2 The song, with lyrics by Harry Graham, was a substantial number, with five verses and choruses. The full lyrics are reprinted in Holroyd, *Augustus John*, Appendix Five, 610–12. See also 337, n. 67.

3 Holroyd observes: 'In later years everyone would recognise readily enough the manly and melodramatic form of Augustus John. But he himself did not know who he was. His lack of stylistic conviction as a painter, the frequent changes of handwriting and signature in his letters, his surprising passivity and lack of initiative in everyday matters, the abrupt changes of mood… the theatricality: all these suggested a lack of self-knowledge.' Ibid., 26.

4 Quoted ibid., 135. The exhibition was at the Carfax Gallery in April. Of the 48 works, 45 were by Augustus. On professionalism in the London context, see below in this chapter.

5 Holroyd, *Augustus John*, 208.

6 Both Holroyd and Tickner have invaluable accounts of the history of this culture and lifestyle, and its life-changing significance for John from the moment he discovered it: see Tickner, *Modern Life and Modern Subjects*, 54–65, and Holroyd, *Augustus John*, 100–04, 111–12, 280–82.

7 Tickner, *Modern Life and Modern Subjects*, 54.

8 Arthur Symons, 'In Praise of Gypsies', *Journal of the Gypsy Lore Society*, April 1908, 296, quoted ibid.

9 Douglas Goldring, *South Lodge: Reminiscences of Violet Hunt, Ford Madox Ford and the 'English Review' Circle,* London: Constable, 1943, 57. As the title of his memoir indicates, Goldring was a member of the Ford/Hunt circle, and editorial secretary of the former's *Review*. 'The intention', he notes of *The Tramp* (he was its founder and editor), 'was to combine literary merit with what is now called hiking'. Not only literary merit, it turned out, but also the most up-to-date of avant-gardist movements, since in the August 1910 issue it published Marinetti's *Founding Manifesto of Futurism* – it seems because Marinetti had published 'a number' of Goldring's poems in his own magazine *Poesia*. (ibid.)

10 Peter Brooker, *Bohemia in London: The Social Scene of Early Modernism*, Basingstoke: Palgrave Macmillan, 2007.

11 On Slade teaching methods see Andrew Forge, 'The Slade I', *Motif*, 4, 1960, 29–43, and 'The Slade II', *Motif*, 5, 1960, 16–31 (which discusses both of these first phases, Poynter's (and Legros') and Brown's); and Simon Watney, *English Post-Impressionism*, London: Studio Vista, 1980, ch. 3 (which considers the second). Overviews of the role and history of the Slade in this period can be found in Kenneth McConkey, *The New English: A History of the New English Art Club*, London: Royal Academy, 2006, 69–76, and Edward Morris, *French Art in Nineteenth-Century Britain*, New Haven, C.T., and London: Yale University Press, 2005, chs 22 and 23.

12 Quoted in Joseph Hone, *The Life of Henry Tonks*, London: Heineman, 1939, 9.

13 Watney, *English Post-Impressionism*, 22.

14 Forge, 'The Slade II', 20.
15 Forge, 'The Slade I', 33.
16 See Chapter 4.
17 Watney, *English Post-Impressionism*, 21; Augustus John, *Chiaroscuro: Fragments of an Autobiography* (1952), London: Readers Union, 1954, 24–5.
18 Forge, 'The Slade II', 25. The group he refers to were John's co-students, and included William Orpen, Ambrose McEvoy and Albert Rutherston. It was through the latter that they knew his older, Paris-trained brother William Rothenstein and his friend Charles Conder, who were acquainted with the Nabi group and with Anquetin.
19 On the experience of its female students seen through that of Gwen John, see Alicia Foster, 'Gwen John's *Self-Portrait*: Art, Identity and Women Students at the Slade School', in David Peters Corbett and Lara Perry, eds, *English Art 1860–1914: Modern Artists and Identity*, Manchester: Manchester University Press, 2000, 168–79. An excellent survey of this scholarship, as well as detail on the issue (and number and circumstances) of female students at the Slade, is provided in Catherine Heathcock, 'Jessica Dismorr (1885–1939): Artist, Writer, Vorticist', unpublished PhD thesis, University of Birmingham, 1999, 5–15.
20 Heathcock notes that between 1871 and 1945 three-quarters of Slade students were women (she does not disaggregate this total). Heathcock, 'Jessica Dismorr', 9.
21 See Chapter 4.
22 Heathcock, 'Jessica Dismorr', 15–19. See also Gillian Perry, *Women Artists and the Parisian Avant-Garde: Modernism and 'Feminine' Art, 1900 to the Late 1920s*, Manchester and New York: Manchester University Press, 1995; Lisa Tickner, 'Bohemianism and the Cultural Field: *Trilby* and *Tarr*', *Art History*, vol. 34, no. 5, November 2011, 978–1011.
23 Barnaby Wright, 'Modern Art and the Professionalisation of Culture: The Development of Modern Painting in England at the Beginning of the Twentieth Century', unpublished PhD thesis, London: Courtauld Institute of Art, 2004, 54, 51. Brown is quoted in Forge, 'The Slade I', 33.
24 Wright, 'Modern Art and the Professionalisation of Culture', 24.
25 D.S. MacColl, 'Augustus John', in John Fothergill, ed., *The Slade: A Collection of Drawings and Some Pictures Done by Past and Present Students of the London Slade School of Art, MDCCCXCIII–MDCCCCVII*, London: Richard Clay & Sons, 1907. In all of these affinities and allegiances can be discerned the inheritance of Grosvenor Gallery aestheticism.
26 Wright, 'Modern Art and the Professionalisation of Culture', 64.
27 Intriguingly, this positioning, in Wright's argument for it, is comparable in its alternative professionalism to that of the Parisian avant-garde – with the crucial differences that, first, the Slade's was anchored in the tradition of Old Masters, and not – *especially not* – in technicist innovation; and, second, that this traditionalism was not seen as self-consciously oppositional, but assumed to have the authority of art history as a discipline.
28 See Chapter 4.
29 On these social and artistic connections see Wendy Baron, 'Sickert's Links with French Painting', *Apollo*, 91, March 1970, 186–97; Anna Gruetzner Robins, 'Degas and Sickert: Notes on their Friendship', *Burlington Magazine*, vol. 130, March 1988, 225–8; Andrew Stephenson, 'Buttressing Bohemian Mystiques and Bandaging Masculine Anxieties', *Art History*, vol. 17, no. 2, June 1994, 269–78; Matthew Sturgis, *Walter Sickert: A Life*, London: HarperCollins, 2005, esp. 108–23.

30 Walter Sickert, 'The New *Life of Whistler*', *Fortnightly Review*, December 1908; reprinted in Anna Gruetzner Robins, *Walter Sickert: The Complete Writings on Art*, Oxford and New York: Oxford University Press, 2000, 178–88; this citation, 183.
31 Walter Sickert, 'Manet and the Impressionists', *Art News*, 17 February 1910, repr. ibid., 196–9; here, 197 (translated as 'rigged out for a few pence but with the air of the great Condé').
32 Sickert, 'The New *Life of Whistler*', ibid., 183.
33 Walter Sickert, 'Where Paul and I Differ', *Art News*, 10 February 1910; ibid., 194. Sickert had been reading 'Mrs Herringham's *Cennino Cennini*' (London: George Allen, 1899), which he here cited for this point of historical one-upmanship.
34 Of the 27 pictures he showed at the New English Art Club exhibitions between 1890 and 1895, 16 were portraits.
35 Walter Sickert, 'New Wine', *The New Age*, 21 April 1910; reprinted in Robins, *Walter Sickert*, 219.
36 Walter Sickert, 'Idealism', *Art News*, 12 May 1910; ibid., 229.
37 Walter Sickert, 'The Spirit of the Hive', *The New Age*, 26 May 1910; ibid., 235.
38 Walter Sickert, 'Stones from a Glass House', *Art News*, 27 January 1910; ibid., 191.
39 Walter Sickert, 'The Language of Art', *The New Age*, 28 July 1910; ibid., 264.
40 As I have noted in Chapter 5, Signac's treatise *D'Eugène Delacroix au néo-impressionnisme* of 1899 was a case in point. On these overlaps and rivalries in Paris, see Linda Goddard, *Aesthetic Rivalries: Word and Image in France, 1880–1926*, Oxford: Oxford University Press, 2012. As familiar as he was with artistic debate across the Channel, Sickert would doubtless have been aware of such rivalries and allegiances, and influenced by them. On the professionalisation of art criticism in late Victorian England, see Elizabeth Prettejohn, 'Aesthetic Value and the Professionalization of Victorian Art Criticism 1837–78', *Journal of Victorian Culture*, vol. 2, no. 1, spring 1997, 71–94.
41 Sickert, 'The Spirit of the Hive'; reprinted in Robins, *Walter Sickert*, 235.
42 *The Pall Mall Gazette*, 2 February 1889; ibid., 10.
43 Sickert, 'New Wine'; ibid., 218.
44 Walter Sickert, 'Impressionism', *The New Age*, 30 June 1910; ibid., 252.
45 Walter Sickert, 'Post-Impressionists', *Fortnightly Review*, January 1911; ibid., 274–5.
46 See, e.g., Walter Sickert, 'Encouragement for Art', *The New Age (Supplement)*, 7 April 1910; ibid., 214: 'I do believe that those of us who are intellectuals owe much more to those who work with their hands than we ever pay…. We, relatively skilled in thought, as they are in deed, should be ashamed to offer them, in return for their faithful labour, their plumbing, their ploughing, their washing, their dustmanship, and what not, the selfish and callous insincerities of our lying political philanthropies, in which, it is needless to say, we do not believe for ourselves.'
47 See, e.g., Walter Sickert, 'Fathers and Sons', *Art News*, 7 April 1910: 'The good craftsman is… a pious worshipper of his artistic ancestors…. You may be certain that any painter who has done anything at all has, as the very foundation of his art, a devoted buttoning-on, as they say in German (*anknüpfen*) to the past.' Ibid., 211, 212. Also 'The Spirit of the Hive': 'You are not to consider that every new and personal beauty in art abrogates past achievement like an Act of Parliament does preceding ones, or that it is hostile to the past. You are to consider these beauties, these innovations, as enrichments, as variations, as additions to an existing family.' Ibid., 237.
48 Sickert, 'New Wine'; ibid., 218.

49 Walter Sickert, 'Solomon J. Solomon', *Art News*, 17 March 1910; ibid., 205.
50 Sickert, 'New Wine'; ibid., 218.
51 Gilles Philippe, *French Style: l'Accent français de la prose anglaise*, Paris: Les Impressions Nouvelles, 2016.
52 David Peters Corbett, *The World in Paint: Modern Art and Visuality in England, 1848–1914*, Manchester and New York: Manchester University Press, 2004, 170–71.
53 See, e.g., Barnaby Wright, ed., *The Camden Town Nudes*, exh. cat., London: Courtauld Institute Gallery, 2007.
54 These works have been exhaustively discussed by modern scholars. See especially Wendy Baron and Richard Shone, eds, *Sickert: Paintings*, exh. cat., New Haven, C.T., and London: Royal Academy of Arts in association with Yale University Press, 1992; Tickner, *Modern Life and Modern Subjects*; Corbett, *The World in Paint*; Wright, ed., *The Camden Town Nudes*.
55 Tickner, *Modern Life and Modern Subjects*, 19, citing Penelope Curtis, 'Introduction', *W.R. Sickert: Drawings and Paintings 1890–1942*, exh. cat., Liverpool: Tate Gallery, 1989, 6.
56 Wendy Baron, *Perfect Moderns: A History of the Camden Town Group*, Aldershot: Ashgate, 2000, 16–17, 19.
57 Ibid., 19.
58 Ibid., 27, 28.
59 From letters in the Tate Gallery Archives, London; quoted ibid., 24, 26. The Salon d'Automne, founded three years earlier, catered to both a fashionable stratum of Parisian society (on the demand side of the market) and its progressive artists (on the supply side) – and thus to the pan-European 'Secessionist' network (on both sides). It would seem that Sickert was thinking more about the supply side (the artists he wished to attract), since his targeted clientele was more modest than that of the Automne.
60 Charles Ginner, 'The Camden Town Group', *Studio*, November 1945, vol. 130, no. 632, 130–31.
61 Baron, *Perfect Moderns*, 39.
62 Ibid., 43–4.
63 Ginner, 'The Camden Town Group', 130.
64 Sickert, letter to Nan Hudson, quoted in Baron, *Perfect Moderns*, 45 (no citation).
65 Grant studied at Westminster School of Art from 1901 to 1905, and at the Slade for two terms in 1906 and 1908; before and between the latter he attended La Palette, which was then headed by Sickert's friend Jacques-Émile Blanche, from February to the autumn of 1906 and from January to June 1907. 'Chronologies', in Richard Shone, *The Art of Bloomsbury*, exh. cat., London: Tate Gallery, 1999, 282.
66 Fry had studied at the Académie Julian, the oldest and best-known *académie libre* in Paris, for a term in 1892. Appointed curator of paintings at the Metropolitan Museum of Art, New York, in 1906, he had travelled widely in Europe on purchasing trips on its behalf by 1908. 'Chronologies', in Shone, *The Art of Bloomsbury*, 275–6.
67 Richard Shone, 'The Friday Club', *The Burlington Magazine*, 117, May 1975, 279–84. As Shone points out elsewhere, neither Bell nor Grant, nor any others of their circle, had any idea that they were Bloomsbury painters or producing Bloomsbury art; this term only began to be used as an art-historical category retrospectively – decades later, in fact, in the 1960s. Shone, *The Art of Bloomsbury*, 11.
68 The Bells met art historian, critic and painter Fry by chance at Cambridge railway station in January 1910. He had by then marked his debut as a theorist and critic of

contemporary art with an 'Essay in Aesthetics' a year earlier in *The New Quarterly*; in the January and February 1910 issues of the newly founded *Burlington Magazine*, of which he was co-founder and joint editor, he published his translation of Maurice Denis's essay on Cézanne of 1907; in February he lectured to the Friday Club. 'Chronologies', in Shone, *The Art of Bloomsbury*, 276.

69 At the Galerie Barbazanges, a rentable exhibition space owned by the couturier Paul Poiret. The exhibition, in May 1912, was entitled *Exposition de quelques artistes indépendants anglais* and included, besides the Bloomsbury trio, work by Spencer Gore, Wyndham Lewis, Eric Gill and Stanley Spencer. According to Shone, it was 'a trial run for the English section of the Second Post-Impressionist Exhibition' at the Grafton Gallery in 1912–13. Shone, ibid., 74.

70 Shone, *The Art of Bloomsbury*, 16.

71 Fry, 'An Essay in Aesthetics', *The New Quarterly*, April 1909, reprinted in Roger Fry, *Vision and Design* (1920), New York: Meridian Books, 1966, 16–38. In his *A Roger Fry Reader* (Chicago, I.L., and London: University of Chicago Press, 1996) Christopher Reed includes a previously unpublished lecture by Fry, entitled 'Expression and Representation in the Graphic Arts', which he gave to a philosophical society at Oxford University in 1908, which anticipated the key ideas, and even phrasing, of the 'Essay in Aesthetics', and which named the author of this definition as John Collier R.A., an academic painter of portraits and social scenes in the Pre-Raphaelite style. Ibid., 61–71; 61.

72 Fry, 'An Essay in Aesthetics', 33–4.

73 See Chapter 6, n. 2. Fry was possibly translating Denis's essay on Cézanne for the *Burlington* (see n. 68) as he wrote his own 'Essay'.

74 Denis noted in his journal that year, 'Je deviens royaliste'. Maurice Denis, *Journal*, 3 vols, Paris: La Colombe, 1957–59, vol. 1, 1884–1904, 222.

75 '[L]a jeunesse est devenue résolument classique… En littérature, en politique, les jeunes gens ont la passion de l'ordre. Le retour à la tradition et à la discipline est aussi unanime que l'était dans notre jeunesse le culte du moi et l'esprit de révolte… En somme le moment est venu où il a fallu choisir… le nationalisme intégral a l'avantage de tenir compte… des expériences *réussies* du passé.' Denis, 'De Gauguin et de Van Gogh au classicisme', *L'Occident*, 90, May 1909, reprinted in Maurice Denis, *Le Ciel et l'Arcadie*, ed. Jean-Paul Bouillon, Paris: Hermann, 1993, 161–2.

76 Michel Décaudin, *La Crise des valeurs symbolistes. Vingt ans de poésie française, 1895–1914*, Toulouse: Privat, 1960, esp. ch. 3.

77 'The Post-Impressionists', in *Manet and the Post-Impressionists*, exh. cat., London: Grafton Galleries, 1910. The essay was written up by the exhibition secretary, Desmond MacCarthy, from notes by Fry. Reprinted in Reed, *A Roger Fry Reader*, 81–5; 82.

78 Whether Fry had read this text is uncertain. He may have learned of it via Denis.

79 'An Essay in Aesthetics', in Fry, *Vision and Design*, 32; 'Post Impressionism', *The Fortnightly Review*, 1 May 1911, reprinted in Reed, *A Roger Fry Reader*, 107; 'The French Group', *The Second Post-Impressionist Exhibition*, exh. cat., London: Grafton Galleries, 1912, repr. as 'The French Post-Impressionists' in Fry, *Vision and Design*, 240.

80 An apperception and treatment that was fully exemplified by the profusion of decoration with which Bell, Grant and others filled the rooms of Charleston, the Sussex farmhouse where they lived from 1916.

81 There was some discussion of the concept within the late Fauvist milieu of *c.* 1907; it is possible that, as his interest in Matisse grew, Fry became aware of this, but his idea of the concept is far vaguer. See Roger Benjamin, 'The Decorative Landscape, Fauvism, and the Arabesque of Observation', *The Art Bulletin*, vol. 25, no. 2, June 1993, 295–316.

82 'Rhythm' as an explanatory concept first appeared in his writing in the 'Essay in Aesthetics' in *The New Quarterly* of April 1909, as I have noted, the first of five 'emotional elements of design' that he enumerated without elaboration: Fry, *Vision and Design*, 33, 35. At the end of 1910, explaining his then-current Grafton Gallery Post-Impressionism exhibition, he referred in passing to Matisse's 'masterly sense of rhythmic design': Reed, *A Roger Fry Reader*, 93. A few weeks later, in his January 1911 lecture, he began to invest more deeply in the concept, describing rhythm as 'the fundamental and vital quality of painting', and explaining that '[p]articular rhythms of line and particular harmonies of colour have their spiritual correspondences', adding '[t]he artist plays upon us by the rhythm of line, by colour, by abstract form, and by the quality of the matter he employs': ibid., 105. His closing assertion that 'art, like religion, appeals to the non-mechanical parts of our nature, to what is rhythmic and vital' (ibid., 110) suggests an engagement with Bergsonian ideas that was becoming increasingly fashionable among London critics; three months later, a magazine entitled *Rhythm* was launched that confirmed its status as the catch-all epithet for the new art. See Chapter 10.

83 In his *Revolution in Art: An Introduction to the Study of Cézanne, Gauguin, Van Gogh and Other Modern Painters*, London: Art News Press, 1910, 54, Rutter wrote about Picasso's Cubism to date that 'it is highly logical, but to me it appears very complicated, but I confess for its proper elucidation at the moment *je ne suis pas à la hauteur*', and added: 'But for what I have seen of the work that preceded this last stage I have so high a respect that I ask nothing more than opportunity for its better understanding.'

84 Roger Fry, 'The French Group', in *The Second Post-Impressionist Exhibition*, exh. cat., London: Grafton Galleries, 1912, repr. as 'The French Post-Impressionists' in Fry, *Vision and Design*, 239. In a reply to critics of his *Second Post-Impressionist Exhibition* ('The Grafton Gallery, An Apologia', *The Nation*, November 1912), Fry 'confessed' that '[a]s to the latest works of all, those in which Picasso frankly abandons all direct reference to natural appearance... I take them to some extent on trust... which is surely justified by his previous work'; he saw these works as based on 'the construction of a fugal arrangement of forms'. Reprinted in Reed, *A Roger Fry Reader*, 116. See also Chapter 10.

85 Bell, letter to Virginia Stephen, 19 October 1911, reprinted in Regina Marler, ed., *Selected Letters of Vanessa Bell*, London: Bloomsbury, 1993, 109. £4 was equivalent to about £315 in 2020: https://www.nationalarchives.gov.uk/currency-converter/.

86 Bell, letter to Grant, 29 January 1914, in Marler, ed., *Selected Letters of Vanessa Bell*, 160–61, misdated 25 March.

87 It is likely that Grant knew the Picasso painting; it was in the collection of Gertrude Stein in Paris, together with 14 related gouache and oil studies for it, by the time he called on her in April 1909: 'visited Stein. Interesting conversation', he noted in his diary (Grant, diary entry, April 1909, private collection; quoted in James Beechey, 'Duncan Grant and Picasso', in James Beechey and Chris Stephens, eds, *Picasso and Modern British Art*, exh. cat., London: Tate Publishing, 2012, 62 and 216 n. 1). The borrowing of its stylistic hallmarks may well, therefore, be direct, albeit based on recollection, although the comparison does not depend upon this.

88 On these *papiers collés* and this distancing, see David Cottington, *Cubism in the Shadow of War: The Avant-Garde and Politics in Paris, 1905–1914*, New Haven, C.T., and London: Yale University Press, 1998, ch. 5.

89 Grant also painted the still life pictured by Bell, and included pasted paper in doing so, but less boldly or extensively. Shone, *The Art of Bloomsbury*, 124. Grant did not finish his *papier collé* until early in 1915, and (as Shone notes) it 'was never completely realised to his conception and remained rolled up and stored for nearly sixty years until acquired by the Tate Gallery' in 1973. Ibid., 155.

90 Ibid.

91 Watney, *English Post-Impressionism*, 146 n. 13. Watney notes: 'Grant doodled on the cover of his copy of this edition of *Les Soirées de Paris* with surrounding designs which pre-figure some aspects of the scroll.'

92 On this distinction, and these two 'wings', see Chapter 5, n. 35.

93 As of 1910, Fry seems not to have been aware either of Kahnweiler or of Cubism as a style; the only Picasso that displayed any of its features was the (not very Cubist) *Portrait of Clovis Sagot* of 1909. As a sometime dealer in Cubism from about that year, Sagot may have been a conduit to Kahnweiler for Fry's 1912 Post-Impressionism exhibition. Druet's position in the hierarchy of the Paris art market was mid-range; less heavyweight than Bernheim-Jeune, more reputable than Sagot, his clientele was that oriented primarily to the Salon d'Automne and the Société Nationale: progressive but not, unlike Kahnweiler, very adventurous. On the Paris market at this time Malcolm Gee remains invaluable: Malcolm Gee, 'Dealers, Critics and Collectors of Modern Painting: Aspects of the Parisian Art Market 1910–30', unpublished PhD thesis, University of London, 1977.

94 Jeffrey Weiss, *The Popular Culture of Modern Art: Picasso, Duchamp and Avant-Gardism*, New Haven, C.T., and London: Yale University Press, 1994, esp. 56–9. On Picasso's reputation reaching London see Chapter 10.

95 Pierre Daix and Joan Rosselet, *Picasso: The Cubist Years 1907–1916*, London: Thames & Hudson, 1979, cats 615 and 578. The *Head*, although at first sight a *papier collé*, was in oil, gouache, varnish, ink, charcoal and pencil on paper masquerading as one.

96 James Beechey, 'Picasso in Britain 1910–1914', in *Picasso and Modern British Art*, 60, 216 n. 27. The record of Fry's opinion was made by Nina Hamnett, the exhibition's secretary.

97 Fry, 'The French Group', 15.

98 Fry too experimented with such 'radical' abstraction, but less certainly. See his study for an abstract painting of 1914–15, reproduced in Christopher Reed, *Bloomsbury Rooms: Modernism, Subculture and Domesticity*, New Haven, C.T., and London: Yale University Press, 2004, fig. 113.

99 This relation has been fairly widely recognised; e.g., and most recently, by Matthew Affron: 'Both Bell and Grant adopted collage as a primary model of abstraction. Visits to Picasso's studio in the early months of 1914, where they were exposed to his collage and related practices, were surely decisive in this regard.' Matthew Affron, 'Abstraction and Decoration in Bloomsbury', in Leah Dickerman, ed., *Inventing Abstraction 1910–1925: How a Radical Idea Changed Modern Art*, exh. cat., London and New York: Thames & Hudson, 2012, 182.

100 Reed, *Bloomsbury Rooms*, 147–53. The literature on the Omega is extensive; see in particular, besides Reed: Judith Collins, *The Omega Workshops*, Chicago, I.L.: University of

Chicago Press, 1984; Isabelle Anscombe, *Omega and After: Bloomsbury and the Decorative* Arts, London: Thames & Hudson, 1981; Gerstein, ed., *Beyond Bloomsbury: Designs of the Omega Workshops 1913–19*, exh. cat., London: Courtauld Gallery in Association with Fontanka, 2009; Ben Angwin, 'Repositioning the Omega Workshops: Modern Patrons and Modern Markets', unpublished PhD thesis, Kingston University London, 2022.

101 Alexandra Gerstein and Lucia Floriana Savi have noted that one other artist who designed rugs and textiles for the Omega was the painter Frederick Etchells, a Bloomsbury friend who joined the venture early and also contributed abstract geometric designs – and that, as with Bell and Grant, his paintings of the time bore some relation to these. However, their analysis does not extend beyond design into his fine-art practice. Gerstein, ed., *Beyond Bloomsbury*, 81–129.

102 See Chapter 10.

103 Tickner, *Modern Life and Modern Subjects*; Mark Antliff and Scott W. Klein, eds, *Vorticism: New Perspectives*, Oxford: Oxford University Press, 2013. The 'spectacular' character of this vogue for the edge-of-abstraction is worth noting; see Chapter 9.

104 A dismantling that was pioneered by Peter Wollen's essay 'Fashion, Orientalism and the Body' (1987), reprinted in his *Raiding the Icebox: Reflections on Twentieth-Century Culture*, London: Verso, 2008. See Chapter 10.

105 Shone, *The Art of Bloomsbury*, 145.

106 Reed, *A Roger Fry Reader*, 56, 57.

107 Ibid., 58.

108 It is arguable, however, that this residual utopianism too was being co-opted, by the aristocracy's 'raiding of Bohemia' (see Chapter 9), catered to by the Omega Workshops set up in 1913 by Fry, who marketed the group's individualist Post-Impressionist *facture* as a brand. See also Ben Angwin, 'Repositioning the Omega Workshops'.

CHAPTER 9

1 Richard Ellmann, *Oscar Wilde*, London: Penguin, 1988, 45.

2 Deborah Cohen, *Household Gods: The British and their Possessions*, New Haven, C.T., and London: Yale University Press, 2006, 79.

3 On the 'saturation of spectacle and consumption' in Edwardian Britain see Andrea Wolk Rager, 'The Glittering World: Spectacle, Luxury and Desire in the Edwardian Age', in Andreas Trumble and Andrea Wolk Rager, eds, *Edwardian Opulence: British Art at the Dawn of the Twentieth Century*, New Haven, C.T.,: Yale Center for British Art, 2013, 41. The consecration of this national cornucopia, the opening of Selfridges on Oxford Street, came in 1909. See John Benson, *The Rise of Consumer Society in Britain, 1880–1980*, London: Longman, 1994, chs 1 and 2; also Erika Rappaport, Mark J. Crowley and Sandra Trudgeon Dawson, eds, *Consuming Behaviours: Identity, Politics and Pleasure in Twentieth-Century Britain*, London: Bloomsbury Academic, 2015; Peter Gurney, *The Making of Consumer Culture in Modern Britain*, London: Bloomsbury Academic, 2017.

4 Thorsten Veblen, *Theory of the Leisure Class* (1899), London: Unwin Books, 1970, 35, 70. Veblen was writing about the late nineteenth-century USA, but his analysis is equally apposite for the UK at that time.

5 I am indebted to the pioneering research of Richard Cork, Lisa Tickner and David Peters Corbett on which the argument of this chapter builds. See in particular Richard Cork, *Art Beyond the Gallery in Early Twentieth-Century England*, New Haven, C.T., and London: Yale University Press, 1985; Lisa Tickner, *Modern Life and Modern Subjects: British Art in the Early Twentieth Century*, New Haven, C.T., and London: Yale University Press, 2000; David Peters Corbett, *The Modernity of English Art*, Manchester: Manchester University Press, 1997.

6 David Cannadine, *The Decline and Fall of the British Aristocracy*, New Haven, C.T., and London: Yale University Press, 1990; Lawrence Stone, *An Open Elite?: England, 1540–1880*, Oxford: Clarendon Press, 1984; Pamela Horn, *High Society: The English Social Elite, 1880–1914*, Stroud: Alan Sutton, 1992.

7 The term is that of one of its members: Mary Jeune (Lady St Helier), 'More on Society', *The Pall Mall Magazine*, vol. 1, no. 3, July 1893, 422–8; 424.

8 See Chapter 7, n. 21.

9 Cannadine, *The Decline and Fall of the British Aristocracy*, 347.

10 Ibid.

11 Ibid.

12 In the year that The Souls was founded, *Vanity Fair* editorialised on 'The New Society and its Sets': 'Our reputation as the leaders, not only of English but the world's Society, is slowly leaving us, and will leave us, if the present state of things is tolerated as it is being tolerated. Sets are being formed without number. For a few weeks, perhaps months, they dazzle the eyes of the unthinking.... A rotten and showy fabric has been built up.' *Vanity Fair*, 2 November 1889, cited in Nancy W. Ellenberger, 'The Souls and London "Society" at the End of the Nineteenth Century', *Victorian Studies*, vol. 25 no. 2, winter 1982, 133–160; 144.

13 See Chapter 7, n. 49.

14 'A Woman of the World', 'Society in Retrospect', *The Pall Mall Magazine*, vol. 1, no. 4, August 1893, 577.

15 Mary Jeune, 'More on Society', 423.

16 Ibid.

17 Ibid., 425.

18 Eve Adam, ed., *Mrs J. Comyns Carr's Reminiscences*, London: Hutchinson, 2nd edn, 1926, 243. (See Chapter 7.) The letters, now in the Bodleian Library, Oxford, in which Lady Lewis kept a record of her dinner guests, reveal a galaxy of talent: Edward Burne-Jones (a close friend and frequent visitor), James Abbott McNeill Whistler, George du Maurier, Lawrence Alma-Tadema, John Singer Sargent, Sir Arthur Sullivan, Ignacy Jan Paderewski, Arthur Rubinstein, Robert Browning, Henry James, Oscar Wilde, J.M. Barrie, Ellen Terry, Henry Irving and Lillie Langtry are some of the more famous names. See https://archives.bodleian.ox.ac.uk/repositories/2/archival_objects/70164.

19 On Violet Rutland see Caroline Dakers, *The Holland Park Circle: Artists and Victorian Society*, New Haven, C.T., and London: Yale University Press, 1999; K.D. Reynolds, 'Manners, (Marion Margaret) Violet, Duchess of Rutland (1856–1937)', *Oxford Dictionary of National Biography* (online edn): Oxford University Press, 2004; doi:10.1093/ref:odnb/49527.

20 Including G.F. Watts. *Oxford Dictionary of National Biography* (online edn): doi:10.1093/:odnb/49527.

21 Angela Lambert, *Unquiet Souls: The Indian Summer of the British Aristocracy, 1880–1918*, Basingstoke: Macmillan, 1984, 149.
22 Ibid.
23 C.R.W. Nevinson, *Paint and Prejudice*, London: Methuen, 1937, 57–8.
24 The recollection is worth quoting more fully. 'As a result of these sociable activities', Lewis writes, 'I did not sell a single picture, it is perhaps superfluous to say. But it was an object-lesson in the attitude of what remained of aristocratic life in England to the arts I practised… these good people of the British *beau monde* looked upon the artist as an oddity, to be lion-hunted for expensive howdahs.' Wyndham Lewis, *Blasting and Bombardiering: Autobiography (1914–1926)* (1937), London: Imperial War Museum, 1992, 50–51. Tickner notes that Lewis's claim not to have sold a single picture 'is economical with the truth', in that *Kermesse* was rented to Mme Strindberg, founder of the Cave of the Golden Calf nightclub (see Chapter 10) for £30 and he received 'several hundred pounds' worth of decorative commissions' from his several aristocratic patrons. Lisa Tickner, 'The Popular Culture of *Kermesse*: Lewis, Painting and Performance, 1912–13', *Modernism/Modernity*, vol. 4, no. 2, April 1997, 67–120; 104. In 1912 £100 was equivalent to *c.* £8,000 in 2017: https://www.nationalarchives.gov.uk/currency-converter/#currency-result.
25 Tickner, *Modern Life and Modern Subjects*, 82.
26 Tickner, 'The Popular Culture of *Kermesse*', 68.
27 Ibid.
28 Quoted in Judith Collins, *The Omega Workshops*, Chicago, I.L.: University of Chicago Press, 1984, 16. Fry was hoping to secure a decorative commission from Lady Cunard to succeed the one he had obtained for his Bloomsbury artist friends that year for a mural project at the Borough Polytechnic at the Elephant and Castle in London. On this project see ibid., 11–14. Collins adds: 'Fry was in his element as impresario and organiser, trying to wheedle commissions out of society people. This adumbrates the role he was to play within his Omega Workshops.' Ibid., 16.
29 In 1908 and 1909 the club held balls at the Royal Opera House in Covent Garden, and from 1910 at the Albert Hall, which remained its venue for most of the next 50 years: https://chelseaartsclub.com/the-club/history/, accessed 8 September 2021.
30 Nevinson, *Paint and Prejudice*, 60. On this event see the *Sketch* supplement, 10 December 1913, 3–10, and Tickner's acute account of it in 'The Popular Culture of *Kermesse*', 92–5.
31 This was the start, for Muriel Paget, of a lifetime of humanitarian work. See Wilfrid Blunt, *Lady Muriel: Lady Muriel Paget, her Husband, and her Philanthropic Work in Central and Eastern Europe*, London: Methuen, 1962, 287–8.
32 Lambert, *Unquiet Souls*, 148–9.
33 'The Wave of Unrest', *The Tatler*, 618, 30 April 1913, 132.
34 Tickner, 'The Popular Culture of *Kermesse*', 69.
35 Ibid., 95.
36 'The Enlargement of London Society', *The Saturday Review*, 5 May 1900, 552–3. This may be a conservative estimate, but it is from the period, and substantiated by research. Leonora Davidoff suggests 'four thousand families', while Nancy Ellenberger uses the phrase 'Society's upper ten thousand' as a familiar estimate, but without substantiation. Leonora Davidoff, *The Best Circles; Society Etiquette and the Season*, London: Croom Helm, 1973, 61; Ellenberger, 'The Souls and London "Society"', 138.

37 In his letter to Grant (see n. 28), Fry wrote of Lady Cunard that 'she's promised our group a room at her house, and says she'll make Lord Curzon do likewise'. Collins, *The Omega Workshops*, 16. Since his *Manet and the Post-Impressionists* exhibition of the winter of 1910–11, Fry had been making efforts to develop the link he saw between the French art he had exhibited there and Byzantine decorative art, in part by securing such commissions for Bloomsbury artists. See Denys Sutton, ed., *Letters of Roger Fry*, London: Chatto and Windus, vol. 1, 338.

38 Obituary, *The Times*, 12 July 1948, 7. The biographer Alan Jefferson wrote that having moved to London with her daughter Nancy in 1911, leaving her husband at the country home in Leicestershire, '[s]oon she had captured all London society, and her… salon became the most important Mecca for musicians, painters, sculptors, poets and writers as well as for politicians, soldiers, aristocrats'. Alan Jefferson, *Sir Thomas Beecham – A Centenary Tribute*, London: Macdonald and Jane's, 1979, 38–9.

39 'A Classical Beauty and a Celtic Marriage', *The Tatler*, 3 March 1909, 233.

40 'Small Talk', *The Sketch*, 11 March 1914, 320. The columnist did not give the name of the decorator. Black seems to have become – as a result? – the *décor du jour* (or rather *de la nuit*) from that time, since not only did the Countess repeat it in her 1914 makeover, but Lady Jean Hamilton followed suit.

41 Charles Drogheda, *Double Harness. Memoirs By Lord Drogheda*, London: Weidenfeld and Nicholson, 1978, 12. The Countess led the vogue for Society's embrace of aviation, visiting the London Aerodrome, Hendon (the centre of British aviation) in January 1914 and flying with air ace Grahame White, an adventure noted in the press: see 'Society Ladies and Aviation', *The Birmingham Mail*, 12 January 1914, 7. On this fashion, both aristocratic and popular, and its relation to artists see Bernard Vere, 'A "Modern Rendezvous" in London: Painters, Pilots, and Edward Wadsworth's "A Short Flight" (1914)', *British Art Studies*, 5, spring 2017, http://dx.doi.org/10.17658/issn.2058-5462/issue-05/bvere.

42 Cork, *Art Beyond the Gallery*, 179.

43 The speculation is Cork's: ibid., 184. Cork states that Boulestin had only opened his London business in November 1913 (ibid., 154), but in his autobiography Boulestin himself dates the launch of this to November 1911. *Ease and Endurance*, trans. Robin Adair, London: Home & Van Thai Ltd., 1948, 58. I am indebted to Ben Angwin for this reference.

44 *The Times*, 28 February 1914.

45 See Chapter 10.

46 Letter from Lady Drogheda to Wyndham Lewis, n.d. but probably near the end of 1913, owned by the Department of Rare Books, Cornell University. Quoted in Cork, *Art Beyond the Gallery*, 178. It has not been ascertained just why the Countess gave *Kermesse* the title *Norwegian Dance*; *Kermesse* was the title in the Doré exhibition, noted as such by Clive Bell in his review, as Paul Edwards observes: *Wyndham Lewis: Painter and Writer*, New Haven, C.T., and London, Yale University Press, 2000, 73 and 553 n. 26. Its contemporary critics did not use her name for the work, and subsequent historians have not come up with a reason for it. Perhaps the Countess, associating the painting with the Cave of the Golden Calf where it originally hung, took Mme Frida Strindberg, its founder and hostess, as Norwegian (she was Austrian, and her late husband, the playwright August Strindberg, was Swedish). If so, this perhaps underlines the tenuousness of the Countess's familiarity with this milieu.

47 See Chapter 10.

48 On the Countess's 'strong feelings for art' see Drogheda, *Double Harness*, 12.
49 On the details of the décors see Cork, *Art Beyond the Gallery*, ch. 4. Cork suggests that the Countess's own ideas played a part in the conception of her decorations; if so, it is significant that the photograph of the drawing room (pl. 42) shows a silver ball on a pedestal positioned so obtrusively in the space of the room that this could only have been for 'spectacular' effect rather than domestic convenience. On Lewis's part in such staging in his scheme for the dining room, see the next chapter.
50 *The Times*, 28 February 1914; *The Sketch*, 4 March 1914.
51 Cork, *Art Beyond the Gallery*, 187.
52 See the next chapter on the question of the status of this formation in terms of avant-gardehood.
53 *The Egoist*, 16 March 1914; letter to Harriet Monroe, 9 November 1914; D.D. Paige, ed., *The Letters of Ezra Pound, 1907–1941*, London: Faber and Faber, 1951, 87.
54 The standard reference on this initiative to date is Collins, *The Omega Workshops*, but see also Ben Angwin, 'Repositioning the Omega Workshops'. Angwin reveals and explores the complex discursive matrix of class, consumerism and taste that shaped the Omega's aims and achievements. On Fry's decorative predilections see Chapter 10.
55 *Née* Jean Muir, daughter of a recently ennobled Glasgow businessman, she married Colonel (later General) Sir Ian Hamilton in 1887, and had been painted by Sargent in 1896, and thus possessed economic, genealogical and cultural capital sufficient to Fry's aspirations for Omega.
56 Collins, *The Omega Workshops*, 86–7. Entries in Lady Hamilton's diary from mid-June 1913 until February 1915 reveal her passion for designing both the architecture and the decorations of her new home, and the progress of this project. See https://kingscollections.org/catalogues/lhcma/collection/h/ha30-001/16-21/h0-2001.
57 *The Sketch*, 23 June 1915. On 2 February 1915 Lady Hamilton wrote in her diary: 'Had a delightful dinner party to-night – all the women charming and I sat between the two most delightful men which seldom happens to me at my own party or elsewhere – Lord Ribblesdale took me in and I sat next to Roger Fry: Me, Roger Fry, Frances, Mr. [Henry] (Bogey) Harris, Lady Mond, Florrie, Mr. Harold Baker (who did not eat/come), Norah, Freddy, Lady Ancaster, Ian. The black drawing-room looked well to-night, but I don't think anyone likes it much, and I feel rather depressed about it. I have kept it locked up till to-night – I did not want Roger Fry to make any suggestions about it, and to do it all myself; I have painted the fireplace green myself and stood over the workmen while they painted the wood like malakite [*sic*; malachite]': https://kingscollections.org/catalogues/lhcma/collection/h/ha30-001/16-21/h0-2001.
58 It was also sufficiently acknowledged as to be ridiculed on stage. In June 1914 a play entitled *Idle Women* by Magdalen Ponsonby, a theatre professional and campaigner for women's rights, was performed at the Little Theatre, London by the Pioneer Players, and reviewed by several critics. Subtitled 'A Study in Futility', it satirised the purposelessness of fashionable Society women who, in order to pass the time, pursued the latest fads and fancies and formed new committees and societies to legitimise such trivial pursuits. The sets included 'Futurist furniture and decorations' by the Omega Workshops. On the obsession with exclusivity in the consumer behaviour of aristocratic women in this period see Mary Schoeser, *Fabrics and Wallpapers (Twentieth Century Design)*, London: Bell & Hyman Ltd., 1986. I am indebted for this information to Ben Angwin.

59 Cohen, *Household Gods*, ch. 3. The first and most successful of these was Mary Eliza Haweis, who published *The Art Dress* in 1879, *The Art of Decoration* in 1881, and *Beautiful Houses: Being a Description of Certain Well-Known Artistic Houses* in 1882. According to her biographer, 'Her own taste was renowned. After the publication of her fashion manual, *The Art of Dress*, society ladies shrank from meeting Mrs Haweis, lest she cast a critical eye over their raiment.' Bea Howe, *Arbiter of Elegance: A Biography of Mary Eliza Haweis*, London: Harvill Press, 1967, 78, 175.

60 Cohen notes: 'By the turn of the century, the siren song of art had echoed through the ranks of the lower middle classes, sweeping up Britain's rapidly growing numbers of clerks, shopkeepers, and schoolteachers in its wake.... High art's "homely" quality encouraged imitation down the social scale.... One decorating columnist advised that an artistic effect in the dining-room might be achieved with china blue paper, woodwork painted white, and cupboards full of blue china: "It is a kind of cottage realization of the magnificent dining-room which was decorated by Mr Whistler for Mr Leyland."' Cohen, *Household Gods,* 75, 232, citing Mrs Talbot Coke, 'House Furnishing', *Woman at Home*, 1895, no issue or page numbers given.

61 See Chapter 3.

62 David Garnett, 'Nancy Cunard', in Hugh Ford, ed., *Nancy Cunard: Brave Poet, Indomitable Rebel, 1896–1965*, Philadelphia, P.A.: Chilton Book Co., 1968.

63 The espousal of the 'Omega values' of handicraft, amateurism and authenticity may have underwritten this store-bought bohemianism, except that such purchases themselves made Omega's Post-Impressionism into a brand (see Chapter 8, n. 108).

64 On the growth of the advertising industry see Gurney, *The Making of Consumer Culture in Modern Britain.*

65 Hence, on the one hand, *The Sketch*'s designation, noted above, of the Countess of Drogheda as 'Futurist' along with her new decoration; on the other, its description of Lady Randolph Churchill as 'the best of the numerous Society ladies who dance the Tango'. (*The Sketch*, 26 November 1913, 224, on her costume for the Albert Hall Picture Ball.) This observation is one also made, if indirectly, by Tickner: 'The impact of Diaghilev and the Russian Ballet has been allowed to eclipse the reputations of their contemporaries (many of them women).... Edward Marsh, an early patron of Mark Gertler, Stanley Spencer and Duncan Grant, certainly went to see Vaslav Nijinsky, but he also went ten times to *Hello Ragtime at the Alhambra*'. Tickner, *Modern Life and Modern Subjects*, 80, citing Christopher Hassall, *Edward Marsh, Patron of the Arts: A Biography*, London: Longman, 1959, 204. In the postmodernist conjuncture, 'cultural omnivorousness' became a defining (and celebrated) feature of dominant cultural attitudes. See T.W. Chan and J.H. Goldthorpe, 'Social Stratification and Cultural Consumption: The Visual Arts in England', *Poetics*, vol. 35, nos 2–3, April–June 2007, 168–90.

66 On the financial benefit see n. 24. On the social, Frank Rutter noted early in 1914 that Lewis's Drogheda decorations had 'lately attracted so much attention in the daily press'. Rutter, 'Art and Artists – The English Cubists', *The New Weekly*, 1, 1914, 85.

67 Elizabeth Wilson, *Bohemians: The Glamorous Outcasts*, London and New York: I.B. Tauris, 2000, 24.

68 For an account by an *aficionado* of the music hall of the variety of upper-class (male) patrons this was attracting by 1909 see Peter Gilchrist, 'Where Men Foregather, IV: The Music Hall', *Modern Man*, 27 March 1909, 10.

69 On the Café Royal see Chapter 8, 188–89.
70 Evelyn Silber, *Gaudier-Brzeska: Life and Art*, London: Thames & Hudson, 1996, 54–5.
71 D. Goldring, *Odd Man Out: The Autobiography of a 'Propaganda Novelist'*, London: Chapman & Hall, 1935, 100; Marsh is cited by W.C. Wees, *Vorticism and the English Avant-Garde*, Manchester: Manchester University Press, 1972; Etchells's remark, as reported by Duncan Grant, is noted by Richard Cork in *Vorticism and Abstract Art in the First Machine Age*, vol. 1, *Origins and Development*, London: Gordon Fraser Gallery, 1976, 110.
72 Lisa Tickner, 'Men's Work? Masculinity and Modernism', in Norman Bryson, Michael Ann Holly and Keith Moxey, eds, *Visual Culture: Images and Interpretations*, Hanover, N.H., and London: University Press of New England, 1994, 42–82.
73 Lisa Tickner, 'Now and Then: The *Hieratic Head of Ezra Pound*', *Oxford Art Journal*, vol. 16, no. 2, 1993, 59. See also Corbett, *The Modernity of English Art*, which builds on Tickner's question, noting the 'assiduous and systematic character' of Lewis's posturing, but does not answer it.
74 See Chapter 6.
75 T.J. Clark, 'Cubism and Collectivity', in his *Farewell to an Idea: Episodes from a History of Modernism*, New Haven, C.T., and London, Yale University Press, 1999, 169–223; 180. 'But the pretending in cubism is done with such imaginative vehemence and completeness', Clark adds, 'that it constantly almost convinces – both the viewer and no doubt the painter in the first place. Pretending is cubism's power.' Ibid.
76 On the relation of consumerism, and of the advertising industry that drove it, to the consolidation of monopoly capitalism in the decades after 1880 see Raymond Williams, 'Advertising: The Magic System', in *Problems in Materialism and Culture*, London: Verso, 1980; more recently, Gurney, *The Making of Consumer Culture in Modern Britain*, ch. 4.

CHAPTER 10

1 Wyndham Lewis, *Blasting and Bombardiering: Autobiography (1914–1926)* (1937), London: Imperial War Museum, 1992, 258.
2 For the Paris figures see Chapter 4, 121 and n. 65. For those for London see Faith Binckes, *Modernism, Magazines, and the British Avant-Garde: Reading Rhythm, 1910–1914*, Oxford: Oxford University Press, 2010, 87. On such magazines in London see the 'General Introduction' to the first volume of the recent major publishing project, the three-volume *Oxford Critical and Cultural History of Modernist Magazines*, which notes that, until this project, 'it would be fair to say that magazines have represented an unexplored place on the map [of Anglophone literary modernism].' Peter Brooker and Andrew Thacker, eds, *The Oxford Critical and Cultural History of Modernist Magazines*, Vol. I: *Britain and Ireland 1880–1955*, Oxford: Oxford University Press, 2009, 3.
3 Rebecca Beasley, 'Literature and the Visual Arts: *Art and Letters* (1917–20) and *The Apple* (1920–22)', in ibid., 485.
4 Mark S. Morrison, *The Public Face of Modernism: Little Magazines, Audiences, and Reception 1905–1920*, Madison: University of Wisconsin Press, 2001, 17. On modernism and the press in the same period see Patrick Collier, *Modernism on Fleet Street*, Aldershot: Ashgate, 2006.

5 Michel Leymarie, 'Introduction: la belle époque des revues?', in Jacqueline Pluet-Despatin, Michel Leymarie and Jean-Yves Mollier, eds, *La Belle Époque des revues, 1880–1914*, Paris: L'IMEC, 2002, 14, 18, 16; and see Chapter 4, nn. 126–30.

6 Laurence Binyon, 'Sacrifice and Emphasis. Fine Prints: The New English Art Club', *The Saturday Review*, 26 November 1910, 675–6; J.M. Murry, 'French Books: A Classical Revival', *The Blue Review*, vol. 1, no. 2, June 1913, 137.

7 J.B. Bullen, *Post-Impressionists in England: The Critical Reception*, London: Routledge, 1988, 144

8 Binckes, *Modernism, Magazines, and the British Avant-Garde*, 21.

9 Fergusson's autobiographical notes, quoted in Margaret Morris, *The Art of J.D. Fergusson: A Biased Biography*, Glasgow: Blackie, 1974, 64.

10 J.M. Murry in John Lehmann, ed., *Coming to London*, London: Phoenix House, 1957, 106.

11 J.M. Murry, 'The Influence of Baudelaire', *Rhythm*, March 1913, Literary Supplement, xxvii.

12 This was not a Cubist work, a fact that appears to have prompted Orage of the rival *The New Age* to publish Picasso's very Cubist *La Mandoline et la Pernod* (*Mandolin and Glass of Pernod*), painted only earlier that year, in its issue of 23 November, to accompany critic Huntly Carter's piece, 'The Plato-Picasso Idea'. This in turn provoked *Rhythm* contributor Dorothy Banks to suggest this was motivated by intermagazine one-upmanship. Dorothy Banks, 'Carter-Murry-Picasso', *The New Age*, 14 December 1911, 166. The squabble gives an indication of the new feverishness over art from Paris in the London field from 1911.

13 On the craze for 'futurism' see the last section of this chapter.

14 Murry's biographer F.A. Lea notes that it was a young Frenchman, Maurice Larrouy, whom he met in 1910, who urged him to go to Paris, 'pointing out the absurdity of studying Rimbaud or Mallarmé before one could converse intelligibly with a French porter'. F.A. Lea, *The Life of John Middleton Murry*, London: Methuen, 1959, 18.

15 Painters Sonia Terk (later, Delaunay) and Marie Wassilief graduated in 1905, Amedée Ozenfant and Roger de La Fresnaye attended from 1906, sculptor Josef Czaky in 1910–11, Chagall in 1911, painters Liubov Popova and Nadezda Udaltsova in 1912–13. On La Palette see the informative and well-referenced (and reliable) entry in Wikipedia: https://en.wikipedia.org/wiki/Acad%C3%A9mie_de_La_Palette.

16 In a review of the 1909 Salon d'Automne for critic and curator Frank Rutter's London magazine *Art News* he aligned himself explicitly with the 'Matisseites'. J.D. Fergusson, 'The Autumn Salon', *Art News*, 21 October 1909, 7.

17 For illustrations see Elizabeth Cumming, ed., *Colour, Rhythm and Dance: Paintings and Drawings by J.D. Fergusson and his Circle in Paris*, Edinburgh: Scottish Arts Council, 1985. On the way in which Fauvist principles informed Fergusson's teaching at La Palette *c.* 1910, see Elizabeth Cumming, 'Les Peintres de l'Écosse Moderne: The Colourists and France', in Philip Long and Elizabeth Cumming, *The Scottish Colourists 1900–1930*, Edinburgh: National Galleries of Scotland with Mainstream Publishing, 2000, 46.

18 Although space does not permit further elaboration of the group's theoretical debt, such as it was, to Matisse's *technie*, it does illustrate the broader context of Murry's exploratory Parisian networking which, as Faith Binckes notes, also had a distinctly Anglophone character, and which owed more, it would seem, to the *New Age* critic Huntly Carter's

example than to any contact with Parisians. In his reviews of Paris exhibitions in 1911 Carter, a frequent visitor to the city and a keen Francophile, energetically promoted Fergusson's group, adopting for the purpose a critical lexicon peppered with labels for current 'isms' that appear to have been his own invention, appearing nowhere in the equivalent reviews of French critics ('the Expansionists, as I may now call them, had sorted themselves into groups.... These I will name for convenience Radiationists, Chrystallisationists, Vibrationists, Rhapsodists – terms having no connection with those manufactured by the married critics of the Harmsworth press and their wives during week-end visits to Paris.') This brass-necked gesture of one-upmanship both belied the fact that these labels were themselves made up by him, and suggests the competitive Parisophilia of the London 'little magazine' milieu. Huntly Carter, 'Letters from Abroad. The Post-Expressionists', *The New Age*, vol. 9, no. 26, 26 October 1911, 617. Prominent among these invented labels was 'the Rhythmists', which owed much to Carter's personal aesthetic predilections, which were probably influential on the consolidation of Murry's own. See Binckes, *Modernism, Magazines, and the British Avant-Garde*, 73–9.

19 It was only in London that this group was, indeed, recognised as such, largely by a circle led by the collector Michael Sadler and the critic P.J. Konody. Upset that Fry's second Post-Impressionist exhibition had ignored it, Sadler persuaded the Stafford Gallery in London to exhibit *Pictures by J.D. Fergusson, A.E. Rice and Others (The Rhythm Group)* to run concurrent with the Grafton show. See Binckes's account of these rivalries in her *Modernism, Magazines, and the British Avant-Garde*, ch. 5. Sadler changed his surname to Sadleir in 1914, to distinguish himself from his father who was an esteemed academic and collector of modernist art; see Michael T.H. Sadleir, *Michael Ernest Sadler, 1861–1943. A Memoir by his Son*, London: Constable, 1943.

20 See in particular Mark Antliff, *Inventing Bergson: Cultural Politics and the Parisian Avant-Garde*, Princeton, N.J.: Princeton University Press, 1993, ch. 3, who argues for Fergusson's familiarity with Bergson's writings as the theoretical basis for his approach to painting.

21 Mary Ann Gillies, 'Bergsonism: Time Out of Mind', in David Bradshaw, ed., *A Concise Companion to Modernism*, Oxford: Blackwell, 2003, 97. *Time and Free Will* appeared in 1910; *Matter and Memory*, *Laughter* and *Creative Evolution* in 1911; *Introduction to Metaphysics* in 1912 (in an American edition; in England, in 1913). See also Mary Ann Gillies, *Henri Bergson and British Modernism*, Montreal, Kingston and London: McGill-Queen's University Press, 1996.

22 On these threats and opportunities see Morrison, *The Public Face of Modernism*.

23 'It is a job to write a reasoned, critical letter with Yvonne and the rest of them clasping your neck, and reading every word, that they can't understand', wrote Murry in a letter from Paris to his friend Philip Landon, 31 December 1910; quoted in Lea, *The Life of John Middleton Murry*, 22.

24 Roger Fry's *Manet and the Post-Impressionists* exhibition at the Grafton Gallery, which ran from 8 November 1910 to 15 January 1911.

25 Letter to Philip Landon of April 1911, quoted in Lea, *The Life of John Middleton Murry*, 24–5.

26 J.M. Murry, *Between Two Worlds: An Autobiography*, London: Jonathan Cape, 1937, 156. See Chapter 8, 218.

27 Frank Rutter, *Art in my Time*, London: Rich and Cowan, 1933, 132–3.

28 See Chapter 8.

29 Roger Fry, 'Post-Impressionism', *The Fortnightly Review*, 1 May 1911, 856–67. Reprinted in Christopher Reed, *A Roger Fry Reader*, Chicago, I.L., and London: University of Chicago Press, 1996, 105–6.

30 Ibid., 105. The vagueness of Fry's last phrase quoted here suggests his uncertainty.

31 *The Nation*, 20 July 1912. See Chapter 9.

32 'Aims and Ideals', *Rhythm*, vol. 1, no. 1, summer 1911, 36; 'The Meaning of Rhythm', *Rhythm*, vol. 2, no. 5, June 1912, 20. Mansfield was also co-founder of the magazine itself.

33 The poets Georges Duhamel and Charles Vildrac, of the Abbaye de Créteil group, in 1910 together published a treatise, *Notes sur la Technique poétique*, in which they proposed the usefulness for the writing of *vers libre* of a 'rhythmic constant'. This fed into discussions in the winter of 1910–11 among the nascent salon Cubist coterie centred on the painting *L'Abondance* (*Abundance*) (see pl. 23) on which Henri Le Fauconnier was then at work; exhibited in the notorious Room 41 of the 1911 Salon des Indépendants which launched Cubism as a public movement, it gained a wide reputation across the burgeoning network of the European avant-garde as a pictorial manifesto of Bergsonism (see David Cottington, *Cubism in the Shadow of War: The Avant-Garde and Politics in Paris, 1905–1914*, New Haven, C.T., and London: Yale University Press, 1998; also Antliff, *Inventing Bergson*). But explorations in this direction were soon replaced within this milieu by an engagement, prompted by several factors including the innovations of Gallery Cubism and the 'modernolatry' of Italian Futurism, with 'simultaneity', a concept which became the *concept du jour* in the Paris of 1912–14; tellingly, it was not taken up by Fergusson's group of Rhythmists.

34 As indeed, Fergusson himself acknowledged: when J.M. Murry and Michael Sadler visited him in Paris in March 1911 to ask if he would join them as Art Editor of their proposed new 'little magazine', he replied that 'I didn't think Rhythm was a good title—it was (at that time) a word hardly ever used and to most people meant nothing.' Fergusson, 'Chapter from an Autobiography', in Morris, *The Art of J.D. Fergusson*, 64.

35 Efforts have been made by some scholars of British literary modernism to find cross-Channel links over concerns with 'rhythm' via a *petite revue*, *Le Rythme*, founded in Paris early in 1911 shortly before *Rhythm* in London. Their analyses are somewhat impressionistic and brief, however, and offer no accounts of this *revue*'s relation, or lack of it, to the artistic avant-garde. It appears to have been fairly unadventurous aesthetically and more engaged with writing, music, theatre and dance than with visual art. See Binckes, *Modernism, Magazines and the British Avant-Garde*, 87; Claire Davison, 'On Unknowing French? *Rhythm* and *Le Rythme* on a Cross-Channel Exchange', in Claire Davison, Jane Goldman and Derek Ryan, eds, *Cross-Channel Modernisms*, Edinburgh: Edinburgh University Press, 2020, 19–49. On the popularity of dance see Lisa Tickner, *Modern Life and Modern Subjects: British Art in the Early Twentieth Century*, New Haven, C.T., and London: Yale University Press, 2000, 80–88, 99–111; Sherril Dodds and Susan C. Cook, *Bodies of Sound: Studies Across Popular Music and Dance*, Farnham: Ashgate, 2013; Gabriele Brandstetter, *Poetics of Dance: Body, Image and Space in the Historical Avant-Gardes*, Oxford: Oxford University Press, 2015.

36 See Chapter 8.

37 J.M. Murry, 'The Art of Pablo Picasso', *The New Age*, 30 November 1911, 115. The last remark shows how little Murry was aware of the frames of interpretation offered in Paris

by numerous Cubists and critics by late 1911, including Apollinaire, Metzinger, Allard, Rivière, Salmon and Soffici. See Mark Antliff and Patricia Leighten, eds, *A Cubism Reader: Documents and Criticism, 1906–1914*, Chicago, I.L., and London: University of Chicago Press, 2008.

38 O. Raymond Drey, 'The Autumn Salon', *Rhythm*, vol. 2, no. 11, December 1912, 327.

39 O. Raymond Drey, 'Indépendants and the Cubist Muddle', *The Blue Review*, vol. 1, no. 2, June 1913, 148. Picasso did not exhibit in this Salon, in keeping with his dealer Kahnweiler's abstentionist policy, but remained the focus of attention of the London critics.

40 Roger Fry, 'The French Group', *The Second Post-Impressionist Exhibition*, exh. cat., London: Grafton Galleries, 1912, 15.

41 Drey, 'Indépendants and the Cubist Muddle', 148.

42 Examples are Matisse's *Notes of a Painter* of 1908, theoretical statements by Cubists such as Le Fauconnier ('Das Kunstwerk', September 1910) and Metzinger ('Note sur la peinture', October 1910), and elaborations of them by critics such as Allard ('Sur quelques peintres', June 1911) and Olivier-Hourcade ('La Tendance de la peinture contemporaine', February 1912); for all of these, reprinted in English translation, see Antliff and Leighten, eds, *A Cubism Reader*.

43 On this filiation see Alan Robinson, *Poetry, Painting and Ideas, 1885–1914*, Basingstoke: Macmillan, 1985, 40–57. Symons was the leading conduit for the transmission of Parisian Symbolist poetry and its aesthetic to London at the turn of the century. He had attended Mallarmé's Tuesday gatherings in the early 1890s, invited Verlaine to lecture in London, edited the *Savoy* magazine and in 1908 published *The Symbolist Movement in Literature*, whose considerable influence owed much to his discussions with the poet W.B. Yeats. Yeats himself was among the founders, in 1904, of the Abbey Theatre in Dublin, which sought to promote native Irish culture and integrate it with modern European theatrical methods. See Peter Brooker, *Bohemia in London: The Social Scene of Early Modernism*, Basingstoke: Palgrave Macmillan, 2007, 29–39.

44 Frank Kermode, *The Romantic Image*, London: Routledge, 1957, 81–7, and 'Poet and Dancer before Diaghilev', *Partisan Review*, 28, 1961, 48–75. See also Ian Fletcher, 'Explorations and Recoveries II: Symons, Yeats and the Demonic Dance', *The London Magazine*, vol. 7, no. 6, 1960, 46–60.

45 Robinson notes that for Symons, Wagner's opera *Parsifal* combined stage tableaux and music to make abstract pictures, producing a *mise-en-scène* that offered 'the lesson that, in art, rhythm is everything'; and that Rodin's sketches of naked women in motion, and the sculptures that resulted from them, 'seized an essential *rhythm* of nature.... When a woman combs her hair... she is making a gesture which flows into the *eternal rhythm*.' Robinson, *Poetry, Painting and Ideas*, 55.

46 The 'unreserved concurrence' of these ideas on the part of the critic and the poet in this respect is noted by Robinson, who quotes from Symons's review of Yeats's volume of poetry of 1899, *The Wind among the Reeds*, implicitly comparing it to Wagner's work. Robinson, *Poetry, Painting and Ideas*, 54; Symons, 'Mr Yeats as a Lyric Poet', *Saturday Review*, 6 May 1899, 553.

47 Robinson, *Poetry, Painting and Ideas*, 54–5.

48 See Chapter 1.

49 'Aims and Ideals', *Rhythm*, 36.

50 For a more substantial iteration of this observation and its implications see David Cottington, 'The Transnational Hierarchies and Networks of the Artistic Avant-Garde,

ca.1885–1915', in Marja Jalava, Stefan Nygård and Johan Strang, eds, *Decentering European Intellectual Space*, Leiden and Boston, M.A.: Brill, 2018, 65–87.

51 Richard Cork, *Art Beyond the Gallery in Early Twentieth-Century England*, New Haven, C.T., and London: Yale University Press, 1985, ch. 2. This was a development of an article Cork had published three years earlier, 'The Cave of the Golden Calf', *Artforum*, December 1982, 56–68.

52 See Tickner, *Modern Life and Modern Subjects*, esp. ch. 3; idem, 'The Popular Culture of *Kermesse*: Lewis, Painting and Performance, 1912–13', *Modernism/Modernity*, vol. 4, no. 2, April 1997, 67–120; Lisa Appignanesi, *The Cabaret* (1975), New Haven, C.T., and London: Yale University Press, 2004; Jo Cottrell, 'Killing John Bull with Art: Vorticism, Nationalism and Race, in the Cave of the Golden Calf', MA dissertation, Birkbeck, University of London, 2018, and idem, 'London: Cave of the Golden Calf, 1912–14', in Florence Ostende with Lotte Johnson, eds, *Into the Night: Cabarets and Clubs in Modern Art*, exh. cat., London: Barbican Art Gallery with Prestel, 2019, 85–101.

53 Monica J. Strauss, *Cruel Banquet: The Life and Loves of Frida Strindberg*, New York: Harcourt, 2000.

54 See Chapter 3.

55 Harold B. Segel, *Turn-of-the-Century Cabaret: Paris, Barcelona, Berlin, Munich, Vienna, Cracow, Moscow, St Petersburg, Zurich*, New York: Columbia University Press, 1987; J.T. Grein, 'Cabaret: The Panacea', in 'Premières of the Week', *Sunday Times*, 19 March 1911, 6; Cottrell, 'London: Cave of the Golden Calf', 86.

56 Cork, *Art Beyond the Gallery*, 65. The Cave was not, it seems, her first attempt to do so. The painter C.R.W. Nevinson recalled in his memoirs, *Paint and Prejudice*, London: Methuen, 1937, 41, that Mme Strindberg had been 'the originator of night clubs in London, starting first, I think, with a supper club in Percy Street, and later, with the aid of the Arts and Dramatic, moving to Hanover Square'. His not always reliable memory is corroborated, if a little fancifully, by an account in *The New York Daily Herald*, on 28 January 1912, 39, of an initiative by the Arts and Dramatic Club to establish an artists' meeting place in London (cited in Cottrell, 'London: Cave of the Golden Calf', 90 and 326 n. 37). This does not seem to have been the Golden Calf.

57 According to a press-clipped account of the opening ('New Sensation for London. Night in "Cave of Golden Calf". Exotic atmosphere.') quoted by Cork, who was unable to trace its origin, and which at the time of his research in the mid-1980s was in the collection of Spencer Gore's son Frederick. Cork, *Art Beyond the Gallery*, 104.

58 'The Cabaret Club', *The Times*, 27 June 1912.

59 Appignanesi, *The Cabaret*, 208 (as noted earlier, see Chapter 7, n. 74). Segel concurs, declaring it to be 'alien [to London] from its very inception', though without suggesting why. Segel, *Turn-of-the-Century Cabaret*, xxv.

60 Douglas Goldring, *Reputations: Essays in Criticism*, London: Chapman and Hall, 1920, 138. On the Café Royal, and his remark, see Chapter 7. Mme Strindberg's choice of a basement in Heddon Street as the venue was also perhaps bravely provocative since it offered the very opposite ambiance to the Café Royal's gilt opulence and Regent Street swagger no more than a stone's throw from it. As Jo Cottrell notes, Regent Street itself was the borderline between wealthy, aristocratic Mayfair and bohemian Soho. Cottrell, 'Killing John Bull with Art', 8.

61 *The Sphere*, 9 March 1912, 272. The title of the article, 'Will the Cabaret System Become Acclimatised?', indicates their fashionability.
62 *The Sketch*, 21 January 1914.
63 Quoted in Cork, *Art Beyond the Gallery*, 63, 67.
64 Ibid., 61.
65 Ibid. As Cork observes, the nearest precedent for the Golden Calf was the Cabaret Fledermaus in Strindberg's native Vienna, but its decorations were minimal in comparison with her scheme. Ibid., 67–8.
66 Extract from an undated press review from *The Standard*, quoted in 'The Press and the Cabaret Club', in an unpaginated Cabaret Club brochure dated September 1913, printed from 9 Heddon Street, London W1. Cited by Cottrell, 'London: Cave of the Golden Calf', 88 and 326 n. 25.
67 Unidentified clipping cited by Cork, *Art Beyond the Gallery*, 104.
68 See Chapter 8.
69 Cork, *Art Beyond the Gallery*, 64. *Kermesse* was lost, and survives only as a small (35 × 35 cm) gouache study.
70 *The Sunday Times*, 27 June 1912; Augustus John, *Chiaroscuro: Fragments of an Autobiography* (1952), London: Readers Union, 1954, 177.
71 *The Times*, 18 July 1912, 3.
72 'New Sensation for London. Night in "Cave of Golden Calf". Exotic atmosphere', quoted in Cork, *Art Beyond the Gallery*, 106. Maud Allan was a Canadian actor, dancer and choreographer, famous for what were termed 'impressionistic mood settings'. A less well-known rival of Isadora Duncan, she had little training but much imagination and ambition; her 1906 version of Wilde's *Salomé* gained some notoriety.
73 Author of detective stories Edgar Jepson later recalled that it was 'an expensive club… frequented by the intelligent wealthy, interested in letters and the arts'. Edgar Jepson, *Memories of an Edwardian and Neo-Georgian*, London: Richards, 1937, 154.
74 On the Café Royal's clientele see Chapters 7 and 9, including David Garnett's recollection of Nancy Cunard as both gracing the Café Royal and marrying a Guards officer. Lisa Appignanesi underscores the anomalous character of its patronage by Guards officers, noting that Ezra Pound 'rued' their presence, while 'relish[ing] the unbuttoned vitality of the place'. Appignanesi, *The Cabaret*, 93–4, no source given.
75 Ashley Gibson, *Postscript to Adventure*, London: J.M. Dent, 1930, 105. The Cabaret Theatre Club rulebook stated that membership was 5 guineas, but the rule was administered idiosyncratically: reduced to 1 guinea for 50 supporters representing the arts. Noting this, Peter Brooker adds that 'out of deference to their personalities', certain artists were given honorary membership and had their bills shifted to wealthier patrons, and quotes Ezra Pound: 'you cd/even get eats for free if you took 'em at Frida's table.' Brooker, *Bohemia in London*, 74, citing Eustace Mullins, *This Difficult Individual, Ezra Pound*, New York: Fleet Publishing, 1961, 99.
76 Charles Marriott, *Subsoil*, London: Hurst and Blackett, 1913, 9–10.
77 Ibid., 10.
78 Ibid., 11.
79 Ibid., 13.
80 Ibid., 14.
81 Gilbert Cannan, *Mendel*, London: T. Fisher Unwin, 1916, 236, 238.

82 Ford Madox Ford, *The Marsden Case: A Romance*, London: Duckworth, 1923, 87–92.
83 Osbert Sitwell, *Left Hand, Right Hand! An Autobiography*, 4 vols, London: Macmillan, 1948, 3:208.
84 Violet Hunt, *I Have This to Say: The Story of My Flurried Years*, New York: Boni and Liveright, 1926, 116, 267.
85 Nathan Waddell, 'Bohemian Retrospects: Ford Madox Ford, Post-War Memory and the Cabaret Theatre Club', in Kate McLoughlin, ed., *The Modernist Party*, Edinburgh: Edinburgh University Press, 2013, 241. He elaborates: 'The elegiac overtones of [*The Marsden Case*'s hero] Jessop's recollections are primarily a consequence of his status as a recovering participant in the First WW, but they are also a product of his longing for a moment of social and cultural import when "to be in London", in his words, "was to be in the centre of the world"' (247); 'Jessop's reconstruction of that moment imbues it with a liveliness which contrasts suggestively with the post-war present from which it is viewed' (249).
86 'Mr Sickert on Futurism. The Mayor and "Tumultuous Youth"', *The Brighton Herald*, 20 December 1913, 3. However, Sickert wrote to his painter friend Nan Hudson two months later: 'At Brighton the Epstein-Lewis-Etchells room made me sick and I publicly disengaged my responsibility.' Quoted in Wendy Baron, *Perfect Moderns: A History of the Camden Town Group*, Aldershot: Ashgate, 2000, 69. The ambivalence is intriguing; it seems likely, from the tone of his remarks overall as reported, that in his speech Sickert was being diplomatic (and perhaps also showing solidarity with other progressive artists), in the presence of the mayor and others unfamiliar with, even unsympathetic to, avant-garde art.
87 Cork, *Art Beyond the Gallery*, 91.
88 As Cork notes, there was 'a distinctly cosmopolitan flavour' to the list of performers from the start, although the 'Aims and Programme' brochure was careful to reassure potential clients that 'we do not want to Continentalize, we only want to do away, to some degree, with the distinction that the word "Continental" implies, and with the necessity of crossing the Channel to laugh freely, and to sit up after nursery hours'. 'Aims and Programme of the Cabaret Theatre Club', May 1912 (author's copy). Cork, *Art Beyond the Gallery*, 101.
89 I borrow this phrase from Jo Cottrell's 'Killing John Bull with Art'.
90 On Kandinsky's exhibits at the AAA in London, see Cork, *Vorticism and Abstract Art in the First Machine Age*, vol. 1, *Origins and Development*, London: Gordon Fraser Gallery, 1976, 216. On Ginner's possible debt in his mural to Picasso's primitivist, expressionistic early Cubism of 1907, in particular the lozenge-shaped, hatched wedges on works such as *Nu à la draperie* (*Nude with Drapery*) of 1907 (Hermitage, St Petersburg) (see pl. 30), see Paul Edwards, *Wyndham Lewis: Painter and Writer*, New Haven, C.T., and London: Yale University Press, 2000, 59.
91 Bell's decoration of her children's nursery at 46 Gordon Square was painted in summer 1912 (thus postdating the Golden Calf's murals, which she is very likely to have seen); it was re-created in collage form for the Omega Workshops late in 1913. See Christopher Reed, *Bloomsbury Rooms: Modernism, Subculture and Domesticity*, New Haven, C.T., and London: Yale University Press, 2004, 116–17, 152–3, 291 n. 14.
92 Cork, *Art Beyond the Gallery*, 111.
93 Edwards, *Wyndham Lewis: Painter and Writer*, 9.
94 Ibid., 53–4.

95 Ibid., 56. On its reflexive character see the discussion of Edward Fry's analysis of this Cubism in Chapter 5.

96 The *Exhibition of Works by the Italian Futurist Painters* was held at the Sackville Gallery in London's West End in March 1912. At the Paris Indépendants of mid-March to mid-May 1912, each of the Cubists who regularly exhibited at this Salon showed their biggest picture to date: Léger, *La Noce* (*The Wedding*) (257 × 206 cm) (see pl. 51), Delaunay, *La Ville de Paris* (*The City of Paris*) (267 × 406), Le Fauconnier, *Le Chasseur* (*The Hunter*) (203 × 167), Gleizes, *Les Baigneuses* (*The Bathers*) (105 × 170) and Metzinger, *Femme au cheval* (*Woman on a Horse*) (162 × 131). Lewis would have owed it to himself not to miss this Indépendants; he was better versed in the work of the Cubist movement in Paris – both wings of it – by the time of his work on the Golden Calf, than anyone else in London, and would have recognised the significance of this collective declaration of Parisian *simultanéité*.

97 On this transaction see Chapter 9, n. 24.

98 Cork, *Art Beyond the Gallery*, 87.

99 Tickner, 'The Popular Culture of *Kermesse*', 106, 95. On London's aristocrats and the tango see Chapter 9.

100 Frank Kermode, *Modern Essays*, London: Fontana, 1970, 12–13.

101 Paul O'Keeffe, *Some Sort of Genius: A Life of Wyndham Lewis*, London: Pimlico, 2000, 116–21.

102 See, e.g., Edwards, *Wyndham Lewis: Painter and Writer*.

103 On the introduction of this device, as between the salon Cubists and the Futurists, see Cottington, *Cubism in the Shadow of War*, 100–04. The innovation led directly to the first artistic use of photomontage a few years later; it was perhaps the most notable innovation of salon Cubism to be taken up by the European avant-garde.

104 '[W]hat must be rendered is the *dynamic sensation*, that is to say, the particular rhythm of each object, its inclination, its movement, or, more exactly, its interior force.... Every object reveals by its lines how it would resolve itself if it were to follow the tendencies of its forces.' 'The Exhibitors to the Public', in *Exhibition of Works by the Italian Futurist Painters*, exh. cat., London: Sackville Gallery, 1912. Reprinted in Umbro Apollonio, ed., *Futurist Manifestos*, London and New York: Thames & Hudson, 1973, 45–50; 47–8. For the works exhibited see Anna Gruetzner Robins, *Modern Art in Britain 1910–1914*, exh. cat., London: Barbican Art Gallery with Merrell Holberton, 1997, 56–63 and 189.

105 Edwards, *Wyndham Lewis: Painter and Writer*, 61.

106 For that of Paris see Jeffrey Weiss, *The Popular Culture of Modern Art: Picasso, Duchamp and Avant-Gardism*, New Haven, C.T., and London: Yale University Press, 1994. See also Chapter 8, 226–7.

107 On Fry's theories see Chapter 8. Clive Bell, *Art*, London: Chatto & Windus, 1914; Wassily Kandinsky, *The Art of Spiritual Harmony* (now known as *Concerning the Spiritual in Art*), intro. and trans, by M.T.H. Sadler, London: Constable, 1914. Hulme's writings about Worringer's *Abstraktion und Einfühlung* (*Abstraction and Empathy*), which were not translated into English until 1940, and whose ideas were 'unknown, except to Hulme' in London in 1913, according to the painter David Bomberg, are in T.E. Hulme, *Speculations* (1924), ed. Herbert Read, 2nd edn, London: Kegan Paul, 1936. Robert Ferguson, *The Short Sharp Life of T.E. Hulme*, London: Allen Lane, 150 and 286 nn. 37, 38.

108 Edwards, *Wyndham Lewis: Painter and Writer*, pl. 53.

109 Ibid., 124.

110 A reading of them shared by Edwards, see *Wyndham Lewis: Painter and Writer*, 115.

111 Günter Berghaus, *Italian Futurist Theatre 1909–1944*, Oxford: Clarendon Press, 1998, 59.

112 It was published in the major Parisian newspaper *Le Figaro* – apparently with the help of a family friend with shares in that paper; as a result of which it was picked up and published very soon after by numerous dailies across the continent. London, however, was not included. Walter L. Adamson, *Embattled Avant-Gardes: Modernism's Resistance to Commodity Culture in Europe*, Berkeley and London: University of California Press, 2007, 85.

113 On Marinetti's early career see Chapter 6; also Günter Berghaus, *The Genesis of Futurism: Marinetti's Early Career and Writings 1899–1909*, Leeds: Society for Italian Studies, 1995; Luca Somigli, *Legitimizing the Artist: Manifesto Writing and European Modernism 1885–1915*, Toronto: University of Toronto Press, 2003; and Adamson, *Embattled Avant-Gardes*, ch. 2. For the multiple futurisms, Pontus Hulton's *Futurisme & Futurismes*, Venice: Palazzo Grassi and Milan: Fabbri, 1986, remains the most useful single-volume yet comprehensive survey. For an edited collection of the manifestos in English translation see Apollonio, ed., *Futurist Manifestos*.

114 This was not only in keeping with the manner of his founding manifesto's publication, but also in contrast to avant-garde practice, which was usually to address fellow avant-gardists, often via the network of *petites revues* as well as café-based milieux such as, in Paris, the Closerie des Lilas.

115 Jamie Wood, '"On or about December 1910": F.T. Marinetti's Onslaught on London and Recursive Structures in Modernism', *Modernist Cultures*, vol. 10, no. 2, June 2015, 135–58; 143. Wood cites several London press reports of material received from Marinetti between 1908 and 1910.

116 The date of Marinetti's first visit was universally accepted by historians and memorialists of Futurism as having been in April 1910, until Wood's painstaking, forensic and persuasive reassessment of 2015 (ibid.), which after examining the historiography and primary sources offers the date, location and content presented in this paragraph.

117 Ibid., 142–3. The Lyceum Club, founded in 1906, was conceived as a challenge to the culture of elite men-only clubs, intended, in the words of its founder, Constance Smedley, 'for ladies engaged with literature, journalism, art, science and medicine'. Elizabeth Crawford, *The Women's Suffrage Movement: A Reference Guide 1866–1928*, Abingdon: Routledge, 2003, 124, quoted ibid., 144.

118 Ibid., 145–6.

119 On the *serate* see below.

120 Barbara Pezzini, 'The 1912 Futurist Exhibition at the Sackville Gallery, London: An Avant-Garde Show within the Old-Master Trade', *Burlington Magazine*, June 1913, 471–9.

121 However, this critical response did not prevent the exhibition from attracting substantial numbers of visitors; in a letter to F.B. Pratella of 12 April 1912, Marinetti claimed that well over 10,000 catalogues had been sold (at sixpence each, equivalent to £2 today); see M. Gambillo and T. Fiori, eds, *Archivi del Futurismo*, 2 vols, Rome: De Luca, 1959–62, 1: 37–8. On the art-market context of this exhibition see Pezzini, who describes it as 'an event organised by a group of dealers who commodified the avant-garde, exploited the artists and controlled the media': 'The 1912 Futurist Exhibition', 478. On the Futurists'

reception in general see Jonathan Black, 'Taking Heaven by Violence: Futurism and Vorticism as Seen by the British Press', in J. Black, C. Adams, M.J.K. Walsh and J. Wood, eds, *Blasting the Future! Vorticism in Britain 1910–1920*, London: Estorick Collection of Modern Italian Art with Philip Wilson Publishers, 2004, 30. On the convention of such ridicule see Weiss, *The Popular Culture of Modern Art*.

122 Lawrence Rainey, 'The Creation of the Avant-Garde: F.T. Marinetti and Ezra Pound', ch. 1 of *Institutions of Modernism: Literary Elites and Public Culture*, New Haven, C.T., and London: Yale University Press, 1999, 28 and 182 n. 42. For the figures (which may be unreliable, given his habit of hyperbole), Rainey cites the letter to F.B. Pratella of 12 April 1912 (see n. 121); 11,000 francs equalled £400 in 1912, or approximately £30,000 in today's money (https://www.nationalarchives.gov.uk/currency-converter/#currency-result).

123 Rainey, 'The Creation of the Avant-Garde', 14. On the link with anarchism see Black, 'Taking Heaven by Violence', 30. On the convention of such linkage, see Weiss, *The Popular Culture of Modern Art*.

124 A Severini solo exhibition had been held at the Marlborough Gallery in April, and an exhibition, *Post-Impressionists and Futurists*, of October at the Doré Gallery, curated by Frank Rutter, broadened its connotations. It included two works by Severini, *Dance* and *Polka*, as well as work by Lewis, Wadsworth, Hamilton, Etchells and Nevinson, among 38 European and 25 British artists selected. Robins, *Modern Art in Britain 1910–1914*, 29 and 36–8.

125 *The Times*, 18 November 1913, 5.

126 On this history see Victor Glasstone, *Victorian and Edwardian Theatres*, Cambridge, M.A.: Harvard University Press, 1975.

127 F.T. Marinetti, 'The Meaning of the Music Hall, by the Only Intelligible Futurist', *The Daily Mail*, 21 November 1913, 6. The manifesto, 'Il teatro di varietà', was first published in the Futurist periodical *Lacerba* on 1 October 1913 in a slightly longer version. Reprinted in translation by R.W. Flint in Apollonio, ed., *Futurist Manifestos*, 126–31. On the music hall and the variety theatre, see Rainey, 'The Creation of the Avant-Garde', 35–7; Lee Jackson, *Palaces of Pleasure: From Music Halls to the Seaside to Football, How the Victorians Invented Mass Entertainment*, New Haven, C.T., and London: Yale University Press, 2019.

128 The press responses to these performances are too numerous to detail here; see Valerio Gioé, 'Futurism in England: A Bibliography (1910–1915)', *Bulletin of Bibliography*, vol. 44, no. 3, 1987, 172–88.

129 Felix Barker, *The House That Stoll Built: The Story of the Coliseum Theatre*, London: Frederick Muller, 1957, 11.

130 Glasstone, *Victorian and Edwardian Theatres*, 116.

131 *The Sketch* also covered the Futurists' musical concerts at the Coliseum, reporting on 'Noise-Makers for the Futurist Concert of Noises' on 17 June 1914, 324, with photos of performers and their instruments.

132 Rainey, 'The Creation of the Avant-Garde', 35, who cites Barker, *The House That Stoll Built*, 186, as well as the account by a member of the first audience, the painter C.R.W. Nevinson, in his memoirs *Paint and Prejudice*, 83. Ironically, 'throwing things' and booing were precisely what Futurist performances sought to provoke (see below).

133 Ibid., 33.

134 See Black, 'Taking Heaven by Violence', 32, who notes as an example a 'Lucky Futurist Cat… [with] meow-meow notes printed on the animal's porcelain body – a weird sort of music which it would be quite impossible for any but a futurist musician to read', as reported in June 1914 by *The Daily Express* as currently on sale.

135 Adamson, *Embattled Avant-Gardes*, 83–4, who borrows the term 'taste professional' without reference or elaboration from Leora Auslander's *Taste and Power: Furnishing Modern France*, Berkeley and London: University of California Press, 1996, ch. 5. For both it refers to professional cultural critics, 'the growing [in late nineteenth-century France] number of men and women (but mostly men) engaged in commenting on matters of taste and style' (Auslander, *Taste and Power*, 195). Effectively, the first two options are those of sociologist Pierre Bourdieu's two 'principles of hierarchisation', the struggle between which shapes the 'field of cultural production': the heteronomous principle ('e.g. "bourgeois art"') and the autonomous principle ('e.g. "art for art's sake"'). Bourdieu does not suggest a third, intermediate principle. Pierre Bourdieu, 'The Field of Cultural Production, or: The Economic World Reversed', in Pierre Bourdieu, *The Field of Cultural Production: Essays on Art and Literature*, ed. Randal Johnson, Cambridge: Polity, 1993, esp. 40–45.

136 These *serate* were held in cities across Italy (but until 1914, nowhere else). For an invaluable, detailed and entertaining account and analysis of them see Berghaus, *Italian Futurist Theatre 1909–1944*, 85–155.

137 Ibid., 59–84.

138 Nevinson, *Paint and Prejudice*, 83.

139 Reprinted in English translation in Lawrence Rainey, Christine Poggi and Laura Wittman, eds, *Futurism: An Anthology*, New Haven, C.T., and London: Yale University Press, 2009, 96–9.

140 Mario Dessy, quoted by Berghaus, *Italian Futurist Theatre 1909–1944*, 140 and 155 n. 172.

141 Ibid., 59–60; Adamson, *Embattled Avant-Gardes*, 95–9, 108.

142 Lewis, *Blasting and Bombardiering*, 39–40. See n. 1 above, and Chapter 9.

143 Lewis, *Blasting and Bombardiering*, 51–2. Also quoted in Chapter 9 (n. 24). As that chapter showed, although Lewis may not have sold any pictures as a result of this celebrity, he received lucrative commissions for schemes of interior decoration.

144 Paul Edwards, 'Lewis's Myth of the Artist: From Bohemia to the Underground', in Paul Edwards, ed., *Volcanic Heaven: Essays on Wyndham Lewis's Painting and Writing*, Santa Barbara, C.A.: Black Sparrow Press, 1996, 25–39; Wyndham Lewis, 'The Pole', in *The Complete Wild Body*, ed. Bernard Lafoucade, Santa Barbara, C.A.: Black Sparrow Press, 1982, 210–11.

145 Lewis wrote two drafts of it between 1908 and 1911, then put it aside, returning to it in 1915; it was first published in 1918. See Edwards, *Wyndham Lewis: Painter and Writer*, 35–7.

146 Edwards, 'Lewis's Myth of the Artist', 26, 33.

147 Pound, 'The New Sculpture', *The Egoist*, vol. 1, no. 4, 16 February 1914, 221; Upward, 'The Order of the Seraphim' I, 10 February 1910, 349; Pound, 'The Order of the Brothers Minor', in 'Correspondence', *The New Freewoman*, 15 October 1913, 176. See Chapter 1.

148 Pound, whose talents as an editor and organiser were evident, wrote to fellow America poet William Carlos Williams in December 1913 that '[w]e are getting our little gang

after five years of waiting'. *The Letters of Ezra Pound, 1907–1941*, ed. D.D. Paige, London: Faber and Faber, 1951, 27.

149 For further assessment of Nevinson's particular position, see Michael J.K. Walsh, ed., *A Dilemma of English Modernism: Visual and Verbal Politics in the Life and Work of C.R.W. Nevinson, 1889–1946*, Durham, N.C.: Duke University Press, 2007.

150 For details of the Centre's programme and brief history see, e.g., Cork, *Art Beyond the Gallery*, ch. 4; Andrew Wilson, 'Rebels and Vorticists: "Our Little Gang"', in Paul Edwards, ed., *Blast: Vorticism 1914–1918*, Aldershot: Ashgate, 2000, 31 and 124 n. 59; Edwards, *Wyndham Lewis: Painter and Writer*, 99–100.

CODA

1 Nancy J. Troy, *Modernism and the Decorative Arts in France: Art Nouveau to Le Corbusier*, New Haven, C.T., and London: Yale University Press, 1991.

2 Thomas Crow, 'Modernism and Mass Culture in the Visual Arts' (1982), in Francis Frascina, ed., *Pollock and After: The Critical Debate*, New York and London: Harper & Row, 1985, 233–66.

3 Raymond Williams, *Marxism and Literature*, Oxford: Oxford University Press, 1977, 113.

4 Piotr Piotrowski, 'Toward a Horizontal History of the European Avant-Garde', in Sascha Bru et al., eds, *Europa! Europa? The Avant-Garde, Modernism, and the Fate of a Continent*, Berlin: De Gruyter, 2009, 49–58.

SELECT BIBLIOGRAPHY

Alsdorf, Bridget, *Fellow Men: Fantin-Latour and the Problem of the Group in Nineteenth-Century French Painting*, Princeton, N.J.: Princeton University Press, 2013

Annan, N.G., 'The Intellectual Aristocracy', in J.H. Plumb, ed., *Studies in Social History*, London: Longmans, Green & Co., 1955

Antliff, Mark, and Patricia Leighten, eds, *A Cubism Reader: Documents and Criticism, 1906–1914*, Chicago, I.L., and London: University of Chicago Press, 2008

—, and Scott W. Klein, eds, *Vorticism: New Perspectives*, Oxford: Oxford University Press, 2013

Appignanesi, Lisa, *The Cabaret* (1975), New Haven, C.T., and London: Yale University Press, 2004

Baron, Wendy, *Perfect Moderns: A History of the Camden Town Group*, Aldershot: Ashgate, 2000

Beasley, Rebecca, *Ezra Pound and the Visual Culture of Modernism*, Cambridge: Cambridge University Press, 2007

Benson, John, *The Rise of Consumer Society in Britain, 1880–1980*, London: Longman, 1994

Berghaus, Günter, *The Genesis of Futurism: Marinetti's Early Career and Writings 1899–1909*, Leeds: Society for Italian Studies, 1995

—, *Italian Futurist Theatre 1909–1944*, Oxford: Clarendon Press, 1998

Binckes, Faith, *Modernism, Magazines, and the British Avant-Garde: Reading* Rhythm, *1910–1914*, Oxford: Oxford University Press, 2010

Bock, Catherine, *Henri Matisse and Neo-Impressionism 1898–1908*, Ann Arbor, M.I.: UMI Research Press, 1981

Bois, Yve-Alain, 'On Matisse: The Blinding: For Leo Steinberg' (trans. Greg Sims), *October*, 68, spring 1994, 60–121

Bouillon, Jean-Paul, 'Sociétés d'artistes et institutions officielles dans la seconde moitié du XIXe siècle', *Romantisme*, 54, 1986, 89–113

Bourdieu Pierre, 'The Field of Cultural Production, or: The Economic World Reversed', in Pierre Bourdieu, *The Field of Cultural Production: Essays on Art and Literature*, ed. Randal Johnson, Cambridge: Polity, 1993, 29–73

—, *The Rules of Art: Genesis and Structure of the Literary Field* (1992), trans. Susan Emanuel, Cambridge: Polity, 1996

Brooker, Peter, *Bohemia in London: The Social Scene of Early Modernism*, Basingstoke: Palgrave Macmillan, 2007

—, and Andrew Thacker, eds, *The Oxford Critical and Cultural History of Modernist Magazines, Volume I: Britain and Ireland 1880–1955*, Oxford: Oxford University Press, 2009

Brown, Marilyn, *Gypsies and Other Bohemians: The Myth of the Artist in Nineteenth-Century France*, Ann Arbor, M.I.: UMI Research Press, 1985

Bru, Sascha, *The European Avant-Gardes, 1905–1935: A Portable Guide*, Edinburgh: Edinburgh University Press, 2018

Bürger, Peter, *Theory of the Avant-Garde* (1974), trans. Michael Shaw, foreword by Jochen Schulte-Sasse, Manchester: Manchester University Press, 1984

Calinescu, Matei, *Five Faces of Modernity: Modernism, Avant-Garde, Decadence, Kitsch, Postmodernism*, Durham, N.C.: Duke University Press, 1987

Campos, Christophe, *The View of France: From Arnold to Bloomsbury*, London: Oxford University Press, 1965

Cannadine, David, *The Decline and Fall of the British Aristocracy*, New Haven, C.T., and London: Yale University Press, 1990

Carter, Karen L., and Susan Waller, eds, *Foreign Artists and Communities in Modern Paris, 1870–1914*, Farnham: Ashgate, 2015

Cate, Phillip Dennis, and Mary Shaw, eds, *The Spirit of Montmartre: Cabarets, Humor and the Avant-Garde, 1875–1905,* New Brunswick, N.J.: Zimmerli Art Museum, Rutgers University, 1996

Charpin, Catherine, *Les Arts incohérents (1882–1893)*, Paris: Syros, 1990

Cherry, Deborah, *Painting Women: Victorian Women Artists*, London: Routledge, 1993

Chevrefils-Desbiolles, Yves, *Les Revues d'art à Paris, 1905–1940* (1993), Paris: Presses Universitaires de Provence, 2014

Clark, T.J., *Farewell to an Idea: Episodes from a History of Modernism*, New Haven, C.T., and London: Yale University Press, 1999

Clawson, Mary Anne, *Constructing Brotherhood: Class, Gender, and Fraternalism*, Princeton, N.J.: Princeton University Press, 1989

Cole, Sarah, *Modernism, Male Friendship, and the First World War*, Cambridge: Cambridge University Press, 2003

Comentale, Edward, *Modernism, Cultural Production, and the British Avant-Garde*, Cambridge: Cambridge University Press, 2004

Conner, Tom, *The Dreyfus Affair and the Rise of the French Public Intellectual*, Jefferson, N.C.: McFarland, 2014

Corbett, David Peters, *The World in Paint: Modern Art and Visuality in England, 1848–1914*, Manchester and New York: Manchester University Press, 2004

—, and Andrew Thacker, 'Raymond Williams and Cultural Formations: Movements and Magazines', *Prose Studies*, vol. 16, no. 2, August 1993, 84–106

Cork, Richard, *Art Beyond the Gallery in Early Twentieth-Century England*, New Haven, C.T., and London: Yale University Press, 1985

Cottington, David, *Cubism in the Shadow of War: The Avant-Garde and Politics in Paris, 1905–1914*, New Haven, C.T., and London: Yale University Press, 1998

—, *Cubism and its Histories*, Manchester and New York: Manchester University Press, 2004

—, 'The Formation of the Avant-Garde in Paris and London, c. 1880–1915', *Art History*, vol. 35, no. 3, June 2012, 596–621

—, *The Avant-Garde: A Very Short Introduction*, Oxford: Oxford University Press, 2013

—, 'The Transnational Hierarchies and Networks of the Artistic Avant-Garde, ca. 1885–1915', in Marja Jalava, Stefan Nygård and Johan Strang, eds, *Decentering European Intellectual Space*, Leiden and Boston, M.A.: Brill, 2018, 65–87

Crossley, Ceri, and Ian Small, eds, *Studies in Anglo-French Cultural Relations: Imagining France*, Basingstoke: Macmillan, 1988

Crow, Thomas, 'Modernism and Mass Culture in the Visual Arts' (1982), in Francis Frascina, ed., *Pollock and After: The Critical Debate*, New York and London: Harper & Row, 1985

David, Hugh, *The Fitzrovians: A Portrait of Bohemian Society 1900–1955*, London: Sceptre, 1989

Davison, Claire, Derek Ryan, Jane A. Goldman, eds, *Cross-Channel Modernisms*, Edinburgh: Edinburgh University Press, 2020.

Debord, Guy, *Society of the Spectacle* (1967), English trans., Detroit, M.I.: Black & Red Press, 1973

Décaudin, Michel, *La Crise des valeurs symbolistes. Vingt ans de poésie française, 1895–1914*, Toulouse: Privat, 1960

Deghy, Guy, and Keith Waterhouse, *Café Royal: Ninety Years of Bohemia*, London: Hutchinson, 1955

Delap, Lucy, *The Feminist Avant-Garde: Transatlantic Encounters of the Early Twentieth Century*, Cambridge: Cambridge University Press, 2007

Dellamora, Richard, *Masculine Desire: The Sexual Politics of Victorian Aestheticism*, Chapel Hill: University of North Carolina Press, 1990

Denis, Maurice, 'Cézanne' (1907), reprinted in Olivier Revault d'Allonnes, ed., Maurice Denis, *Du Symbolisme au classicisme. Théories*, Paris: Hermann, 1964, 155–72

Denis, Maurice, *Le Ciel et l'Arcadie*, ed. Jean-Paul Bouillon, Paris: Hermann, 1993

Deslandes, Paul R., *Oxbridge Men: British Masculinity and the Undergraduate Experience, 1850–1920*, Bloomington: Indiana University Press, 2005

Dessy, Clément, *Les Écrivains et les Nabis. La littérature au défi de la peinture*, Rennes: Presses Universitaires de Rennes, 2015

Destremeau, Frédéric, 'L'Atelier Cormon (1882–1887)', *Bulletin de la Société de l'histoire de l'art français*, 1996, 171–83

Durão, Fabio A., and Dominic Williams, eds, *Modernist Group Dynamics: The Politics and Poetics of Friendship*, Newcastle upon Tyne: Cambridge Scholars, 2008

Duret, Théodore, *Critique d'avant-garde* (1885), preface by Denys Riout, Paris: ENS des Beaux-Arts, 1998

Eagleton, Terry, 'The Flight to the Real', in Sally Ledger and Scott McCracken, eds, *Cultural Politics at the 'Fin de Siècle'*, Cambridge: Cambridge University Press, 1995, 11–21

Edwards, Paul, 'Lewis's Myth of the Artist: From Bohemia to the Underground', in Paul Edwards, ed., *Volcanic Heaven: Essays on Wyndham Lewis's Painting and Writing*, Santa Barbara, C.A.: Black Sparrow Press, 1996

—, *Wyndham Lewis: Painter and Writer*, New Haven, C.T., and London: Yale University Press, 2000

Ellenberger, Nancy W., 'The Souls and London "Society" at the End of the Nineteenth Century', *Victorian Studies*, vol. 25, no. 2, winter 1982, 133–60

Fénéon, Félix, *Oeuvres plus que complètes*, textes réunis et présentés par Joan U. Halperin, tome I, *Chroniques d'art*, Geneva–Paris: Droz, 1970

Figura, Starr, Isabelle Cahn and Philippe Peltier (eds), *Félix Fénéon: The Anarchist and the Avant-Garde*, New York: The Museum of Modern Art, 2020

Fletcher, Pamela, and Anne Helmreich, eds, *The Rise of the Modern Art Market in London, 1850–1939*, Manchester: Manchester University Press, 2011

Forge, Andrew, 'The Slade I', *Motif*, 4, 1960, 29–43; 'The Slade II', *Motif*, 5, 1960, 16–31

Frèches-Thory, Claire, and Antoine Terrasse, *The Nabis: Bonnard, Vuillard and their Circle*, trans. Mary Pordoe, New York: Abrams, 1991

Freidson, Eliot, *Professional Powers: A Study of the Institutionalization of Formal Knowledge*, Chicago, I.L.: University of Chicago Press, 1986

Fry, Edward, 'Picasso, Cubism and Reflexivity', *Art Journal*, vol. 47, no. 4, winter 1988, 296–310

Gamboni, Dario, '"Après le Régime du sabre le régime de l'homme de lettre": la critique d'art comme pouvoir et comme enjeu', in J.-P. Bouillon, ed., *La Critique d'art en France 1850–1900*, Saint-Étienne: C.I.E.R.E.C., 1987

Gandhi, Leela, *Affective Communities: Anticolonial Thought, Fin-de-Siècle Radicalism, and the Politics of Friendship*, Durham, N.C., and London: Duke University Press, 2006

Garb, Tamar, *Sisters of the Brush: Women's Artistic Culture in Late Nineteenth-Century Paris*, New Haven, C.T., and London: Yale University Press, 1994

Gee, Malcolm, 'Dealers, Critics and Collectors of Modern Painting: Aspects of the Parisian Art Market 1910–30', unpublished PhD thesis, University of London, 1977

Glinoer, Anthony, and Vincent Laisney, *L'Âge des cénacles. Confraternités littéraires et artistiques au XIXe siècle*, Paris: Fayard, 2013

Gluck, Mary, *Popular Bohemia: Modernism and Urban Culture in Nineteenth-Century Paris*, Cambridge, M.A., and London: Harvard University Press, 2005

Goddard, Linda, *Aesthetic Rivalries: Word and Image in France, 1880–1926*, Oxford: Oxford University Press, 2012

Goudeau, Émile, *Dix Ans de Bohème*, Paris: La Librairie Illustrée, 1888

Grojnowski, Daniel, 'Une Avant-garde sans avancée. Les "Arts Incohérents", 1882–1889', *Actes de Recherche en Sciences Sociales*, November 1981

Grojnowski, Daniel, and Bernard Sarrazin, *L'Esprit fumiste et les rires fin-de-siècle*, Paris: Corti, 1990

—, and Denys Riout, *Les Arts incohérents et le rire dans les arts plastiques*, Paris: Corti, 2015

Hadjinicolaou, Nicos, 'On the Ideology of Avant-Gardism', *Praxis*, 6, 1982, 39–106

Haine, W. Scott, *The World of the Paris Café: Sociability among the French Working Class, 1789–1914*, Baltimore, M.D., and London: Johns Hopkins University Press, 1996

Hall, Stuart, and Bill Schwarz, 'State and Society, 1880–1930', in Mary Langan and Bill Schwarz, eds, *Crises in the British State 1880–1930*, London: Hutchinson, 1985

Halperin, Joan U., *Félix Fénéon, Aesthete and Anarchist in Fin-de-Siècle Paris*, New Haven, C.T., and London: Yale University Press, 1988

Hamnett, Nina, *Laughing Torso*, London: Constable, 1932

Harris, Jose, *Private Lives, Public Spirit: Britain 1870–1914*, Harmondsworth: Penguin, 1994

Harrison, Carol E., *The Bourgeois Citizen in Nineteenth-Century France: Gender, Sociability, and the Uses of Emulation*, Oxford: Oxford University Press, 1999

Helmreich, Anne, and Ysanne Holt, 'Marketing Bohemia: The Chenil Gallery in Chelsea, 1905–1926', *Oxford Art Journal*, vol. 33, no. 1, March 2010, 43–61

Helt, Brenda and Madelyn Detloff, eds, *Queer Bloomsbury*, Edinburgh: Edinburgh University Press, 2016

Hobson, Suzanne, *Angels of Modernism: Religion, Culture, Aesthetics 1910–1960*, Basingstoke: Palgrave Macmillan, 2011

Holroyd, Michael, *Augustus John: The New Biography*, London: Vintage, 1997

Hynes, Samuel, *The Edwardian Turn of Mind*, London: Pimlico, 1992

Jackson, Lee, *Palaces of Pleasure: From Music Halls to the Seaside to Football, How the Victorians Invented Mass Entertainment*, New Haven, C.T., and London: Yale University Press, 2019

Jensen, Robert, *Marketing Modernism in Fin-de-Siècle Europe*, Princeton, N.J.: Princeton University Press, 1994

Joyeux-Prunel, Béatrice, 'L'Art de la mesure. Le salon d'Automne (1903–1914), l'avant-garde, ses étrangers et la nation française', *Histoire et mesure*, 2007, 1, 145–82

—, *Nul n'est prophète en son pays? L'internationalisation de la peinture des avant-gardes parisiennes 1855–1914*, Paris: Musée d'Orsay/Nicolas Chaudun, 2009

—, 'L'Art mobilier. La circulation de la peinture avant-gardiste et son rôle dans la géopolitique culturelle de l'Europe', in Christophe Charles, ed., *Le Temps des Capitales culturelles, XVIIIe–XXe Siècles*, Paris: Champ Vallon, 2009

—, *Les Avant-gardes artistiques 1848–1918. Une histoire transnationale*, Paris: Gallimard, 2015

Knott, Stephen, *Amateur Craft: History and Theory*, London: Bloomsbury, 2015

Kuper, Adam, *Incest and Influence: The Private Life of Bourgeois England*, Cambridge, M.A., and London: Harvard University Press, 2009

Lambert, Angela, *Unquiet Souls: The Indian Summer of the British Aristocracy, 1880–1918*, Basingstoke: Macmillan, 1984

Larson, Magali Sarfatti, *The Rise of Professionalism: A Sociological Analysis*, Berkeley: University of California Press, 1977

Leighten, Patricia, *The Liberation of Painting: Modernism and Anarchism in Avant-Guerre Paris*, Chicago, I.L., and London: University of Chicago Press, 2013

Levenson, Michael, *A Genealogy of Modernism: A Study of English Literary Doctrine 1908–1922*, Cambridge: Cambridge University Press, 1984

Levitine, George, *The Dawn of Bohemianism: The 'Barbu' Rebellion and Primitivism in Neoclassical France*, University Park and London: Pennsylvania State University Press, 1978

Levy, Paul, *Moore: G.E. Moore and the Cambridge Apostles*, London: Weidenfeld and Nicolson, 1979

Lewis, Wyndham, *Tarr*, London: Egoist, 1918

—, *Blasting and Bombardiering: Autobiography (1914–1926)* (1937), London: Imperial War Museum, 1992

—, *Rude Assignment: An Intellectual Autobiography* (1950), ed. Tobu Foshay, Santa Barbara, C.A.: Black Sparrow Press, 1984

Livesey, Ruth, *Socialism, Sex, and the Culture of Aestheticism in Britain, 1880–1914*, Oxford: Oxford University Press, 2007

Lübbren, Nina, *Rural Artists' Colonies in Europe, 1870–1910*, Manchester: Manchester University Press, 2001

Lubenow, W.C., *The Cambridge Apostles, 1820–1914: Liberalism, Imagination and Friendship in British Intellectual and Professional Life*, Cambridge: Cambridge University Press, 1998

Lutz, Deborah, *Pleasure Bound: Victorian Sex Rebels and the New Eroticism*, New York and London: W.W. Norton, 2011

Marès, Antoine, 'Pourquoi des étrangers à Paris?', in *L'École de Paris 1904–1929, la part de l'Autre*, exh. cat., Paris: Musée d'Art Moderne de la Ville de Paris, 2000, 138–47

Marlais, Michael, 'Conservative Style/Conservative Politics: Maurice Denis in Le Vésinet', *Art History*, vol. 16, no. 1, March 1993, 125–46

Marriott, Charles, *Subsoil*, London: Hurst and Blackett, 1913

Marsh, Jan, *The Pre-Raphaelite Sisterhood*, New York: St Martin's Press, 1985

Mayeur, J.-M., and M. Rebérioux, *The Third Republic from its Origins to the Great War 1871–1914*, Cambridge: Cambridge University Press, 1984

McConkey, Kenneth, *British Impressionism*, London: Phaidon, 1989

McGuinness, Patrick, *Poetry and Radical Politics in Fin de Siècle France. From Anarchism to 'Action Française'*, Oxford: Oxford University Press, 2015

McLoughlin, Kate, ed., *The Modernist Party*, Edinburgh: Edinburgh University Press, 2013

Merrick, Jeffrey, and Bryant T. Ragan, eds, *Homosexuality in Modern France*, Oxford: Oxford University Press, 1996

Milner, John, *The Studios of Paris: The Capital of Art in the Late Nineteenth Century*, New Haven, C.T., and London: Yale University Press, 1988

Milne-Smith, Amy, *London Clubland: A Cultural History of Gender and Class in Late Victorian Britain*, New York: Palgrave Macmillan, 2011

Moffett, Charles, ed., *The New Painting: Impressionism 1874–1886*, exh. cat., Geneva: Burton with Fine Arts Museums of San Francisco and the National Gallery of Art, Washington, D.C., 1986

Morowitz, Laura, and William Vaughan, eds, *Artistic Brotherhoods in the Nineteenth Century*, Aldershot: Ashgate, 2000

—, and Elizabeth Emery, *Consuming the Past: The Medieval Revival in Fin-de-Siècle France*, London: Routledge, 2018

Morris, Edward, *French Art in Nineteenth-Century Britain*, New Haven, C.T., and London: Yale University Press, 2005

Morris, William, *News from Nowhere* (1890), facsimile edn, London: Victoria and Albert Museum/Thames & Hudson, 2017

Nevinson, C.R.W., *Paint and Prejudice*, London: Methuen, 1937

O'Day, Alan, ed., *The Edwardian Age: Conflict and Stability 1900–1914*, London and Basingstoke: Macmillan, 1979

Orfila, Jorgelina, '*Blague*, Nationalism and Incohérence', in June Hargrove and Neil McWilliam, eds, *Nationalism and French Visual Culture, 1870–1914*, Washington, D.C., New Haven, C.T., and London: Yale University Press, 2005, 173–93

Patry, Sylvie, ed., *Inventing Impressionism: Paul Durand-Ruel and the Modern Art Market*, exh. cat., London: National Gallery/Yale University Press, 2015

Perkin, Harold, *The Rise of Professional Society: England since 1880*, London: Routledge, 1989

Perry, Gillian, *Women Artists and the Parisian Avant-Garde: Modernism and 'Feminine' Art, 1900 to the Late 1920s*, Manchester and New York: Manchester University Press, 1995

Philippe, Gilles, *French Style: L'Accent français de la prose anglaise*, Paris: Les Impressions Nouvelles, 2016

Pierson, Stanley, *British Socialists: The Journey from Fantasy to Politics*, Cambridge, M.A., and London: Harvard University Press, 1979

Piotrowski, Piotr, 'Toward a Horizontal History of the European Avant-Garde', in Sascha Bru et al., eds, *Europa! Europa? The Avant-Garde, Modernism, and the Fate of a Continent*, Berlin: De Gruyter, 2009, 49–58

Pluet-Despatin, Jacqueline, Michel Leymarie and Jean-Yves Mollier, eds, *La Belle Époque des revues, 1880–1914*, Paris: L'IMEC, 2002

Poggioli, Renato, *The Theory of the Avant-Garde* (1962), New York: Harper & Row, 1971

Pollock, Griselda, *Avant-Garde Gambits 1888–1893: Gender and the Colour of Art History*, London and New York: Thames & Hudson, 1993

Prettejohn, Liz, *Art for Art's Sake: Aestheticism in Victorian Painting*, New Haven, C.T., and London: Yale University Press, 2007

—, ed., *After the Pre-Raphaelites: Art and Aestheticism in Victorian England*, Manchester: Manchester University Press, 1999

Rainey, Lawrence, *Institutions of Modernism: Literary Elites and Public Culture*, New Haven, C.T., and London: Yale University Press, 1999

Ransome, Arthur, *Bohemia in London* (1907), London: Read Books, 2013

Rappaport, Erika, Mark J. Crowley and Sandra Trudgeon Dawson, eds, *Consuming Behaviours: Identity, Politics and Pleasure in Twentieth-Century Britain*, London: Bloomsbury Academic, 2015

Reed, Christopher, *A Roger Fry Reader*, Chicago, I.L., and London: University of Chicago Press, 1996

—, *Bloomsbury Rooms: Modernism, Subculture and Domesticity*, New Haven, C.T., and London: Yale University Press, 2004

Robins, Anna Gruetzner, 'Degas and Sickert: Notes on their Friendship', *Burlington Magazine*, vol. 130, March 1988, 225–8

—, *Modern Art in Britain 1910–1914*, exh. cat., London: Barbican Art Gallery with Merrell Holberton, 1997

—, *Walter Sickert: The Complete Writings on Art*, Oxford: Oxford University Press, 2000

—, and Richard Thomson, *Degas, Sickert and Toulouse-Lautrec: London and Paris, 1870–1910*, exh. cat., London: Tate Publishing, 2005

Rooksby, Rikky, *A.C. Swinburne: A Poet's Life*, London: Scolar Press, 1997

Rose, Jonathan, *The Edwardian Temperament, 1885–1919*, Athens: Ohio University Press, 1986

Rowbotham, Sheila, *Edward Carpenter: A Life of Liberty and Love*, London: Verso, 2008

Schneer, Jonathan, *London 1900: The Imperial Metropolis*, New Haven, C.T., and London: Yale University Press, 1999

Searle, G.R., *A New England? Peace and War, 1886–1918*, Oxford: Oxford University Press, 2004

Sedgwick, Eve Kosofski, *Between Men: English Literature and Male Homosocial Desire*, New York and London: Columbia University Press, 1985

Segel, Harold B., *Turn-of-the-Century Cabaret: Paris, Barcelona, Berlin, Munich, Vienna, Cracow, Moscow, St Petersburg, Zurich*, New York: Columbia University Press, 1987

Seigel, Jerrold, *Bohemian Paris: Culture, Politics and the Boundaries of Bourgeois Life, 1830–1930*, New York: Viking, 1986

Sénéchal, Christian, *L'Abbaye de Créteil*, Paris: Delpeuch, 1930

Shiff, Richard, *Cézanne and the End of Impressionism: A Study of the Theory, Technique, and Critical Evaluation of Modern Art*, Chicago, I.L., and London: University of Chicago Press, 1984

Shryock, Richard, 'Becoming Political: Symbolist Literature and the Third Republic', *Nineteenth-Century French Studies* 33, nos 3–4, spring–summer 2005, 385–98

Signac, Paul, *D'Eugène Delacroix au néo-impressionnisme*, Paris: Revue Blanche, 1899

Simpson, Juliet, 'The Société Nationale: The Politics of Innovation in Late Nineteenth-Century France', *Apollo*, vol. 149, no. 444, February 1999, 49–55

Somigli, Luca, *Legitimizing the Artist: Manifesto Writing and European Modernism 1885–1915*, Toronto: University of Toronto Press, 2003

Stephenson, Andrew, 'Buttressing Bohemian Mystiques and Bandaging Masculine Anxieties', *Art History*, vol. 17, no. 2, June 1994, 269–78

Strychacz, Thomas, *Modernism, Mass Culture, and Professionalism*, Cambridge: Cambridge University Press, 1993

Sutherland, Edwin H., ed., *The Professional Thief, by a Professional Thief*, Chicago, I.L.: University of Chicago Press, 1937

Szczerski, Andrzej, *Views of Albion: The Reception of British Art and Design in Central Europe, 1890–1918*, Berne: Peter Lang, 2015

Thatcher, David S., *Nietzsche in England, 1890–1914: The Growth of a Reputation*, Toronto: University of Toronto Press, 1970

Tickner, Lisa, 'Men's Work? Masculinity and Modernism', in Norman Bryson, Michael Ann Holly and Keith Moxey, eds, *Visual Culture: Images and Interpretations*, Hanover, N.H., and London: University Press of New England, 1994, 42–82

—, 'The Popular Culture of *Kermesse*: Lewis, Painting and Performance, 1912–13', *Modernism/Modernity*, vol. 4, no. 2, April 1997, 67–120

—, *Modern Life and Modern Subjects: British Art in the Early Twentieth Century*, New Haven, C.T., and London: Yale University Press, 2000

—, 'Bohemianism and the Cultural Field: *Trilby* and *Tarr*', *Art History*, vol. 34, no. 5, November 2011, 978–1011

Tillyard, Stella, *The Impact of Modernism 1900–1920: Early Modernism and the Arts and Crafts Movement in Edwardian England*, London: Routledge, 1988

Troy, Nancy J., *Modernism and the Decorative Arts in France: Art Nouveau to Le Corbusier*, New Haven, C.T., and London: Yale University Press, 1991

—, *Couture Culture: A Study in Modern Art and Fashion*, Cambridge, M.A.: MIT Press, 2003

Turner, Sarah Victoria, '"Spiritual Rhythm" and "Material Things": Art, Cultural Networks and Modernity in Britain, c.1900–1914', unpublished PhD thesis, Courtauld Institute of Art, 2009

Ward, Martha, 'Impressionist Installations and Private Exhibitions', *The Art Bulletin*, vol. 73, no. 4, December 1991, 599–622

—, *Pissarro, Neo-Impressionism and the Spaces of the Avant-Garde*, Chicago, I.L.: University of Chicago Press, 1996

Watkins, Nicholas, 'The Genesis of a Decorative Aesthetic', in Gloria Groom, ed., *Beyond the Easel: Decorative Painting by Bonnard, Vuillard, Denis and Roussel*, New Haven, C.T., and London: Yale University Press, 2001, 1–28

Watney, Simon, *English Post-Impressionism*, London: Studio Vista, 1980

Weiss, Jeffrey, *The Popular Culture of Modern Art: Picasso, Duchamp and Avant-Gardism*, New Haven, C.T., and London: Yale University Press, 1994

Williams, Raymond, 'The Significance of "Bloomsbury" as a Social and Cultural Group', in D. Crabtree and A.P. Thirlwell, eds, *Keynes and the Bloomsbury Group*, London: Macmillan, 1980

—, *Culture*, London: Fontana, 1981

Wilson, Elizabeth, *Bohemians: The Glamorous Outcasts*, London and New York: I.B. Tauris, 2000

Wood, Jamie, '"On or about December 1910": F.T. Marinetti's Onslaught on London and Recursive Structures in Modernism', *Modernist Cultures*, vol. 10, no. 2, June 2015, 135–58

Wright, Barnaby, 'Modern Art and the Professionalisation of Culture: The Development of Modern Painting in England at the Beginning of the Twentieth Century', unpublished PhD thesis, London: Courtauld Institute of Art, 2004

Yeo, Stephen, *A New Life: The Religion of Socialism in Britain, 1883–1896: Alternatives to State Socialism*, Brighton: Edward Everett Root, 2018

INDEX

Plates are denoted by pl.; *italic* numbers refer to the illustrations in the text

PICTURE CREDITS

FIGURES

© ADER: 4
© Courtauld Gallery / Bridgeman Images: 6
Photo © Musée d'Orsay, Dist. RMN-Grand Palais / Patrice Schmidt: 5
Private Collection Europe, Courtesy Piano Nobile, Robert Travers (Works of Art) Ltd: 7
Photo © RMN-Grand Palais (Musée d'Orsay) / Hervé Lewandowski: 8
© UCL Art Museum, University College London / Bridgeman Images: 3

PLATES

The Albertina Museum, Vienna. The Batliner Collection. © Succession Picasso / DACS, London 2021: 28
Collection Albright-Knox Art Gallery, Buffalo, New York; General Purchase Funds, 1957 (1957:1). © Estate of Jean Metzinger / Artists Rights Society (ARS), New York / ADAGP, Paris. Image courtesy the Albright-Knox Art Gallery: 21
Archivart / Alamy Stock Photo: 2
The Art Institute of Chicago / Art Resource, NY / Scala, Florence: 10, 16
© Ashmolean Museum: 26
Photo by Birmingham Museums Trust, licensed under CC0: 4
© Bridgeman Images: 8, 9, 15, 50, 52
Photo © Centre Pompidou, MNAM-CCI, Dist. RMN-Grand Palais / Philippe Migeat and © ADAGP, Paris and DACS, London 2021: 51
Photo © Christie's Images / © Estate of Vanessa Bell. All rights reserved, DACS 2020 / Bridgeman Images: 31, 39
British Council, London. © Bridgeman Images: 53
Photo © The Courtauld, London. © Bridgeman Images: 54, 55
© The Courtauld, London (Samuel Courtauld Trust). © Estate of Duncan Grant. All rights reserved, DACS 2021: 40
Photo © Mary Evans Picture Library: 56
Kunsthaus Zürich, Donated by the Holenia Trust in memory of Joseph H. Hirshhorn, with a contribution from Rolf and Margit Weinberg, 1998. © Succession H. Matisse / DACS 2021: 19
Image © The Metropolitan Museum of Art / Art Resource, NY / Scala, Florence: 11
Mildred Lane Kemper Art Museum, Washington University in St. Louis. University purchase, Kende Sale Fund, 1946. © Succession Picasso / DACS, London 2021: 34
Photo © Musée d'Orsay, Dist. RMN-Grand Palais: 6
Museum of Fine Arts, Boston: 7
Digital image, The Museum of Modern Art, New York / Scala, Florence: 12, 13, 24, 36

Digital image, The Museum of Modern Art, New York / Scala, Florence. © Succession Picasso / DACS, London 2021: 20, 36

© The National Gallery, London: 14

Photo © Paris Musées, Musée d'Art Moderne, Dist. RMN-Grand Palais / image ville de Paris: 27

Courtesy National Museums Liverpool, Walker Art Gallery: 5

Philadelphia Museum of Art: The Louise and Walter Arensberg Collection, 1950, 1950-134-59 © Artists Rights Society (ARS), New York / ADAGP, Paris / Succession Marcel Duchamp: 22

Philadelphia Museum of Art: A.E. Gallatin Collection, 1952, 1952-61-79 / Artwork: © Succession H. Matisse, Paris / Artists Rights Society (ARS), New York: 17

The Picture Art Collection / Alamy Stock Photo: 3

Photo © RMN-Grand Palais (Musée du Louvre) / Michel Urtado: 1

Photo © RMN-Grand Palais (Musée d'Orsay) / Hervé Lewandowski / Artwork: © Succession H. Matisse, Paris / DACS 2021: 18

Photo © The State Hermitage Museum. Photo by Vladimir Terebenin, and © Artists Rights Society, Inc. (ARS) / https://arsny.com/licensing-requests: 30, 32

Photo © Tate: 46

Photo © Tate and © Estate of Duncan Grant. All rights reserved, DACS 2021: 29, 35, 38

Photo © Tate and © Estate of Vanessa Bell. All rights reserved, DACS 2021: 37 Photograph © 2022

© TfL from the London Transport Museum collection: 48

© Estate of Vanessa Bell. All rights reserved, DACS 2020: 33

Volgi archive / Alamy Stock Photo: 23

© Estate of Wyndham Lewis. Courtesy of the British Council Collection. Photo © The British Council: 53

Yale Center for British Art, Paul Mellon Collection. Object Number: B1993.30.11. © Bridgeman Images: 25

Yale Center for British Art, Paul Mellon Fund and Gift of Neil F. and Ivan E. Phillips in memory of their mother, Mrs. Rosalie Phillips. Object Number: B1982.1. © Bridgeman Images: 49